Contemporary Issues in Strategic Management

Traditional narratives on strategic management no longer fulfil the needs of students, practitioners, consultants and business owners operating within contemporary society. This textbook provides a differentiated approach to the topic, highlighting the dichotomy between theory and practice, and guiding readers towards an understanding of the future of strategic management.

Moving beyond the short-sighted goal of profit maximization, *Contemporary Issues in Strategic Management* shines a light on measures that really matter, such as value. A wealth of global examples provides an illustration of competitive advantage from market-based and state-based perspectives, giving an insight into the activities that lead to the formation of successful and unsuccessful strategies.

Written by two distinguished scholars in the field, this global textbook is essential reading for postgraduate students of strategic management worldwide.

Paul Phillips is Professor of Strategic Management at Kent Business School, The University of Kent, UK.

Luiz Moutinho is Visiting Professor of Marketing at Suffolk Business School, University of Suffolk, UK; Adjunct Professor of Marketing at Graduate School of Business, University of the South Pacific, Fiji; Visiting Professor of Marketing at Universidade Europeia and the Marketing School, Portugal.

Contemporary Issues in Strategic Management

Paul Phillips and Luiz Moutinho

LONDON AND NEW YORK

First published 2018
by Routledge
2 Park Square, Milton Park, Abingdon, Oxon OX14 4RN

and by Routledge
711 Third Avenue, New York, NY 10017

Routledge is an imprint of the Taylor & Francis Group, an informa business

© 2018 Paul Phillips and Luiz Moutinho

The right of Paul Phillips and Luiz Moutinho to be identified as authors of this work has been asserted by them in accordance with sections 77 and 78 of the Copyright, Designs and Patents Act 1988.

All rights reserved. No part of this book may be reprinted or reproduced or utilised in any form or by any electronic, mechanical, or other means, now known or hereafter invented, including photocopying and recording, or in any information storage or retrieval system, without permission in writing from the publishers.

Trademark notice: Product or corporate names may be trademarks or registered trademarks, and are used only for identification and explanation without intent to infringe.

British Library Cataloguing-in-Publication Data
A catalogue record for this book is available from the British Library

Library of Congress Cataloging-in-Publication Data
A catalog record has been requested for this book

ISBN: 978-1-138-93963-9 (hbk)
ISBN: 978-1-138-93964-6 (pbk)
ISBN: 978-1-315-67482-7 (ebk)

Typeset in Times New Roman
by Swales & Willis Ltd, Exeter, Devon, UK

"To my truly inspirational mother, Joyce." – Paul Phillips
"To my best . . . nagging . . . friend, Andrea Douglas." – Luiz Moutinho

Contents

List of figures	ix
List of tables	xii
Acknowledgements	xiii
1 Introduction	1

PART 1
Strategic management primer   23

2 Strategy	25
3 Strategic analysis	46
4 Case study analysis	80

PART 2
Globalisation   **99**

5 Creating the global organisation	101
6 Creating value in a global context	118
7 Emerging economies	143

PART 3
Contemporary themes   **157**

8 Strategic agility and design	159
9 Business ethics	178
10 Digital strategy	195

viii *Contents*

11	Small and medium-sized enterprises	210
	PAUL PHILLIPS AND SIMON RABY	
12	Strategic performance measurement	228

PART 4
Radical/futures themes **249**

13	Strategic thinking	251
14	The future of the future	268
	Index	287

Figures

1.1	Strategic planning efforts	2
1.2	Scope, scale, speed	2
1.3	Key trends	4
1.4	Old-fashioned business values	8
1.5	New problems demand new vision	12
1.6	The "parallel lines test"	15
2.1	Two questions	25
2.2	The world is changing – fast!	26
2.3	Different contexts for strategy	27
2.4	Strategy content – how to identify company strategy?	28
2.5	Strategic management	28
2.6	View on management trends	34
2.7	Deliberate and emergent strategies	39
2.8	Beware!	40
3.1	Where is the profit?	47
3.2	Determinants of company performance	47
3.3	A question	52
3.4	SWOT analysis	54
3.5	Five forces model	56
3.6	Mendelow's (1981) stakeholder mapping matrix	60
3.7	Stakeholder analysis matrix	61
3.8	Scenario analysis	62
3.9	The world automobile industry	63
3.10	Elements of organisational structure	65
3.11	Span of control	65
3.12	Functional organisational structure	66
3.13	Matrix structure	67
3.14	Network organisational structure	67
3.15	Tall vs flat structures	68
3.16	Porter's value chain analysis	71
3.17	BCG growth/share matrix	73
3.18	BCG matrix – balanced portfolio	74
3.19	Ansoff matrix	75

x   *List of figures*

3.20	Porter's (1980) generic strategy framework	76
4.1	AccorHotels brands and segments	95
5.1	Some basic questions in global strategy	103
5.2	Issues in global strategy?	103
5.3	Porter's Diamond	111
5.4	Government policy and chance	112
5.5	Integration/responsiveness framework	113
5.6	Entry mode strategies	115
6.1	Corporate mistakes	120
6.2	Market share hints	122
6.3	Is market share dead?	123
6.4	Am I managing for volume growth or value growth?	125
6.5	New forces	126
6.6	Curses of growth	127
6.7	Managing in a downturn	128
6.8	Re-inventor companies	128
6.9	Profitability	129
6.10	Cross-functional metrics	130
6.11	Shareholder value – two-sided coin. . .	130
6.12	The other side of the stakeholder value two-sided coin. . .	131
6.13	The parallel lines test	134
6.14	Shifts in metrics	135
6.15	The only acceptable metric is a stakeholder value-driven metric	136
6.16	ROI becomes. . .	137
6.17	Does meaningful marketing have a future?	139
6.18	Profit sharing – the performance marketing model of the future	141
6.19	The formula for (MS) success	142
7.1	Emerging economies outlook	144
7.2	Changing landscape	145
7.3	BRICS and MINT countries	146
7.4	2010–2016 upturn?	146
7.5	Emerging economies 2010–2016 downturn?	147
7.6	Some questions to consider	148
7.7	Haier strategy 1984–2012	155
8.1	Reality #1	162
8.2	Strategy today is gridlocked by a growing overload of strategic disruptors	162
8.3	Dilemma management	162
8.4	And. . . some new terms emerging	165
8.5	Companies vs individuals	169
9.1	Ethics	178
9.2	Ethical behaviour	181
9.3	Scandals	182
9.4	Sustainability is a differentiator	185
9.5	Sustainability 2.0	185

9.6	Sustainability 3.0 Stanford University	186
9.7	Key trends and issues in CSR	188
10.1	The impact of the Internet	195
10.2	The impact of the Internet: issues	196
10.3	Changing business relationships	197
10.4	E-organisational dimensions	198
10.5	What we know about online relationships	200
10.6	Agility and flexibility	202
10.7	E-procurement: strategic performance measurement system	202
10.8	The social media situation	204
10.9	Social media trending	205
10.10	Facebook alternatives	205
10.11	Social media is not a strategy	206
12.1	Shortcomings of performance measurement	229
12.2	Contingency approach	229
12.3	Relationship between lead and lag indicators	230
12.4	Managing strategic performance in 3-dimensions	233
12.5	Determining measures	236
12.6	Primary problems	236
12.7	Balanced scorecard	238
12.8	The strategy map	239
12.9	Triple bottom line	241
12.10	Common marketing measures used by board	241
12.11	Common marketing measures used by finance	242
12.12	Driving performance with the marketing dashboards	242
12.13	A new mindset	243
13.1	It's a VUCA world	254
13.2	Age of anxiety	255
13.3	New economy	255
13.4	Dear Business as Usual, It's time for a revolution	258
13.5	The end of Business as Usual	259
14.1	Paradigm shifts	272
14.2	Strategic thinking: Strategy's orphan	275
14.3	Major trends in new strategic thinking	275
14.4	Stretch	280
14.5	Business colonies	281
14.6	Dilemma management	284
14.7	Strategic agility	284

Tables

2.1	Putting a price on health	38
2.2	Top management consulting firms	41
2.3	Strategy firms' practice areas and sectors	42
3.1	PESTEL analysis	55
4.1	Generic 10-step procedure in case study analysis	82
4.2	Selected financial ratios	86
4.3	Summary of profit measures	87
5.1	The top paid footballers in China (January 2016)	110
7.1	Top ten largest banks in the world by market capitalisation	147
7.2	Examples of leading MINT companies	150
9.1	Ethics in action	191
11.1	Factors that influence the formation and execution of strategy in SMEs	213
11.2	The "BIG ten" capabilities of growing SMEs	214
11.3	Factors that influence HRM formulation and implementation in SMEs	218
11.4	EU definition for micro, small and medium enterprises	220
11.5	The 1,000 companies to Inspire Europe report 2016	221
11.6	Chinese SME definitional characteristics	223

Acknowledgements

This book could not have been completed without the collaboration between the authors and publisher. The authors would like to thank the work of the editorial team at Routledge.

The authors are appreciative of the contributions from Dr Michael E. Dobbs, EIU School of Business, Eastern Illinois University, USA – Chapter 3; Dr Alexandra Lipitakis, Kent Business School, University of Kent, UK – Chapter 10; Dr Simon Raby, Bissett School of Business, Mount Royal University, Canada – Chapter 11.

The authors would also like to thank the following individuals and organisations for giving permission to reproduce material within the text:

Martin Gibbs, News Syndication, The News Building, London Bridge Street, London l SE1 9GF – Chapter 2.

Edward Barbini, Vice President, Corporate Communications, IBM, Armonk, NY 10504 – Chapter 2.

Denise Williams, Director of Corporate and Government Affairs, Flow, Jamaica – Chapter 3.

Ganeshan Wignaraja, formerly Advisor, Economic Research and Regional Cooperation Department, Asia Development Bank – Chapter 11.

Tea Banic, Communications and Marketing Director, AdvisoryHQ News – Chapter 2.

Pippa Watts, Rights and Permissions, McGraw-Hill Education, 8th Floor, 338 Euston Road, London, NW1 3BH – Chapter 10.

Lee-Ann Anderson – Senior Permissions and Licensing Executive, Journals, Taylor & Francis Group, 3 Park Square, Milton Park, Abingdon, Oxon, OX14 4RN, UK – Chapter 10.

Laura Stingelin, Permissions Helpdesk Associate, ELSEVIER, Global E-Operations Books – Chapter 10.

1 Introduction

1.1 Learning objectives

After completing this chapter you will:

- be able to describe the forces affecting success and failure in today's commercial world
- be able to locate the salient literature relating to the evolution of business strategy
- appreciate the nuances of strategic planning and implications for organisations seeking competitive advantage
- be familiar with some of the recent thrusts in strategic management and implications for today's CEO
- comprehend the effect of organisational context on strategy development and organisational success
- be aware of the objectives and structure of the book.

1.2 Introduction

The field of strategy is concerned with formulating, implementing and evaluating effective proactive responses. Academics and consultants advocate a plethora of approaches to develop effective strategies but the media is replete with examples of failed strategies. Problems cited relate to a failure by the CEO to deliver increased value added, or powerful stakeholders may feel that the strategy is being implemented too slowly. After two years in the role of Barclays' CEO, Anthony Jackson got ousted in July 2015 over "slow pace of growth". Tellingly, Jackson was appointed with the brief that included reforming the bank's culture, which had been tarnished by a series of scandals under the previous CEO. In terms of growth the share price rise under Jackson had been a respectable 65 per cent, but for the corresponding period, that of its peer, Lloyds, was 180 per cent. On a broader European dimension other banking CEOs left their posts too. Deutsche Bank's co-CEOs Anshu Jain and Jurgen Fitschen, Standard Chartered's Peter Sands, and Credit Suisse's Brady Dougan were ousted as investors lost patience with the rate of recovery. The banking industry went through regulatory changes and together with the duality of economic and market cycles led to the need for new growth oriented business models. Figure 1.1 illustrates the frustration with strategic planning efforts.

In contrast, if we adopt a longitudinal perspective, some companies have appointed a series of CEOs who collectively have failed to compete effectively in their marketplaces. Organisations such as Marks and Spencer, and HP, have made a series of bold statements

2 *Introduction*

Figure 1.1 Strategic planning efforts

highlighting their new strategies with varying attempts to be innovative and customer oriented. But they still lag behind their respective peer groups. Marks and Spencer suffered 14 consecutive quarters of declining growth before there was an upturn for the quarter to 28 March 2015. The then CEO, Marc Bolland, had spent billions of pounds investing in the redesign of new products, stores, and logistics. Moreover, its general merchandising poor performance was unaltered during declining sales, and despite hyped new fashion teams and a new website, customers were being lured to other organisations.

The world advances in terms of scope, scale and speed (see Figure 1.2). The information technology industry is fast-paced and demanding. Firms competing in this industry have to be continually making growth announcements to satisfy shareholders. HP has had a turbulent past and since the beginning of the third millennium has made three significant acquisitions: Compaq (in 2001), Palm (in 2010) and Autonomy (in 2011). All three have been arguably an error of strategy. Meg Whitman became CEO of HP in 2011, after her predecessor Leo Apotheker got rid of the HP PC business and spent US$7bn in acquiring Autonomy to focus on software. The Autonomy debacle led to HP making an $8.8bn write-down in its books. As part of its turnaround plan, on 1 November 2015, HP split

Figure 1.2 Scope, scale, speed

itself into two publicly traded businesses, HP Enterprises providing technology infrastructure, software and services for corporate IT, and HP Inc. focusing on personal systems and printing markets.

The UK public sector too has a litany of failures. Mergers within the National Health Service (NHS) have cost billions, but according to leading health think tank, The King's Fund (Collins, 2015) they do not solve the issues that they were formed to address. Similar to its private sector counterparts, mergers are proposed to help reduce debt-ridden trusts with the process taking up to five years. Collins states that "senior management can be over confident about their ability to lead major projects, while systematically overestimating the benefits and underestimating the risks". The NHS has to deliver its mandate from government and fulfil its duty to enhance outcomes for people. Charities can also be casualties of the current economic climate. Kids Company, a charity founded in 1996 by Camila Batmanghelidjh provided practical, emotional and educational support to inner-city children and young people in the cities of London, Bristol and Liverpool. Despite its high profile, Kids Company suffered from funding difficulties and closed in August 2015, causing the government to find alternative support for 6,000 vulnerable children. In the case of the public sector, failure ultimately reinforces the importance of the business–society relationship. These examples highlight a waste of healthcare resources, and vulnerable children having to find other interventions for their problems. Both represent high social costs to vulnerable members of society.

Big brands too have had notable product failures such as Nike, Mercedes, and Home Depot in China. Nike's design of white sneakers created for the year of the monkey, incorporated special Chinese characters printed on both heels. The sneakers looked smart but the character on the left shoe, Fa, means good fortune and the character on the right shoe, Fu, symbolises wealth. Unfortunately, when both characters are combined the meaning changes to become fat. Mercedes Benz, too, suffered from a phonetic nightmare. The company chose the name Ben Si, which sounds like Benz, but actually means rushing to die. This is somewhat worrying for a motor vehicle. Home Depot is a market-leading American firm that provides supplies for Do It Yourself (DIY) work at home. The firm was excited by the size of the commercial opportunity in China. Sales never took off in China. On reflection, management realised that the majority of potential customers in the major cities lived in modern buildings, which did not need the attention of DIY. Also, in the Chinese culture, DIY is perceived as a sign of poverty. Collectively, these examples show that having a large budget cannot prevent causing major organisational trauma from mistakes. Some of the key trends shaping the business context are shown in Figure 1.3.

The opening to this chapter uses practical examples to illustrate failure at the corporate and product level. We also reiterate the fact that strategic management outcomes are not always the same as we teach in universities. Following a precise set of instructions does not always translate into success. By reviewing the evolution of strategy theory over the last five decades and comparing this with managerial practice, we briefly draw attention to strategic planning. The salient strategic planning literature is highlighted, and observations suggest that much of the prior strategic management literature is replete with rigorous quantitative and qualitative empirical studies, but currently lacks behavioural rigor and practical relevance. While an abundance of textbooks consider the general nature of strategic management, few texts really focus on how organisations create value in today's business environment. Next, we consider the new thrusts of the strategic management literature. Organisational success through a theoretical lens is briefly explored. Then, the chapter overviews the remaining chapters of the textbook, which seek not to necessarily advocate a

4 Introduction

> ## Some key trends that are shaping tomorrow:
>
> 1. Globalisation/Glocalisation
> 2. Asia and new economics
> 3. Convenience technology
> 4. Connected
> 5. Smart technology
> 6. Transparency
> 7. Global sustainers
> 8. Rethinking energy
> 9. The creative class
> 10. Ageing population
> 11. Health and wellbeing

Figure 1.3 Key trends

single solution or approach, but to introduce the reader to a variety of insights to allow them to make up their own mind. The chapter summary reinforces the salient messages, and then concludes with self-reflection questions.

Strategy nugget

Sir Alex Ferguson

Sir Alex Ferguson was born on 31 December 1941 in Glasgow, Scotland. He made his first team football debut for Queen's Park FC (1957–60), and moved on to St. Johnstone FC (1960–64). Sir Alex turned professional after joining Dunfermline Athletic FC (1964–67). In 1967, he was transferred to Rangers FC for a Scottish record fee of £65,000, which ended abruptly in 1969. Sir Alex joined Falkirk FC in 1969 and spent four years with the club, and spent one season with Ayr United FC. In 1974, Sir Alex Ferguson retired as a player after scoring 167 goals in 327 appearances.

At the age of 32, Sir Alex entered football as a manager on a part-time basis with the East Stirlingshire FC. After a few months, he joined St. Mirren FC and won the Scottish First Division in 1976–77. Sir Alex quickly progressed to Aberdeen Football Club and as a young manager won the respect of the club. This led to him gaining a reputation as a strict disciplinarian with superb man-management skills. This culminated in Aberdeen clinching the Scottish Premier Division title in 1979–1980. By the end of his managing career he won two more premier titles, four Scottish cups, a league cup, super cup and a European Cup Winners' Cup in eight seasons.

After not winning the Football League since 1967, Manchester United appointed Sir Alex on 6 November 1986. Unfortunately, success was not immediate and there was much media speculation that Sir Alex was at one stage only one game from getting the sack. Manchester United's first success was the League Cup during 1991–92, and the all important Premier

League* in 1993–94. Much success continued and culminated in the famous quadruple in the unforgettable 1998–99 season: FA Cup, Premier League, UEFA Champions League, and Intercontinental Cup.

In terms of non-football honours, Sir Alex Ferguson received the Order of the British Empire (OBE) in 1983, for his services to football. The Commander of the Order of the British Empire (CBE) which he received in 1995 was well deserved. Sir Alex Ferguson was inducted into the English Football Hall of Fame in 2002 and was made Knight Bachelor in 1999 for Manchester United's spectacular efforts in the 1998–99 season.

The 2011 season was a pivotal moment in the history of Manchester United, as the team moved ahead of Liverpool on the all-time championship list. By winning the Premier League, Manchester had won 19 League title trophies compared to Liverpool's 18. Sir Alex had transformed Manchester United into the most successful club in the country and he himself was the most successful football manager of his generation.

In his last season (2012–13), Manchester United won the Premier League title by an 11-point margin. After 27 years of Sir Alex in charge in the role of manager, Manchester United had overtaken Liverpool for winning the Football League Championship/Premier League with 19 wins. Manchester United won the Premiership title three years in succession (2006/7; 2007/8; 2008/9). Under Sir Alex's reign Manchester United won the Premier League (13 times), the FA Cup (5 times), the League Cup (4 times) the FA Charity/Community Shield (10 times), the UEFA Champions League twice, UEFA Cup Winners' Cup and UEFA Super Cup once each.

*The Premier League commenced in the 1992/3 season, and became the top division of English football. Prior to this it was the Football League Championship.

Questions:

1. Define what is meant by the term organisational success. How did Sir Alex Ferguson achieve so much success during his 27-year reign as manager of Manchester United?
2. Discuss ways in which Sir Alex Ferguson managed to maintain his team's success for nearly three decades?

1.3 Evolution of business strategy theory

The first book of strategy emanates from the works of Sun Tzu. His book *The Art of War* was written more than 2,500 years ago and a number of Sun Tzu's thoughts and strategies are still relevant in today's marketplaces. Sun Tzu's strategy without tactics is the slowest route to victory and his four general types of warfare strategy: offensive, defensive, flanking and guerrilla strategies continue to influence today's researchers. The old Chinese saying, "the marketplace is a battlefield", remains apt.

The evolution of business strategy can be grouped into six decades from the 1960s to the 2010s.

1960s

In terms of context, strategy is a youthful sub-speciality of the management discipline (Boyd, Finkelstein & Gove, 2005), which commences with a variety of strategy works (Andrews, 1971; Ansoff, 1965; Chandler, 1962; Hofer & Schendel, 1978; Steiner, 1979). Chandler (1962) presents in-depth case studies illustrating strategic problems facing managers, which have, in turn, been used as a platform by subsequent researchers to develop theories. This classical view of strategy emanates from a military tradition. The orientation towards long-term goals and a choice of action plans for achieving them were made explicit by early pioneers (Andrews, 1971; Ansoff, 1965). Definitions of action plans, programmes or orientations were stressed (Hofer & Schendel, 1978; Rumelt, 1974). During this period, senior executives were concerned with the general direction and long-term policy of their enterprises.

During the 1960s, these earlier strategy documents were essentially financial budgeting-oriented and eventually became part of a separate business function from accounting, marketing, operations etc. The value system within organisations was one of "meeting the budget". This philosophy led to a focus on the annual budget with investment decisions being made based on capital budgeting procedures. Corporate planners were employed to help coordinate decisions and maintain control. Such systems evolved into making multi-year forecasts and predictions.

1970s

During the 1970s, organisations developed scientific approaches that led to the creation of corporate planning departments. The outputs of these departments were five-year long-range plans, which frequently led to the development of diversification strategies. A flurry of academics, practitioners, and consultants writing about strategic planning together with the need to think strategically were prevalent. Trust in strategic planning initially took off. At first, all appeared well until the oil crisis in 1973, when organisations suddenly realised the need to continually seek re-alignment with the external environment.

Unfortunately, instead of closely analysing assumptions, projections had merely become an extrapolation of the annual budget. This would be fine as long as there were no shocks in the external environment. Unfortunately, as we now know only too well, the world does not behave in a linear manner. The 1973 oil crisis disrupted the business environment, and organisations were unable to make forecasts with much confidence. The old rules no longer could be deployed, and corporate chiefs shifted from a long-range planning perspective to one of thinking strategically.

In one sense, the term "long-range planning" became the corporate tool, with the value system being to predict the future. The corporate objectives of enhancing productivity, profitability, and measurement were key. After a while, long-range planning became ill-suited to the turbulent environments. What became necessary was the need to develop and conceptualise strategy, i.e. engage in strategic thinking. A large-sample time series study performed by Rumelt (1974), had an enduring and pertinent effect, with his finding that "strategy matters". The case study work of Miles et al. (1978) was also appropriate, with the strategic typologies of prospector, analyser, defender and reactor being vivid illustrations of how organisations can adjust to their environments.

In terms of the economics of organisations, the key to success was profit maximisation. Salient contributions during the 1970s were made by the concepts of agency theory (Jensen & Meckling, 1976) and transaction cost theory (Williamson, 1976; 1977). According to agency theory the utility functions of principals and agents diverge, and the efficiency loss can be mitigated if the principal adopts appropriate incentive mechanisms. Agency theory has grown dramatically since its emergence and asserts that the process of economic selection favours governance structures that reduce agency costs. Transaction cost economics asserts that transactions (exchanges) are the basic unit of economic analysis, and that there are costs for each transaction. Maximising efficiency requires mechanisms that minimise each transaction cost (Coase, 1937).

1980s

As strategic planning began to fall from grace, Michael Porter's influence grew. The 1980s became famous for the Porterian view of the world (Porter, 1980), whose thoughts and tools remain the bedrock of business school strategy syllabus. Strategic management textbooks inevitably possess his models, theories and frameworks. The quest for competitive advantage became the holy grail for CEOs. The failure of diversification strategies together with the shocks in the oil industry led to a greater focus on profitability and business level strategy. Michael Porter (1980) applied industrial economics to analysing industry profitability. Porter's five forces model (1980) of supplier, customer, substitutes, threat of new entrants, and intensity of rivalry enabled organisations to understand the structure of an industry and to assess its attractiveness. By successfully engaging in competitor analysis organisations could achieve competitive advantage. Chapter 3 will consider the efficacy of the strategic planning tools and techniques which originated during the 1980s.

1990s

Alternatively, internal resources and capability were also seen as potential sources of differential performance levels over time. Researchers began asking fresh questions, such as why do some firms outperform others? This challenged the previous exaggerated view of the impact of industry on firms' performance. Why do performance differences persist over time? Wernerfelt's (1984) resource-based theory view of the firm articulated a new methodological perspective, with the emphasis on the relationship between firm resources and performance. The resource-based theory perspective also includes dynamic capabilities (Teece et al., 1997) and knowledge-based approaches (Grant, 1996). Barney (1991) made significant theoretical development with the resource-based view. During the 1990s, other influential researchers such as Prahalad and Hamel (1990) offered a rebuttal to the argument that industry matters more than the firm. Collectively, this weakened the Porterian view, and provided further evidence that resources and capabilities at the firm-level, not external characteristics at industry level, are prominent determinants of firms' performance.

Importantly, this swing in the pendulum from external and industry-level to internal factors was a major landmark in the strategy literature. An excellent critique of the ten schools of strategy is provided by Mintzberg, Ahlstrand and Lampel (2008), with the strategy literature emphasising deliberate rather than emergent approaches (Bower & Gilbert, 2005). Mintzberg, Ahlstrand and Lampel (2008) distinguish between prescriptive schools' (e.g. Andrews, 1971; Ansoff, 1965; Chandler, 1962; Farjoun, 2002) *design, planning*, and *positioning*; and descriptive schools' (e.g. Bower, 1970; Lovas & Ghoshal 2000; Quinn, 1980) *cognitive, cultural, environmental, learning*, and *power* (e.g. Marsh & Simon, 1958; Pugh, Hickson, Hinings, & Turner, 1968). Two schools have elements of both *configuration* and *entrepreneurialism*. Prahalad and Hamel's (1990) dynamic capabilities approach with core competence, strategic intent and stretch overlap across the schools. The resource-based view (e.g. Barney, 1991; Grant, 1991; Wernerfelt, 1984) is categorised by Mintzberg and Lampel (1999) as descriptive and a hybrid of the cultural and learning schools. Contrary to some opinions, the ten schools do not have to be viewed as fundamentally different.

8 *Introduction*

2000s

In the beginning of the third millennium, Hamel (2000) argues that the optimal strategy is geared towards radical change and creating a new future. Knowledge and its management can assist organisations to enhance performance. As Pfeffer and Sutton (2000) stress, converting knowledge into tangible outcomes is the key. They assert that knowing and doing is more important than the gap between ignorance and knowing. Implementation of new ideas can be troublesome, if the management of knowledge over-emphasises technology and the storage of codified information such as facts, statistics, presentations and written reports. Alternatively, when CEOs and general managers actively select a knowledge management approach that supports a coherent strategy, both the company and its customers benefit (Hansen, Nohria & Tierney, 1999).

The dot.com crash of 2001 led organisations to swiftly identify and build core competencies for the digital economy. Organisations were under increasing pressure from stakeholders to find new ways to compete effectively in dynamic markets. Accordingly, organisations sought structures and technologies that improve agility and flexibility through the implementation of e-business models. During the earlier commercial phases of the Internet, a plethora of e-business models were advocated, prompting management to search for the best model (Phillips, 2003). Magretta (2002) felt that differences between the e-business model and an e-business strategy was a significant issue for any organisation. Ultimately, the e-business model in itself could not replace an e-business strategy.

2010s

Professor Luiz Moutinho (2015) raises a number of pertinent questions. These include: Are we experiencing a conventional economic cycle? Or did the financial crisis of 2008 and subsequent global economic downturn mark the beginning of a "new normal", characterised by fundamental changes in the use of leverage, trajectory of globalisation, nature of consumption patterns, and appetite for risk taking? For some organisations, near-term survival is the only agenda item. Others are peering through the fog of uncertainty, thinking about how to position themselves once the crisis has passed and things return to normal. The question is, "What will normal look like?" While no one can say how long the crisis will last, what we find on the other side will not look like the normal of recent years. The new normal will be shaped by a confluence of powerful forces – some arising directly from the financial crisis and some that were at work long before it began. Figure 1.4 reinforces the need for good old-fashioned business values.

> The "new normal" represents a return to old-fashioned business values of using leverage judiciously, watching cash flow rigorously, investing in people and systems, and keeping an eye out for growth.
>
> Adjusting to the "new normal" is about managing people better.

Figure 1.4 Old-fashioned business values

Organisational learning and knowledge were dominant themes, but there is now growing interest in the area of behavioural strategy. Powell, Lovallo & Fox (2011) draw attention to research on micro foundations and behavioural strategy, which emphasise the individual level, and the behaviours that have an impact on strategy. This continues the swing of the pendulum to an internal view of the firm. Strategy research now covers macro and micro levels and both internal and external domains. As strategic management continues to evolve as a field, its theoretical underpinnings have become empirical. Both quantitative and qualitative empirical studies, which often include deductive or inductive hypotheses have failed to keep abreast of the changing environments. In 2014, this particular point was raised in a call for papers for a special issue of the *Strategic Management Journal* entitled "New theory in strategic management". The editorial team of the special issue solicited opinions if there are important questions in the field not well covered by existing theories. We feel that despite the rapid expansion of researchers' tools there has been limited progress of strategic management theories. So having considered the past six decades of strategic management research, together with the leading strategic management academic journal questioning the need for new theories, we shall now briefly consider the process of strategic planning and some of the new thrusts in strategic management.

Strategy nugget

Rihanna

From her Bajan roots, Rihanna is now one of the world's most successful artists. She is now a global brand, with her hit-making music, and is constantly in the public eye. Each of her records becomes a best seller and in 2015 the Recording Industry Association of America announced that Rihanna has "more than 100 million gold and platinum song certifications" (digital sales), in contrast to artists such as Taylor Swift (88m), Katy Perry (79m), Kanye West (46.5m), and Lady Gaga (39.5m).

Rihanna was born in 1988, with the full name Robyn Rihanna Fenty in the small but popular Caribbean island of Barbados. When she was 15 years old, Rihanna and two friends secured an audition with music producer Evan Rodgers. It was successful for Rihanna personally. Less than one year later, Rihanna left Barbados to live with Rodgers and his wife in Connecticut, USA.

In January 2005, Rihanna landed an audition for Def Jam Records and its president, the legendary rapper Jay-Z. The hip-hop icon felt the same as Evan Rodgers had two years earlier and signed her on the spot. Eight months later, Rihanna released her first single "Pon de Replay", which went to number two on the Billboard singles chart. In 2007, Rihanna became a superstar with the release of her third Album *Good Girl Gone Bad*. The smash hit single "Umbrella" featuring Jay-Z was number 1 in the British charts for 10 weeks and was in the top 100 for 71 weeks. Rihanna had other hits with her 2010 Album *Loud* with the singles "What's My Name", "Only Girl (In The World)" and "S&M". Aside from Jay-Z, she has collaborated with countless stars including Coldplay, Kanye West, Drake, Nicki Minaj, Calvin Harris, Paul McCartney, and Shakira.

Rihanna has made branding work for her, to obtain a loyal following. With nearly 40m Twitter followers together with her willingness to share what she is doing in her life, the Rihanna brand goes from strength to strength. She is PUMA's global brand ambassador for women's training and serves as a creative director, bringing her styling and innovation to PUMA's collections. The celebrity appeared in Dior's "Secret Garden" video shoot in

Versailles. During the designer Raf Simons' spring-summer 2016 Paris Fashion Week presentation, Rihanna appeared in a billowing peach-pink cape with a knit neckline and black latex Dior boots.

Questions:

1 Define what is meant by success in the music industry. How did Rihanna achieve so much success in a relatively short time period?
2 Discuss ways in which Rihanna has made herself into a global brand in the fast-paced music industry.

1.4 Strategic planning

Four decades later, empirical studies still demonstrate that strategic planning remains deeply embedded in organisations (Grant, 2003). Phillips and Moutinho (2014) note that since its earliest days, strategic planning approaches were preoccupied with the economic and planning-performance perspective (e.g. Fulmer & Rue, 1974; Grinyer & Norburn, 1975; Herold, 1972; Thune & House, 1970) and the process of strategy formulation (e.g. Mintzberg & Waters, 1985; Pascale, 1984). Greenley (1994) identified 29 empirical studies, where the aim of the study was to investigate the association between strategic planning and performance. He classifies the studies into three groups. In the first group of nine studies, the researchers found no association between strategic planning and performance. In the second group of 12 studies, there was an association between strategic planning and performance. In the third group, it was found that companies with strategic planning outperformed companies without strategic planning. In contrast, strategic planning research is now being influenced by wider concerns to humanise management and firm research (Whittington, Pettigrew & Thomas 2002).

The design school adopts a deliberate approach to setting objectives and goals, formulating targets and metrics, and allocating resources (Ansoff, 1991). Mintzberg, Brunet & Waters (1986) argue that the reality of strategic planning processes bore little resemblance to the advocated formal, rational, strategic planning process. Mintzberg and Lampel (1999) state that scholars and consultants should continue to probe into the design school. The strategy literature appears captivated by the notion of "design versus process", which encapsulates the differences between deliberate and emergent strategies (Mintzberg & Waters, 1985). Emergent strategies derive from strategic patterns despite or in the absence of intentions (Mintzberg & McHugh, 1985).

Miller and Cardinal (1994) refer to the debate of the value of strategic planning in the management literature. Grant (2003) observes that as strategic management grew as an area of academic study, the interest in strategic planning waned. With only 11 per cent of managers reporting satisfaction with the results of strategic planning (Mankins & Steele, 2006), some ambivalence remains. Criticisms of strategic planning research continue in terms of methodology, treatment of mediating variables and studies being limited to financial measures of performance (Rudd, Greenley, Beatson & Lings, 2008).

The absence of people-related interactions and effects on strategies led to a change of focus. At first during the earlier studies the human factor was seen more as a potential source of trouble (Lyles & Lenz, 1982), rather than a potential source of competitive advantage. For Eppler and Platts (2009), strategic planning processes are challenging for managers and pose a number of cognitive, social and emotional challenges that need managing. Little is known about the actual activities, which lead to the formation of a strategic plan, or the purposes that these activities serve within the organisation (Spee & Jarzabkowski, 2011). These gaps in knowledge are reflected in the strategy-as-practice (SAP) perspective, which analyses the micro processes involved in strategic planning (Jarzabkowski, Balogun & Seidl, 2007; Johnson, Merlin & Whittington, 2003; Whittington, 2006). As well as SAP studies in the traditional profit-making context, some researchers have a particular interest in not-for-profits, including universities Jarzabkowski (2003), and not-for-profit cities (Vaara, Sorsa & Palli, 2010; Kornberger & Clegg, 2011). Formal procedures such as strategy workshops (Johnson, Prashantham, Floyd & Bourque, 2010) and meetings (Jarzabkowski & Seidl, 2008) have considered strategising activities (Vaara & Whittington, 2012). Phillips and Moutinho (2014) opine that the recent micro-foundations approach to strategy (Eisenhardt, Furr and Bingham, 2010; Foss, 2011) provides insights into how actors are enabled by organisational and wider social practices in decision-making. The efforts of SAP researchers during the last decade have enabled strategic planning research to move away from the sole preoccupation with macro processes.

Recent research on practice theories is becoming increasingly influential in the management literature (e.g. Tengblad, 2012), organisations (e.g. Miettinen, Samra-Fredericks and Yanow, 2009), management learning (e.g. Gherardi, 2009), and technology (e.g. Orlikowski, 2007). Practice approaches can be distinguished as being empirical, theoretical and philosophical (Feldman and Orlikowski, 2011). Collectively, SAP has led to a breakthrough from the economic performance dominance in earlier strategic planning research. The growing theoretical and practical relevance of SAP is evidenced with special issues in *Journal of Management Studies* and *Human Relations* and with a more than 2000-member website (http://www.sap-in.org/) covering more than 100 countries.

Strategy nugget

Why are non-profit-making social media companies so attractive to investors?

During the first decade of the third millennium the financial markets suffered from the dot.com crash. Dot.com companies were acquired for extraordinary sums in some cases, such as Excite@Home's purchase of BlueMountain.com for $780m in 1999. The firm at this stage was without revenue or profits. Such valuations lay in the prospects for the future. The authors of this texbook wonder if there is a case of déjà vu?

Today, the rise of the digital consumer is characterised by more time and money being spent online. Increasingly, consumers are attracted to social media such as Facebook, Twitter, Tumblr and Snapchat. Arguably, financial investors are not solely looking for firms that provide smartphones and tablets, but rather for the generation of cash from applications. Such business models convert usage into money from advertisements or in-app purchases. Firms such as Google, Facebook and Twitter are in pole positions. Games producers are trying to follow this trend too.

Looking back over recent events does raise some pertinent points. In 2013 the $1.8bn initial public offering of Twitter saw a share price movement of 90 per cent on its opening day. Today, 10 years after sending its first tweet, it has still not generated a profit. Since 2011, Twitter has lost $2bn. Tumblr, the blogging platform was acquired by Yahoo for $1bn in May 2013. In Yahoo's financial statements, Tumblr's tangible and intangible assets were just $353m and it had liabilities of $114m. The $750m goodwill has already been written down by a third. After receiving more than $1bn from investors, the privately held firm was valued at $416m. Snapchat, like Spotify, Instagram, Pinterest and Yelp, does not make a profit.

12 *Introduction*

While the traditional accounting model of start-ups focuses on generating revenue, profits and healthy ratios, investors focus on the projected customer base. This user base is the key and it is anticipated that revenues and profits will follow. With the salient phases of (i) offering a free service, (ii) adjusting business to generate revenue by advertising, and (iii) removing dependence on advertising, maintaining and growing the user base is imperative. It seems that value is being placed more on brands, customer databases and algorithms.

Questions:

1 To what extent do you believe social media financial valuation models are fit for purpose?
2 What steps can a start-up social media firm take to maximise their chances of success? Justify your answers using material from an existing social media firm.

1.5 New thrusts in strategic management

Strategy remains the CEO's tool to sustain and grow business value. Hamel, in the book *The Future of Management* (Breen and Hamel, 2007) laments that the management paradigm of the last century centred on control and efficiency, which no longer suffices in a world where adaptability and creativity drive business success. To be competitive in the future, organisations must reinvent management, with efforts to remove the toxic effects of traditional management beliefs. Radical principles will need to become part of every company's "management DNA". CEOs and their "dream" teams must select the right path for their organisations.

POD

Jeremy Corbyn

In September 2015, the north London MP Jeremy Corbyn won a stunning first-round victory for leader of the British Labour Party. Jeremy Corbyn won more than 59 per cent of first-preference votes, beating more prominent rivals such as Andy Burnham (19 per cent), Yvette Cooper (17 per cent) and Liz Kendall (4.5 per cent). He persuaded Labour members and supporters to draw a line under the New Labour era of Tony Blair and Gordon Brown. Corbyn sent a clear message that people are "fed up with the injustice and the inequality" of Britain.

Despite the stunning victory, Corbyn's first 365 days were a challenge. After the results of the Brexit referendum, Corbyn faced calls for his resignation because of his alleged absence of leadership during the vote on exiting the European Union. A string of Labour MPs resigned from the front bench en masse saying that they had no confidence in his ability to win a general election. Twenty-six ministers resigned, but Corbyn stood firm and insisted that he had no intention of quitting. Corbyn even lost a vote of no confidence after a motion with 172 Labour MPs voting for the motion and 40 against. The Labour leader stated that the vote was

> That is, there is simply no way to create /build tomorrow's key/critical organisational capabilities – resilience, innovation and employee engagement – atop the scaffolding of past century management principles.

Figure 1.5 New problems demand new vision

non-binding and that he would remain. Eventually a leadership challenge was mounted by Owen Smith, but Jeremy Corbyn confounded his critics by winning the Labour leadership contest for the second time in two years. He won by a large majority, winning 313,000 votes compared to Owen Smith's 193,000.

New thinking (see Figure 1.5) about strategy comes with a whole lexicon of buzzwords. Forget Porter's value chain, and cash cows and dogs. Today's enlightened discussion of strategy can include terms such as "organisation ecosystem" – creating new networks of relationships with customers, suppliers and rivals to gain leverage and competitive advantage. In an ecosystem, organisations need to compete and cooperate with the same firms to create new innovative products to serve customers. It changes the organisation's vision of the business in the future. The CEO needs to start thinking about how they can enhance value from all segments of the company, and bring in new perspectives for salient processes.

An organisation should not be seen to belong to a single industry, but be considered as an entity that permeates a variety of industries. This cross-sectional view presents new areas for potential conflict. In a business ecosystem, organisations should align their needs and wants and co-evolve capabilities around a new holistic innovative thread.

Environments in which setting strategy has become more complex include: faster velocity environments; shrinking planning cycles; future growth trajectories that are harder to predict; business assumptions that once seemed indisputable and are now coming into question. Managers face a multitude of choices when designing new corporate strategies. Some organisations have little idea of what's going to happen within their industry, and need to build their organisation into an engine of possibility. Technology creates disruption and is chaotic. It affects every industry, often in ways that are difficult (if not impossible) to anticipate. An evolving portfolio of strategic experiments can be developed. Alternatively, emergent strategy is an organic approach to growth that lets companies trial and test ideas, with no deliberate expectations of outcomes. Increasing numbers of organisations want to be positioned to take advantage of opportunistic decision-making.

The business landscape is replete with CEOs who implemented strategies that create value for customers and other stakeholders by satisfying their needs and wants better than their peers. However, some fail to remember that their competitive strategy should have a dual purpose: (1) protecting their current source of competitive advantage against the actions of competitors, and (2) making a continual investment in the development of new capabilities to maintain its leadership position. Ultimately, value if left unattended will erode over time. CEOs should seek "values beyond value". The corporate emphasis remains on short-term rather than long-term earnings. Executives' pay is rising faster than corporate earnings with shares and options giving executives in excess of $50m per annum. Perhaps more encouragingly, there is a shift in consciousness with some organisations, such as Kingfisher with its net positive strategy, Unilever considering becoming a B-Corp, and an increasing number of organisations wishing to become more self-managing, organic and decentralised. We shall return to such topics in Chapter 9.

Organisations are now faced with the challenges of trying to operate within a sustainable business model and having to deal simultaneously with environmental, economic and community issues. This focus has raised the importance of the public sector. New Public Management seeks to improve public sector performance.

Major new thrusts in the strategic management literature now include globalisation, or more precisely "global strategy". As Peng (2013) states in his global strategy textbook, the broader definition of global strategy covers the large MNE and small entrepreneurial firms, and firms from both developed and emerging economies. The year 2009 was a landmark year in terms of emerging markets, which for the first time in 200 years contributed more to the global economy than developed markets. Part II of this textbook assesses the topic of globalisation in greater depth.

Strategy nugget

Failures

Caterham F1 commenced life as a Malaysian-owned Formula One team. The team was launched by the aviation entrepreneur Tony Fernandes in 2010. Fernandes owned Air Asia airline and Queens Park Rangers football club. The team did not score a single point in three years of F1, and the company that built the cars for Caterham F1 went into administration. Bailiffs seized Caterham assets including pit equipment and even a test car. Caterham were desperate to complete the 2014 season, and sought to raise £2.4m through crowdfunding. This was successful, and Caterham were able to race in the final F1 grand prix of the 2014 season.

La Senza – in 2014, the British franchise arm of Canadian lingerie chain La Senza went into administration for the second time in two years. The company made losses of £26.2m on a turnover of £43.3m in 2012 due to a combination of poor trading and costly property leases. Kuwaiti-based retail group Alshaya bought 60 of La Senza's stores in 2012 saving 1,100 jobs. At the time of acquisition Alshaya stated the acquisition would lead to a first phase of an anticipated £100m investment spread over two years. In the year to December 2013 La Senza made a pre-tax loss of £24m. The market in which La Senza competes is dominated by strong department stores and clothing retailers and changing customer buying habits. The younger, value end of the consumer market is looking at the offerings of Primark, New Look and H&M for lingerie.

Questions:

1 Define what is meant by the term organisational failure. Why is it so hard to become successful in F1 racing?
2 Discuss ways in which La Senza could have competed better against firms targeting the younger, value end of the market.

1.6 Organisational success

Porter's (1980) generic strategies of cost leadership, differentiation and focus remain a core topic in business school education. Even when supported with a SWOT analysis together with Porter's five forces, implementation of the desired strategy may not lead to organisational success. CEOs of profit-making organisations tend to focus on growth, profitability, and shareholder value, while individuals focus on values, personal productivity, family and friends. Figure 1.6 presents the full picture of this dichotomy between the view of the individual and the company. Miles (2007) continues these thoughts by highlighting this emerging perspective in management education by claiming that the economic emphasis in classrooms is too much on stock incentives and too little on trust.

In terms of organisational success, the strategic management literature presents three main models for organisational success, these being the structure-conduct-performance (SCP), resource-based view (RBV) and dynamic capabilities. In brief, the SCP paradigm of traditional industrial organisation has been embraced within the strategic management discipline.

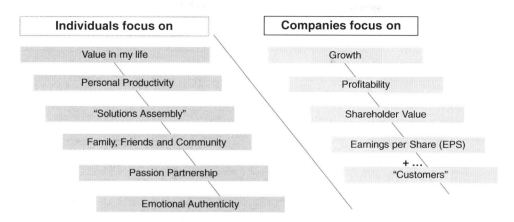

Figure 1.6 The "parallel lines test"

However, the assumption that the industry is more important than the decisions managers actually make continues to be challenged by other approaches. SCP asserts that the economic success of an industry is a function of the conduct of buyers and sellers, which is dependent upon industry structure (Bain, 1956; Mason, 1939). As aptly stated by McWilliams and Smart (1993) the SCP paradigm emphasises structural characteristics of an industry, particularly the level of concentration of firms and level of entry barriers. This, in turn, will have a notable influence on the ability of firms within an industry to price above the competitive price. Over the last four decades, the SCP paradigm is evidenced in research and prescriptions pertaining to generic strategies, business typologies, strategic groups, diversification, mergers and acquisitions, and strategic planning.

The RBV approach grew in prominence during the 1980s, but its seminal ideas relate to the work of Edith Penrose (Penrose, 1959). Barney (1991) defines competitive advantage as when a firm implements a value-creating strategy not simultaneously being implemented by any current or potential competitor. A firm derives sustained competitive advantage when it implements value-creating strategy not simultaneously being implemented by any current or potential competitor and when these other firms are unable to duplicate the benefits of this strategy. The RBV literature stresses that for a resource to be a potential source of sustained competitive advantage it must possess four attributes: valuable, rare, inimitable and non-substitutable. The resource-based view relaxes assumptions of rationale and positioning planning and concentrates upon factors internal to the firm. RBV operates upon the assumption that organisations are heterogeneous in terms of control of strategic resources and that resources are not perfectly mobile between firms. As Barney (1991) argues, firms' resources can be defined as strengths that firms use to conceive and implement their strategies.

More recently, dynamic capabilities have had a recent resurgence with the incorporation of the social and behavioural sciences to help ascertain the capabilities necessary to lead to organisational success. Teece (2007) reminds us that enterprises with strong dynamic capabilities are intensely entrepreneurial. These organisations adapt to business ecosystems by using innovation and by collaboration with other enterprises, entities and institutions. Ultimately, this form of entrepreneurial managerial capitalism requires recognising problems and trends, directing (and redirecting) resources, and reshaping organisations' structures and systems. Augier and Teece (2009) summarise that strategic, organisational and human resource decisions lie at the heart of successful enterprise performance. Helfat et al. (2007) disaggregate technical fitness (how effectively a capability is performed) and dynamic fitness (whether the right activity is being performed).

1.7 Overview of textbook

Contemporary Issues in Strategic Management provides a differentiated approach to the topic of strategic management. The traditional approach is usually built around the design school with an overview of the strategic management process, establishing direction, industry and competitive analysis, resources and capabilities, and competitive advantage. However, the fact remains that these traditional approaches use a narrative that no longer sits well in the world in which students, practitioners, consultants, and business owners operate. The fundamental structural transitions in a wide variety of industries brought about by major catalysts such as deregulation, global competition, technological discontinuities, and changing customer expectations are imposing new strains on managers around the world. Old recipes no longer work. Managers, concerned with restoring competitiveness of their firms, are abandoning traditional approaches to strategy; they are searching for new approaches that give guidance in a turbulent environment.

This textbook reflects, identifies and discusses some of the new approaches and uses academic and practitioner literature bearing upon the contemporary issues, with clear procedures for students at the undergraduate and postgraduate level to produce strategic plans that relax the pure assumption of profit maximisation and incorporate a focus on the measures that really matter, i.e. value is a guiding virtue. We use examples to consider competitive advantage in terms of market-based and state-based perspectives, and seek to use in-depth case studies where the reader gains insights into the actual activities that lead to the formation of a strategic plan, or the purposes that these activities serve within the organisation. As the world as we know it continues to change, the inconsistency between strategic planning popularity in theory and practice is worrying. Recognising the existence of this dichotomy is important for the future development of strategic management practice.

Contemporary Issues in Strategic Management provides a detailed examination of the essential challenges facing the international business practitioner. This first chapter has the primary objective of helping students to locate the salient literature relating to the evolution of business strategy. The authors note that students sometimes write exam "theory free" answers to questions. This is extremely pertinent at the postgraduate level, where there is the expectation that the student should engage in writing at a level which demonstrates being aware of the core and wider literature. There is expectation of full and perceptive awareness of strategic management issues, demonstrating an appreciation of all major points and a clear grasp of their wider significance. The evidence should include integration in their reading and knowledge, and understanding, analysis and argument. Human actors involved in strategy are now realised to be the major barriers to successful implementation of strategy. A focus on greater practice-based approaches to the study of strategy and organisations continues to emerge. New thrusts in strategic management continually force strategists to incorporate greater complexity into their models, but academic research appears to lag behind practice. The following section provides a brief overview of the book.

Part 1, Strategic management primer, contains three chapters – Strategy (Chapter 2); Strategic analysis (Chapter 3); Case study analysis (Chapter 4). These three chapters provide students with the basics of strategic management. Chapter 2 focuses upon the planned strategy vs emergent strategy approaches and considers the strengths and limitations.

The majority of students studying strategic management have to engage in performing strategic analysis, which can be at the operational, business, corporate and global level. Chapter 3 provides a summary of the key managerial tools that can be used to perform strategic analysis. Chapter 4 introduces the concept of case study analysis and provides students with a variety of insights on how to apply theory to practical situations. Chapter 4 also provides approaches for analysing, discussion and writing up case studies.

Part 2, Globalisation, consists of three chapters – Creating the global organisation (Chapter 5); Creating value in a global context (Chapter 6); and Emerging economies (Chapter 7). According to a McKinsey (2014) report to mark their 50th anniversary, in 2009 for the first time in 200 years emerging markets contributed more to global economy growth than the developed economy. Also, the growth of urban populations, 65 million per year, in emerging economies creates new cities, which shift the locus of economic power within a single country. For example, previously unknown cities in China are becoming powerful economic players. This section considers the globalisation of world markets with an emphasis on developing and implementing global strategies. Chapter 5 describes how profit and non-profit firms create the infrastructure to operate on a global context. This chapter seeks to address some of the business environment challenges mentioned in the introduction. Chapter 6 argues that perhaps market share is dead and has been replaced by value share. This chapter considers the concept of creating value in a global context. Chapter 7 considers the decline in the BRICs and the apparent potential and growing influence of urban areas and the MINT economies.

Part 3, Contemporary themes, consists of five chapters. This section is based on contemporary issues – Strategic agility and design (Chapter 8); Business ethics (Chapter 9); Digital strategy (Chapter 10); Small and medium-sized enterprises (Chapter 11); Strategic performance measurement (Chapter 12), with each chapter incorporating theoretical and practitioner sources. These chapters will provide a variety of insights, which shed light on the themes, but leave it for the student to make up their own mind. The focus is to provide the student with some solid theoretical and practical knowledge, which can assist them in decision-making. Chapter 8 dissects strategy problems and raises issues about corporate identity. It defines a number of orientations, roles and responsibilities. It also introduces a discussion behind the failure of strategic plans. The new normal and the concept of strategic agility and design are revisited. Chapter 9 makes the case for the importance of business ethics and its impact on business and society. Chapter 10 reviews digital disruption and provides the reader with a reflection on its evolution. The rise of social media is also noted. Despite their contribution to the economy in terms of turnover and number of jobs created, small and medium-sized enterprises (SMEs) are often neglected in books about strategy. Chapter 11 acknowledges this influence and considers high-performing SMEs. Ultimately, strategy is about performance, which is no longer solely about the financial aspect. A core tenet of Chapter 12 is the need for the CEO to be continually improving performance. Given the array and role of stakeholders, the journey needs to be measured in terms of performance, which should be outcome-based.

The final part, Radical/futures themes, contains two chapters, on Strategic thinking (Chapter 13), and The future of the future (Chapter 14), which combine to cover the evaluation of major trends and the assessment of new ones. In short, we are attempting to design an analytical reasoning and structure that evolves around the dyad society evolution and its impact on management. It's a VUCA world: Volatility – rate of change, Uncertainty – unclear about the present situation and future outcomes, Complexity – multiplicity of key decision factors, and Ambiguity – lack of clarity about the meaning of an event. The new economy requires fresh perspectives on: social capital; voluntary simplicity; benefit corporations; attention economy; emotionomics; consumers in control: made of/by/for consumers; glocal; deglobalisation; not made in China; locavores; new business ecosystems; sense and respond models; evenomics.

1.8 End of chapter self-reflection questions

1. What is strategy and why is it important?
2. Who are the primary practitioners involved in the formulation, implementation and evaluation of strategy? What roles are they responsible for?
    - CEOs, Chief Strategy Officer, strategy teams, middle managers and strategy consultants.
3. What economic and social drivers are making the world change so fast?
4. What do you believe has been the major contribution to strategy? You should provide some examples to support your thoughts.
5. What are the differing contexts for strategy and how do they affect the CEO? You can use one example from: small medium-sized enterprises, multinational enterprises, manufacturing, voluntary and not-for-profit, and social enterprises to illustrate your answer.

References

Andrews, K. (1971). *The concept of corporate strategy*. Homewood, IL: Dow-Jones-Irwin.
Ansoff, I. H. (1965). *Corporate strategy: An analytic approach to business policy for growth and expansion*. New York: McGraw Hill.
Ansoff, I. H. (1991). Critique of Henry Mintzberg's 'The design school: Reconsidering the basic premise of strategic management'. *Strategic Management Journal*, *12*(6), 449–462.
Augier, M., & Teece, D. J. (2009). Dynamic capabilities and the role of managers in business strategy and economic performance. *Organization Science*, *20*(2), 410–421.
Bain, J. S. (1956). *Barriers to new competition*. Cambridge, MA: Harvard University Press.
Barney, J. B. (1991). Firm resources and sustained competitive advantage. *Journal of Management*, *17*, 99–120.
Bower, J. L., & Gilbert, C. G. (Eds.) (2005). *From resource allocation to strategy*. Oxford: Oxford University Press.
Bower, J. L. (1970). *Managing the resource allocation process*. Boston, MA: Harvard Business School Press.
Boyd, B.K., Finkelstein, S., and Gove, S. (2005). How advanced is the strategy paradigm? The role of particularism and universalism in shaping research outcomes. *Strategic Management Journal*, *26*(9), 841–854.
Breen, B., & Hamel, G. (2007). *The future of management*. Boston, MA: Harvard Business School Press.
Chandler, A. (1962). *Strategy and structure: Chapters in the history of American Industrial Enterprise*. Cambridge, MA: MIT Press.
Coase, R. H. (1937). The nature of the firm. *economica*, *4*(16), 386–405.
Collins, B. (2015). *Foundation trust and NHS trust mergers 2010 to 2015*. The King's Fund. Online at: https://www.kingsfund.org.uk/sites/files/kf/field/field_publication_file/Foundation-trust-and-NHS-trust-mergers-Kings-Fund-Sep-2015_0.pdf
Eisenhardt, K. M., Furr, N. R., & Bingham, C. B. (2010). Micro-foundations of performance: Balancing efficiency and flexibility in dynamic environments. *Organization Science*, *21*(6), 1263–1273.

Eppler, M., & Platts, K. W. (2009). Visual strategizing. The systematic use of visualization in the strategic-planning process. *Long Range Planning, 42*, 42–74.

Farjoun, M. (2002). Towards an organic perspective on strategy. *Strategic Management Journal, 23*(7), 561–594.

Feldman, M. S., & Orlikowski, W. J. (2011). Theorizing practice and practicing theory. *Organization Science, 22*(5), 1240–1253.

Foss, N. J. (2011). Invited editorial: Why micro-foundations for resource-based theory are needed and what they may look like. *Journal of Management, 37*(5), 1413–1428.

Fulmer, R. M., & Rue, W. L. (1974). The practice and profitability of long range planning. *Managerial Planning, 22*(6), 1–7.

Gherardi, S. (2009). Introduction: The critical power of the "practice lens". *Management Learning, 40*(2), 115–128.

Grant, R. M. (1991). The resource-based theory of competitive advantage: Implications for strategic formulation. *California Management Review, 33*(3), 113–135.

Grant, R. M. (1996). Toward a knowledge-based theory of the firm. *Strategic Management Journal, 17*(S2), 109–122.

Grant, R. M. (2003). Strategic planning in a turbulent environment: Evidence from the oil majors. *Strategic Management Journal, 24*(6), 491–517.

Greenley, G. E. (1994). Strategic planning and company performance: An appraisal of the empirical evidence. *Scandinavian Journal of Management, 10*(4), 383–396.

Grinyer, P. H., & Norburn, D. (1975). Planning for existing markets: Perceptions of executives and financial performance. *Journal of the Statistical Society, 138*(1), 70–97.

Hamel, G. (2000). *Leading the revolution*. Boston, MA: Harvard Business School Press.

Hansen, M. T., Nohria, N., & Tierney, T. (1999). What's your strategy for managing knowledge? *Harvard Business Review, 77*(2), 106–116.

Helfat, C. E., Finkelstein, S., Mitchell, W., Peteraf, M. A., Singh, H., Teece, D. J., & Winter, S. G. (2007). Dynamic capabilities: Understanding strategic change in organizations. Malden, MA: Blackwell.

Herold, D. M. (1972). Long-range planning and organisational performance: A cross-valuation study. *Academy of Management Journal, 15*(1), 91–102.

Hofer, C. W., & Schendel, D. (1978). *Strategy formulation: Analytical concepts*. St Paul, MN: West Publishing Company.

Jarzabkowski, P. A. (2003). Strategy practices: An activity theory perspective on continuity and change. *Journal of Management Studies, 40*(1), 23–55.

Jarzabkowski, P. A., & Seidl, D. (2008). The role of meetings in the social practice of strategy. *Organization Studies, 29*(11), 1391–1426.

Jarzabkowski, P. A., Balogun, J., & Seidl, D. (2007). Strategizing: The challenges of a practice perspective. *Human Relations, 60*(1), 5–27.

Jensen, M. C., & Meckling, W. H. (1976). Theory of the firm: Managerial behavior, agency costs and ownership structure. *Journal of Financial Economics, 3*(4), 305–360.

Johnson, G., Merlin, L., & Whittington, R. (2003). Micro strategy and strategizing: Towards an activity-based view. *Journal of Management Studies, 40*(1), 3–22.

Johnson, G., Parashantham, S., Floyd, S. W., & Bourque, N. (2010). The ritualization of strategy workshops. *Organization Studies, 31*(12), 1589–1618.

Kornberger, M., & Clegg, S. (2011). Strategy as performance practice: The case of Sydney 2030. *Strategic Organization, 9*(2), 136–162.

Lovas, B., & Ghoshal, S. (2000). Strategy as guided evolution. *Strategic Management Journal, 21*, 875–896.

Lyles, M. A., & Lenz, R. T. (1982). Managing the planning process: A field study of the human side of planning. *Strategic Management Journal, 3*, 105–118.

Magretta, J. (2002). Why business models matter. *Harvard Business Review, 80*(5), 86–92.

Mankins, M. C., & Steele, R. (2006). Stop making plans: Start making decisions. *Harvard Business Review*, *84*(1), 76–84.

Marsh, J. G., & Simon, H.A. (1958). *Organizations*. New York: Wiley.

Mason, E. S. (1939). Price and production policies of large-scale enterprises. *American Economic Review Supplement* 29.

McKinsey (2014). Online at: http://www.mckinsey.com/quarterly/digital-newsstand/2014-issue-3-mckinsey-quarterly

McWilliams, A., & Smart, D. (1993). Efficiency v structure-conduct-performance: Implications for strategy research and practice. *Journal of Management*, *19*(1), 63–78.

Miettinen, R., Samra-Fredericks, D., & Yanow, D. (2009). Re-turn to practice: An introductory essay. *Organization Studies*, *30*(12), 1309–1327.

Miles, R. (2007). Innovation and leadership values. *California Management Review*, *50*(1), 192–201.

Miles, R. E., Snow, C. C., Meyer, A. D., & Coleman, H. J. (1978). Organizational strategy, structure, and process. *Academy of Management Review*, *3*(3), 546–562.

Miller, C. C., & Cardinal, L. B. (1994). Strategic planning and firm performance: A synthesis of more than two decades of research. *Academy of Management Journal*, *37*, 1649–1665.

Mintzberg, H., & Lampel, J. (1999). Reflecting on the strategy process. *Sloan Management Review*, *40*(3), 21–30.

Mintzberg, H. & McHugh, A. (1985). Strategy formation in an adhocracy. *Administrative Science Quarterly*, *30*, 160–197.

Mintzberg, H., & Waters, J. A. (1985). Of strategies, deliberate and emergent. *Strategic Management Journal*, *6*(3), 257–272.

Mintzberg, H., Ahlstrand, B., & Lampel, J. (2008). *Strategy Safari*, 2nd edition. London: Financial Times Prentice Hall.

Mintzberg, H., Brunet, J. P., & Waters, J. (1986). Does planning impede strategic thinking? Tracking the strategies of AirCanada 1937–1976. In R. Lamb & P. Shrivastava (Eds.), *Advances in Strategic Management*, Vol. 4. (pp. 3–41). Greenwich, CT: JAI Press.

Moutinho, L. (2015). The age of anxiety and methodolatry. Available at: https://lovedoc.org/combined-paradigm-2

Orlikowski, W. J. (2007). Sociomaterial practices: Exploring technology at work. *Organization Studies*, *28*, 1435–1448.

Pascale, R. T. (1984). Perspective on strategy: The real story behind Honda's success. *California Management Review*, *26*(Spring), 47–72.

Peng, M. (2013). *Global strategy*. London: Cengage Learning.

Penrose, E. T. (1959). *The theory of the growth of the firm*. Oxford: Basil Blackwell and Mott Ltd.

Pfeffer, J. and Sutton, R.I. (2000). *The knowing-doing gap*. Boston, MA: Harvard Business School Press.

Phillips, P. A. (2003). *E-business strategy: Text and cases*. Maidenhead: McGraw-Hill.

Phillips, P. and Moutinho, L. (2014). Critical review of strategic planning research in hospitality and tourism. *Annals of Tourism Research*, *48*, 96–120.

Porter, M. E. (1980). *Competitive strategy: Techniques for analyzing industries and competitors*. New York: Free Press.

Powell, T. C., Lovallo, D., & Fox, C. R. (2011). Behavioral strategy. *Strategic Management Journal*, *32*(13), 1369–1386.

Prahalad, C. K., & Hamel, G. (1990). The core competence of the corporation. *Harvard Business Review*, *68*(Spring), 79–91.

Pugh, D.S., Hickson, D.J., Hinings, C.R. and Turner, C. (1968). Dimensions of organization structure. *Administrative Science Quarterly*, *13*, 65–105.

Quinn, J. B. (1980). *Strategies for change: Logical incrementalism*. Homewood, IL: Irwin.

Rudd, J. M., Greenley, G. E., Beatson, A. T., & Lings, I. N. (2008). Strategic planning and performance: Extending the debate. *Journal of Business Research*, *61*, 99–108.

Rumelt, R. P. (1974). *Strategy, structure, and economic performance*. Boston, MA: Harvard University Press.
Spee, A. P., & Jarzabkowski, P. A. (2011). Strategic planning as communicative process. *Organization Studies*, *32*(9), 1217–1245.
Steiner, G. A. (1979). *What every manager must know*. New York: Free Press.
Teece, D. J. (2007). Explicating dynamic capabilities: The nature and microfoundations of (sustainable) enterprise performance. *Strategic Management Journal*, *28*(August), 1319–1350.
Teece, D. J., Pisano, G., & Shuen, A. (1997). Dynamic capabilities and strategic management. *Strategic Management Journal*, *18*(7), 509–533.
Tengblad, S. (2012). *The work of managers: Towards a practice of management*. Oxford: Oxford University Press.
Thune, S. S., & House, R. J. (1970). Where long range planning pays off. *Business Horizons*, *13*, 82–87.
Tzu, S., 2015. *The Art of War*. Sheba Blake Publishing (ebook).
Vaara, E., & Whittington, R. (2012). Strategy-as-practice: Taking social practices seriously. *The Academy of Management Annals*, *6*(1), 285–336.
Vaara, E., Sorsa, V., & Palli, P. (2010). On force potential of strategy texts: A critical discourse analysis of a strategic plan and its power effects in a city organization. *Organization*, *17*(6), 685–702.
Wernerfelt, B. (1984). A resource-based view of the firm. *Strategic Management Journal*, *3*, 171–180.
Whittington, R. (2006). Completing the practice turn in strategy research. *Organization Studies*, *27*(5), 613–634.
Whittington, R., Pettigrew, A.M., & Thomas, H. (2002). Conclusions: Doing more in strategy research. In A. M. Pettigrew, H. Thomas, & R. Whittington, *Handbook of Strategy and Management* (pp. 447–490). London: Sage.
Williamson, O. E. (1976). The economics of internal organization: Exit and voice in relation to markets and hierarchies. *The American Economic Review*, *66*(2), 369–377.
Williamson, O. E. (1977). Markets and hierarchies. *Challenge*, *20*(1), 70–72.

Part 1
Strategic management primer

2 Strategy

2.1 Learning objectives

After completing this chapter you will:

- be able to demonstrate an understanding of, and ability to assess strategies in today's world where adaptability and creativity drive business success
- be able to define strategy and strategic management
- be aware of the strategy levels from the CEO and stakeholder perspectives
- distinguish between strong and weak vision, mission and objectives
- critically explain some of the various perspectives of strategy
- be aware of some insights into the strategy consulting profession.

2.2 Introduction

After more than 50 years, the theory of business strategy is well developed and widely disseminated. Most senior executives have been trained in its principles, and large corporations have their own skilled strategy personnel and in-house strategy expertise. Yet the business world remains littered with examples of bad strategies. Why? What makes chief executives back them when so much know-how is available? Notwithstanding the changing world which includes greater regulation, threats of terrorism, more demanding customers, changing technology and growth of the silver economy, excessive ambition, greed, and other corporate vices are all possible causes. This is a worry, given the rise of the emerging markets and the digital revolution. Some commentators, such as Henry Mintzberg, argue that strategic planning is dead. But as per Mark Twain, who remarked on learning that his death had been incorrectly reported, "the reports of my death are greatly exaggerated", this textbook contends that such missives tend to be based on faulty assumptions. More specifically, this chapter will closely consider strategy terminology; vision, mission and objectives; perspectives of strategy; the strategy consulting profession. Figure 2.1 raises two pertinent questions, which can be answered after reading this chapter.

There has been a plethora of academic and airport-type books offering simplistic approaches to a complex subject. *Contemporary Issues in Strategic Management* seeks to investigate how to drive organisational change, but realises that those responsible for leading

> What is strategy?
> Why is it important?

Figure 2.1 Two questions

organisations cannot afford to adopt a blueprint approach. For example, the past is no longer a guide to the future. To meet the challenges of discontinuity and to maintain/enhance market position, organisations must learn to change. Recession aftershocks, huge new risks, and persuasive uncertainty together with the challenges defining today's business environment place a greater premium than ever on good corporate strategy. Yet the strategic-planning approaches that many organisations devised for such times are ineffective. The world continues to change at a pace (see Figure 2.2), which is not making it easier for the CEO.

One question to consider is whether CEOs with good strategies that could lead to creating value for investors should be rewarded. A thought provoking *Harvard Business Review* article by Zenger (2013) raised the question "are unique or complex strategies systematically ignored by analysts or undervalued by capital markets?" His findings found factors such as company size and trade volumes influence analysts' decisions about which companies to cover. Zenger concluded that capital markets routinely undervalue companies with complex or unique strategies.

Yet, the literature holds that good strategies will be reflected favourably in the capital markets. Generally, this may be the case, but sometimes this does not hold in practice. During the 1990s, hotel CEOs often complained that the financial markets did not appear to understand or appreciate their strategies. Financial analysts at the time did sometimes acknowledge the quality of the strategy, but admitted that the hotel sector was not that attractive to their clients. They cited reasons such as the lack of size in terms of market capitalisation, and that these organisations possessed businesses that needed to be unbundled. Over the next two decades, at least in terms of the London Stock market, the majority of hotel companies disappeared. The British company Intercontinental Hotel Group (IHG), the world's largest hotel group has pursued an asset-light business model. A feature of the asset-light business model is its focus on franchising and managing hotels rather than tying up capital owning them. In 2015, IHG operated under one of three business models, owned and leased (7 hotels), managed (806 hotels), franchised (4,219 hotels). Ninety per cent of IHG operating profit was generated from its asset-light franchise and management contracts. The CEO of IHG sees this as a strategy that creates greater returns for owners, whilst using their skills managing the hotel asset.

2.3 Strategy terminology

The following section will briefly take stock of some of the salient strategy terminology and some of its challenges facing academics and practitioners. A good starting point is to consider the core lexicon in use and taught during introductory business school modules

- Regulation
- Terrorism
- Global market
- Environment
- Demanding customers and other stakeholders
- Complex supply chains
- Technology – channels of communication/intellectual property
- Emerging markets

Figure 2.2 The world is changing – fast!

in strategy. The terms strategy and strategic management, although not synonymous, are often treated as such. Schendel (1994) posits that strategic management is the field of study and strategy is the main topic of study. We shall now look at definitions for strategy, and strategic management, but need to be cognisant of the varying contexts for strategy (see Figure 2.3).

Definition of strategy

The kernel of the strategic management field is strategy. The absence of a sufficiently agreed-upon definition has led to confusion among academics and managers (Markides, 2004). Nevertheless, some academics feel that if strategic management is a science then the field should not be dependent upon a singular view of strategy (Mintzberg, 1987; Pfeffer, 1993). A co-word analysis study for the period 1962–2008 by Ronda-Pupo and Guerras-Martin (2012) found that the essence of the strategy concept is the dynamics of the firm's relation with its environment, for which the necessary actions are taken to achieve its goals and/or increase performance by means of the rational use of resources. In the second part of the Ronda-Pupo and Guerras-Martin (2012) study the internal perspective was included in the definition of strategy.

Definition of strategic management

Ramos-Rodríguez and Ruíz-Navarro's (2004) analysis of strategic management found that books had greater influence than academic journal articles in the primeval phases of the strategic management history field. With strategic management now becoming a mature enough topic to be treated as a research topic in its own right, it may be the case that the field should not be dependent upon a singular view of strategic management. Researchers are drawn to the reviews of the strategic management field. For example, Nag et al.'s (2007) large-scale survey of strategic management scholars defines strategic management as dealing "with the major intended and emergent initiatives taken by general managers on behalf of owners, involving utilisation of resources, to enhance the performance of firms in their external environments". This definition is of interest, as it notes that strategic management consists of both deliberate and emergent processes. Nerur, Rasheed and Natarajan's (2008) study complements Ramos-Rodríguez and Ruíz-Navarro's (2004) analysis and provides the reader with a useful historical trace of the intellectual structure of strategic management. Their results show the influence of individual authors and changes in their influence over time. Strategy content and the identification of the firm's strategy need to take into account a variety of subjects (see Figure 2.4).

- Small medium-sized enterprises (SMEs)
- Multinational enterprises (MNEs)
- Manufacturing/service organisations
- Public sector
- Voluntary and not for profit
- Social enterprises

Figure 2.3 Different contexts for strategy

28 *Strategic management primer*

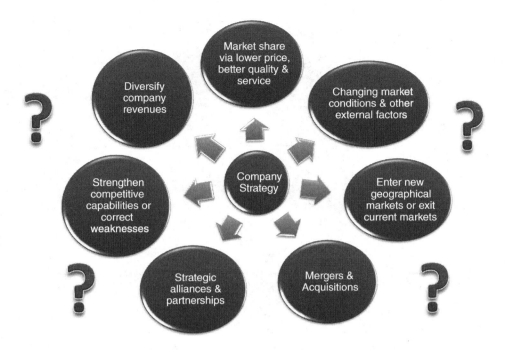

Figure 2.4 Strategy content – how to identify company strategy?

Strategy levels

From an organisation's vision and mission, a strategy will emanate. A single strategy is no longer sufficient. Multiple levels need strategies in varying contexts. The "Why" question is strategic; the "What" question is tactical; the "How" question is operational. So, the CEO and their team must develop strategies at various levels of the firm – alliance, corporate, business and functional. In terms of implementation, structure, processes and culture are core enablers, which can result in higher levels of strategic performance (see Figure 2.5).

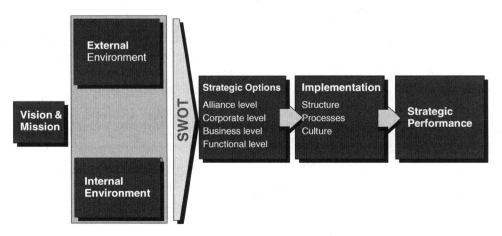

Figure 2.5 Strategic management

POD

Alibaba

The numbers behind China's e-commerce giant Alibaba's IPO in September 2014 were mind boggling. The $25bn raised netted the underwriters more than $300m with Alibaba paying $121.8m in commissions. The $25bn raised was more than the record set by Agriculture Bank of China Ltd in 2010. Jack Ma, a former English teacher and founder, had smiles as the share price jumped from $68 to $96.29. After peaking at $120, one year later in September 2015 the share price has plummeted to nearly $60. In terms of comparison Alibaba lost a third of its value but the S&P was down less than 2 per cent for the period.

Today, Alibaba consists of a number of key businesses such as Taobao, a Chinese consumer-to-consumer website much like eBay. Tmall acts as a storefront to consumers in China. AliExpress and Alibaba connect businesses in China with buyers around the globe. Jack Ma and his team possess an online payment platform called Alipay. Strategic stakes are placed in Sina Weibi, and YouKu Tuduo, Chinese versions of Twitter and Youtube. Investments are also made in cloud computing and internet infrastructure firms. The Chinese economic slowdown has meant that a drop in spending growth and the share price is not at the level it reached on its spectacular first day of trading.

Alliance strategy

Whether measured in terms of sales, assets or market capitalisation, alliances now account for a significant share of organisations' corporate value. From its origin position of being at the periphery of corporate strategy, discussions at the alliance level now take greater importance. The consequences of getting the alliance strategy wrong can lead to corporate failure. The Swissair Group's failure in 2001 is a prime example of the dangers of pursuing a global strategy. The airline's failure to define a clear direction and make the appropriate decisions when faced with the crisis led to its demise. The literature does state that strategic alliances offer huge opportunities, but sometimes they are formed as the last throw of the dice.

So why do strategic alliances prove so challenging? Inter-organisational collaboration can be complex and risky, and such alliances exhibit low rates of success. Kale and Singh (2009) state that between 30 per cent and 70 per cent of alliances fail, with termination rates of over 50 per cent (Lunnan & Haughland, 2008), in many cases destroying shareholder value (Kale, Dyer & Singh, 2002). The starting point is usually one organisation desiring access to another organisation's strength, which could be in terms of distribution, technology, marketing, or knowledge in exchange for providing either resources or access to an ingredient for overcoming the partner's weakness. But the overwhelming majority of academic studies assert partners' failures to cooperate, due to misaligned incentives of self-interested agents (Gulati, Wohlgezogen & Zhelyazkov, 2012).

Case study

Apple and IBM form a strategic alliance

APPLE AND IBM FORGE GLOBAL PARTNERSHIP TO TRANSFORM ENTERPRISE MOBILITY

CUPERTINO, California and ARMONK, New York—July 15, 2014—Apple® and IBM (NYSE: IBM) today announced an exclusive partnership that teams the market-leading strengths of each company to transform enterprise mobility through a new class of business apps—bringing IBM's big data and analytics capabilities to iPhone® and iPad®.

The landmark partnership aims to redefine the way work will get done, address key industry mobility challenges and spark true mobile-led business change—grounded in four core capabilities:

- a new class of more than 100 industry-specific enterprise solutions including native apps, developed exclusively from the ground up, for iPhone and iPad;
- unique IBM cloud services optimised for iOS, including device management, security, analytics and mobile integration;
- new AppleCare® service and support offering tailored to the needs of the enterprise; and
- new packaged offerings from IBM for device activation, supply and management.

The new IBM MobileFirst for iOS solutions will be built in an exclusive collaboration that draws on the distinct strengths of each company: IBM's big data and analytics capabilities, with the power of more than 100,000 IBM industry and domain consultants and software developers behind it, fused with Apple's legendary consumer experience, hardware and software integration and developer platform. The combination will create apps that can transform specific aspects of how businesses and employees work using iPhone and iPad, allowing companies to achieve new levels of efficiency, effectiveness and customer satisfaction—faster and easier than ever before.

As part of the exclusive IBM MobileFirst for iOS agreement, IBM will also sell iPhones and iPads with the industry-specific solutions to business clients worldwide.

"iPhone and iPad are the best mobile devices in the world and have transformed the way people work with over 98 percent of the Fortune 500 and over 92 percent of the Global 500 using iOS devices in their business today," said Tim Cook, Apple's CEO. "For the first time ever we're putting IBM's renowned big data analytics at iOS users' fingertips, which opens up a large market opportunity for Apple. This is a radical step for enterprise and something that only Apple and IBM can deliver."

"Mobility—combined with the phenomena of data and cloud—is transforming business and our industry in historic ways, allowing people to re-imagine work, industries and professions," said Ginni Rometty, IBM Chairman, President and CEO. "This alliance with Apple will build on our momentum in bringing these innovations to our clients globally, and leverages IBM's leadership in analytics, cloud, software and services. We are delighted to be teaming with Apple, whose innovations have transformed our lives in ways we take for granted, but can't imagine living without. Our alliance will bring the same kind of transformation to the way people work, industries operate and companies perform."

Apple and IBM's shared vision for this partnership is to put in the hands of business professionals everywhere the unique capabilities of iPads and iPhones with a company's knowledge, data, analytics and workflows. Specifically, the two companies are working together to deliver the essential elements of enterprise mobile solutions:

- Mobile solutions that transform business: The companies will collaborate to build IBM MobileFirst for iOS Solutions—a new class of "made-for-business apps" targeting specific industry issues or opportunities in retail, healthcare, banking, travel and transportation, telecommunications and insurance, among others, that will become available starting this fall and into 2015.

- Mobile platform: The IBM MobileFirst Platform for iOS will deliver the services required for an end-to-end enterprise capability, from analytics, workflow and cloud storage, to fleet-scale device management, security and integration. Enhanced mobile management includes a private app catalog, data and transaction security services, and productivity suite for all IBM MobileFirst for iOS solutions. In addition to on-premise software solutions, all these services will be available on Bluemix—IBM's development platform on the IBM Cloud Marketplace.
- Mobile service and support: AppleCare for Enterprise will provide IT departments and end users with 24/7 assistance from Apple's award-winning customer support group, with on-site service delivered by IBM.
- Packaged service offerings: IBM is introducing IBM MobileFirst Supply and Management for device supply, activation and management services for iPhone and iPad, with leasing options.

Announced at Apple's Worldwide Developer Conference in June and available later this year, Apple's iOS 8 is the biggest release since the launch of the App Store^{SM}, giving users incredible new features and developers the tools to create amazing new apps. For enterprise, iOS 8 builds on the new IT model for a mobilised workforce by improving the way users are informed of how their devices are configured, managed or restricted, with expanded security, management and productivity features.

Apple designs Macs, along with OS X, iLife, iWork and professional software. Apple leads the digital music revolution with its iPods and iTunes online store. Apple has reinvented the mobile phone with its revolutionary iPhone and App Store, and is defining the future of mobile media and computing devices with iPad.

IBM's 5,000 mobile experts have been at the forefront of mobile enterprise innovation. IBM has secured more than 4,300 patents in mobile, social and security, that have been incorporated into IBM MobileFirst solutions that enable enterprise clients to radically streamline and accelerate mobile adoption, help organisations engage more people and capture new markets.

IBM has made a dozen acquisitions in security in the past decade, has more than 6,000 security researchers and developers in its 25 security labs worldwide that work on developing enterprise-class solutions.

IBM has also established the world's deepest portfolio in Big Data and Analytics consulting and technology expertise based on experiences drawn from more than 40,000 data and analytics client engagements. This analytics portfolio spans research and development, solutions, software and hardware, and includes more than 15,000 analytics consultants, 4,000 analytics patents, 6,000 industry solution business partners, and 400 IBM mathematicians who are helping clients use big data to transform their organisations.

For more information regarding the new Apple and IBM solutions, please visit www.ibm.com/MobileFirstForiOS or www.apple.com/ipad/business.

Press Contacts:

Edward Barbini

IBM

barbini@us.ibm.com

(914) 499-6565

Corporate level strategy

A corporate level strategy determines the goals of the organisation and creates appropriate structure and processes. CEOs, have to lead on corporate level activities, making the necessary decisions that will add value at the corporate level. Yet, contingency theory, which posits that there is no optimal strategy for all organisations, and that the most desirable strategy depends upon a number of factors (Donaldson, 1996), leads to CEOs facing abundant choices for pursuing a growth strategy. The corporate level strategy lexicon has traditionally been based around diversification, differentiation, and strategic positioning, and also involves making decisions around (i) where to compete, (ii) which value creating activities should be pursued, and (iii) how the organisation should enter the marketplace. Ideally, the perspective is long-term together with the mechanisms in place to monitor changes taking place externally and internally within the organisation.

CEOs remain under pressure to sustain top line growth and too much emphasis on external positioning may lead to organisations chasing opportunities where they do not have the capabilities to succeed. Moreover, in chasing too many opportunities resources become stretched too thinly. Successful organisations today tend to figure out what they are really best-in-class at and ensure that their capabilities are aligned with marketplace opportunities. The opportunities actually pursued are not solely based on external market analysis using financial metrics, but based upon internal capabilities such as knowledge, people, processes, systems and tools that can create enhanced levels of stakeholder value.

In terms of broader goals of the organisation, these should include incorporating the relationship between business and society. Problems in society are becoming increasingly complex, and the expectation that companies should play a more prominent role in addressing these issues will escalate. The Committee Encouraging Corporate Philanthropy (2010) concluded that to reach a state of sustainable value creation, organisations should begin by rigorously selecting the social issues on what to lead and engage, ensuring that the issues are integral to the achievement of larger organisational goals. Despite these compelling reasons, it also raises the question of whether such types of organisational social engagement are genuinely altruistic. If one takes the view that businesses exist to serve society, then the starting point is that organisations should add value for society as well for themselves. Chapter 9 adopts this expansive view and delves into the ethical challenges faced by the CEO.

Business level strategy

Making business level strategies work may be part of the annual strategic planning exercise, a transformational effort or a response to a business failure. The emphasis is upon making decisions about what services and products the business should provide. Strategic business units can be distinguished from each other in terms of product line, division, and profit centres. Yet, decision-making can be somewhat confusing, as the literature proposes a broad array of strategy typologies to pursue. These tend to assess the attractiveness of the industry or competitive environment, and organisational capabilities. Organisations consist of a portfolio of businesses, and attempts to categorise the complex phenomenon of business strategy into a limited number of strategy typologies may involve over-simplification. Chapter 3 will articulate prior dimensions of business level strategy and outline strategies being pursued by organisations in mature and declining industries.

Information technology is a conduit to organisational success as it can directly affect the mechanism through which the firm can create and capture value to earn a profit (Drnevich & Croson, 2013). The continued advancements in information technology have had a profound effect upon business infrastructure. Organisations of all shapes, sizes and cultures have become digital with increased information flows among products, processes and services. As businesses continue to invest in information technology, such as going more mobile, using more complex analytics and enhancing the online experience, a strategic perspective is now imperative. Today's fusion of IT strategy and business strategy, which advances the prior view that IT strategy is a mere functional level strategy (Phillips, 2003) is compelling. The previous under-appreciation of the business level role of IT indicates a need for a reconceptualisation of its role in strategy together with the complex and interdependent relationships with the mechanisms through which organisations generate profit (Drnevich & Croson, 2013). Bharadwaj et al. (2013) propose a working definition of digital business strategy as "organisational strategy formulated and executed by leveraging digital resources to create differential value." They go on to identify four key themes to help managers think strategically on digital business strategy, these being (i) scope of digital business strategy, (ii) scale of digital business strategy, (iii) speed of digital business strategy, and (iv) source of business value creation and capture in digital business strategy.

Functional level strategy

Functional level strategy creates the action plans to achieve objectives as outlined in the corporate and business strategies. These action plans can lead to organisations obtaining superior efficiency, quality, innovation and customer responsiveness. Effective management of core functions such as accounting and finance, marketing, productions and operations, human resource management and research and development are a prerequisite for effective strategic planning, implementation and control. How each function contributes to business strategy, and determining their priorities is a concern for the CEO. Organisations can become market leaders based on their unique functional skills and competencies. This can either enable the execution of functional activities more efficiently or lower cost, or derive a differentiation advantage from their competitors. Functional strategies can build resources and capabilities that enhance an organisation's distinct competencies. Marketing now needs to be reinvented as the business environment is now more fragmented. With a less fragmented world consumers did not have digital megaphones that could influence the masses, but now they are able to. Such conditions now stifle the agility of marketing.

Many executives openly state that they work in siloed organisations. Information is seen as power and is not shared for the benefit of others. This type of behaviour reduces efficiency, morale and productivity. CEOs need to practice true customer-centric behaviour that is integrated into all business processes, i.e. not a silo. Many departments (including marketing) are now being examined, analysed and turned inside out. They can no longer avoid getting swept up by the latest management thinking about how companies operate, which is without rigid functional silos. The focus now is on siloed functions being replaced by a more fluid, cross-functional, and integrated way of working.

Strategy tools

Students, researchers and practitioners possess a bank of strategy tools and techniques that they use to help formulate strategies. Scenarios can range from a case study based exam paper, research being written up in an academic journal paper to an analysis being performed as part of due diligence during a potential merger and acquisition. In such circumstances a tool should not be seen as a panacea in its own right. Also knowing the popular tools in use in practice helps to ensure that the strategy knowledge is current.

Rigby and Bilodeau (2015), based on a survey of 1,067 executives, reports that executives were confident and upbeat, with 74 per cent saying that their current financial performance is strong, and 55 per cent believe economic conditions are improving in their industry (see Figure 2.6). The report states that the sectors of pharma and biotech, construction and real estate, and financial services are the most optimistic. In terms of the most popular tools in use, customer relationship management was in pole position with benchmarking, employee engagement surveys and strategic planning highly ranked. Tool preferences and satisfaction levels did vary by region with strategic planning ranking ninth and fifth in EMEA and APAC respectively. Both EMEA and Latin America had balanced scorecards ranked in third position. Another observation is the number one position of big data analytics in APAC, with it being ranked low in other regions (Rigby & Bilodeau, 2015).

The growth in customer relationship management usage is a consequence in part of social media. CRM tools can be used to retrieve data from social media networking sites and scrape data from various sources. These actions will enhance interaction with the customer. By tracking and interacting with customers, organisations will increase their business by improving their service and/or product offer. Collectively they will help the organisation to be continually updating the marketing agenda. Employee engagement enables the CEO to tap into their workforce creativity and innovation. Such enthusiasm for the organisation's strategy and vision will translate into greater trust and greater levels of discretionary effort and predisposition behaviour. Employee engagement surveys can raise potential issues of concern prior to them affecting employee performance. Ideally each employee engagement survey should be based on the precise requirements of the organisation, and depend upon the target group. Basic issues to consider include views of management style, and satisfaction with remuneration and benefits. Leading organisations do stress that competitive advantage can be obtained by measuring, recognising and enhancing employee engagement levels.

	Agree (%)	Disagree (%)
Our ability to adapt and change is a significant competitive advantage	75	13
Innovation is more important than cost reduction for long-term success	74	9
Our financial performance is strong	74	10
Over the next three years, our it spending must increase as a percentage of sales	64	16
Customers are less loyal to brands than they used to be	62	19

Figure 2.6 View on management trends

Both benchmarking and strategic planning have been continually ranked as leading management tools and a core feature of this textbook will be to ensure that management are incorporating contemporary issues in their benchmarking and strategic planning activities.

POD

Brexit

The then Prime Minister David Cameron called a referendum, which was held on Thursday 23 June 2016, the vote being to decide whether the UK should leave or remain in the European Union. The turnout was nearly 72 per cent with more than 30 million people voting. Surprisingly, the leave vote won by 52 per cent to 48 per cent.

England and Wales voted strongly for Brexit with 53.4 per cent and 52.5 per cent respectively, while Scotland and Northern Ireland voted to remain, with 62 per cent and 55.8 per cent respectively. The term "Brexit" (Britain and exit) is now synonymous with a way of saying leaving the EU. The consequences of Brexit have been far reaching, with a change in Prime Minister when David Cameron resigned on the day after losing the referendum. Theresa May, the former home secretary took over from David Cameron. Despite Theresa May saying "Brexit means Brexit", there appears to be a lack of clarity over how British firms will work in the EU and what restrictions will be placed on EU nationals who live and work in the UK. The value of Sterling slumped to a three-decade low, and prices of both commodity and luxury items have increased in prices. The loss of the AAA credit rating has increased the cost of government borrowing, and the Bank of England had to cut interest rates from 0.5 per cent to 0.25 per cent, to curb threats of a recession and to stimulate investment.

2.4 Vision, mission and objectives

Strategy will lie in the mind of the CEO but needs to be made explicit to stakeholders. Much secrecy may surround the actual discussions of strategy held at strategy away-days and board meetings, but there comes a time when it needs to be made explicit. A vision statement should describe the desired future position of the organisation. A mission statement defines how the organisation will turn the vision into reality together with the underlying philosophy. Both vision and mission statements can be inspiring, complete with self-description, or rather bland. Ideally, they should be succinct and to the point but also with caveats, now that so many consultants and online providers are offering template-type products.

There have been some notable examples. The 2013 1,200-word jargon-filled "mission statement" of Warwickshire Police, which did not even include the word crime is something to be avoided. Tellingly, its vision was subsequently changed to "protecting people from harm" and they listed the following values:

- take pride in our professionalism and standards of behaviour
- listen and engage
- use professional judgement and be courageous in making decisions
- seek out better ways of working
- lead with confidence and do the right thing
- work in partnership to provide the best service we can

Warwickshire Police end their vision and values statement by stating that the vision and values will form the basis of the alliance developing organisational culture – a set of shared attitudes, goals, practices and aspirations. We can see that elements of mission and vision statements can be combined to provide a statement of the company's purposes, goals and values. A statement outlines the tools for the organisation to accomplish its aspirations. The values will demonstrate the core ideology and behaviours that the organisation wishes to portray. The CEO should ensure that the mission should be adapted as the organisation evolves.

Objectives are necessary to provide the quantitative numbers, which can quickly indicate if the desired strategy is on or off track. Key performance indicators can be effectively used to enable managers and subordinates to keep track of organisational performance. When monitoring achievement of objectives, the underlying action plans i.e. how exactly the results will be achieved, are crucial. Too many KPIs can be harmful. For example, Tesco Plc in its 2015 strategy report stated "for a long time, we measured our performance using the Steering Wheel. This served us well for many years, but as time has gone on, it has become too complex, with over 40 different measures. We now have just six simple, key business performance measures" (Tesco 2015):

- customers recommend us and come back time and again
- colleagues recommend us as a great place to work and shop
- we build trusted partnerships
- grow sales
- deliver profit
- improve operating cash flow.

Strategy nugget

Foreigners to pay for emergency healthcare

From the article "Putting a price on health" by Francis Elliott and Chris Smyth in *The Times*, 31 October 2015.

JEREMY HUNT WILL ANNOUNCE THE CHANGES NEXT MONTH

Foreigners will be forced to pay for using an ambulance or visiting A&E under a £500 million crackdown on "health tourism".

Jeremy Hunt, the health secretary, will announce charges for emergency treatment and travel on all non-British residents for the first time next month, *The Times* has learnt.

Emergency care should not be delayed by the need for payment, officials say, but any treatment judged non-urgent – even in A&E departments – should be withheld until fees are paid.

The move comes amid pressure to find more savings before next month's spending review. Mr Hunt believes that the charges, combined with the present fees for foreigners' routine care, could help the NHS to recoup £500 million a year. It faces an annual £30 billion shortfall in the next parliament.

All visitors to the UK, including British expats, already have to pay up to 150 per cent of the cost of elective care, but ministers excluded A&E, ambulances and visits to the GP because of fears that it would cause anger among doctors and patients, and undermine public health.

The latest decision could leave patients facing bills for thousands of pounds. Seeing an A&E doctor costs the NHS a minimum of £56 if no treatment is needed, and £316 with more extensive care. Scans and tests can cost more than £200 each. Crisis maternity care would fall under the new charging system; it was previously exempt.

The Department of Health said that it was fair to charge non-UK taxpayers for using the health service. "International visitors are welcome to use the NHS, provided they pay for it – just as families living in the UK do through their taxes," a spokesman told *The Times*. "This government was the first to introduce tough measures to clamp down on migrants accessing NHS care and we have always been clear we want to look at extending charges."

Visitors from the EU must present a European Health Insurance Card so that the NHS can send the bill to their government, while those from outside Europe will be chased for the fees. The government concedes, however, that little can be done if patients leave the country and ignore a letter demanding payment.

Doctors said yesterday that they would refuse to act as border guards, with health leaders warning that the "half-baked" plans could stop the sick from seeking treatment.

John Ashton, president of the Faculty of Public Health, said: "You only have to look at America: people without insurance are intimidated from seeking care, and you have to produce a visa card before anyone will look at you. So this must affect the willingness of people to seek the help they need."

He questioned how much the plan would raise if it needed "armies of clerks collecting small amounts of money" and added: "In terms of our standing in the world, for what is a small amount of money, are we prepared to throw away our reputation of being a humane country?"

The British Medical Association has previously refused checks on patients' status. Mark Porter, chairman of its governing council, said: "A doctor's duty is to treat the patient in front of them, not to act as border guard. Any plans to charge migrants and short-term visitors need to be practical, economic and efficient."

Roger Goss, of Patient Concern, said: "The average patient would think 'quite right too!' In other countries they won't touch you until you get out your credit card and that's how they ought to operate here . . . But the main issue is not whether patients are supposed to pay, it's the failure of hospitals to collect the money."

Officials say that no one will be denied urgent treatment and that refugees and other vulnerable groups will be exempt from charges. The plans are to go out to consultation next month.

The scale of "health tourism" in Britain is disputed, with a government report two years ago estimating it at between £70 million and £300 million. Much concern has centred on claims that pregnant women from overseas are flying in to give birth on the NHS.

Officials have calculated that only £73 million of the £461 million that should be charged to overseas visitors is recouped, estimating that half a billion could be raised by chasing payment and barring health tourists.

A spokesman for the Royal College of Emergency Medicine said that A&E doctors "cannot reasonably be expected to take on the burden on identifying who is eligible for free treatment, and who should be charged."

Questions

1 Do you believe that it's reasonable to place on price on healthcare?
2 Outline the impact of charging foreign nationals for healthcare. What are the potential unintentional consequences of such a policy?

Table 2.1 Putting a price on health

Activity	£
Ambulance call-out	180
Ambulance call-out with trip to hospital	231
Immediate A&E treatment of broken leg	224
MRI scan of several areas	282
Normal birth with epidural	3,345
ECG monitoring and stress testing	794
Minor arm treatment	216
Dental fitting	176

2.5 Perspectives of strategy

The strategic management literature gets divided into differing opinions. These include ten schools of strategy (Mintzberg, Ahlstrand & Lampel, 2008), and the deliberate and emergent schools.

Ten schools of strategy

- Design – as a process of conception. Despite being widely advocated, it possesses weaknesses that are exposed in turbulent environments.
- Planning – as a formal process. Strategy can be too static, which makes prediction difficult.
- Positioning – as an analytical process. Ignores the soft management areas such as power, politics, culture and is the approach for large firms.
- Entrepreneurial – as a visionary process. Being the architect is an extremely demanding approach for the CEO.
- Cognitive – as a mental process. Problems occur beyond the initial conceptual stage.
- Learning – as an emergent process. Runs the risk of not adopting a clear strategy.
- Power – as a process of negotiation. Can be a divisive process where muddling along becomes the norm.
- Cultural – as a collective process. The vagueness of culture can make it difficult to know how things should be done.
- Environment – as a reactive process. The complexity of the environment makes it difficult to know the salient force affecting the firm.
- Configuration – as a process of transformation. Within the top management team there may be differing views of the reality facing the firm – pattern is in the eye of the beholder.

Deliberate vs. emergent strategy

Figure 2.7 advocates five kinds of strategy: deliberate, intended, realised, unrealised and emergent strategies. If an intended strategy is an input and realised strategy is an output, this can be distinguished from an emergent strategy, where observations in the absence of intentions are derived from an unrealised strategy. Deliberate strategy is the link between intended strategy and realised strategy. This outcome may be successful or unsuccessful, resulting in aspirations being realised or unrealised. This deliberate approach concurs with the strategies being pursued in the period from the 1950s to the 1980s, evident in the early schools of strategy, including design school, strategy as position, strategy as culture and strategy as organisational learning. During this period, implementation of the corporate level strategy involves a series of management interventions. From a middle managerial perspective, these interventions include: organisational structures, key personal actions, control systems (Hrebiniak & Joyce, 1984) together with the alignment of organisational action, with strategic intentions being the fourth (Floyd & Wooldridge, 1992). However, academics such as Eisenhardt and Brown (1998) forcefully stated that deliberate strategy does not adequately cope with the future.

Interestingly, despite Mintzberg's polemic statements he does note that few, if any strategies are purely deliberate, just as few are purely emergent. Mintzberg et al. (2008) do distinguish strategy as either deliberate or emergent. One requires no learning, the other requires no control. All real-world strategies need to mix these in some way: to control while fostering learning. Raisch and Birkinshaw (2008) posit that academics recognise the importance of balancing seemingly contradictory tensions. As Goold and Quinn (1990) remark, "detailed and precise plans and strategies" don't work for modern organisations as decisions are often "messy and political" and firms need to possess the flexibility to take advantages of new opportunities.

Emergent strategy should be a critical element when dealing with turbulent environments. CEOs cannot overlook the usefulness of emergent strategy and ensure that space is allowed for such endeavours to occur. If the CEO chooses an action that is explicitly planned then it cannot be emergent. The emergent strategy can be the result of a series of actions culminating as a pattern of behaviour in a quest to take advantage of an opportunity.

Ambidexterity

One of the key business drivers that emanate throughout this book is the need for organisations to continually adapt to a dynamic environment and implement innovative strategies to meet or create future demand. Given the dichotomy of deliberate and emergent strategies, organisations must resolve such tensions harmoniously. As aptly stated by Tushman and O'Reilly (1996), managers suffer from problems in overcoming inertia and implementing innovation and change.

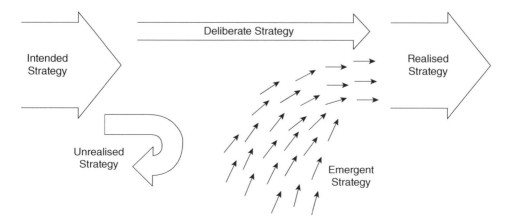

Figure 2.7 Deliberate and emergent strategies

In terms of organisational learning modes, ambidexterity can help CEOs reconcile exploration and exploitative approaches. The academic literature informs us that organisations need to balance exploitation and exploration (Levinthal & March, 1993). Despite their differences, both learning modes are necessary to ensure long-term success and survival. The term ambidexterity is also used as an organisational metaphor, when organisations attempt to balance deliberate and emergent approaches to strategy. Tushman and O'Reilly (1996) developed and expanded the metaphor of ambidexterity. Empirical studies reveal two different types of ambidexterity – structural and contextual (Gibson & Birkinshaw, 2004). The former approach relates to the exploitative and exploratory tasks, and the latter approach relates to cultural values and norms of the organisational context. Structural ambidexterity has been the main priority in the literature. In contrast, contextual ambidexterity needs collective sense-making, a common mindset and a mutual absorptive capacity among individuals with a broad knowledge on heterogeneous tasks as a prerequisite for alternating between exploitation and exploration (Güttel & Konlechner, 2009).

Gibson and Birkinshaw (2004, p. 210) in their study conclude that organisational ambidexterity is best achieved by "building a set of processes or systems that enable and encourage individuals to make their own judgements about how to divide their time between conflicting demands for alignment and adaptability". During times of organisational change the ability to implement renewal strategies is vital. Ambidextrous organisations can simultaneously exploit their existing capabilities while exploring new opportunities (O'Reilly & Tushman, 2008). Academics have used the insights gained from the ambidexterity literature to link with other key strategic processes. Bodwell and Chermack (2010) describe a useful scenario planning method for fostering organisational ambidexterity. They refer to three capabilities described in the ambidexterity literature – sensing, seizing and reconfiguring. Kortmann et al. (2014) illustrate the link between strategic flexibility and operational efficiency using innovative ambidexterity (Jansen et al., 2006) as a key construct. The SME focus of the Voss and Voss (2013) study is a welcome addition to the literature. The authors note the challenges for SMEs in balancing exploitation and exploration. They tend to lack resources, capabilities, and the experience to implement ambidexterity. Voss and Voss's findings include that smaller theatres have greater difficulty than larger theatres when dealing with the ambidexterity challenge. There appears to be some economy of scale effects when considering the ambidexterity–performance relationship.

2.6 Strategy consulting

This section briefly considers strategy consulting. Figure 2.8 reaffirms the problems of being too over-focused on analysis and extrapolation.

> Being too over-focused on analysis and extrapolation rather than creativity and invention, the strategic planning effort can create the illusion of certainty for senior management. But in today's world certainty is anything but guaranteed.

Figure 2.8 Beware!

Strategy 41

Firms

The strategy consultant is an influential external actor well versed in the practice of strategy. Strategy firms are hired to support the CEO and their team in strategic decision-making. The consulting industry can trace its origins back to the late nineteenth century and the major firms evolving from the 1930s. The internationalisation process began to take off in the early 1960s, when large US firms entered Europe. These US firms, such as McKinsey, soon brought their models and tools to impact the structures of European MNEs. Now the top strategy firms include McKinsey, The Boston Consulting Group, and Bain & Co. In 2014, PwC acquired Booz Allen Hamilton and branded themselves Strategy&. The attraction of high-end, high-margin work has attracted other large accounting professional firms, Deloitte, EY and KPMG into the strategy consulting field too. Their scale enables them to push their one-stop shop approach with its cost savings for clients. Other points of differentiation include being a trusted advisor across accounting, tax and legal matters. Table 2.2 provides a summary of the top management consulting firms.

According to recent research by Gartner, in terms of the broader consulting market Deloitte Consulting, PwC / Strategy& and EY Advisory are the largest consulting firms on the globe. The Big Four accounting and consulting giants together hold 40 per cent of the market, and the top 200 firms globally distributing nearly 80 per cent of an advisory market are worth more than $125 billion. The traditional management consulting model has not significantly altered in a century. The model of hiring bright graduates and sending them out of the office to work on identifying solutions for the most difficult organisational problems has been the approach to strategy consulting. Strategy consulting can be broken down into the following areas: corporate strategy; business model transformation; economic policy; organisational strategy; functional strategy; mergers and acquisitions; strategy and operations in digital environments. Yet, the latter area is now cause for concern for strategy consulting. Table 2.3 illustrates the strategy firms' practice areas and sectors.

Disruptive forces

The digital age remains one of the driving forces behind the period of profound change the business world is currently undergoing. The development and diffusion of information and communication technologies have reached the point where they are bringing about structural changes to all aspects of business and society. Try as they may, strategy consultants help their

Table 2.2 Top management consulting firms

Name of consulting firms	Founded	Total Revenue	#of Employees
McKinsey & Co	1926	$7.8 billion	17,000
The Boston Consulting Group	1963	$3.95 million	6,200
Bain & Company	1973	$1.6 billion	5,000
Strategy& (Formerly Booz & Company)	1914	$1.3 billion	3,000
PricewaterhouseCoopers	1998	$32.1 billion	184,235
Deloitte Consulting	1845	$32.41 billion	203,000
Accenture	1989	$28.6 billion	293, 000
Oliver Wyman	1984	$1.36 billion	3,000
A.T. Kearney	1926	$1 billion	3,200
Ernst & Young	1989	25.8 billion	190, 000

Table 2.3 Strategy firms' practice areas and sectors

Firms	Practice areas	Sectors
McKinsey & Co	Marketing and sales planning, corporate financing, organisation, business technology.	Chemicals, media and entertainment, private equity, oil and gas, public sector, healthcare provider, telecommunication and automotive.
The Boston Consulting Group	Change management, cost and supply chain management, performance improvement, private equity, mergers and acquisitions, corporate renewal, financial management.	Healthcare, retail, education and public sector, technology, automotive, telecommunication, media, financial services, nonprofit organisations and pharmaceuticals.
Bain & Company	Performance improvement, change management, private equity investments, organisation, working capital management.	Nonprofit, technology, telecommunication, education, retail, public sector, energy and utilities, consumer products, mining, transportation and automotive.
PricewaterhouseCoopers	Corporate finance, operations, risk management, forensic services, performance and capital management.	Asset management, healthcare, construction and engineering, technology, real estate, capital market and banking, entertainment, energy, insurance, public sector, chemicals, aerospace and communications.
Deloitte Consulting	Tax advisory, strategic financial management, capital and operational management.	Health industry, federal and state government, entertainment, insurance, aerospace, technology, tourism, telecommunication, hospitality, life science, mutual funds and hedge funds.
Accenture	Strategic financial management, business valuation, capital, and operational management.	Healthcare and public sector, retail, financial institutions, media, technology and communication.
Olive Wyman	Marketing and sales planning, risk leadership, finance and risk management, leadership development, and actuarial services.	Communication, health care, retail, energy, industrial products, technology, aviation, media, transportation and automotive.
A.T. Kearney	Strategic financial management planning, mergers and acquisitions, organisation, sales and marketing planning and procurement.	Gas and oils, health, retail, mining, financial industry, public sector, utilities, private equity and infrastructure.
Ernst & Young	Financial and tax advisory, performance management, business valuation, strategic growth management and specialty services.	Oil and gas, healthcare, insurance, media, capital and banking markets, real estate, power utilities, technology, mining, and automotive.

Source: Advisoryhq.com 17 May 2016.

clients to tackle the repercussions of digital technologies in their industries, yet the consulting industry is braced for change itself.

What happens next for the strategy consulting industry has the potential to be disruptive. Aside from PwC acquiring Booz Allen Hamilton, there have been a number of significant transactions. Market changes have already affected the strategy consulting industry with firms such as Monitor (co-funded by Michael Porter) being acquired by Deloitte after being placed in bankruptcy, and LECG Corporation being liquidated in 2011. EY bought the strategy consulting firm Parthenon Group. According to Consultancy.uk, the online platform for the consultancy industry, KPMG sought to bundle its services and enter the strategy consulting market for three reasons. The global market is in a growth phase due in part to rapidly changing business models to new technologies, increased regulatory pressure and disruptions within sectors. Second, aligning strategy consulting within its advisory space will help grow market share. KPMG itself was lagging in terms of growth rate in comparison with its Big Four rivals. Third, by creating a strategy platform this will enable KPMG to respond more effectively to global requests.

Christensen, Wang and van Bever (2013) remark that the industry that assisted CEOs to sidestep strategic threats is no longer immune from disruption. They mention McKinsey & Company, McKinsey Solutions, software and technology-based analytics and tools. An early sign of change at other big strategy firms such as Bain and Boston Consulting Group is a decline in classical strategy work, which is now about 20 per cent down from about 60 to 70 per cent, according to Tom Rodenhauser, managing director of Kennedy Consulting Research & Advisory. The sacred cow of per diem billing is gradually being replaced by value-based pricing.

Christensen et al. (2013) articulate that lessons can be taken from the legal field, which saw a disruption in the general counsel model. It resulted in reducing organisations' reliance on law firms. The in-house law function grew as organisations got to compare the value derived from law firms with the fees that they were being charged. Statistics such as profits per partner highlighted the fees generated, which were traditionally hidden from organisations. This lack of transparency helped to maintain the traditional legal business model. Once knowledge is democratised traditional business models will change. Evidence of this is noted with organisations' in-house consulting teams ranging from ad hoc to teams in excess of 100 consultants.

2.7 Chapter summary

In this chapter we investigate some of the theoretical and practical strategy challenges facing the CEO. The hotel sector was used as an illustration of the communication challenges facing the CEO and how the sector has evolved via its asset-light strategy. Some facets of strategy terminology are introduced to provide the reader with a theoretical base for this and later chapters. This foundation enables the reader to consider strategy dilemmas from a variety of perspectives, which reinforces the array of solutions for any challenge. Through the examples provided, it is anticipated that readers will appreciate the various levels of strategy and ask the appropriate questions at each level. From our experience, students of strategy often fail to articulate answers which place sufficient context in their discussions.

The strategic issues raised in this chapter will hopefully get the reader to re-consider their initial thoughts and apply a range of approaches which are truly strategic rather than tactical. A key insight can be obtained from considering the ten schools of strategy, which can be used to get a more complete picture of strategy practice. Ambidexterity reinforces the message that the CEO needs to be continually adapting to both the internal and external environments.

Overcoming inertial and strategic implementation issues can bring about enhanced performance levels. External experts such as strategy consultants were introduced. The modern strategy firm and their clients currently face contradictory demands, and management thinking still matters.

2.8 End of chapter self-reflection questions

1 Why is the business world littered with examples of bad strategies? What are the salient reasons for this observation?
2 What are the priorities at alliance, corporate, business, and functional levels during the strategy formulation process? What are the key questions which should be addressed?
3 Explain the practical differences between vision, mission and objectives? What makes for a good vision and mission?
4 How do the ten schools of strategy assist the CEO during the strategy process?
5 To what extent are deliberate and emergent strategy processes mutually exclusive? Justify your thoughts with some practical examples.

References

Bharadwaj, A., El Sawy, O. A., Pavlou, P. A., & Venkatraman, N. (2013). Digital business strategy: Toward a next generation of insights. *MIS Quarterly*, *37*(2), 471–482.
Bodwell, W., & Chermack, T. J. (2010). Organizational ambidexterity: Integrating deliberate and emergent strategy with scenario planning. *Technological Forecasting and Social Change*, *77*(2), 193–202.
Christensen, C. M., Wang, D., & van Bever, D. (2013). Consulting on the Cusp of Disruption. *Harvard Business Review*, *91*(10), 106–14.
Committee Encouraging Corporate Philanthropy (2010). *Shaping the future: Solving social problems through business strategy. Pathways to sustainable value creation*. New York: McKinsey.
Donaldson, L. (1996). *For positivist organization theory*. London: Sage.
Drnevich, P. L., & Croson, D. C. (2013). Information technology and business-level strategy: Toward an integrated theoretical perspective. *MIS Quarterly*, *37*(2), 483–509.
Eisenhardt, K. M., & Brown, S. L. (1998). Patching: Restitching business portfolios in dynamic markets. *Harvard Business Review*, *77*(3), 72–82, 208.
Floyd, S. W., & Wooldridge, B. (1992). Middle management involvement in strategy and its association with strategic type: A research note. *Strategic Management Journal*, *13*(S1), 153–167.
Gibson, C. B., & Birkinshaw, J. (2004). The antecedents, consequences, and mediating role of organizational ambidexterity. *Academy of Management Journal*, *47*(2), 209–226.
Goold, M., & Quinn, J. J. (1990). The paradox of strategic controls. *Strategic Management Journal*, *11*, 43–57.
Gulati, R., Wohlgezogen, F., & Zhelyazkov, P. (2012). The two facets of collaboration: Cooperation and coordination in strategic alliances. *The Academy of Management Annals*, *6*(1), 531–583.
Güttel, W. H., & Konlechner, S. W. (2009). Continuously hanging by a thread: Managing contextually ambidextrous organizations. *Schmalenbach Business Review*, *61*, 150–171.
Hrebiniak, L. G., & Joyce, W. F. (1984). *Implementing strategy*. New York: Macmillan.
Jansen, J. J., Van den Bosch, Frans A. J., & Volberda, H. W. (2006). Exploratory innovation, exploitative innovation, and performance: Effects of organizational antecedents and environmental moderators. *Management Science*, *52*(11), 1661–1674.
Kale, P., & Singh, H. (2009). Managing strategic alliances: What do we know now, and where do we go from here? *Academy of Management Perspectives*, *23*(3), 45–62. doi:10.5465/AMP.2009.43479263
Kale, P., Dyer, J. H., & Singh, H. (2002). Alliance capability, stock market response, and long-term alliance success: The role of the alliance function. *Strategic Management Journal*, *23*(8), 747–767.

Kortmann, S., Gelhard, C., Zimmermann, C., & Piller, F. T. (2014). Linking strategic flexibility and operational efficiency: The mediating role of ambidextrous operational capabilities. *Journal of Operations Management*, *32*(7), 475–490.

Levinthal, D. A., & March, J. G. (1993). The myopia of learning. *Strategic Management Journal*, *14*(S2), 95–112.

Lunnan, R., & Haugland, S. A. (2008). Predicting and measuring alliance performance: A multidimensional analysis. *Strategic Management Journal*, *29*(5), 545–556.

Markides, C. (2004). What is strategy and how do you know if you have one? *Business Strategy Review*, *15*(2), 5–12.

Mintzberg, H. (1987). *Crafting strategy*. Boston, MA: Harvard Business School Press.

Mintzberg, H., Ahlstrand, B., & Lampel, J. (2008). *Strategy Safari*, 2nd edition. London: Financial Times Prentice Hall.

Nag, R., Hambrick, D. C., & Chen, M. (2007). What is strategic management, really? Inductive derivation of a consensus definition of the field. *Strategic Management Journal*, *28*(9), 935–955.

Nerur, S. P., Rasheed, A. A., & Natarajan, V. (2008). The intellectual structure of the strategic management field: An author co-citation analysis. *Strategic Management Journal*, *29*(3), 319–336.

O'Reilly, C. A., & Tushman, M. L. (2008). Ambidexterity as a dynamic capability: Resolving the innovator's dilemma. *Research in Organizational Behavior*, *28*, 185–206.

Phillips, P. A. (2003). *E-business strategy: Text and cases*. Maidenhead: McGraw-Hill.

Pfeffer, J. (1993). Barriers to the advance of organizational science: Paradigm development as a dependent variable. *Academy of Management Review*, *18*(4), 599–620.

Raisch, S. & Birkinshaw, J. (2008). Organizational ambidexterity: Antecedents, outcomes, and moderators. *Journal of Management*, *34*(3), 375–409.

Raisch, S., Birkinshaw, J., Probst, G., & Tushman, M. L. (2009). Organizational ambidexterity: Balancing exploitation and exploration for sustained performance. *Organization Science*, *20*(4), 685–695.

Ramos-Rodríguez, A. R., & Ruíz-Navarro, J. (2004). Changes in the intellectual structure of strategic management research: A bibliometric study of the Strategic Management Journal, 1980–2000. *Strategic Management Journal*, *25*(10), 981–1004.

Rigby, D., & Bilodeau, B. (2015). *Management tools and trends 2015*. London: Bain & Company.

Ronda-Pupo, G.A., & Guerras-Martin, L.Á. (2012). Dynamics of the evolution of the strategy concept 1962–2008: A co-word analysis. *Strategic Management Journal*, *33*(2), 162–188.

Schendel, D. (1994). Introduction to the summer 1994 special issue – 'Strategy: Search for new paradigms'. *Strategic Management Journal*, *15*(S2), 1–4.

Tesco (2015) Key performance indicators. Available at:https://www.tescoplc.com/media/264150/strategic_report_15.pdf

Tushman, M., & O'Reilly, C. (1996). Evolution and revolution: Mastering the dynamics of innovation and change. *California Management Review*, *38*(4), 8–30.

Voss, G. B., & Voss, Z. G. (2013). Strategic ambidexterity in small and medium-sized enterprises: Implementing exploration and exploitation in product and market domains. *Organization Science*, *24*(5), 1459–1477.

Zenger, T. (2013). Strategy: The uniqueness challenge. *Harvard Business Review*, *91*(11), 52–58.

3 Strategic analysis

3.1 Learning objectives

After completing this chapter you will:

- appreciate the concept of strategic analysis and underlying salient theory
- be able to critically analyse the competitive context in which an organisation operates
- be able to explain what is meant by an external and internal analysis
- be familiar and describe and apply some key tools of external and internal analysis
- be able to critically evaluate the future prospects of an organisation
- understand the necessity to develop successful strategies in today's world where adaptability and creativity drive business success.

3.2 Introduction

The structural transitions taking place in terms of speed, scale and scope are imposing new strains on managers. In many cases, old strategy recipes no longer work. New discontinuities can undermine a successful strategy. Managers are anxious about maintaining the competitive positioning of their firms, and continue to seek new approaches to guide their firm in turbulent environments (Prahalad & Hamel, 1994). With an out-dated strategy paradigm, managers turned their attention to "implementation" as their saviour, more or less abandoning strategy as either unimportant or uninteresting. Our view is that it is necessary to be acquainted with core strategy tools and then apply them appropriately in the correct context.

Currently, the business world is recovering after a deep economic recession in 2008. As a result, the business landscape has altered and new emerging drivers mean that the CEO needs new tools to analyse the firm. One of the changes can be characterised as the "corporate social responsibility" effect, which has radically changed customer consumption patterns and behaviour, and often creates public scepticism and lack of trust in senior managers. This theme will be elaborated upon in Chapter 9. Some of yesterday's thinking continues to be challenged (see Figure 3.1).

The corporate "I don't know factor" is higher than ever before, because business leaders lost their sense of direction in the global economic crisis and were unable to identify and focus on growth opportunities appropriate for their business. Figure 3.2 illustrates that the shift beyond economic profit evolves and customer value is increasingly a valuable strategic asset.

Strategic analysis 47

Figure 3.1 Where is the profit?

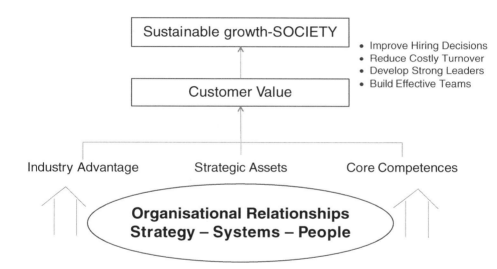

Figure 3.2 Determinants of company performance

Strategy nugget

CWC agrees to acquire Columbus International Inc. to accelerate growth strategy and deliver superior customer service - Nov 6, 2014

The combined business will:

- Deliver broader pro-consumer product offerings and improved services
- Inject state-of-the-art TV and next-generation broadband technology into CWC
- Deliver huge opportunities to the Business and Government sectors
- Provide rapid lead in fixed-mobile convergence through premier network platform

Cable and Wireless Communications PLC (CWC) has reached a conditional agreement to acquire Columbus International Inc. The proposed acquisition, valued at US$3.025bn will enable the combined company to significantly accelerate their growth strategy, improve service delivery to customers in the region, offer customers a comprehensive portfolio of high-quality products and services, and strengthen their position against larger competitors. The increased scale and capabilities of the combined company will provide the technical platform and financial capacity to help enable CWC to drive greater innovation and expand our geographic footprint.

The combination of the two companies is consistent with global industry trends, where convergence of fixed and mobile networks, increasing content consumption growth, and continuing development of online applications are driving requirements for high bandwidth, fixed line networks and TV capabilities. Operators in Europe and North America, as well as regional competitors, are acquiring and constructing networks that are capable of supporting ever-growing data needs along with new video capabilities.

The combination of the two businesses supports CWC's new strategy and its four primary areas of focus: Drive Mobile Leadership; Accelerate Fixed-Mobile Convergence; Reinforce TV Offer; and Grow Business to Business and Business to Government sectors. This strategy is underpinned by our announced US$1.05 billion Project Marlin capital investment programme. Additionally, CWC believes that the combination of the two businesses will generate material operating cost and capital expenditure synergies. Similarly, Columbus believes that the combined strengths of both companies will accelerate growth, provide the necessary scale to enhance the customer experience, and help to allow Columbus to achieve its goal to become the "Best service provider" and "Employer of Choice" in the region.

The proposed combination of CWC's region-leading mobile footprint and existing fixed line infrastructure with Columbus' pay TV capabilities and next-generation, state-of-the-art fibre networks will significantly expand the product and service offerings for customers and also advance the companies' quad-play ambitions. The combined business will also deliver the benefits of superior quality network infrastructure, fixed-mobile products and bundles, superior TV content at competitive rates, and a more attractive portfolio of products and services in the B2B and B2G segments.

Phil Bentley, CWC's Chief Executive Officer said: "This is a transaction that transforms CWC, providing a step-change in growth and returns. Columbus offers complementary TV, Broadband and B2B capabilities in complementary markets. Together, we will create the best-in-class quad-play offering in the region, delivered on a superior mobile, fibre and subsea network. This is a significant opportunity to better serve our customers and improve the ICT infrastructure of the communities in which we operate, whilst accelerating our strategy and delivering materially enhanced returns and synergy benefits."

Similarly, Columbus' chairman and CEO, Brendan Paddick, indicated that, "Together we will form a truly world-class company focused on our customers in the Caribbean, Central America and the Andean regions. The proposed acquisition makes both companies stronger, faster and smarter in competing with their larger competitors. The proposed transaction reinforces our commitment to transform connectivity in the region, to increase the attractiveness of the region to investors, to support the growth of the communities we serve by making them more globally accessible and to ensure that our customers always have access to the best products and services available."

For both companies, the proposed acquisition also enables greater focus on the Caribbean, Andean and Latin American markets as a region that offers attractive growth. The proposed acquisition will provide new opportunities and focus in Colombia, Guatemala, Costa Rica, Honduras, El Salvador, Dominican Republic, Puerto Rico and Peru.

"Our goal is to provide customer-focused solutions and the highest level of service across the region. This agreement will accelerate our efforts through a strengthened set of assets and capabilities," Bentley affirmed.

The recent acquisition of both Groupo Sonitel in Panama, combined with Columbus' Lazus acquisition in Colombia will accelerate CWC's progress against the new streamlined strategy.

About Cable & Wireless Communications

Cable & Wireless Communications PLC (CWC) is a full-service communications provider operating in 16 countries throughout the Caribbean and Latin America. Operating four leading businesses: Cable and Wireless Panama, LIME, (the Caribbean excluding The Bahamas), BTC (The Bahamas) and Cable and Wireless Seychelles, CWC offers mobile, broadband, TV, domestic and international fixed line services in most of our markets serving over 5.6m customers. CWC also provides premium data centre hosting, telecoms, domestic and international managed data network services and custom IT Service Solutions to businesses and governments through the new unit, Cable & Wireless Business Solutions. Our mission is to grow customer relationships and lifetime value by becoming #1 for Customer Service. We are the market leader in most products they offer and territories they serve.

For more information visit: www.cwc.com

About Columbus International Inc.

Columbus International Inc. is a privately held diversified telecommunications company based in Barbados. The Company provides digital cable television, broadband Internet and digital landline telephony in Trinidad, Jamaica, Barbados, Grenada, St. Vincent & the Grenadines, St. Lucia and Curacao under the brand name Flow and in Antigua under the brand name Karib Cable. Columbus also provides next-generation connectivity and IT solutions, managed networking and cloud-based services under the brand Columbus Business Solutions. Through its subsidiary, Columbus Networks, the Company provides capacity and IP services, corporate data solutions and data centre hosting throughout 42 countries in the greater Caribbean, Central American and Andean region. Through its fully protected, ringed submarine fibre optic network spanning more than 42,300 km and its 38,000 km terrestrial fibre and coaxial network, Columbus' 3,150-plus professionals provide advanced telecom services to a diverse residential and corporate client base of over 700,000 customers.

    Contacts:
    Columbus International Inc.
    Media
    Denise Williams
    Dwilliams@columbus.co
    Cable & Wireless Communications
    Media

Questions

1 What are the core reasons for Cable and Wireless Communications PLC acquiring Columbus International Inc?
2 Outline the key threats to Cable and Wireless Communications PLC in the external environment due to convergence of fixed and mobile networks, increasing content consumption growth, and continuing development of online applications.

3.3 Strategy

Setting the scene

A primary outcome of a good strategy is the creation of value, be it shareholder value, economic value, and/or social value. CEOs in the 1970s, 1980s and 1990s tended to focus on shareholder and economic value, but until recently, most businesses assumed that being green and making money were diametrically opposed. The 2008 financial melt-down was an illustration that organisations did not generate true value. Mindsets changed to looking beyond shareholder value. Making products more ecologically friendly was seen as a cost, not an opportunity. Now, leading companies have recognised that sustainability and growth go hand-in-hand. Unfortunately, too many companies look at green products through a features and benefits lens. In today's intensely cost-obsessed economy, a product's greenness is rarely enough to make up for the typically higher upfront price. But this does not mean that green investments are a waste of effort.

While it is great to think that at least for the big data consultants, one day all strategic analysis will be entirely analytical and based on some algorithm somewhere in the computing cloud, we have to remember that we live and work in the real world of human wants, needs, desires, psychology, sociology and physiology. Successful organisations will be those that can learn to manipulate these variables, and they may very well create the leap in the advancement of strategy practice. After more than 50 years, the theory of business strategy continues to develop. Most senior executives have been trained in its principles through MBA programmes and have a good understanding of the core tools and techniques. But, many organisations have diminished the actual meaning of strategy. Ultimately, staff now label anything that bears the CEO's signature as strategic – a definition based on the decider's pay grade, not the decision. Given these observations, the following section starts by considering the cognitive dilemma, and the external and internal environment.

POD

SWOT analysis

How can the CEO and his management team:

(1) Ensure that any strength be used and developed to align with strategic objectives?
(2) Convert any weakness into a strength?
(3) Exploit and benefit from each opportunity?
(4) Address any threat and possibly converted into an opportunity?

The cognitive dilemma

CEOs need to lead with vision, manage resources and provide the inspiration for their teams. The lack of clarity of purpose can make it difficult to make good decisions. As previously stated and now becoming a core theme in this textbook, the business world remains littered with examples of bad strategies. Any lack of clarity of purpose makes it difficult to make good decisions. Another often neglected contributing factor that affects every strategist is the human brain (Ohmae, 1983). Over the last four decades, science has uncovered a greater understanding of individuals' cognitive capabilities. Through studies in human resource management, we know that humans are not always rational. Leading organisations in the twenty-first century require a broader range of skills than ever before. Brain elasticity can help develop leaders. The ability to change the way a leader thinks may enhance the individual's capacity to lead teams through challenging times.

Strategic decisions can be influenced by cognitive biases which can include overconfidence, self-interest, and being risk averse. Heskett (2014) raises the thought-provoking question, "Will you be taking a brain-scan for your next job interview?" The electrical testing of various chemicals in the brain may detect changes in certain stimuli and present some ideology and mind-boggling issues. But the unravelling of minds has been part of behavioural and organisational psychologists' work to analyse leadership and workplace behaviour. In terms of educational courses, the multidisciplinary aspects of management and leadership can incorporate neuroscience too. The role of emotional and cognitive aspects in effective managerial decision-making are assessed. It appears important to consider how neuroscience can help to further understand, predict or influence human behaviour.

Big data

With the geometric expansion of consumer data, the need for management of this data becomes intense (see Figure 3.3). The corporate narrative has now moved on from whether there is a payoff. Evidence does show productivity gains (Barton & Court, 2012). Data-driven businesses now need new strategies to win customers, beat competitors and enhance profits.

Rapid advances in technology are further reshaping traditional business relationships. For example, in tourism, the application of a smart tourism approach can enhance the quality and performance of hotels. The term "smart tourism" relates to the increasing reliance of tourism destinations, private and public sector firms, and tourists on digitised data for decision-making. The transition from traditional tourism to smart tourism does not just happen. Success is dependent upon the ability to make informed decisions and upon their meaningful execution. Innovative businesses have come to realise that smart mobile applications are a way to optimise and extract data analytics for competitive advantage. In addition, if the visitor infrastructure is improved and modernised this could drive up economic and social benefits for the entire region through more visitors, higher occupancy and spend. The USP for the firm is in its ability to cope with attitudinal, conversational and behavioural issues, which will be subsumed in big data. Managers need to make decisions based at the granular level, which will involve the use of human cognition to make sense and create useful knowledge.

Big data ability to make information transparent by capturing new sources in digital form can create competitive advantage. Falling costs together with easier methods of collection and better analytical tools and techniques make the big data proposition more compelling.

> Could strategic analysis become entirely analytical and based on some algorithm?

Figure 3.3 A question

Collecting the right kind of data is imperative and it's not all about size. Quality matters and each customer needs to be easily identifiable. Then experts need to mine the data in order to create, interpret and capture sources of value.

So, if data is the new resource for the firm, consumers will demand their share of its value. This is an essential part of the big data discussion, obtaining competitive advantage from the value of customer data to businesses. Now, informed consumers are reversing the flow by seeking to own and make the most of their lifestyle data. This data mining can help firms to work with the customer to provide advice, help, and save money. Giving the customer greater control has been exploited by social media companies. Facebook allows users to download their data and at its launch in 2010 included a video demonstrating the value.

POD

Verizon agree to acquire Yahoo

In July 2016, Verizon agreed to pay $4.83 billion for Yahoo, which was the end of an era for the takeover victim. Despite still possessing one billion active users, Yahoo became another dominant brand which had lost its way. In 2008 Microsoft were willing to pay more than $45bn for Yahoo, an offer that was rebuffed by cofounder Jerry Yang. CEO Marissa Meyer remained attached to turning around Yahoo, and did outline a "three-legged stool" strategy of focusing on three platforms: search, mail, and microblogging property Tumblr, the message being get rid of one and the rest will fail.

Now Yahoo's days as an independent company appear to be over. Yahoo remained squeezed by Google and Facebook, and the question many analysts ask is if an organisation with one billion people using it each month cannot increase its revenues and if a media company cannot make money, then who can? Verizon is placing a huge bet that combining the purchases of Yahoo with AOL, which was acquired for $4.4bn in May 2015 will create another competitive offer for advertisers who flock to Google and Facebook.

The $4.48 billion Verizon deal was completed in June 2017.

3.4 External environment

CEOs select strategies they hope will allow the organisation to deploy its scarce resources most effectively. The selection is reliant on internal and external analysis. The uncertain environment makes spotting new opportunities and anticipating threats that much more difficult. Over the last six decades, the strategy pendulum that swings from an external to internal orientation is illustrative of the need to incorporate both perspectives.

If forecasts are reliable, the earth will have more than nine billion inhabitants by 2050, and the United Nations now asks everyone to "consume with care." The sustainability agenda in terms of climate change, conserving water, a carbon constrained planet, and smart cities is now engrained into CEOs' mindsets when thinking about strategy. Previously, CEOs left governments to provide leadership in coping with the threats of the sustainability agenda, but now the emphasis is more on business–government collaboration. At board meetings, the onus should be on protecting the interests of those outside of the organisation too. Reputation now depends upon its compliance with a broad range of social issues, and failure to comply can jeopardise its image among consumers, current and potential staff.

Kim and Mauborgne's (2005) use of blue ocean metaphor elegantly summarises their vision of the kind of expanding, competitor-free markets that innovative companies can navigate. With "red oceans" being well explored and crowded with competitors, "blue oceans" represent "untapped market space" and the "opportunity for highly profitable growth." The primary reason large companies ignore "blue oceans" is that the dominant focus of strategy work over the past three decades has been on competition-based red ocean strategies, i.e., finding new ways to cut costs and grow revenue by taking away market share from the competition. They urge companies to "focus on the big picture, not the numbers." This holistic view is a central theme for this chapter.

Macro-environment

The external macro-environment sits outside the firm's industry and markets. Changes in the macro-environment can be cyclical or structural. The former changes require a temporary tactical response, and the latter a more permanent response. The firm is unable to control the macro-environment, but it seeks to stay abreast of external shifts. Any analysis should lead to a strategy that will leverage external shifts to the firm's advantage. The firm needs to be flexible enough to deal with these future impacts. Such shifts are symptoms of the key drivers of change, which impact industries, markets and firms differently.

No firm is an island, as it does not operate in isolation. The strategies and operations of the firm are influenced by the environment. The firm can take the form of any enterprise – small, medium, large, private sector, public sector, and third sector – and will be affected in differing ways. The CEO of each enterprise has to determine how they are affected and ascertain what are the current structural changes that have taken place. For example, if their market is growing or shrinking, they need to identify the salient factors that are responsible for each phase. Looking forward, analysis should identify the current stage of the industry lifecycle. This will impact the type and timing of the products/service brought to the marketplace. Unfortunately, external factors are uncontrollable.

Micro-environment

The micro-environment consists of firms and their suppliers and buyers. Also, other actors such as the public, employees, media and shareholders are important aspects of a firm's local environment. Any problems in the micro-environment are usually noticed almost immediately, so these should be closely monitored. A clearer understanding of the micro-environment can provide better insights into higher levels of firm performance. The firm can influence the micro-environment with full appreciation of the special characteristics of each factor and force.

When performed well, analysis of the industry and market enables opportunities to leverage core competencies in other industries and markets. To better illustrate these points, markets can be defined in terms of product, utility (need), or customer identity. Market segmentation supports the assertion that a firm cannot be all things to all buyers. The one-size-fits-all approach no longer works. Understanding the needs and wants of a smaller group of potential customers is more efficient. From a resource perspective it is easier to compete in fewer markets. Intermediaries are now affecting all markets with roles such as travel, financial resellers, physical distributions, and market service agencies. Digital platforms are now ubiquitous with firms looking to Google to refer customers. The easier connections between buyers and sellers via digital platforms have resulted in some firms over-relying and paying too much money for the privilege.

There are many approaches to external analysis and the following sections illustrate some of them.

SWOT analysis

A key attribute of the Strengths, Weaknesses, Opportunities and Threats (SWOT) analysis is that it is straightforward and can be effective. It is also widely taught and used in practice. Its durability and longevity remains compelling. Its popularity and ease of use can condense a large number of issues identified into manageable and important points. Nevertheless, knowing what is and what is not relevant is subjective and debatable. Like any tool it should guide the strategy process and not be prescriptive. It can be a useful tool to get brainstorming sessions started and commence discussions. A good SWOT analysis will critique the internal perspective (strengths and weaknesses) and external (opportunities and threats) from the perspective of the customer. The user is able to identify and address weaknesses, enhance strengths, maximise opportunities, and overcome threats. Inherent "strengths," such as old and established can be a "weakness" in terms of the organisation being able to respond to new and nimble competition. Weaknesses should be addressed by management, as if left unattended they may prevent the firm from achieving its mission and goals.

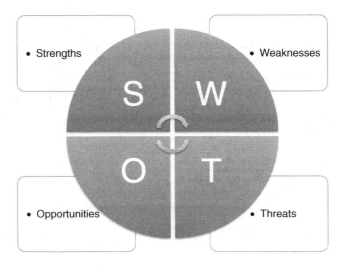

Figure 3.4 SWOT analysis

Yet, the simplistic nature of SWOT analysis (see Figure 3.4) is perhaps its greatest limitation. Factors beyond the control of management can affect the analysis. The economic environment may adversely affect demand for one product/service, but increase the demand for another. For example, during times of economic slowdown, organisations seek to spend less on overnight hotel accommodation for employees and may trade down from a four-star to a three-star or even a budget hotel. Thus, the budget hotel sector can thrive during times of economic slowdown to the detriment of mid-scale hotels. Another constraint to potential opportunities that may be unable to be pursued is a lack of skilled labour. Threats have the potential to harm the organisation, its ventures and/or products/services. The organisation is unable to avoid threats and needs to decide how to deal with them. Irrespective of size and sector focus, the CEO needs to create the intelligence to monitor threats. One of the key tests of SWOT analysis is that the organisation pursues a strategy and capability, which is not a strength of a competitor. Organisations tend to use SWOT analysis as part of their strategy review processes, when performance is below that expected by influential stakeholders. Making the SWOT analysis actionable by providing top-down clarity will help to formulate renewal strategies.

PESTEL

As previously stated, the business environment consists of two elements, macro and micro, with the former and latter covering areas uncontrollable and controllable by the organisation. The macro-environment can be systematically assessed by PESTEL analysis (see Table 3.1).

Table 3.1 PESTEL analysis

	Issues
Political	• Government regime
	• Legislation
	• Social policies
Economic	• Growth rates
	• Unemployment rates
	• Exchange rates
	• Taxation
	• Inflation
	• International trade
	• Minimum wage
Social	• Demographics
	• Lifestyle trends
	• Consumer attitudes
	• Ethical issues
	• Culture
Technological	• Internet
	• Social media
	• Technology obsolescence
Environmental	• Global warming
	• Sustainability
	• Pollution
	• Re-cycling and waste
Legal factors	• Employment law
	• Health and safety
	• Corporate law

An appreciation of the basic forces in the macro-environment can aid understanding and enable the prediction of how an industry might change and evolve.

PESTEL can provide a comprehensive assessment of the environment and market in which the firm operates. However, users sometimes ignore its limitations. External factors can change over time, and in complex environments monitoring needs expert analysis. Simplistic approaches will be dangerous. From a practitioner viewpoint an effective PESTEL can be costly. Weaker students tend to produce bullet point lists regurgitated from lecturer presentations. In such instances there will be a failure to capture the important signals in the external environment. The quality of PESTEL will also depend upon the quality of data. Primary and secondary data may be subjective. Factors need to be prioritised and implemented. But as such factors are beyond the control of the firm, they represent risks.

Michael Porter's Five Forces Model

We now move to the micro-environment, which was a prominent feature of the work of Michael Porter (1980). His five forces framework depicts threat of substitutes; threat of new entrants; intensity of rivals; supplier power; buyer bargaining power, with complementors sometimes being mentioned as a sixth force. When proposing his model Porter argued that a strong force limits the ability of established companies to increase prices and earn a greater return. A strong competitive force can be likened to a threat as it reduces profits. The picture that emerges in the analysis depends upon a number of variables. Heterogeneity in the strength of each force is derived from horizontal and vertical levels of competition in Figure 3.5. Horizontal levels of competition include threat of new entrants, substitutes and competitive rivalry with vertical competition being the power of suppliers and buyers.

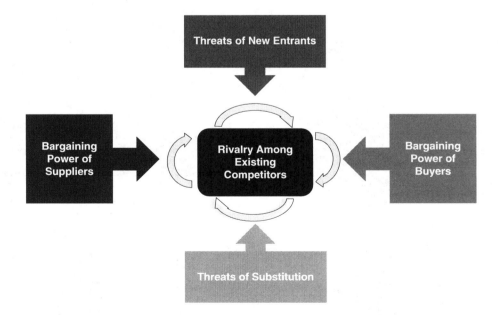

Figure 3.5 Five forces model

Threat of new entrants

Profitable markets that produce high returns for incumbents will attract new firms. If the entry of new firms is unabated, the high returns will normalise. As more firms compete for market share, profits will tend to fall. If incumbents can block new firms they can maintain their profits. Threats of new entrants are high when:

- existing firms do not have established brands, patents and trademarks
- low amount of capital is required to enter the market
- customer switching costs are low
- economies of scale are relatively easy to achieve
- there is a lack of firms to retaliate
- products are similar
- there is scarce government regulation

Bargaining power of suppliers

Groups of suppliers can exert differing influences based on their strengths. If we consider the idea that the bargaining power of suppliers is high, then suppliers are able to sell higher priced or low quality raw materials. In the supermarket sector, many small suppliers are a weak threat to the large firm. Together with low switching costs, management are able to switch from one supplier to another. However, with few suppliers, switching costs are higher and if the item is vital to product quality then the firm is in a weak position.

Suppliers have strong bargaining power when:

- there is high concentration of suppliers
- supplier numbers are limited but there are many buyers
- switching costs of raw material are high
- suppliers possess scarce resources
- large numbers of suppliers possess the ability to forward integrate

Bargaining power of buyers

The position of buyers is opposite from that of suppliers for the firm. If the bargaining power of buyers is high, then they are able to demand low prices or higher quality. The drive towards lower prices and higher quality will reduce margins for the firm. In the clothing industry the newer firms with online presence are quicker and more flexible in getting their products to customers together with aggressive pricing strategies.

Buyers have strong bargaining power when:

- small numbers of buyers exist
- buyer switching costs are low
- buyers are price sensitive
- buyers possess the ability to backward integrate

Threat of substitutes

If potential buyers are able to locate substitute products, then switching costs are low. Substitute products may come from outside the industry too. This places the firm in a relatively weak position. If the substitute is close, buyers will be price sensitive and will switch to the substitute in response to price increases. Also, if the substitute is better quality and of similar cost, buyers will switch. Disruptive technology such as the Internet has provided many sources of substitute products with increased competition. Firms operating in industries such as travel, newspapers, sports and telecommunication have had to rethink their strategies during the last decade. In the newspaper sector, substitute products currently include: online news, iPads, mobile phones, and 24hr news channels.

Threat of substitute products is higher when:

- switching costs are low
- products are lower price
- products have higher quality
- products offer better performance

Intensity of rivals

We have referred to four of the five forces. These set the stage for determining how competitive and profitable an industry is. As the firm evolves within a mature industry, the strategic posture has to be aggressive to maintain and increase market share. In such environments, profit margins are slim. Firms strive to achieve competitive advantage over their peers. The level of intensity varies within each market the firm competes in. Industries that are concentrated are more intense than their fragmented counterparts. There are a number of strategic postures available to the firm, which are a key feature of this textbook. Common moves include increasing value for money, improving product differentiation, and enhancing distribution channels and supply relationships. Within the supermarket sector, common consequences are price wars, aggressive advertising campaigns and customer oriented innovations.

Intensity of rivals is intense when:

- number of competitors is high
- competitors are of similar size
- customer loyalty levels are low
- products are mainly commodity type (i.e. not differentiated)
- exit barriers are high

Complementors

The sometimes forgotten sixth force – complementors – has the opposite effect to substitutes. Complementors provide another mechanism for adding value. They will not be competitors in an industry, but have a contractual relationship which can influence demand. Complementors increase the demand for a primary product. Complementary product examples include a hotdog and the hotdog bun, as a consumer would tend not to buy one without the other. In the case of iTunes and the iPod, the former creates added value, and generates revenue from iTunes and increased sales for the iPod. For example, if one considers a car and petrol, the combined benefit is more than the car and petrol individually. Porter's six forces provide a quick assessment of the macro-environment, but the analysis should form only part of the overall checklist.

Limitations of Porter's five forces model include:

- level of strategy analysis
- assumes homogeneous firms
- assumes largely antagonistic relationships
- cross-sectional, one moment in time
- disregards the behavioural aspects within the firm
- role of governmental regulations
- the Internet and e-commerce
- globalisation (see session on global strategies)
- changes in PESTEL affect "five forces"
- green issues and green awareness
- competition law
- changes in industry growth rate (see industry lifecycle).

The misuse of Porter's five forces escalates if the user ignores the level of analysis and that the tool assumes homogeneous firms, so it will not suit highly diversified companies. Bearing in mind that a typical UK FTSE company operates in a number of industries, the analysis needs to cover discrete business units. The analysis is also static, akin to the balance sheet and only depicts the organisation at that precise moment in time. Thus, given the long-term perspective of strategy, Porter's five forces' timescale is too short. The majority of strategy tools should only be used as part of the beginning of a discussion. The CEO should not use the analysis in itself to make stand-alone decisions. Previously in this textbook part of the narrative has been about the new normal environment created as a consequence of the crisis of 2008. Industries have been affected differently by the events of 2008, and Porter's framework does not account for changes in industry growth rates, in addition to the fundamental changes in the use of leverage, trajectory of globalisation, nature of consumption patterns, and appetite for risk taking. Technology with emphasis on digitisation now increases the importance of globalisation and deregulation fundamentally changes the basic conditions of any industry. The behavioural issues of strategy will affect implementation and government regulation can change the structure and conduct of industries. Those organisations operating in the airline, railways, electricity, and telecommunications industries are acutely aware of government policy. Responses to regulatory changes are demanding, as organisations must consider complicated trade-offs between profit maximisation and broader social factors.

Intriguingly, Dobbs (2014) queries the actual use of the five forces model, when users deploy it in a shallow way. He asserts that this lack of depth is dangerous, as at best it can lead to incomplete, inaccurate and unhelpful analysis. He mentions that users of Porter's five forces model – academics, students and practitioners – have a number of other challenges: lack of structural analysis; lack of strategic insight; and millennial generation preferences. Porter (2008) himself does lament the paucity of quantitative measures in typical applications of the five forces model. The qualitative measures are frequently arbitrary and make poor substitutes for rigorous analysis. This lack of structural analysis diminishes the quality of the output.

A lack of strategic insight is another disappointment, which Porter (1980) actually acknowledges. This is in part due to the tool being perceived by users to assess attractiveness levels of industries rather than gain strategic insight into how to compete more effectively. The authors of this textbook can attest to these observations, as when marking student assignments at the postgraduate and undergraduate levels, remarks regarding lack of insight are frequently mentioned in our comments. The contextual setting for any classroom exercise should indicate that blueprint solutions are inappropriate (just as in the business environment).

Stakeholder analysis

As a result of the post-financial crisis, values among business and society are being rethought. From a corporate perspective, firms need to show that they have a conscience and profit and growth can no longer be the sole justification for "immoral actions." Hence, stakeholders are now becoming increasingly influential during the decision-making process. The Board need to be aware of understanding and managing stakeholder interests. Technology disruptions such as social media now enable small groups of stakeholders to impact quickly on organisational affairs. The other dimension that should be proactively managed is stakeholder power. When interests and power are considered together, they provide management with an indication of the type of relationship to form with each group. This becomes pertinent when the CEO wishes to push certain projects. Quickly identifying who is important and who can positively and negatively influence the project is desirable. A classic example often mentioned is when an organisation wishes to expand its footprint, and needs to get the local council planning committee and local community on board, in terms of identifying primary stakeholders, those who are ultimately affected, and secondary stakeholders who act as intermediaries. Mendelow's (1981) stakeholder mapping matrix (see Figure 3.6) provides the user with ways to depict, understand and manage stakeholder power.

An effective stakeholder analysis will enable management to improve their relationships with stakeholders. This will also allow stakeholders to better understand organisational traumas and needs for their strategies and actions. Many organisations stress on their websites how employees are an invaluable resource, but do not treat employees as such, and possess

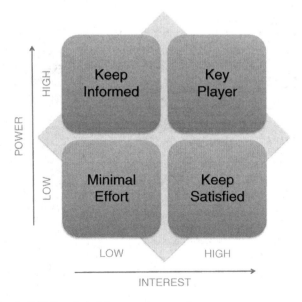

Figure 3.6 Mendelow's (1981) stakeholder mapping matrix

Strategic analysis 61

Stakeholder	Stakeholder Interests (H),(M), (L)	Assessment of Impact (+),(-), (?)	Potential Strategies
Primary – directly affected–employees & shareholders			
Secondary – indirectly affected govt & media			
Key – Most significantly affected			

Figure 3.7 Stakeholder analysis matrix

high staff turnover rates. Companies have to invest considerable sums in terms of resources to recruit and retain good staff. Talent management is now high up on the CEO agenda, so ensuring the values of the organisation are explained to employees is crucial. Also, trade unions, despite being of less influence than in the past, can still create havoc for the CEO leading a management of change agenda. Although stakeholder analysis may be subjective, it is useful to perform it on a continuous basis with a focus on the most important stakeholders for each particular situation. The end column of Figure 3.7 considers potential strategies, and these can include ways of strengthening stakeholders' commitment to the project, reassuring their sensitivities, maintaining support, turning neutral views into support and coping with resistance. Specific strategies can bring certain benefits to key stakeholder groups, enhanced levels of communication and involvement.

Scenario analysis

As we live in an uncertain world, strategic analysis should create and understand perceptions about alternate future states. Executives need to deploy forecasting tools that can be integrated with strategy assumptions. The robustness of a strategic plan can be stress-tested by using a variety of "what-if" analyses. Organisations should test their financial resilience to macro-economic or market-driven scenarios. Each sector will have its salient operating models, risk methodologies and investment priorities for the next decade and beyond. Figure 3.8 illustrates the situations when scenario analysis is beneficial.

The scenario analysis matrix is a deductive method for illustrating scenarios in uncertain and volatile situations. Four scenarios are depicted in the matrix. The two uncertain dimensions for the x and y axis form the context of the analysis. Timeframes should match the length of the strategic planning exercise. To perform effective scenario analysis four steps can be employed: identification of salient factors for inclusion in the scenario analysis; which scenarios to analyse for each factor; estimation of asset cash flows; and assignment of probabilities.

Well-run scenario planning exercises will involve subject-matter experts coming together to debate a range of issues such as economic, technology and increasingly geo-political futures. Essentially, scenario analysis can enable the Board to consider multiple plausible futures and inherent risks. Scenarios can be for periods well in excess of a decade. For example, in a 17-page communiqué issued after the summit at Schloss Elmau under the slogan

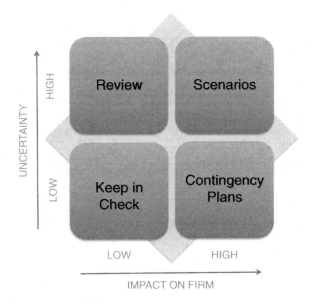

Figure 3.8 Scenario analysis

"Think Ahead, Act Together", the G7 leaders supported the recommendations of the United Nations' climate control panel to reduce greenhouse gas emissions by 70 per cent by 2050, the overall goal being to phase out the use of fossil fuels by the end of the century. This will have a huge impact on energy companies and world governments and commercial organisations will be expected to help develop global solutions.

Given this level of high uncertainty and high impact, businesses and governments have to create integrated scenario models, highlighting the effects of decarbonisation. International cooperation will be necessary at the individual, community, organisational, government, and country levels. At the country level there appears to be a view that those countries that were chiefly responsible for the carbon crisis from their past behaviour should be playing a leading role in seeking a solution. In some quarters matters are made more exasperating as the technology is available to revolutionise clean energy, but the global legislative frameworks and the capital investment models need to evolve to facilitate implementation. Parameters and metrics are required to develop a common framework to compare and contrast scenarios.

Customer analysis

Previously, the energy in the relationship was with the brand and the brand owner, and now that energy is with consumers. Knowing your customer base and ascertaining their needs helps to effectively target and position your strategy. Customer analysis helps to develop existing products/services for existing and new customers. Unfortunately, there are numerous examples of institutional blindness, compounded by dangerously misleading survey results. The UK's 2015 General Election results did not resonate with the polls. During campaigning the polls had Labour and Conservatives neck-and-neck at 34 per cent, but the actual result was a Conservative win of 38 per cent to 32 per cent.

Consumers change their minds, often faster than research methodologies and methods can make new predictions. What customer analysis should provide is insight, not just data. With firms such as Facebook possessing more data on individuals than ever before, CEOs are still starved of a holistic understanding of the whole consumer. Basic customer analysis should segment by contribution to sales and profits. However, keeping the focus on low profitable customers can be a myopic approach. Apple continues to demonstrate that by selecting certain customer groups to serve with selected and limited products/services together with premium process can yield extraordinary results.

The ability to tailor products individually to customers has long been widely available. The credit-card industry has long been able to provide such a service. Organisations grow and invest significant sums in database marketing tools. The return on investment in terms of hardware and software costs sometimes becomes negative, especially when the human element is ignored. The initial focus of attention should be upon the actual business problem. Matters are not usually helped by fluctuating demand, lower prices, and fierce competitive actions by peers.

Strategic groups

A widespread theme used in strategic analysis is that of strategic groups, which exist within an industry and where members possess similar strategic characteristics, pursue similar strategies or compete on similar bases. From Hunt's (1972) doctoral thesis, the link between strategic groups and performance has been a popular research theme with tenuous findings. Nevertheless, economic and cognitive theories suggest that there may be differences between the performances of firms that belong to different groups. What we do know is that some organisations remain stable core members of strategic groups over time, while others may switch. Such observations appear to be moderated by organisational situational variables including the degree of profitability. What has become evident is the emergence of resource-based theory at the expense of strategic group theory with Barney and Hoskisson (1990) arguing that strategic groups, in some cases, may be mere artefacts of the algorithms utilised to generate clusters.

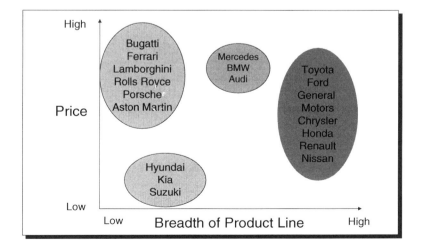

Figure 3.9 The world automobile industry

Despite the dissatisfaction with strategic groups, there is benefit to integrating the two perspectives (Leask & Parnell, 2005). The different but complementary perspectives of strategic groups and RBV on competitive strategy and performance present a synergistic insight into how clusters of organisations compete. Over the last five decades, the SCP paradigm is evident in research and prescriptions including strategic groups. Today's business is unlikely to operate in a discrete operating environment, but will be part of a strategic group. Understanding the intra-industry strategic groupings can enhance performance for the CEO. From a research perspective, gaining insight can be performed at the firm and industry level. As businesses tend to be multiproduct, selling in more than one market, blurring may occur, and depicting and understanding strategic groups may assist in understanding the salient drivers. If the CEO considers a strategic group to be a cluster of firms with similar behaviours, then mobility barriers together with technology can enable meaningful comparative analysis.

Strategic group mapping can assist in providing an illustration of the salient differentiating forces. For example, start by identifying the peer group in the selected industry. Then select two key variables for the x and y-axis. Using the appropriate axis plot each organisation with the size of the circle being proportional to market share, or another critical dimension. Then assess the overall map. The different groups should offer a valuable proposition to the customer, which in turn requires the CEO to create a compelling strategy. Figure 3.9 elucidates the world automobile industry.

3.5 Internal analysis

Strategies can fail for two reasons: external and internal issues. The previous section provides tools to help the CEO to gain sufficient knowledge about the external environment, anticipate changes in the external environment and determine some competitive actions. In contrast to external analysis, internal analysis is the process of identifying and evaluating resources, capabilities and competencies that are available for strategy implementation and for attaining strategic objectives. The internal analysis process should look closely at the alignment of vision, mission, strategic objectives and strategies.

The changing corporate landscape into a more caring society is undoing the traditional efforts of organisations of all shapes and sizes. Executives spend more time at work than pursuing any other activity, and the behavioural aspects of strategy tends to be ignored in the literature. From a strategic management perspective, the literature lacks behavioural rigour together with practical relevance. Powell, Lovallo and Fox (2011), in their special *Strategic Management Journal* issue on the psychological foundations of strategic management, note that behavioural strategy merges cognitive and social psychology, but the topic remains unclear. For the purpose of this textbook behavioural strategy is beyond the boundaries, but there is a gap between individual cognition and collective strategy (Powell, Lovallo & Fox, 2011). The strategy formulated may not always reflect the sole choices of the CEO or top management team.

Individuals responsible for strategic analysis need to evaluate the internal environment of the organisation. The strengths and weaknesses of the SWOT analysis provide an initial snapshot view of activities. In addition to the vision and mission statements, the internal environment consists of management, employees, organisational structures, culture, other resources intangible and tangible, capabilities and competencies. Each of the following topics is of huge importance during the strategic planning process, but will be covered briefly to demonstrate some practical relevance.

Strategic analysis 65

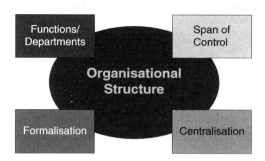

Figure 3.10 Elements of organisational structure

Organisational structure

CEOs need to acquire high levels of performance by simultaneously exploring and exploiting their internal environment. Figure 3.10 depicts the key elements of organisational structure. Arranging the organisational architecture in terms of formal structures is one of the keys to success. The traditional organisational structure is hierarchical with the CEO at the top, with tasks and people allocated in terms of decision-making power flows. One dilemma is the balance between centralisation and decentralisation. Decision-making is best associated with authority, which can rest with senior management or be delegated down the hierarchy. The twentieth century belonged to a scenario of centralisation of both capital, resources and decision-making. We are now experiencing a shift in the twenty-first century towards decentralisation. The challenge today is about finding the right balance, and how CEOs navigate these conflicting pressures will have both economic and societal consequences for their organisations.

Since the 1980s, as organisations strive for better customer service, the number of direct relationships between a manager and subordinates has widened. This has led to a widening of the span of control (see Figure 3.11). Factors such as external environmental turbulence, the nature of job task and budgetary constraints may affect the span of control. The formal structure clearly shows the official lines of enquiry and communication within the organisation. Figure 3.12 illustrates a typical formal organisational structure, which shows a deliberate division of labour with each employee knowing rules, policies and procedures. The formal organisational structure should not stifle informal structures, such as communities of

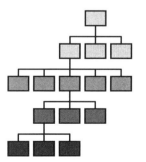

Figure 3.11 Span of control

Figure 3.12 Functional organisational structure

practice, which are prevalent in learning organisations. Such structures can help crosslink organisational units and are thematic rather than hierarchical based. They provide linkages among the individual, group and the broader strategy themes. Wenger and Snyder (2000) pertinently state that the economy runs on knowledge, and despite the use of cross-functional teams, customers of product-focused business units' community of practice are radically galvanising knowledge sharing, learning and change. The impact of the digital age has accelerated the benefits of community of practice and new theories can be located in the *Learning in Landscapes of Practice* textbook (see Wenger-Trayner & Wenger-Trayner, 2014).

The functional structure departmentalises activities into core business functions. Each department enables specialisation by grouping employees with shared skills and knowledge, and is easily scalable as the organisation grows. Typically, this works best in environments involving routine operations with little variation of the end product. Organisations may deploy structures in terms of product/service line, customer and location, depending on their strategic posture. Functional structures do possess a number of benefits and limitations. A functional structure enables economy of scale, which can reduce unit costs, and a conduit for career aspirations in terms of promotions and paths. Limitations include the provable silo mentality, which can lead to dysfunctional conflict and less coordination.

Working in teams has become effective in problem solving, increasing productivity and product innovation. Advocates such as Henry Ford and the late Steve Jobs have stated that working together is one of the major keys to success. Due to the decentralised structure, members should decide how to work together. Self-directed work teams are usually organic and organised around salient work processes. This structure is flexible and responsive, increases staff commitment to tasks, and enables quicker management decisions. However, limitations include higher interpersonal training costs, slow start-up efficiency due to the learning curve effect, and in some situations stress levels can be higher.

Matrix structures (see Figure 3.13) tend to evolve when there is a need to utilise the skillset of a functional structure without affecting day-to-day operations. This form keeps the desirable aspects of being both functional and stand-alone. Staff are appointed to specific projects with the aim of meeting the project criteria, which will be around time, cost and quality. Resources can be allocated efficiently and staff can move from project to project in case of delays. In highly complex environments it is possible to develop a cadre of experts that can be deployed using the latest state-of-the art techniques, which can focus on clients and products. However, conflicts may arise due to split loyalties between the project manager and departmental manager. In complex environments there can be more conflict, organisational politics, and stress.

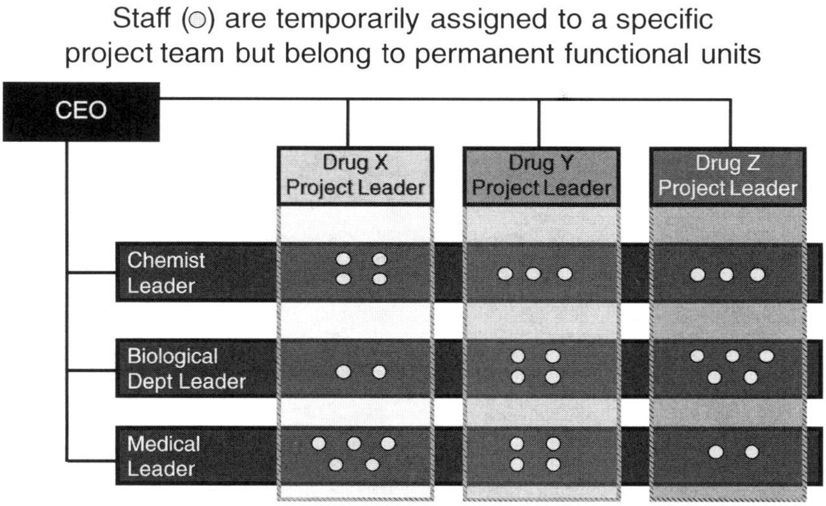

Staff (○) are temporarily assigned to a specific
project team but belong to permanent functional units

Figure 3.13 Matrix structure

As organisations seek to position themselves in global markets and take advantage of digitisation, the network structure (see Figure 3.14) has evolved as a way of coordinating and delegating tasks among a number of parties with a common goal. This can be a specific product or service. Collaboration is vital, as competitive advantage is desired. The network organisational structure is highly flexible and efficient. Each party is carefully selected and has responsibility for a specific task. This can operate across borders and can make the best use of skills and technology for products. Limitations include being exposed to external forces and being over-reliant on each party, which can reduce synergistic effects.

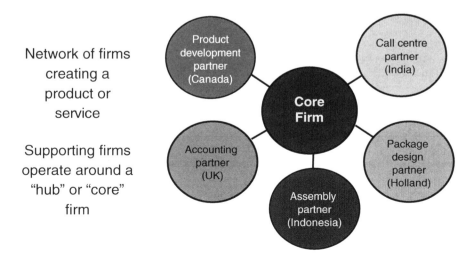

Figure 3.14 Network organisational structure

68 *Strategic management primer*

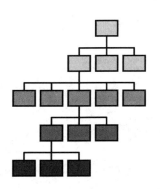

Traditionally as companies develop and grow, they:

- Create a taller hierarchy of structure and widen span of control

Problems with tall hierarchies

- Higher overhead costs
- Poor quality information flows
- Greater bureaucracy
- Less empowered staff
- Focus power around managers

Figure 3.15 Tall vs. flat structures

Flat organisational structures can help to reduce bureaucracy and empower staff at all levels. Functional silos become blurred and cross-functional activities enhance the flow of communication. Moreover, informal networks of employees can help to bind the newer type of structures. As well as enhancing staff satisfaction, morale and talent retention, they are crucial in knowledge intensive industries. Informal structures can be conduits for official rules to be negotiated or subverted by staff. From a strategy perspective informal structures can increase the flow of communication and can help solve management staff problems. Debates about tall versus flat organisational structures continues (see Figure 3.15). Tall organisations can provide a career path for newly appointed ambitious employees, but flat structures can work successfully even in large firms. Ultimately, structures are created to regulate and provide control mechanisms for management and employees.

Organisational culture

CEOs hugely influence culture and this interaction is related to consequential organisational outcomes. Culture represents a system of shared values and beliefs of organisational members. Leaders shape culture and send signals via formal and informal mechanisms to reinforce desired behaviours and prevent undesired behaviours. Culture is passed from generation to generation and shapes behaviour and perceptions. Defining and analysing culture is problematic, and as pronounced by Williams (1983) is one of the two or three most complicated words in the English language. Schein (2004) suggests that the confusion of defining culture is due to a failure to differentiate the levels at which culture permeates the organisation. Values underlie norms and artefacts and lead to a consistency of behaviour (Hogan & Coote, 2014). If the CEO wishes to pursue an innovative strategy, then innovative behaviours need to be developed via norms that support new processes. These in turn can derive from values and are manifest in artefacts from stories, rituals and symbolic behaviour.

Organisations realise that being old and traditional is not necessarily a strength, but can be a potential weakness. Being slow to respond to imminent danger has brought some organisations to a quick demise. Using the analogy of an iceberg, the image of culture above the water can be seen as how staff look, dress and communicate, being the observable elements. However, it is the values, beliefs, norms, customs and nonverbal behaviour that can lead to difficulties in implementing a change management strategy, these being the non-observable elements. In addition, organisational culture may be misaligned with the external environment and if strong cultures exist they may suppress dissenting subcultures.

One form of organisational culture is bureaucratic and a theme of this textbook is the need to be innovative. Part of being innovative involves taking calculated risks and being creative. A bureaucratic culture perpetuates stability and works best for those organisations producing standardised goods and services. Hogan and Coote (2014) provide a useful overview of how organisational culture can support innovation. Value dimensions mentioned in the literature include: success; openness and flexibility; internal communication; competence and professionalism; inter-functional cooperation; responsibility; appreciation; risk-taking.

Globalisation takes on additional complexity for culture, as large firms that are patriotic can send confused messages. For example, Carrefour, the French hypermarket, uses PR to send strong messages that it's a thoroughly French enterprise, holding open days showcasing its French offer. However, it is the world's second largest retailer with 10,860 stores in 33 countries and a larger turnover outside of France. With its €2.4bn profits Carrefour is arguably more of a global organisation than a French one. Adam Sage, *Times* correspondent, retorts that Carrefour's claim to be as French as the baguettes that it sells should be taken with a pinch of salt (*The Times*, October 12, 2015 World). As organisations increase their global presence they may suffer from a loss of cultural identity.

Organisational resources

Intangible and tangible resources are recognised as crucial drivers of organisational success, as they can help gain competitive advantage and lead to higher levels of performance. Intangible assets relate to the non-financial assets without a physical presence, which are used to generate products or services, which in turn generate revenue. These assets are under the control of the organisation and include the knowledge, skills and aptitudes of staff. In the 1970s, intangible assets constituted only 5 per cent of total assets, but this has increased to 78 per cent of all assets (Chareonsuk & Chansa-ngavej, 2008). Successful brands tend to be easily recognised, strong innovators, show longevity and have strong balance sheets. Hence the mismanagement of intangible assets in the knowledge era can be costly. Management of organisations need to identify critical groups of tangible and intangible assets to ascertain their precise value drivers. As Kaplan and Norton (2004) state, intangible assets are the primary drivers upon which a firm can establish its identity and frame its strategy.

The term intellectual capital is often treated as synonymous with intangible assets and is used to define "intellectual capital" as "all non-monetary and non-physical resources that are fully or partly controlled by the organisation and that contribute to the organisation's value creation." Despite disagreement in the literature on categorisation approaches, the tripartite taxonomy of human, structural and relational capital is employed in the literature. Human capital comprises the intangible resources embodied by individuals (e.g. knowledge and motivation). Structural capital refers to the infrastructure in organisations, such as information systems, management processes and procedures, as well as organisational systems. Relational capital refers to the value that is derived from and created through continuous relationships with external economic actors. In Chapter 1, the RBV approach states that sustained competitive advantage needs to possess four attributes: valuable, rare, inimitable and non-substitutable.

Organisational capabilities, core competencies, and dynamic capabilities

The relationship between organisational capabilities and competencies cannot be readily inferred from the lexicon used by practitioners. The theoretical objection rests on their distinctiveness. Competitive advantage may be an outcome of a firm's distinctiveness of its capabilities, but capabilities in themselves are insufficient to support competitive advantage. Capabilities occur when resources achieve a specific task or set of tasks. These capabilities may lie within functional areas such as: Wal-mart's distribution; Apple's marketing and product innovation; Zara's clothing production. Using these examples, it is clear how these capabilities enable these firms to perform at much higher levels than their peers.

In general, firms have to ascertain a level for threshold competencies, which are the minimum requirement to compete in an industry. A proficiency that enables a firm to deliver value to customers is consistent with the term core competence. These effects can be leveraged across a wide variety of markets and be a source of competence-based strategies. With collaboration being an increasingly market-based response to scarce resources and turbulence, competence-based strategies are increasingly blurring interfirm boundaries. Collinson and Parcell (2001) describe five key organisational competencies: strategy development; management techniques; collaboration mechanisms; knowledge sharing and learning processes; knowledge capture and storage. Successful organisational change is sustainable when core competencies are integral and aligned with strategy.

IT competencies can assist in the implementation of requisite entrepreneurial and adaptive actions (Chakravarty, Grewal & Sambamurthy, 2013). These findings that managers should consider multiple contingencies both observed and unobserved while assessing the effects of IT competencies on agility and firm performance are the essence of the latest arguments. Understanding the link between IT competencies and innovation is important for several reasons. First, IT is used as an enabler as organisations implement their renewal strategies. Second, the continued growth of digital business strategies requires higher levels of functionalities. These digital strategies reshape existing processes as modular, cross-functional, distributed and global, enabling the CEO to operate across traditional boundaries such as time and distance.

As the environment changes, capabilities need to evolve over time and must be managed dynamically. Successful organisations need to make timely responses to the environment using capabilities to coordinate competencies. This specific source of competitive advantage is referred to as dynamic capabilities. The term "dynamic" applies to the changing character of the environment, and the strategic responses to such situations. The term "capabilities" refers to the specific organisational skills, resources, and functional strengths that can be a core component of the desired strategy. Teece et al.'s (1997) dynamic capabilities framework extends the RBV by incorporating the environment and technological change. Given this advancement, organisational capabilities can moderate the relationship between IT investments and performance.

As outlined continuously in Chapters 1 and 2, in rapidly changing environments organisations need to be proactive, rather than reactive. To fulfil this objective, there is a requirement to integrate, build and reconfigure internal and external competencies. Hence, the concept of dynamic capabilities still remains apt as it can help ascertain the capabilities necessary to lead to organisational success. The protection of output capabilities in terms of the observable product or service is vital, whereas innovation capabilities by contrast are that much harder to imitate. This reinforces the importance of being innovative in rapidly changing

Strategic analysis 71

environments. Teece (2007) stresses that organisations with strong dynamic capabilities are intensely entrepreneurial.

Value chain analysis

Given that we have highlighted the importance of adding value from an internal perspective, the value chain provides some useful additional theory. Porter's value chain analysis (see Figure 3.16) seeks to provide a framework that describes the salient process within and around an organisation which creates a product or service. During the analysis the user should be able to understand how value is created or lost in terms of activities undertaken and to diagnose strategic capability.

Value chain resources and activities are interdependent, and must be evaluated as a whole, so it is possible to optimise and coordinate them so they work together effectively to form a coherent strategy. The links between the strategic resources and the associated activities are as important as the individual resources and activities themselves.

Starbucks (2015 Annual Report)

Formed in 1985, Starbucks purchases and sells high-quality coffees, along with tea, other beverages and a variety of fresh food items.

Primary activities

Inbound Logistics: In 2010, the founder Howard Schultz returned to the firm and commenced a renewal strategy, which involved a major restructuring initiative. The inbound logistics of Starbucks was essentially purchasing unroasted Arabica coffee beans from Africa, Asia, and Latin America. The procurement activity is not outsourced, so as to ensure the highest quality.

Operations: Starbucks operates in 65 countries and sells via direct stores operated by the company or as licensed stores. Starbucks employs approximately 191,000 people worldwide

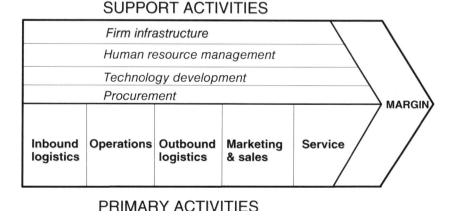

Figure 3.16 Porter's value chain analysis

with 141,000 within the US. In addition to the flagship Starbucks brand, the company sells under the brands of Teavana, Tazo, Seattle's Best Coffee, Evolution Fresh, La Boulange and Ethos. Revenue from company-operated stores accounts for 79 per cent of the 2014 total net revenues. Licensed stores accounts for 10 per cent of 2014 total net revenues. Operating margins tend to be higher for licensed stores, with Starbucks receiving a reduced share of revenue. However, this is offset by the licensee having to share costs and with Starbucks receiving license and royalty fees.

Service: Starbucks' customers welcome the high levels of service. High service levels are a feature of the mission, which is to inspire and nurture the human spirit – one person, one cup and one neighbourhood at a time. And their values are:

With our partners, our coffee and our customers at our core, we live these values:

- creating a culture of warmth and belonging, where everyone is welcome.
- acting with courage, challenging the status quo and finding new ways to grow our company and each other.
- being present, connecting with transparency, dignity and respect.
- delivering our very best in all we do, holding ourselves accountable for results.

We are performance driven, through the lens of humanity.

Marketing and Sales: The company seeks to provide each customer with a unique Starbucks experience, which is built upon superior customer experience and to build customer loyalty. Starbucks strategy for its company-operated stores is to increase market share, by selectively opening stores in new and existing markets. Licensed stores rely on the expertise of local partners who share operating and store development experiences.

Supporting activities

Procurement: The supply and price can be affected by multiple factors in the producing countries, including weather, natural disasters, crop disease, increases in farm input costs, production costs, inventory levels and other macro-economic factors. So, coffee is subject to significant price movements and it is acquired using fixed-price and price-to-be-fixed purchase commitments.

Technological development

Information technology systems include point of sale, web and mobile platforms, including online and mobile payment systems and rewards programmes. Starbucks continuously seeks to connect with customers and its online forum can enable customers to ask questions, provide suggestions and comments.

Results

The brief value chain analysis illustrates how Starbucks are able to gain a competitive edge. Improvements in primary and secondary activities will help the firm to obtain greater profit margins. Competition is intense and Starbuck's customers choose their products on the basis of quality, service and convenience, as well as price. Ultimately, Starbucks is dependent upon the performance of its US operations (73 per cent of net revenues). Encouragingly, net revenues continue to climb from $16.4bn in 2014 to $19.2bn in 2015, and operating margins were 18.7 per cent and 18.8 per cent.

3.6 How to compete

Sources of sustainable competitive advantage remain the holy grail of business and management education and practice. We have considered a range of approaches enabling business leaders to keep on track during times of global economic crisis and economic slowdown. During this chapter we consider a range of strategy tools and techniques, and use the context of external and internal analysis. We now consider some more theory, which is rather dated, but still forms an excellent platform for the student and practitioner to acquire some understanding of the key components to take into account. So, the following section briefly reviews BCG Growth Share Matrix, Ansoff's matrix and Porter's generic strategies.

BCG growth/share matrix

This growth/share matrix (Henderson, 1979) created by the Boston Consulting Group in the 1970s assists managers in making decisions about business objectives (see Figure 3.17). Despite the blurring of discrete business units within some organisations, the analysis focuses some attention on the cash flow of operations. Inherent assumptions include that the margins generated by a product and respective cash flow generation are a consequence of market share. The larger the market share (relative to competitors), the greater the earnings potential. Sales and revenue growth require investment, and this cash should be internally generated by the product portfolio. But we know that sales will only grow if there is effective marketing. High market share is desirable, but requires additional investment. As no business can grow indefinitely, there must be trade-offs between earnings and money spent on them. Profitability is affected also by the product lifecycle, and the user must take a holistic view of the product portfolio. Decisions need to be made about earnings from mature products being invested in other products with future earning potential.

From a cash flow perspective, a balanced portfolio is highly desirous (see Figure 3.18). In summary, each quadrant presents varying challenges.

Question marks (high growth, low market share):

- High expenditure required to develop and launch the product, and later unlikely to be profitable. Further investment will be required if the business wants to claim market share.

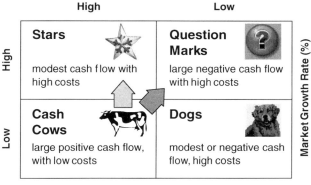

Figure 3.17 BCG growth/share matrix

Stars (high growth, high market share):

- Successful question marks become stars. But investment is still required to maintain growth and defend leadership position. Only marginally profitable, but become more profitable when growth slows down.

Cash cows (low growth, high market share):

- Mature products in well-established markets. As growth slows down, there is less need for high investment, so most profitable. Should be used to fund other products.

Dogs (low growth, low market share):

- May be a previous cash cow which enjoys a loyal market although is mainly replaced by new rival. Marginally profitable, but should be withdrawn when becomes loss maker.
- Guard dog: blocking the competition.
- Guide dog: complement other activities.
- Sheep dog: creating customers at bottom of the range which may trade up to one of its better products later on.

Ansoff

The Ansoff Matrix (1957) provides guidance for the CEO in determining the firm's growth strategy (see Figure 3.19). When faced with a plethora of opportunities it is advisable to consider what products and markets are currently targeted and should be targeted. Outputs can be broken down into four discrete areas. Each option requires different strategies and actions, as well as supporting resources and skills.

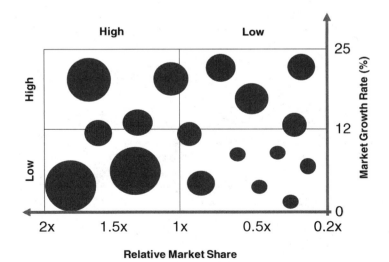

Figure 3.18 BCG matrix – balanced portfolio

Strategic analysis 75

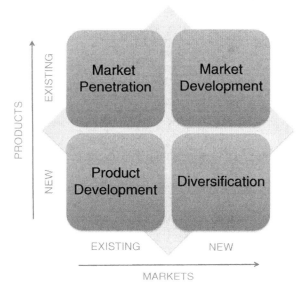

Figure 3.19 Ansoff matrix

Market penetration

This is the easiest and least risky strategy to pursue. The focus on existing products and markets will mean servicing existing customers, and using the existing product range to increase an organisation's share of existing markets. The added advantage is that there is prior knowledge of what works. Loyalty schemes could be promoted to existing customers, which can encourage them to buy more.

Market development

Similar to market penetration but the focus is on existing products/services in new markets. Requires excellent marketing capability, as market research and marketing strategy are needed to provide initial entry, and effective organisational learning about the market. Creating access to a new market takes time, but the high risk can translate into high returns.

Product development

The introduction of new products into existing markets is risky, but this can be mitigated as current customers are already known. During the product development process, customers should be consulted and their feedback incorporated into product development. Good ideas can be solicited from understanding existing customers. It is preferable to return to delighted customers and sell them something new than to find new customers.

Diversification

Contrary to market penetration, diversification is the most risky strategy. With the focus on new products/services in new markets there is potential for high rewards too. It may take time

Strategic management primer

and resources to develop sufficient understanding to compete effectively. The diversification can be related (remain in the same industry) or unrelated (compete in a new industry). The CEO needs to be realistic about strengths and weaknesses when considering this growth strategy. Frequently, help is needed from investors or through mergers and acquisitions.

Porter's generic strategies

During the 1980s Porter's generic strategy, the full range of competitive strategies, gained prominence. The approach became extremely fashionable in western business schools and with executives. Users sought to achieve two things: in the first instance, generic principles, and secondly, customised action plans (Mintzberg, 1992). The four quadrants (see Figure 3.20) built around low cost and differentiation are the basic type of competitive advantage. Originally scholars considered differentiation and cost leadership as two separate types of strategies, i.e. pure strategies.

Cost leadership strategy

- Firms that are successful tend to be the lowest cost producer in the industry. This is achieved by maximising economies of scale and other cost advantages.
- Risks – it may be impossible to reduce cost base. Think about the budget hotel and airline sector.

Differentiation strategy

- Firms that are successful tend to possess a differentiation strategy, which offers its customers something that is unique and valuable. Customers are willing to pay higher prices.
- Risks – the additional costs must be covered by the higher prices. Imitation can be a problem.

Focus strategy

- Focus strategy will concentrate on a specific target segment and seeks to achieve either a cost advantage or differentiation. Firms pursuing such as strategy have lower volumes and therefore gain less bargaining power with their suppliers.
- Risks – it is relatively easy for a broad-market cost leader to adapt its product in order to compete directly.

Target scope	Advantage low cost	Product uniqueness
Broad (industry wide)	Cost leadership strategy	Differentiation strategy
Narrow (market segment)	Focus strategy (low cost)	Focus strategy (differentiation)

Figure 3.20 Porter's (1980) generic strategy framework

Stuck in the middle

Michael Porter argued that to be successful over the long-term, the firm must select only one of his three generic strategies. Otherwise, by pursuing more than one single generic strategy the firm will be "stuck in the middle" and will not achieve a competitive advantage. This apparent dilemma has been subject to debate, and many scholars now see that there is no reason to discriminate against a mixed strategy. For example, insofar as the digital age is concerned, the application of Porter's generic strategies is not clearly delineated. Moreover, with the growing influence of new products and services, Porter's generic strategies do not provide the full range of options to today's strategists and they are not mutually exclusive. As the commercial world becomes more complex, Porter's original blueprint created in the 1980s is limited. In today's dynamism and turbulence, firms now integrate the two elements and can pursue hybrid or combinative, as opposed to pure strategies.

POD

The Five Whys

Sakichi Toyoda, one of the fathers of the Japanese industrial revolution, developed an approach to problem-solving known as the "Five Whys". Typically, a Japanese manager will ask themselves "why?" five times when confronted with a problem. After the fifth "why?" they have often found the root cause of their problem. The questioning can identify systemic relationships, that is, connections and relationships. In practice the activity can involve groups who understand the processes and conditions on the shop floor, rather than at the Board level.

Problem: Your client is refusing to pay an invoice for some posters you have printed.

1   Why? The delivery was too late, and arrived after the event.
2   Why? The posters were more complex than originally thought.
3   Why? The senior artist was on vacation, and a junior artist underestimated the amount of colour ink required.
4   Why? The junior artist had never worked on a poster on their own.
5   Why? The induction did not include how to design, prepare and print a poster.

Counter-measure: We need to ensure that when the senior artist goes on vacation, there is adequate cover. Also, we need to provide better training for junior artists.

3.7 Chapter summary

The corporate "I don't know" factor is higher than ever before because business leaders have lost their sense of direction in the global economic crisis and are struggling to identify and focus on growth opportunities appropriate for their business. They need to look beyond tactical lower prices and cost cutting and repair and rebuild value chain relationships. Many companies obtain a disproportionate benefit from their annual strategic planning in terms of effort and reward, then complain of too few new ideas together with power and political undertones.

So why is there a mismatch between effort and result? The annual strategy review sometimes amounts to little more than a stage show where business unit leaders present updates of last year's presentations, and take few risks in announcing new ideas. This stage performance does not prepare organisations to face the strategic uncertainties ahead or serve as the focal point for creative thinking. The strategic analysis tools considered in this chapter suggests that executives should ask themselves "why?" as well as "how?" By asking "why?", organisations will assess both internal and external environments and by using a broad array of stakeholders will produce more challenging and innovative strategies. Another caveat relates to being too over-focused on the extrapolation of existing thoughts rather than new and stretching aspirations.

3.8 End of chapter self-reflection questions

1. Why are strategic decisions important? Use examples to illustrate your thoughts.
2. How are strategic decisions distinguished from other types of business decisions?
3. How have changes in the external environment in the twenty-first century influenced strategic analysis? What makes for a good external environment analysis?
4. How have changes in the internal environment in the twenty-first century influenced strategic analysis? What makes for a good internal environment analysis?
5. Using Porter's five forces framework, identify the sources of competitive advantage that Aldi, the UK low cost supermarket chain, has over its mainstream rivals.

References

Ansoff, H. I. (1957). Strategies for diversification. *Harvard Business Review*, *35*(5), 113–124.

Barney, J. B., & Hoskisson, R. E. (1990). Strategic groups: Untested assertions and research proposals. *Managerial and Decision Economics*, *11*(3), 187–198.

Barton, D., & Court, D. (2012). Making advanced analytics work for you. *Harvard Business Review*, *90*(10), 78–83.

Chakravarty, A., Grewal, R., & Sambamurthy, V. (2013). Information technology competencies, organizational agility, and firm performance: Enabling and facilitating roles. *Information Systems Research*, *24*(4), 976–997.

Chareonsuk, C., & Chansa-ngavej, C. (2008). Intangible asset management framework for long-term financial performance. *Industrial Management & Data Systems*, *108*(6), 812–828.

Collinson, C., & Parcell, G. (2001). *Learning to fly*. Oxford: Capstone Publishing Ltd.

Dobbs, M. E. (2013). Internal analysis in practice: Templates for firm and case analysis. *Journal of the North American Management Society*, *7*(1), 40.

Dobbs, M. (2014). Guidelines for applying Porter's five forces framework: A set of industry analysis templates. *Competitiveness Review*, *24*(1), 32–45.

Henderson, B.D. (1979). The product portfolio: Growth share matrix of the Boston Consulting Group. *The strategy process: Concepts, contexts, cases*, pp. 678–680.

Heskett, J. L. (2014). Are we entering an era of neuromanagement? Harvard Business School Working Knowledge. Available at http://hbswk.hbs.edu/item/are-we-entering-an-era-of-neuromanagement

Hogan, S. J., & Coote, L. V. (2014). Organizational culture, innovation, and performance: A test of Schein's model. *Journal of Business Research*, *67*(8), 1609–1621.

Hunt, M S. (1972). *Competition in the major home appliance industry 1960-1970*. Unpublished doctoral dissertation, Harvard University.

Kaplan, R.S., & Norton, D.P. (2004). Strategy maps: Converting intangible assets into tangible outcomes. Boston: Harvard Business School Press.

Kim, W. C., & Mauborgne, R. (2005). How to create uncontested market space and make the competition irrelevant. *Harvard Business Review*, *4*, 13.

Kramer, J. P., Marinelli, E., Iammarino, S., & Diez, J. R. (2011). Intangible assets as drivers of innovation: Empirical evidence on multinational enterprises in German and UK regional systems of innovation. *Technovation, 31*(9), 447–458.

Leask, G., & Parnell, J. A. (2005). Integrating strategic groups and the resource based perspective: Understanding the competitive process. *European Management Journal, 23*(4), 458–470.

Mendelow A. (1981). Environmental scanning: The impact of stakeholder concept; *2nd International Conference on Information Systems*. Massachusetts, 407–417.

Mintzberg, H. (1992). Five Ps for strategy in the strategy process. In H. Mintzberg and J. B. Quinn (Eds.), *The strategy process*. Englewood Cliffs, NJ: Prentice-Hall International Editions.

Ohmae, K. (1983). *The mind of the strategist*. Harmondsworth: Penguin.

Porter, M.E. (1980). *Competitive Strategy: Techniques for analyzing industries and competitors*. New York: The Free Press.

Porter, M.E. (2008). *Competitive strategy: Techniques for analyzing industries and competitors*. Simon and Schuster.

Powell, T. C., Lovallo, D., & Fox, C. R. (2011). Behavioral strategy. *Strategic Management Journal, 32*(13), 1369–1386.

Prahalad, C. K., & Hamel, G. (1994). Strategy as a field of study: Why search for a new paradigm? *Strategic Management Journal, 15*(S2), 5–16.

Schein, E. H. 2004. Online at https://static1.squarespace.com/static/57c88c979de4bb44f298d342/t/588fad7bff7c50b31624ecc7/1485811068275/organizational-culture-and-leadership-schein-en-8023-2.pdf

Starbucks (2015). Annual Report, available at: http://s21.q4cdn.com/369030626/files/doc_financials/2015/Starbucks-Fiscal-2015-Form-10-K.pdf

Teece, D. J. (2007). Explicating dynamic capabilities: The nature and microfoundations of (sustainable) enterprise performance. *Strategic Management Journal, 28*(13), 1319–1350.

Teece, D. J., Pisano, G., & Shuen, A. (1997). Dynamic capabilities and strategic management. *Strategic Management Journal, 1*, 509–533.

Wenger, E., & Snyder, W. (2000). Communities of practice: The organizational frontier. *Harvard Business Review*, January–February, 139–145.

Wenger-Trayner, E., & Wenger-Trayner, B. (2014). *Learning in landscapes of practice: Boundaries, identity, and knowledgeability in practice-based learning*. London and New York: Routledge.

Williams, R. (1983). *Keywords: A vocabulary of culture and society*, 2nd edn. New York: Oxford University Press.

4 Case study analysis

4.1 Learning objectives

After completing this chapter you will:

- be able to demonstrate an understanding and appreciation of the case study method
- be aware of the characteristics of successful and failing organisations
- use the results of the case study method to critically evaluate the efficiency and effectiveness of corporate, business and operational level strategies
- structure ideas and arguments in an effective manner
- be familiar with how to synthesise qualitative and quantitative material
- be able to communicate more articulately and concisely in teams.

4.2 Introduction

Case study analysis enables you to bridge the gap between business school and the "real business world." Another benefit from case study analysis is the further development of necessary strategic management skills. Case study analysis requires you to examine a critical point in the life of an organisation. You are put in the position of a decision-maker. In a real business situation, key decisions will have to be made logically, objectively and in a timely manner. In a case study analysis, you will have to apply your analytical skills to identify and solve whatever problems appear. Studying cases will help you to develop the experience to make these decisions in the real world.

An additional benefit will occur as you become involved in the operations of fascinating and dissimilar kinds of organisational situations and dilemmas. You will become familiar with diverse organisational structures, different philosophies of business, and apply alternative strategy techniques, all of which should broaden your knowledge. The whole process of preparation for case study analysis will reap benefits in other ways. You will enhance your communication skills as you write and present your final report. The cases will give you an opportunity to use your initiative, decide on a course of action and follow it through. If you work in groups, you will develop your ability to work with other people, which is a crucial skill in today's business world. Notwithstanding incomplete information, all the relevant information necessary to make critical decisions will be in the case study, and you will learn by doing.

Traditional case study analysis is one of the by-products of the Americanisation of business and management education. It originates from Harvard Business School in 1912, who claim that over 80 per cent of case study analyses sold throughout the world are written by their faculty, and can range from two to twenty-five pages. In a Bloomberg Businessweek report of the top ranked 25 business schools, 19 use case study analysis as one of their main teaching tools. At Harvard Business School 80 per cent of class time is spent on case study analysis.

Being tasked to write reports about specific challenges facing organisations is now an integral part of undergraduate and postgraduate modules in strategic management, executive short courses in strategy, and increasingly in the graduate recruitment process. The case study analysis provides a snapshot picture of a management situation. The emphasis is usually on a situation that is presenting a challenge for management. Situations include large companies, small and medium-sized enterprises, and government organisations, and the student or executive is placed as a decision-maker. Case study analysis will start by the reader assessing events that managers have had to deal with together with changes in the internal and external environment. Issues and problems may relate to corporate, business or operational levels. The management of the organisation may have responded to something such as a strategy renewal project that is either too slow, or has failed. The reader has to use an array of strategic management tools and techniques to solve these problems, as outlined in Chapter 3. The outline processes include analysis, identification of options, selection of a preferred option, and recommendations.

Case study analysis is flexible, as it can be used for semester-long projects, providing ample time for in-depth analysis. Alternatively, case study analysis can be used for seminar classes or even shorter time frames. In these latter instances, issues are simplified and the length is shorter. As Dobbs (2013) suggests, the variety of types and uses of case study analysis can be challenging for students. Not only may the student lack experience of managing others in a business setting, they may have no prior experiences from which to draw on. If not adequately supported, case study analysis can result in superficial analysis that is extemporised, lacks systematic rigour and proposes hasty, ill-informed decisions.

The authors have used the case study method in their classes and use classroom discussions and/or reports for formative assessments (monitor student learning during module) and/or summative ones (evaluate student learning at the end of module). When running executive education courses, vignettes (mini-cases) are normally used during the programme, and case study analysis can be used as a capstone-type exercise towards the end of a programme. Case study analysis is becoming an integral component of the graduate entry position and as part of the consulting interviewing process. Organisations of all sizes and operating in all sectors deploy subject-related or general case studies, which are one of an array of steps to evaluate a candidate's aptitude (strategic, creative, analytical and problem-solving) and employment skills (business, time management, working under pressure and oral communication). Over the years, the feedback from our students is that firms are challenging them by tweaking the process to develop their own methodologies. Sector-specific organisations use case studies based on their scope of activities, financial firms use finance-oriented examples, technology firms use IT-specific examples, marketing organisations may use case studies that seek to reposition firms by creating marketing campaigns.

Nevertheless, despite the wide-scale use of case study analysis, Dobbs (2013) notes the dearth of instruction, examples and guidance provided to students by faculty or in traditional textbooks. This chapter seeks to provide an overview of how to perform case study analysis and help is provided for systematic analysis through the introduction of a series of templates. Although, the majority of undergraduate students do not have business and especially leadership experience, modules in strategic management are taught at either the second or final year of undergraduate degree programmes. In the latter case, strategic management is used as a capstone subject to prepare students for work by consolidating and integrating their knowledge and skills. The lecturer's experience and style together with expectations, backgrounds and abilities of students influence how and what actual cases are employed. At the undergraduate and postgraduate levels, due to experience and age, students tend to have difficulty with analysis and dealing with complex situations. The quality of the actual case study analysis tends to be dependent upon whether the case is realistic or the lecturer's (or author's) personal experiences. On a global basis, the lack of local case studies (non-western) present some frustration to students. Sometimes the student may not even be a business and management student, but could be an engineering student. In such situations, students face the added burden of a lack of time to acquaint themselves with commercial awareness. This can be tackled by reading quality newspapers and business periodicals.

Case study analysis steps

To analyse the current situation, students must closely examine the big issues facing them in the case study. A common mistake is to try and identify every single problem facing the company. Then they prepare a long list to incorporate into the report. There are many ways for students to approach the analysis of business case studies. Each instructor has his or her own ideas on the number and nature of the steps that are involved. A logical format should be used for analysing any business situation. Table 4.1 illustrates a generic ten-step procedure to begin:

Table 4.1 Generic 10-step procedure in case study analysis

Steps	Activities	Questions to consider about the organisation
1	Heritage, development and growth review	Who were the founders? Who are the key individuals? What have been the critical incidents in the organisation's history? Has the development to date been successful? What have been the salient capabilities and competencies? What is the current situation? What are the big questions?
2	External analysis	What are the threats and opportunities?
3	Internal analysis	What are the internal strengths and weaknesses?
4	SWOT analysis	Define the problem. What problems need to be diagnosed? How can weaknesses be converted into strengths? How can threats be converted into opportunities?
5	Corporate strategy review	Is a corporate strategy renewal programme required?
6	Business strategy review	How are the SBUs positioned in their marketplace? What are the SBUs' value propositions? Are the SBUs on track to deliver their targets?
7	Option selection	Formulate the alternatives. What are the alternatives? Analyse the alternatives. What is the most appropriate option? What are the key risks?
8	Develop a strategic plan	What is the vision and mission?
9	Develop a strategic implementation plan	What barriers exist to implement the renewal strategy? What structures and control systems are required to implement the strategy? Is it affordable?
10	Recommendations	How can the strategic problem be solved? Recommend a solution.

4.3 Format for case study analysis

Analysing a business situation needs a formalised plan of action. The case study analyst should try to understand all elements in a particular business situation so that they can recommend action to improve that situation. The entire process must be systematic. In a strategic management case study analysis, there should be a systematic set of principles and procedures in examining a particular situation and making appropriate recommendations. The case study method becomes an effective teaching device when students are encouraged to analyse the data presented and to formulate their own set of recommendations.

Case study overview

Suppose for a moment that you are a strategy consultant who has just been asked to analyse an organisation and advise it on its business strategy. Where would you begin? First, you would acquaint yourself with the entire organisation, including its products, processes, situation and any other relevant general factors. You would try to get a broad picture in your mind of the whole organisation. With this overview, you would then be able to deal with specific elements of the situation.

Your first objective should be to get an overall feel for the case study, an overview of what is going on. Do this by skimming over the case study quickly, perusing its highlights. Try to answer these general types of questions: What kind of organisation is it? What are some of the general factors at work? What kinds of problems is the organisation having?

After you have this overview of the case study, go over it again, reading it carefully, underlining or identifying key statements. During this in-depth reading, you should not only try to understand the case study situation but also identify, at least on a preliminary basis, some of the problem areas. These problems will be formally delineated later. In writing up the first section of your case study analysis, present a brief overview of the situation; this will set the stage for your analysis.

Pre-case analysis

Most students jump to recommendations and conclusions for case studies almost before they have finished reading them for the first time. This section describes a way of forcing students to do more analysis before preparing a formal case study report.

Although strategic management case studies can be used in a number of different ways, most instructors use them, frequently with text material, to get students to apply principles and to develop decision-making abilities. This is supposed to provide an involvement, which builds analytical skills and accelerates learning and understanding rather than rote memory. But experience with this method – both as a student and a teacher – suggests that something is missing. In case study analysis many students find it difficult to sift the data for useful information. But case study analysis offers a new dimension. Practice in making assumptions is extremely valuable since business executives regularly have to make "educated guesses." But this may be one of the weaknesses of the case study method for instruction purposes. The student may avoid careful analysis of the given data by making a strong assumption that overwhelms all other considerations.

Structuring the analysis

A somewhat discouraging observation is that some students do not even know where to begin when given the "raw material," that is, the judgements or assumptions which instructors usually expect students to create for themselves. This can result in the frequent class experience of dominated unstructured case study discussion by students with strong, unsupported conclusions. In other words, in the normal unstructured case study analysis, many students are just guessing. Less extensively, treatment of a few other cases has led to similarly discouraging results. Weaker students give superficial analyses, and may completely miss the underlying difficulties of which the current problem is only a symptom.

Sizing up the situation

A special exercise we sometimes use with students has been developed to force students back one step in their thinking. Students are required to submit a one-page paper entitled "Sizing Up the Situation." They are expected to describe (using strategic management terminology) the situation in the case study, including the underlying situation which gives rise to the present problems and which will affect their solution. They are not permitted to solve any problems or make any recommendations at this stage.

Basically, the students are asked to put down on paper the essential facts and the logical, basic assumptions which they feel they can make on the basis of the material presented in the case study. In the usual case study analysis students are expected to select the key facts. Here more is required. There are certain fundamental, logical assumptions about the nature of the situation, which can be developed from the case study material. Other less fundamental assumptions can be brought out later in the formal report. These modifying assumptions may determine the conclusion.

When pressed in this way, it is surprising how many students differ regarding fundamental considerations, for example, about the nature of the company's product, probable target markets, and even the nature of the market situation. When first starting out, some students even call obvious monopolistic competition situations pure competition (and then are willing to develop policies accordingly).

The steps in "Sizing Up the Situation" for a strategic marketing management problem can include working through the following mental steps:

i) Look at the product or products now being produced or contemplated and provide a tentative classification into categories such as convenience goods, shopping goods, accessories, and so on, and specify the apparent target market of the company. Something about the company's product policy and overall strategy might be noted. The type of market situation (pure competition, monopolistic competition, and so on) and the stage of the product in its lifecycle should also be considered. Further, some thought should be given to the degree of brand preference achieved or sought.

ii) Develop a "reasonable" marketing mix on the basis of the preliminary judgements in step 1. This should be merely a quickly developed "ideal" based primarily on the product classification.

iii) Look at the way the product is actually being handled by the company in the case study.

iv) Rethink the nature of the product and the target market(s) before condemning the company's procedure if it differs from the student's "ideal." The student should try to give the company management the benefit of the doubt, but should not accept everything as "right."

v) Size up the situation, including the strengths and weaknesses of various elements of the marketing mix.

The thinking in step v) is then incorporated into the one-page report. Here students should present the essential facts and any logical, basic assumptions, which seem in order. They should include any major considerations which they feel will have a bearing on the direction of the case study analysis or which they may need in the later analysis. Recommendations and conclusions should be avoided.

This report then becomes the base on which a formal case study analysis can be built. In many cases, if the "Sizing Up the Situation" exercise is done well, the statement of the problem is clear and the rest of the analysis is greatly simplified. It still requires imagination and logic, but it is not a vague guessing game.

Situation analysis

After having understood the case study and identified the key problem areas, you should break the case study down into parts so you can evaluate critically all aspects of the organisation. Look closely at all details of the case, then try to pull this information together into a more manageable form. The situation analysis stage involves analysing four general areas: the organisation, the customer, the competition and the environment. Although these four areas of study are important, one area that can create problems is that of financial analysis. Here is an outline to help you organise your situation analysis:

(1) Financial situation

(A) BALANCE SHEET/INCOME STATEMENT ANALYSIS

You should analyse the financial statements both vertically and horizontally. Vertical analysis involves the calculation of meaningful figures from the financial statements of one year. For the balance sheet, each item may be expressed as a percentage of total assets. For the income statement, each item may be expressed as a percentage of sales. These figures can then be compared with industry figures, competitors, or other divisions of the same company.

Horizontal analysis consists of comparing items on the financial statements, or calculations derived from the vertical analysis, with the same items in other time periods. A comparison of key items over a five-year period can be especially enlightening. For example, you might analyse sales trends over the past five years, calculating the percentage change from one year to the next. You might do the same for other key items such as cost of goods sold or net income. Not only can these figures be compared between years, but they may also be compared with industry trends, those of competitors, or other divisions of the same company.

(B) RATIO ANALYSIS

To obtain an accurate measure of a firm's financial position, it is best to calculate several financial ratios. Some of the more frequently used financial ratios are shown in Table 4.2 and Table 4.3 shows and illustrates a summary of profit measures. These ratios might be calculated for two or more years to uncover any significant trend in the company's financial performance.

(C) OTHER QUANTITATIVE ANALYSES

Depending on the information provided in the case study, you may be able to carry out other quantitative analyses. For example, break-even analysis is a helpful technique for

Strategic management primer

Table 4.2 Selected financial ratios

Ratio	How calculated	What it measures
(1) Liquidity Ratios		
(a) Current ratio	$\dfrac{\text{Current assets}}{\text{Current liabilities}}$	Measures the ability of the firm to meet short-term debt. The rule-of-thumb for this ratio is 2.
(b) Quick {acid test} ratio	$\dfrac{\text{Current assets - Inventory}}{\text{Current liabilities}}$	A more accurate measure of a firm's ability to pay off immediately its short-term debt.
(c) Inventory to working capital	$\dfrac{\text{Inventory}}{\text{Current assets - Current liabilities}}$	Measures the extent to which the firm's working capital is tied up in inventory.
(2) Profitability Ratios		
(a) Return on net worth (return on equity)	$\dfrac{\text{Profit after taxes}}{\text{Net worth}}$	Measures the rate of return on stockholders' equity.
(b) Return on assets (return on investment)	$\dfrac{\text{Profit after taxes}}{\text{Total assets}}$	Measures the return on total investment in the firm.
(c) Net profit margin (return on sales)	$\dfrac{\text{Profit after taxes}}{\text{Sales}}$	Indicates return on sales.
(3) Leverage Ratios		
(a) Debt to assets ratio	$\dfrac{\text{Total liabilities}}{\text{Current assets}}$	Measures the extent to which borrowed funds have been used to finance the operation of the business.
(b) Debt to equity ratio	$\dfrac{\text{Total liabilities}}{\text{Stockholders' equity}}$	Provides a comparison of the equity of the owners with the funds provided by the creditors.
(c) Times interest earned	$\dfrac{\text{Profit before taxes and interest charges}}{\text{Interest charges}}$	Measures the risk that a company might not be able to meet its interest payments.
(4) Activity Ratios		
(a) Inventory turnover	$\dfrac{\text{Sales}}{\text{Inventory}}$	Measures the number of times the average inventory is turned over in the year.
(b) Fixed assets turnover	$\dfrac{\text{Sales}}{\text{Fixed assets}}$	Measures the sales productivity and utilisation of plant and equipment.
(c) Total assets turnover	$\dfrac{\text{Sales}}{\text{Total assets}}$	Measures the sales productivity and utilisation of all the firm's assets.
(d) Average collection period	$\dfrac{\text{Accounts receivable}}{\text{Total sales} \div 365}$	Measures the average collection period for accounts receivable.

analysing the relationship among fixed costs, variable costs and revenue. Marketing profitability analysis examines the profitability of various segments of the company or of various market segments served by the company. You should evaluate carefully all of the quantitative information you are given in a case and ask yourself, "What can I do with this data to make it more meaningful?"

(D) OVERALL FINANCIAL ASSESSMENT

After you have scrutinised all of the financial information in the case study, you should be able to make some general statements regarding the financial position of the firm. For example,

Table 4.3 Summary of profit measures

Method	Definition	Computation
Payback period	Number of years until investment is recouped	If rate of flow is constant, $$\text{Payback} = \frac{\text{Investment Net}}{\text{Cash Flow}}$$ Otherwise, the payback is determined by adding up the expected cash inflows until the total equals the initial investment
Accounting (or Unadjusted) rate of return	Ratio of average annual income after depreciation to the average book value of the investment	$$\frac{\text{Average Annual Cash Flow} - \text{Average Annual Depreciation}}{\text{Half Initial Investment}}$$
Net present value (NPV)	Difference between cash inflows and outflows discounted to the present at a given interest rate	$$NPV = \sum_{t=1}^{T} \frac{F_t}{(1+i)t}$$ Where F_t = net cash flow at time period t i = discount rate T = planning horizon
ROI (Rate of Return of the investment or Internal Rate of Return)	Discount rate which makes the net present value of inflows and outflows equal to zero	The ROI is determined by solving the equation $$\sum_{t=1}^{T} = \frac{F_t}{(1+i)t}$$ Where i is the rate of return of the investment

you may have determined from your ratio analysis that the firm is in a precarious position relative to its liquidity. You should draw attention to this, since it limits what the company is able to do in the short run and, thus, what you are able to recommend. It is imperative that you state concisely the firm's financial position since it directly impacts on future strategy.

Problem identification

Now that you understand the case study and have critically evaluated all of its key elements, you are ready to formalise the problems existing in the organisation. Not only is this normally the most difficult part of the case study analysis, it is also the most crucial. Since the remainder of the case study analysis evolves around solving the problems defined at this stage, it is important to consider the problem areas very carefully. At this stage you should consider strategic management theory and practice. The amount of academic rigour and practice is increased at the postgraduate level. Students often forget the differing programme and module outcomes at the undergraduate and postgraduate levels. At the MBA level we have found that the balance between theory and practice is skewed towards the latter. Conversely at the MSc level students tend to have problems with both the application of theory and appropriate practice.

A good way to start is to define all of the problem areas you see in the case study. Then go over each of these, and try to sort out the symptoms of problems from the actual problems themselves. Having a good grasp of theory can help identify the actual problems themselves. You may have to search to find the problem behind the symptoms in other functional areas. A company may be having problems with increasing inventory costs, declining profitability and declining customer service quality. After examining all aspects of the situation, you may conclude that the company's major problem is poor product management, particularly the lack of a formal product elimination strategy. As you carry out this process, you may find that there is more than one problem in the case study. In this situation you need to prioritise the problems into major and minor. Focus your analysis around what you define as the one major problem. On occasions, you may identify two major problems. If so, treat them separately: solve one completely, and then solve the other. In most situations, try to pick out the one problem that is more immediate than any other and focus your analysis on it. However, you should not disregard the minor problems; deal with them fully at the end of the case study analysis.

In writing up this section of your case study analysis, which should follow what is being asked by the instructor, you should define concisely the major problem (or, occasionally, problems). Also list the appropriate symptoms. Following this statement of the major problem, list all of the minor problems, along with the corresponding symptoms. Problem definition is also a matter of delineating a suitable framework within which to deal with what may be posed in the case as an immediate question. The problem scope should not be unrealistically and unmanageably broad. Good problem definition names the immediate problems and defines them in a way that calls for action-oriented answers.

Statement and evaluation of alternatives

Now that you have identified the major problem, you are ready to solve it. Develop as many possible solutions as you can, and then screen out those ideas that are illogical until you have a set of realistic alternatives. You can then examine the advantages and disadvantages of these remaining alternatives to reach a solution. The initial process of alternative generation is similar to idea generation in the creative process. The objective is to generate as many alternative courses of action as possible. The next step involves mentally making a pass over each of these to eliminate any that are not feasible. This process should leave you with some realistic alternatives to be assessed more critically.

In writing up your case study analysis, list these realistic alternatives, making sure that each relates to the major problem you defined. Each alternative should be a potential solution to the major problem in the case; the alternative should be a completely different way of solving the problem, independent of one another and mutually exclusive. Then list the specific advantages and disadvantages of carrying out each alternative. You may even wish to construct a "T-account" for each alternative, listing the pros on one side and the cons on the other. If you stated more than one major problem, you should follow the same procedure for each. In a poor analysis there is no explicit discussion of the pros and cons of each alternative. Problem and opportunity statements serve as the basis of your pros (opportunities) and cons (problems) discussion. Different ones relate to specific alternatives.

Recommended solution and justification

After following this logical approach to identifying potential solutions to the major problem and evaluating the alternatives, you should be in a position to recommend a course of action.

In this section of your case study analysis, state the alternative you selected and explain why. In cases where you defined more than one major problem and set of realistic alternatives, select and justify an alternative for each problem. Remember that, ideally, no more than one alternative should be selected. If you could select more than one, it is probably because (1) the alternatives in that set were not really independent and mutually exclusive, or (2) your major problem statement is too general and should be more specific. Recommend the solution you think is most suitable, offering reasons for your decision. In your recommendations and implementation, beware of constraints on the organisation. Some important constraints include strength of competition, company resources, production capacity, budgets, and philosophies and capabilities of top management. You must reach a clear decision. Part of the skill of decision-making is to be forced to reach a decision under ambiguous circumstances and then be prepared to defend this decision. A good case study analysis reaches a decision that is logically consistent with the situation analysis that was done. This is the ultimate test of a case study analysis.

Implementation

You may feel that after you have recommended a solution that the case study analysis is finished. Sometimes one of the questions for the case study analysis explicitly asks for an implementation strategy. All you have accomplished so far is to decide on a specific course of action for the future. Now you must answer such questions as:

- How will it be accomplished?
- When will it be accomplished (short term, long term)?
- Who will do it?
- Where will it be done?
- How much is the projected revenue?
- How much is the projected contribution?

You may have a technical appendix at the end of your report in which you specify each part of your plan, along with the corresponding cost and revenue projections. In your recommendations for the organisation, also consider how these plans will impact on the minor problems you identified earlier in the case analysis. Address each of these minor problems and make appropriate recommendations for their solution as well. The final paragraph should attempt to tie a bow around your analysis. Briefly summarise how your recommendations will solve the major and minor problems faced by the organisation. Suggest what the organisation should do in the future and how it will be better off because of it.

Writing the report

Students who prepare written reports do a better job of analysing business problems. Writing a good report takes a certain skill. When instructors read reports, they check to see whether students fully understand the situation and whether their interpretations of the facts are reasonable. They also like to see papers that are objective, balanced, consistent and decisive. Perhaps the most common error made by students in writing case reports is to repeat the facts that have been provided, or merely regurgitate the lecture slides used by instructors. Instead of analysing the data in the light of the alternatives, students frequently repeat statements that appear in the cases, with no clear objective in mind. Another deficiency often observed in writing reports is a lack of organisation. The end result is a paper that has no beginning and no end, and often consists of one long paragraph. To avoid this problem, some instructors require that reports be presented in outline form. The condensed nature of such reports sometimes makes them hard to follow, and the more readable narrative approach is preferred.

There is no optimum length for a written case study analysis. It depends on the preference of the instructor, but is usually measured in the number of words. The report should be long enough to adequately cover the subject and meet the learning objectives of the module. It is fairly obvious that written reports must be neat, legible and free of grammatical and spelling errors. Yet students frequently submit work in a rush, ignoring the fact that instructors expect certain minimum standards of performance in written expression. Also, the conclusions are sometimes missing and the final report does not address the instructors' questions based on the weighting of marks.

Final suggestions

How do you know when you have done a good case study analysis? As you develop your analyses of the case studies, keep the following points in mind:

i) Immerse yourself in the role of a strategy consultant or a particular decision maker in the organisation and address your comments to the appropriate company executive.
ii) As with any report sent to an executive, you should keep it as concise as possible. Do not rehash all the information contained in the case. Stick with a critical evaluation of the facts.
iii) Remember to operate within the time frame of the case. Do not spend your time trying to find out what the organisation actually did and then recommend that as your solution. This destroys the whole purpose of the case study analysis. And just because the organisation did something does not mean it was right. A solution you come up with may be better than what the organisation actually did.
iv) Do not use the expression "I need more information." The information provided for you in each case is sufficient for making a decision. Managers would always like to have more data, but cost and time limitations prevent this. Assume you have all the possible information and make a decision based on it.
v) It is imperative that the case study analysis be thorough. Each area of the situation analysis must be discussed, problems and opportunities must be identified, alternatives must be presented and evaluated using the situation analysis and the relevant financial analysis and a decision must be made. Each area above must be covered in good depth and with insight.
vi) Avoid rehashing case study facts. A good analysis uses facts that are relevant to the situation at hand to make summary points of analysis. A poor analysis just restates or rehashes these facts without making relevant summary comments.
vii) Make reasonable assumptions. Every case study is incomplete in terms of some piece of information that you would like to have. Incomplete information is an accurate reflection of the real world. All strategic management decisions are made on the basis of incomplete information. A good case study analysis must make realistic assumptions to fill in the gaps of information in the case study. It is better to make your assumptions explicit and incorporate them in your analysis than to use them implicitly or not make

them at all. If we make explicit assumptions we can later come back and see if our assumption were correct or not.
viii) Do not confuse symptoms with problems. For example, you might list one problem as decreasing sales volume. This would not be correct. This is a symptom. The real problem is identified by answering the question: Why are sales down? For example, sales volume may be low due to inadequate salesforce training. But this may not yet be the root problem. You still need to ask: Why is sales training inadequate? It may be due to poor sales management policies. What you do is keep asking "why?" until you are satisfied that you have identified the root problem.
 ix) Do not confuse opportunities with taking action. One can recognise a market opportunity but not take any action related to it. A company may decide not to compete in this market due to lack of resources or skills or the existence of strong competition. Decisions involve the complex trading-off of many problems and opportunities.
  x) Recognise alternatives. A good analysis explicitly recognises and discusses alternative action plans. You must do your situation analysis and recognise alternatives before evaluating them and reaching a decision.
 xi) Make effective use of financial and other quantitative information. Financial data (break-even points and so on) and information derived from other quantitative analyses can add a great deal to a good case study analysis. Totally ignoring these aspects or handling them improperly results in a poor analysis.

Case studies give you the opportunity to relate the theoretical content of your strategic management course to the business world and will be helpful in developing your management skills. You will find that your case study analysis technique will improve with practice. Perhaps the greatest pedagogical benefit of the case study method is that it generates a high degree of involvement in the learning process. Much of the challenge and satisfaction of case study analysis teaching comes from the interaction between students and instructors.

(Material kindly extracted with the permission of the author and the publisher, *Worldwide Casebook in Marketing Management*, Luiz Moutinho, 2016 @ World Scientific Publishing.)

4.4 Chapter summary

An increasing number of strategic management courses now assess students at least in part by answering case study questions. However, business and non-business students can find interpreting case studies challenging. This chapter provides an outline of how to approach such case study questions. Students will gain practice in working with strategic management problems by casting themselves in the role of decision-makers. The authors outline approaches for analysing, discussing and writing about cases. Emphasis is placed upon outlining strategic options, making recommendations and arriving at a conclusion.

Case study analysis is flexible, as it can be used for semester-long projects, seminar classes or even shorter timeframes. In these latter instances, issues are simplified and the length is shorter. However, as Dobbs (2013) suggests, the variety of types and uses of case study analysis can be challenging for students at all levels. Not only may the student lack experience of managing others in a business setting, they may have no prior experiences from which to draw on. If not adequately supported, case study analysis can result in superficial analysis that is extemporised, lacks systematic rigour and proposes hasty, ill-informed decisions.

4.5 End of chapter self-reflection questions

1. What is the purpose of case studies?
2. What are the salient key steps in case study analysis?
3. What are the key metrics for assessing an organisation's financial health?
4. Why is it important to consider the statement and evaluation of alternative options?
5. Why is it useful to incorporate theory into the case study analysis?

4.6 Case study

AccorHotels' strategic vision

Information is taken from http://www.accorhotels-group.com/en/finance/accorhotels-strategic-vision.pdf (accessed 2015).

AccorHotels, the world's benchmark hotelier

Present in 92 countries.

Nearly 3,900 hotels and 510,000 rooms.

An extensive brand portfolio, with a comprehensive range of options from luxury to economy: Sofitel, Pullman, MGallery, Grand Mercure, The Sebel, Novotel, Suite Novotel, Mercure, Mama Shelter, adagio, ibis, ibis Styles, ibis *budget*, hotelF1.

TODAY, ACCORHOTELS IS MUCH MORE THAN A GLOBAL LEADER, IT'S A GROUP OF 180,000 HOTELIERS WHO SHARE THE SAME PASSION.

Our ambition is to be the world's benchmark hospitality player so we can offer our guests, employees and partners a unique experience.

In order to fulfil this ambition, on 3rd June 2015, the Group announced that it was entering a new playing field, and would be more open, more connected and more assertive, so it can continue to shake up hospitality industry conventions.

Spurred by Sébastien Bazin, its Chairman and CEO, the Group's strategy is based on several fundamentals:

- A new name, AccorHotels, and a new promise, Feel Welcome, expressed through an updated visual identity.
- Two fields of expertise: operating and franchising hotels (HotelServices) and owning and investing in hotels (HotelInvest).
- A large portfolio of internationally renowned brands covering the full spectrum, with luxury (Sofitel, Pullman, MGallery, Grand Mercure, The Sebel), economy (ibis, ibis Styles, ibis *budget*, adagio access and hotelF1), and midscale (Novotel, Suite Novotel, Mercure, Mama Shelter, adagio) establishments.
- A powerful marketplace and a well-known loyalty program, Le Club AccorHotels.
- Almost half a century's commitment to corporate citizenship and solidarity with the PLANET 21 program.

We express our personality through a strong identity

Accor becomes AccorHotels and reasserts its greatest strengths: its passion for hospitality and for the hotel industry professions.

Feel Welcome is the new signature that illustrates this positioning. It encapsulates the concept of hospitality in just two words and expresses the simplest, warmest and most universal vision of the hotelier profession, as well as everything that makes it enriching and noble.

It is more than a signature, it is a promise that resonates as a pledge from a Group that is always open to cultures, talents and passions, wherever they are.

We bring complementary fields of expertise into play

In order to ensure its long-term expansion, AccorHotels already instigated significant changes at the end of 2013 to leverage the complementarity of its two historical fields of expertise: **operating and franchising hotels**, and **owning and investing in hotels.**

The Group is now organised around two strategic divisions:

HOTELSERVICES (OPERATION AND FRANCHISING)

This division encompasses the 3,000 hotels/510,000 rooms operating under the Group's brands. Its mission is to manage operations at these hotels and provide the best choice of services for partner hotel owners (for example including strong brands and a powerful distribution system).

The goal for HotelServices is to maximize fees, speed up CRM and loyalty-building drives, shift the group deeper into the digital realm, and roll out a strategy in each segment to bolster the Group's brands.

HOTELINVEST (OWNERSHIP AND INVESTMENT)

This division comprises the 1,300 hotels that AccorHotels owns or the Group manages via leases. Its mission is to streamline and manage the existing asset portfolio through disposals and acquisitions based on three criteria: margin, cash generation and location.

The goal for HotelInvest is to establish the leading hotel investor in the economy and midscale segments in Europe, focus on cash-flow generation and reduce result volatility, optimize CAPEX (Capital Expenditure) allocation strategy and support AccorHotels' development by investing selectively in properties.

We put our internationally renowned brands on the map

AccorHotels is the only hotel group spanning the full luxury to economy spectrum. Its extended choice of international brands puts it in a position to cater for customers' new wants, needs and behavior patterns more effectively.

Each Group brand treats customers to a unique hospitality experience. These brands are already organized in three segments: Luxury/Upscale, Midscale and Economy. The goal, here, is to enable the Group to consolidate its expertise and secure its leadership.

Each segment is pursuing clear objectives:

Luxury/Upscale: continuously improve service excellence and develop flagship hotels in cities with a view to enhancing brand value.

This segment encompasses:

> **Sofitel**, France's only luxury hotel chain, which has 121 hotels in almost 41 countries. Sofitel and its Ambassadors (employees), bring French class to the world, in a collection of hotels that treat customers and partners to services with a personal touch, to kindle emotion while driving performance and attaining excellence.

MGallery, a collection of upscale hotels brimming with remarkable character, distinctive design, and history. This brand is building on the success story it has been writing since its inception in 2008, and pushing ahead with its selective development around handpicked hotels featuring unrivalled personalities.

Pullman, an upmarket hotel brand encapsulating the executive lifestyle. It caters to cosmopolitan world travelers from around the world, on business trips or holidays. Pullman is a new-generation hotel for new-generation, hyper-connected customers on the go.

Midscale: expansion and innovation to bolster the range and brand differentiation. This segment encompasses:

Novotel, one of the Group's historical brands, the pacesetter in the midscale hotel segment, and a family hotel expert with its Family&Novotel deals. These hotels cater to businesspeople and holidaymakers in downtown spots in the main international cities, business districts and tourist destinations.

Mercure, the world's third-largest midscale hotel chain and the only midscale hotel brand that combines the muscle of an international network, uncompromising quality and a home-away-from-home experience in hotels steeped in their local ethos, and run by enthusiastic hoteliers who guarantee that no two hotels are alike.

Mama Shelter, which offers more than simply rooms or restaurants. Mama Shelter is a living and meeting space, a true urban refuge that's not just beautiful, modern and lively but also popular, friendly and sexy. Curl up on its sofas and savor its sharing plates, enjoy a drink and relax, you can sleep like a baby. . . Mama takes care of everything!

Economy: take the ibis brand family's success to the next level to cement its leadership.

In September 2011, the Group reorganized its economy brands into a more consistent, clearer and more appealing line-up, harnessing **ibis**, a strong brand with an enviable reputation worldwide. As a result, all seasons is now **ibis Styles** and Etap Hotel **ibis *budget***.

The new **ibis family** encompassed 1,929 hotels at the end of December 2015. The new fully redesigned common areas in ibis and ibis budget hotels guarantee guests will enjoy an all-new experience of hospitality, as well as trailblazing services to take comfort to the next level. Ultimate comfort is particularly important for the ibis family: it entirely revamped its bedding in 2012, and now treats customers to its hallmark great night's sleep in a bed packed with state-of-the-art technology and expertise from specialists across the Group.

We leverage innovation to increase our operational excellence

As the world leader, AccorHotels boasts significant distribution clout.

AccorHotels is the first global hotel group to offer distribution and digital services to partner hotels.

With 329 million visits a year, **AccorHotels.com is establishing itself as the benchmark hotel booking platform**. It is now open to independent hotels, offering visitors exactly selected hotels and powerful solutions. The booking portal is available in 28 languages.

AccorHotels, the Group's single mobile application, is designed to revolutionize the use of mobile devices for tourism. Every user can now enjoy this must-have travel companion,

```
LUXURY AND UPSCALE
Brands:

Sofitel                        Sofitel Legend

SO/ Sofitel                    adagio Premium

M Gallery                      Pullman

Grand Mercure                  The Sebel


MIDSCALE
Brands:

Novotel                        Mercure

Mama Shelter                   adagio aparthotel


ECONOMIC
Brands:

ibis                           ibis styles

ibis budget                    adagio access

Formula 1
```

Figure 4.1 AccorHotels brands and segments

which represents yet another example of AccorHotel's ability to constantly enhance the guest experience at every stage of their journey.

Le Club Accorhotels, the loyalty program, is free of charge, covers every Group brand and every country worldwide, and now boasts around 24 million members.

We think big when it comes to the Group's development

Our development strategy has two main fronts:

- cementing the Group's leadership in Europe
- swiftly developing its presence in emerging countries.

AccorHotels is still looking at significant growth potential in Europe. The Group is leveraging its leadership to roll out its vigorous development strategy, focusing especially on economy hotels because these chains still have low penetration rates in many countries. Repositioning economy hotel brands around ibis will afford us an additional advantage.

AccorHotels is also aiming to bolster its presence in emerging countries in general and in high-potential countries such as Brazil, India and China in particular. Its two hotel network acquisitions in 2012 – Mirvac in Australia and Grupo Posadas in Latin America – and the major strategic alliance sealed with Huazhu for China at the end of 2014, mirror this drive.

The Group is leveraging its expansion by:

- Tailoring its brands more closely to local preferences and enhancing their flexibility;
- Investing selectively in high-margin projects in prime locations, especially in the economy segment in Europe;
- Ramping up franchise development in the midscale and economy segments;
- Harnessing external growth opportunities, i.e. partnerships or acquisitions, to consolidate the Group's leadership in the most attractive markets with asset-light operations.

We develop our in-house talent

The human factor is central to the hospitality industry.

180,000 people are behind the success of AccorHotels. Every day they welcome close to 500,000 guests with the same acclaimed enthusiastic attitude, welcoming spirit and professional flair in 92 countries.

To maintain this quest for excellence, the Group's HR teams are keen on attracting talent across the board, empowering people to grow in sync with our international expansion and technological breakthroughs, and embracing diversity.

AccorHotels is blazing new trails and building skills to tackle this challenge with new career paths and an active training program.

The Group has more than 170 courses, an 18-strong Academy network spanning the globe and a choice of pioneering training methods, making it the world's foremost hotel school.

This is all the more decisive now that job descriptions in the hotel business are undergoing far-reaching changes. AccorHotels is not just building professional management skills (encompassing revenue management) and sales skills: it is shaping the jobs that hotels will need tomorrow, creating new business lines, and building a pool of professional talent that will keep us in the lead on the market.

We reinvent hotels sustainably

Sustainable development and solidarity are key priorities for AccorHotels.

The Group has taken a strong stand on the planet and the communities hosting its hotels with its PLANET 21 program, which it kicked off in 2012.

The Group has not just entered into a buoyant expansion phase: it is also reasserting its vision of smart, responsible development, i.e. development that generates value for everyone to share. PLANET 21 is taking its sustainable development agenda to the next level, to harness it as a decisive competitive advantage for AccorHotels, its brands and its partners.

It is doing this with its customers, who are increasingly aware of social and environmental issues, in mind. It has made 21 commitments, with specific targets that every hotel will be required to achieve this year. PLANET 21 is AccorHotels' way of placing sustainable hospitality at the core of the Group's strategy, development and innovation.

Case study questions

AccorHotels 2015 - Case study analysis example using (Dobbs 2013) internal and external templates.

AccorHotels is a global French hotel group that was created in 1967 by Paul Dubrule and Gérard Pélisson. By 2015 the hotel portfolio covered 92 countries with 3,873 hotels and 511,517 rooms. The group consists of 15 brands covering budget, economy, midscale, and upscale and luxury. Accor, like many of its peers, has been pursuing an asset-light strategy, and split itself into ownership (HotelInvest) and operating (HotelServices).

Questions:

1   AccorHotels is a global French hotel group that was created in 1967 by Paul Dubrule and Gérard Pélisson. Perform an assessment of the critical resources and strategic capabilities of AccorHotels. What are the core value-adding activities?
2   Perform an internal and external analysis of AccorHotels and ascertain what the critical opportunities and threats facing the organisation are. Outline what strategies could be deployed by AccorHotels to maintain its competitive position.
3   How has AccorHotels performed in terms of strategic performance since 2015?

References

Dobbs, M. E. (2013). Internal analysis in practice: Templates for firm and case analysis. *Journal of the North American Management Society*, 7(1), 40.

Dobbs, M. E. (2014). Guidelines for applying Porter's five forces framework: A set of industry analysis templates. *Competitiveness Review*, 24(1), 32–45.

Moutinho, L. (2016). *Worldwide Casebook in Marketing Management*. London: World Scientific.

Part 2
Globalisation

5 Creating the global organisation

5.1 Learning objectives

After completing this chapter you will:

- appreciate the political, economic and regulatory forces which shape globalisation
- be able to understand the differences between internationalisation and globalisation
- be able to critically analyse how globalisation shapes the structures of traditional organisations both large and small
- be able to identify appropriate organisational structures for strategy implementation
- be aware of the national, sector and firm level drivers for global strategy.

5.2 Introduction

Managers often cite growth as a desirable goal for their firm. Growth enables increasing economies of scale and scope of operations. In addition, having to operate in new markets together with new brands and partners requires modern streamlined business models. With heterogeneity rather than homogeneity being the status quo, firms need to embrace such diversity in their strategy processes. As organisations operate beyond their initial markets, they are soon faced with additional levels of complexity.

Internally, the CEO has to reallocate structure and core processes. In today's connected marketplace it is now inappropriate to pursue organisational structures that were built upon a traditional combination of risk, control and money. There is also the issue of knowledge that has traditionally been siloed, which now needs to be leveraged across new markets. To overcome such dilemmas, a response can be to create highly complex structures with a plethora of matrix, geography and service forms. To overcome these problems, the CEO should plan to adopt the appropriate structure for the firm's situation and to get the balance between what needs to be global and local. Market value can be destroyed if stakeholders spot flaws.

Consider for example, no simple solutions and economic and market cycles can disrupt existing business models. Exploring new value drivers present some implications and opportunities, but the ability to extract value is not to be underestimated. New economy firms continue to create business propositions from humble origins and eventually evolve into global market leadership positions. The advent of new venture creation makes it crucial for the CEO to build global organisations around opportunities. Hence, the established firm ought to adapt their business model and approaches to counter the threat of competition, so that they can revitalise their operations and enter new growth paths.

102 *Globalisation*

The CEO may choose a growth path of acquisitions made in different countries. Without controls autonomous businesses can haemorrhage cash. The board needs to integrate its business units and functions globally to reduce costs, enhance efficiency and quality. Support functions such as marketing, accounting, human resources and IT will need to be redesigned and refined. Ultimately, organisations tend not be born global and having to increase the workforce brings challenges in corporate culture and requires maturity of thinking across global teams. The relationships between headquarters and its subsidiaries can be influenced by competencies, responsibilities and partnerships. Success will be partially dependent upon the CEO's ability to absorb and process information for strategic decision-making process.

In recent times there has been a rush to emerging markets, and these situations require local decision-making on core business operations. Local knowledge can enhance the management capability, and the role of the regional office can be an additional cost. Another perspective may be to form strategic groups based on customer needs and wants, together with business growth objectives. The creation of distinct customer interface supported by more seamless back-office functions are priorities. The accelerating pace of communication technologies presents options for the CEO and strategy team.

Moreover, with fading boundaries due in part to trade liberalisation that translates to easier flow of goods, people, capital and knowledge, the world has moved on from the triad markets of North America, Europe and Japan. The trade among triad markets remains significant and the automotive industry is a prime example of this activity. The relaxing of boundaries within Europe has created homogeneity in terms of the Euro currency. But the problems of immigration, failing economies of EU countries and threats of EU exits are new pervasive challenges. Chapter 3 focused on the internal and external business environments and presented tools to comprehend the competitive position of nations and firms.

POD

Barcelona sponsorship with Rakuten

The Spanish football giants Barcelona struck a sponsorship deal worth £47m a year with a Japanese online firm Rakuten. Commencing from the 2017–18 season, over a four-year period the deal will net Barcelona £188m, with bonus clauses inserted if the team wins the Spanish La Liga or the Champions League. Barcelona with its star forward line of Lionel Messi and Luis Suarez have another sponsorship deal with the US Sportswear firm Nike, who are reputably paying in excess of £120m a year over a ten-year period.

As a result of this agreement, Barcelona will surpass Real Madrid's and Manchester United's sponsorship deals and position itself in the number one among professional football clubs. Manchester United signed a ten-year deal with Adidas worth £75m per year and has let its shirts be sponsored by the US carmaker Chevrolet for £47m a year for seven years. At the time of writing it is rumoured that Adidas is ready to renegotiate its current deal with Real Madrid, with Nike willing to pay Real Madrid £100m per year.

5.3 Globalisation

In 2009 for the first time in two centuries emerging markets contributed more to global economy growth than the developed economy (Dobbs, Ramaswamy, Stephenson, & Viguerie, 2014). This trend continues with the rapid growth of urban populations in excess

Creating the global organisation 103

> Why do organisations differ?
>
> What are the strengths, weaknesses and opportunities and threats presented by a global strategy?
>
> What are the cultural differences between Asian and Western firms?
>
> How should global firms behave?

Figure 5.1 Some basic questions in global strategy

> - How should organisations decide upon standardised products and/or services on a global basis?
> - Should standardised products for sale in different countries utilise the locational advantages of emerging low cost countries?
> - How should differentiated products embody variations in local consumer tastes and preferences?
> - How should the organisation position itself between globalisation and localisation?

Figure 5.2 Issues in global strategy?

of 65 million per year. In emerging economies this leads to the creation of new cities, which shift the locus of economic power within a single country. A prime example is China with its economic drive along the Yangtze River, where previously unknown rural areas are being urbanised. The Chinese government has made urbanisation a national priority.

Global strategy (see Figure 5.1) continues to be a significant economic driver, and generates substantial interest amongst academics, practitioners and members of society. Organisations that operate across borders soon realise that the business cases they develop for home markets do not always lead to success in another market. Cross-border business is further complicated by the heterogeneity of markets with differing contexts and customer tastes, and by the nature and scale of competitors. Building on these issues, this chapter seeks to assess a wide variety of organisational and environmental factors that impact structures, markets, products and services. We also consider the concept of parental advantage and the need for global integration and the need for local responsiveness. Some of the dilemmas facing CEOs are depicted in Figure 5.2.

An appetite for new risk?

Globalisation is a driving force that has changed the business landscape. It requires CEOs to adopt new practices and develop new capabilities to enhance competitiveness. As political and economic reforms, technological change, population growth and urbanisation bring nations closer together, this remains a goal for countless organisations of all sizes. Benefits have led to the sharing of wealth, health and prosperity. But at its worst the effects can be contagious. For example, the bad debts in the USA triggered riots in Greece, and the eruption of the Icelandic volcano caused chaos for airlines, costing the European economy £400m a day in lost productivity. The surge in globalisation requires organisations to: adapt to a greater interconnected world with the Internet being a conduit; cope with new systemic risks that can quickly spread across sectors and boundaries; adapt to new infrastructure and scarce resources, threats and challenges.

In health, globalisation has brought immense benefits, with humans now living longer. Improvements to nutrition, lower levels of infant mortality, higher GDP per capita are good. But outbreaks, such as Ebola and Avian influenza are examples of escalating threats and remind us that infectious disease and pandemics continue to pose threats to humans in a globalised marketplace. Education too has suffered from the disruptive force of globalisation and has revolutionised assumptions, practices and strategies of business schools. The reasons for business schools' globalisation aspirations can be related to its mission, networking, reputation, need to satisfy demand, management of change projects or merely to grow revenues and student numbers. Business school deans adopt the globalisation philosophy but problems soon arise if being global becomes a means in itself or a means to an end. It is relatively easy to pronounce that School X is global, but without serious commitment, activities can be at best disjointed and lack a holistic value-added for its stakeholders outside its traditional boundaries. Globalisation as an agent of change extends boundaries beyond traditional borders. Engagement beyond these traditional borders brings new risks. Managing organisations successfully through globalisation will be one of the major challenges leaders face. The following sections will consider some of the issues which need to be surmounted by the CEO.

Financial markets

Accelerating financial market panic put a brake on the strong trend towards globalisation. Prior to 2008 cross-border flows among mature and emerging economies fuelled capital injection in business sectors. Unfortunately, when capital flows are reversed due to tightening external financial conditions or rises in internal imbalances, or a combination of the two, countries can get into trouble. Regulatory reforms have attempted to reduce the risks, to foster a stable and secure financial system. That said, a tightening on capital flow can lead to a lack of investment funds for countries to fund entrepreneurial activity. Governments attempt to look into the future and try to translate internal and external financial market forces into predictable forces. How will the unpredictability of some European economies affect the UK? Will investors panic and seek refuge in the US? The rise of China and its financial banks has rewritten previous economic models.

China's financial markets continue to undergo gradual development with established monetary, bond, stock, insurance, foreign exchange, gold and financial derivatives markets. But the devaluation of the Chinese yuan and the fall in the country's stock market could be the start of a domino effect worldwide. With China's slowing economy, in October 2015 the IMF downgraded its growth forecast to 3.1 per cent, the lowest since 2009. After many years of double-digit growth China is struggling to reach GDP growth of 7 per cent, and the only certainty is that the future will be much tougher than the past. At the time of writing, recovery among G7 countries is strongest in the USA and UK with Germany, Italy, France, Japan and Canada at less than 2 per cent.

When globalisation and digital technologies combine, firms can rapidly gain an international footprint. McKinsey (2010), the strategy consultants, talk about the global grid, with every company now a global company, with the most innovative ones building the global grid into their DNA. The evidence reveals that trillions of large and small transactions synchronise instantly. The vulnerability of interconnected systems can be illustrated by the "butterfly effect" of chaos theory (MacIntosh, Maclean, Stacey, & Griffin, 2013). One ripple, say the collapse of Iceland's financial system, can lead to major disturbances in say the USA mortgage market. CEOs and Heads of governments should expect a bumpy ride – a connected world will be a volatile world. The empirical evidence is fully consistent with these views. The Eurozone has proved tumultuous with high levels of debt, volatile capital and euro markets, levels of unemployment and more recently the refugee crisis.

Polarisation

Despite the uncertainties facing the global economy, certain trends are predictable. The world will become smaller (the "global village"), with a more affluent aged society, be more urban-focused, more risk adverse and with greater polarisation between the rich and the poor. Climate change will continue, food prices will rise and economic power will shift from the West to the East. In his book entitled *The World is Flat*, Thomas Friedman (2005) asserts that globalisation is a leveller of inequalities in societies. Yet, the evidence around us suggests that the world is not flat, and new forms of economic inequalities continue to distort the process. The gap between rich and poor is becoming increasingly large, but global poverty is intrinsically linked to global wealth and vice versa (Bond & O'Byrne, 2014).

MNEs (multinational enterprises) are expected to contribute economically and socially to achieve sustainable development. Yet fairness and exploitation of poor workers by multinationals remains an emotive subject. The media often headlines examples of workers working in extremely challenging conditions for $1 per day. Occasionally the fault may not lie with the MNE apparel firm per se, but with its first-tier suppliers, which cut, sew and assemble, and how these mills recruit their labour force. Problems identified from audits include instances of trafficking and exploitation. The apparel industry operates using a complex supply chain that serves global operations. MNEs now need to determine the optimal number of tier-one suppliers that they can actively manage and ensure that their audits delve deeper into supply chains. Ultimately, the MNE is accountable and needs to create a sustainable footprint.

If economic development continues to be left to business with the state on the sidelines, the outcome will be polarisation. Nations see the engine of globalisation as the economy and are desperate to get a bigger share of the global flow of wealth. In a world without borders, MNEs can operate fluidly taking advantage of incentives from governments. Footloose MNEs can employ locals to build up their manufacturing capability. Then they can seek exit strategies if the plant is uncompetitive and find another location that is better. The weak plants close due to their relatively high labour costs, or when the MNE decides to become an importer rather than a manufacturer.

Changing business production models – offshoring, reshoring and nearshoring

While acknowledging the opportunities and desires to serve a larger market, CEOs are mindful of answering the question, "Which countries are we targeting for job creation in the next three years?" In recent years China was the number one destination for manufacturing start-ups – offshoring – but at the same time for the period 2006–2014, China's average manufacturing wages tripled. This has eroded China's international competitiveness and has displaced low-cost manufacturing of cotton t-shirts, sports shoes, and toys to lower-cost destinations such as Cambodia or Bangladesh. Trends such as reshoring (returning jobs home from overseas countries, such as China) and nearshoring (locating production close to a primary market, say Mexico, to serve the USA) prevail.

General Electric used an outsourcing model to set up production in China to cut costs and improve efficiency. As global conditions change, US supply chain operations have become more efficient, and China is no longer the low-cost option. In September 2015, GE announced plans to bring production of a line of energy-efficient hot water heaters from China to Kentucky. Interests in reshoring remain strong. In their 2014 "Made in America, Again" survey, Boston Consulting Group highlighted the primary reasons for US companies coming home, these being benefits of increased regionalisation, strong workforce and business environment and control over process and quality.

The weaker yen is making reshoring attractive for Japanese manufacturers too. Panasonic Corp announced that it would transfer most of its domestic appliance production in China back to Japan. Reasons cited include a weaker yen and rising labour costs. Panasonic stated that a one yen drop against the dollar reduces profit by about 1.8bn yen ($15.1m) annually.

Traditionally, lawyers are required for complex work with repetitive, routine and back-office services being served using a different business model. For more than a decade the legal profession used its legal process outsourcing (LPO) model. Significant cost savings in terms of salary bills and property overheads can be made by processing legal work outside of the law firm. Instead of operating in top offshoring locations such as the Philippines and India, UK legal firms are looking closer to home. Law firms in London are looking at cities in the provinces with major firms creating wholly owned firms in Bristol and Norwich. Northern Ireland is also attractive and a major firm was also able to receive an initial £2.5m grant from the Northern Ireland Development Agency.

Collaborative economy

The ways individuals consume, contribute, and participate are changing and has led to a new way of thinking about business exchange, value and community (Stokes, Clarence, Anderson, & Rinne, 2014). The connected society has changed not only behaviour, but also fundamentals of virtually every organisation. This trend is about people connecting with each other, with products (and services) and with organisations. People want a purpose and studies show that millennials (individuals born between 1980 and 2000) possess a desire for something other than just profit. Millennials represent a third of the US workforce. A purpose-driven company can be profit or non-profit, but the founders see a need within society and seek to fill that need. Trust in business is on the upturn since 2008, but it is still low. But those organisations with a real sense of purpose can be at the forefront of exploring how organisations with purpose can positively change society.

Individuals have become like a company, getting what they need from each other and bypassing inefficient traditional institutions. By using social networks, they connect with each other instantly and become a powerful "company." But, do not call them consumers. Individuals are consuming less, i.e. there is deconsumption. Instead, they are using marketplaces to re-use and recycle. Those that can make will build and share among the crowd. People can now re-use goods using Nextdoor.com and Yerdle.com to gift to friends. Techshop enables people to become makers of their own products with the crowd functioning like a company.

From an economic standpoint, collaborative established companies such as Airbnb and Uber are currently successful. The mantra for competition is based on price, brand and convenience. A dominant player that enables at least 50 per cent of the peer-to-peer transactions in that category can use this sharing economy model. Samuel (2016) cites brands such as Kickstarter (responsible for 57 per cent of crowdfunding transactions), Uber (86 per cent of ride-sharing) and Etsy (91 per cent of custom products marketplace). The aggregation of a wide range of buyers and sellers in one place is good for the dominant player, but not so attractive for the supplier. Buyers may have high levels of satisfaction, but suppliers can be squashed on price. Ultimately disgruntled suppliers may disrupt the sharing economy model.

The world of tourism has had to evolve due to globalisation. The intangible nature of the tourism experience creates further complications. Phillips and Moutinho (2014) observe that the generation of a valuable tourism experience depends on the provision of intangible services. These intangible assets/resources require the adoption of a greater systemic perspective in strategic planning. Moreover, the practice of strategic planning may differ due to influences on national culture and economic climate.

Global citizens who are the Generation X and Y make an attractive proposition by being at the peak of their earning potential and view business and personal travel as vital. Such hardworking individuals share a passion for the luxury experience. This group has become an authority and they eagerly share their experiences on social media. They possess extremely high expectations and those tourism organisations operating in the luxury marketplace will need to adapt their offer. Global citizens want to feel like a native with a residential experience. Five-star hotels and concierge services are striving to create an authentic, local experience with recommendations for local cuisine and designer boutiques. Hotels are providing living rooms and library spaces.

The rise of the micro-multinational

Prior to the technological disruption, operating in overseas markets was tough and expensive. Having global communication and budgets for global travel were the preserve of large organisations. Small and medium-sized enterprises, which served local markets, can use digitised platforms to enter global markets. Large organisations with global reach can suffer from ineffective bureaucratic structures with blind spots. This leaves them vulnerable to smaller and more nimble entities. The ability to quickly respond to challenging environments and a collaborative DNA makes this a viable proposition for self-service and service-driven SMEs. Strategies can be formulated that enable SMEs to focus on precise areas where they can add value. This also has significant implications for employees. Freelancers and the self-employed can use the enabler of digitisation to scale up and deliver products without the large infrastructures and bureaucracy of traditional enterprises. The formation of ad hoc self-organising teams to accomplish specific strategic tasks will become the norm.

Blurring reality

As a consequence of blurring, over the past decade our perception of what is real (and what is not) has altered. The advance of new technology and globalisation makes this of significance to corporate strategists. Consumers experience a declining trust in the messages projected by firms and politicians. Although consumers seem to long for trust, realness and authenticity, this is only partly true. Society's relationship with "fake" and "real" is ambivalent. There is

108 *Globalisation*

also a huge difference in perception between generations. But we are in the middle of the rise of a new visual culture, created by a young "visual" generation, which grew up surrounded by a total abundance of images. Psychological research shows that this generation thinks visually and learns in images. Gaudin (2015) remarks that Facebook wants to blur the lines between reality and virtual reality. The company is pursuing three things: it wants to connect everyone on the planet via drones and satellites; help individuals sift through the vast sources of information on the Internet to find the images and data that are truly useful; create an immersive technology that "teleports" users to a new place together with new experiences with people they care about.

When considering expanding a business outside of its home market, some questions to consider include:

- Which products/services are suitable?
- Which countries/markets to choose from, and in what order?
- Where to locate value-adding activities?
- What market development method to deploy (internal – exporting, subsidiary, or external – strategic alliance, M&A, franchise and license)?

Strategy nugget

Rugby sevens

The origins of Rugby sevens date back to 1883, at the Melrose Sevens in Scotland (Martin et al., 2013). For more than a century sevens remained in the shadow of the parental 15-a-side rugby union game. However, since the turn of the twenty-first century the sport has seen a rapid injection of global interest and respect. One of the main drivers of global interest and growth relates to the popularity of the HSBC World Sevens series. The HSBC World Sevens circuit currently comprises ten micro-tournaments that are held annually around the world. The micro-tournaments span all seven continents enabling spiralling interests. The showpiece for the HSBC Sevens series is held annually in Hong Kong.

In 2015–16, the series was attended by 715,000 fans (the highest number), with 6,000 hours of broadcast in more than 100 territories and 61m video views. This is in contrast to humble beginnings of 1,147 hours in 2005–06, rising to 4,590 hours in 2013–14 (International World Games Association, 2006; *Telegraph Sport*, 2014). When Rugby sevens was played at the Rio Olympics, it became the first rugby Olympics in 92 years.

Rugby sevens operates under similar rules as its parent rugby union (World Rugby, n.d.). Substantive differences relate to the number of players and match length. As the name suggests, a sevens team consists of 7 players (Forward = 3; Backs = 4) as opposed to 15 players in a rugby union team (Forward = 8; Backs = 7). A sevens match officially lasts 14 minutes (two halves of 7 minutes) as opposed to 80 minutes in rugby union.

HSBC Global Head of Sponsorship and Events Giles Morgan added: "In a pivotal year for rugby sevens, HSBC as a long-standing and proud partner of the game, has been working closely with World Rugby to capitalise on the opportunity.

"The Olympic opportunity has already energised the 2015–16 HSBC World Rugby Sevens Series and sell-out crowds in Dubai, Cape Town, Sydney, Vancouver and Hong Kong are evidence of this. If we can continue to connect rugby sevens to new players, new countries and new audiences, it will be the spark that continues to ignite ground-breaking growth for the game" (Morgan, 2016).

"The Future of Rugby: An HSBC Report" makes seven predictions for 2026 including:

NEW COUNTRIES

- more nations break through
- sevens creates its own big bash

NEW PLAYERS

- participation doubles
- women lead the charge

NEW AUDIENCES

- broadcast pyrotechnics transform coverage
- media value moves to social platforms
- summer sevens becomes self-funding

Questions

1   What have been the salient drivers for the rapid growth in interest of rugby sevens?
2   What steps can the HSBC World Sevens organisers take to maintain the spectacular growth for the next ten years?

Strategy nugget

Chinese football salaries

The January transfer window is usually a battle between the big spending European football powers, such as Manchester United, Real Madrid and Paris Saint-Germain. However, in January 2016 the Chinese Super League spent $278m, outspending the entire English Premier League ($250m). The corresponding figure for clubs in Germany, Italy, Spain and France was $193m.

The Chinese President Xi Jinping's attempt to transform the Chinese Super League into one of the best in the world is beginning to take shape. In contrast to the US Major League Soccer, Chinese clubs have been able to buy players in their prime. The Major League Soccer has tended to be the last career challenge for ageing players.

So how has China been able to lure leading players from leading clubs? The primary incentive has been size of contracts, which have catapulted many players into the top earners of professional football. Table 5.1 illustrates the amount of money involved.

5.4 Analysing nations' competitiveness and MNEs

The traditional building blocks of national competitiveness require consideration of key drivers. Ketels (2016) suggests that traditional building blocks now consist of: rules and regulations; financial markets; physical infrastructure; macroeconomic policies. Identifying the smallest numbers of factors that can drive prosperity and productivity levels can reap economic benefits. Thus the systematic interaction of competitiveness in various contexts

Table 5.1 The top paid footballers in China (January 2016)

Player	Transfer Fee	Salary
Ezequiel Lavezzi 30 years old – Argentina Club: Hebei China Fortune	Transfer fee: $6.1 million to PSG (contract was expiring in the summer)	Salary: $16.8 million per year
Gervinho 28 years old – Ivory Coast Club: Guangzhou Evergrande	Transfer fee: $20 million to Roma	Salary: $9.7 million per year
Jackson Martinez 29 years old – Colombia Club Guangzhou Evergrande	Transfer fee: $45.8 million to Atletico Madrid	Salary: $14 million per year
Paulinho 27 years old – Brazil Club: Jiangsu Suning	Transfer fee: $15.7 million to Tottenham	Salary: $6.3 million per year
Ramires 28 years old – Brazil Club: Jiangsu Suning	Transfer fee: $36.7 million to Chelsea	Salary: $14.5 million per year
Alex Teixeira 26 years old – Brazil Club: Shanghai Shenhua	Transfer fee: $55.6 million to Shakhtar Donetsk	Salary: $11.5 million per year
Demba Ba 30 years old – Senegal Club: Shanghai Shenhua	Transfer fee: $15.7 million to Besiktas	Salary: $6.7 million per year
Fredy Guarin 29 years old – Colombia Club: Shanghai Greenland	Transfer fee: $14.5 million to Inter Milan	Salary: $8 million per year

complicates economic models. Porter's (1990) work on competitiveness is well cited and newer models have been proposed. The following sections consider Porter's diamond and Bartlett and Ghoshal's Integration/responsiveness framework.

Porter's Diamond

Michael Porter's diamond (see Figure 5.3), a competitive advantage model which originates from a study of ten nations, proposes that locational advantages may derive from four main attributes: factor conditions; demand conditions; related and supporting industries and firm strategy; structure and rivalry. The overall size of the diamond can represent competitiveness. Dögl and Holtbrügge (2010) explain how a large diamond represents high competitiveness and a small diamond low competitiveness. But a country with four medium values is more competitive than a country that possesses two high and two low values. Now consider each attribute in turn.

Factor conditions

The "factors of production" may be beneficial when employed in the production process of a product or service. Their mere existence is insufficient for competitive advantage. Abundance of physical resources together with location can bring advantages for certain markets. For example, London is seen as a global financial centre due to its skilled labour force and its favourable time zones. It continues to grow as a foreign exchange market because of financiers'

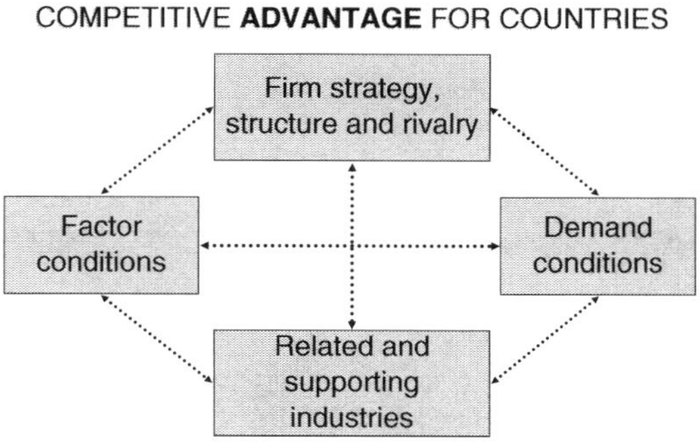

COMPETITIVE **ADVANTAGE** FOR COUNTRIES

Figure 5.3 Porter's Diamond

ability to trade with the East and West on a normal business day. Adverse conditions such as being located in a desert region can be tackled with imagination and resources. For example, the sprawling Jebel Ali plant in the United Arab Emirates can produce in excess of half a million gallons of water a day from the sea. So, for a country afflicted by water scarcity this reliable and efficient source will provide innumerable benefits for its people.

Demand conditions

The home market need can be more challenging than overseas needs. The presence of local demand can be translated into competitive advantage. If local demand forces organisations to innovate, this could be used as an early signalling device for overseas markets. In such cases, this may make products/services more attractive for overseas customers. Key segments in the home market may shape the product. Airbus created larger multi-seat airlines to shuttle passengers short distances within Europe, which illustrates the nature of the home market. The Italians' passion for cars and the US craving for credit has led to both countries being able to anticipate need elsewhere.

Related and supporting industries

The presence of a strong local cluster around a product/service can lead to competitor advantage. If the cluster has like-minded suppliers that provide an efficient and cost-effective access to input, this could enhance co-ordination in the value chain. Collectively they can drive wealth creation in a region. Clusters of supporting industries such as the automotive industry in Germany, with Mercedes Benz, BMW, Audi and Porsche, demonstrate one of the outcomes of intense competition – high quality products with huge driver appeal. With its outstanding engineering, innovation, reliability, safety and design, backed by industry value chain integration, Germany remains the EU's number one automotive market.

Firm strategy, structure and rivalry

The influence of national values and priorities can create fierce competition in the domestic market. When rivalry is fierce, this will enhance productivity and be attractive overseas.

112 Globalisation

Switzerland is landlocked without many natural resources and has four official languages. The Swiss pharmaceutical industry is characterised by large multinational corporations (e.g. Novartis, Roche, Syngenta and Lonza) and also has a vibrant SME presence. To be a winner in this environment will alleviate some of the difficulties of competing globally.

Porter does include another two additional variables – chance and government (see Figure 5.4). Porter's diamond has its critics, which is in part due to the age of the model. A theme throughout this textbook is the change taking place in the internal and external environments. The conditions of international business are now so different. The model could conceptually explain the development of developing states. The advance of the importance of public–private partnerships is not incorporated into the model. The role of chance in the wide-scale use of English language and cheap labour may explain, for example, India's success in the software industry. In terms of the four attributes of the model India would fail the baseline tests, e.g. there is a lack of local demand for software and related and supporting industries. The Indian government arguably challenges Indian firms by acting as a "catalyst and challenger" to push their aspirations. They provided some stimulus by building high-speed data communication infrastructure, which enabled Indians to return home from overseas and create offshore sites for US clients.

Bartlett and Ghoshal's Integration/responsiveness framework

Besides determining locational advantages the MNE should select a model that best suits the environment to obtain global competitiveness. The selection of model can be assessed through drivers that push the MNE's global integration and/or global differentiation. Those MNEs that need innovation to remain competitive will enable autonomy in decision-making in their subsidiaries and companies. Ideas can be created within subsidiaries, which if successful can be dispersed to the entire MNE. CEOs have to cope with the dilemma of economic integration and national responsiveness. How companies achieve integration and responsiveness simultaneously is a challenge.

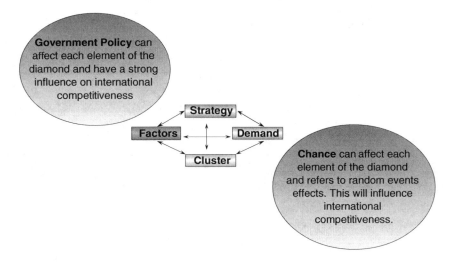

Figure 5.4 Government policy and chance

Creating the global organisation 113

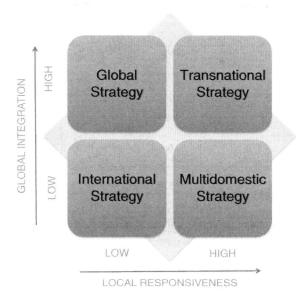

Figure 5.5 Integration/responsiveness framework

A refined analysis of the notion of global integration and responsiveness is depicted in the Bartlett and Ghoshal (1987) Integration/responsiveness framework (see Figure 5.5). Despite the two constructs of integration and responsiveness being much broader than single dimensions the framework is taught on most international business/global strategy programmes. Prahalad and Doz (1987) put forward seven factors that impact global integration.

- importance of multinational customers
- importance of multinational competitors
- investment intensity
- technology intensity
- pressure for cost reduction
- universal needs of customers
- access to raw material and energy

Similarly, Prahalad and Doz (1987) propose five factors that impact local responsiveness:

- differences in customer needs
- differences in distribution channels
- availability of substitutes
- market structure
- local regulations

Despite the opportunities and desires to pursue global competitiveness, some discipline is paramount. The CEO needs to analyse salient industry forces, determine the board preferences and assess the level of global integration and local responsiveness. Clarity and desires have to align the market offer and strategic business unit posture. There are likely to be imbalances between strong and weak interdependencies. Firms need to articulate a position in terms of markets, industry sectors, value chains and business objectives. Interdependencies need to be strong for core functions. Marketing and finance are two such areas. Various segmentation models for identifying country clusters and customer segments need to be translated into financial cash flow models. Bartlett and Ghoshal's Integration/responsiveness framework along with the typology of transnational, multidomestic, international, and global typology are briefly contemplated.

Transnational

Transnational strategies appear attractive as they combine economies of scale and learning with the benefits of locally adapted products and processes. In some instances selected subsidiaries may become centres for technology or products/services. Knowledge flows not only exist between headquarters and subsidiaries, but between subsidiaries. Given these flows, the organisational structure usually employed is the matrix structure, and relies on the relocation of managers across the MNE. Bartlett and Ghoshal assert that MNEs should pursue a transnational strategy combining high levels of integration and local responsiveness. The complex co-ordination is challenging; achieving integration and responsiveness simultaneously demands a balance of collaborative culture and organisational capability. At the heart is an effective matrix, which tends to be over-ambitious and creates conflicts of interest within the firm. Noticeably, over the last couple of decades many MNEs have struggled and reverted to global organisational structures, emphasising integration over local responsiveness.

Multidomestic

Responding to local market needs is imperative, so a portfolio of national companies can fulfil local needs. This portfolio of autonomous national companies possesses the entire value chain, which offers locally adapted products for each market. This empowers managers of companies to pursue local adaptation, and ignores solely seeking economies of scale. Thus, duplication of effort can be seen as relatively expensive in financial terms and it is hard to spread innovation and knowledge beyond the national company level (Meyer & Su, 2015).

International

International strategies are low on both global integration and local responsiveness. This can be the first step of trading overseas and normally begins with exporting for a production company or franchise for a service company. However, it does not seek economies of scale nor fit to local customers and is often mentioned as an inferior strategy. In the early phases, when the majority of customers are local its fine, but when international sales grow it can become a challenge. Typical organisational structures in use include: international division parallel to domestic divisions (Meyer & Su, 2015).

Global

A global strategy seeks integration at the expense of local responsiveness. Economies of scale are sought through highly integrated processes with functional divisions. The HQ will possess the full value chain, as the subsidiaries are weak. Attention is placed on diffusing innovation and development from HQ to its subsidiaries. As mentioned earlier, global strategies are becoming popular and firms tend to centralise operations with top-down information flows. Management adopt a tight control.

In summary, the Bartlett and Ghoshal Integration/responsiveness 2 × 2 matrix remains a popular topic in business school strategy and international business modules, and practitioners still make use of the underlying theory. But in today's contemporary business environment there is urgent need to develop new strategies or to rethink and use other strategies, such as international strategies (Meyer & Su, 2015).

An interesting question to ponder is, why globalise? From the Bartlett and Ghoshal Integration/responsiveness framework, we mention economies of scale, economies of scope and factor costs. CEOs sometimes spot an unexpected opportunity to scale business, or to address a weakness. In many service businesses, the large brands are expected to follow business professionals when they enter new markets. Alternatively, the firm in question may wish to recoup investment in new product development. Sometimes, it could be "the grass is greener" effect which, unfortunately, is not always a good reason to globalise. Also, although firms are affected by globalisation, the response may not be to automatically adopt a global strategy. Essentially the entry mode can vary from exporting to wholly owned subsidiary (see Figure 5.6).

POD

Marriott International

The flurry of hotel mergers, acquisitions, and consolidations that began in 2015 has continued unabated in 2016, even as the value of M&A in other global sectors stagnates. The big chains are out to grab market share and strengthen their positions through scale. This is creating opportunities but also threats for independent hotels.

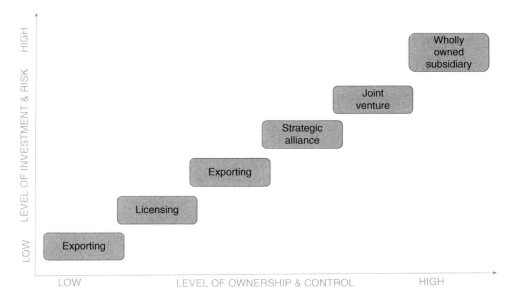

Figure 5.6 Entry mode strategies

Marriott International completed a $13 billion acquisition of Starwood Hotels & Resorts Worldwide, creating the world's largest hotel company. The new company operates or possess franchises in more than 5,700 properties and 1.1 million rooms, representing 30 leading brands from the moderate tier to luxury in over 110 countries. With the completion of the acquisition, Marriott's distribution has more than doubled in Asia and the Middle East and Africa combined.

5.5 Chapter summary

This practical chapter shows the array of political, economic and regulatory forces which impact the CEO's decision-making in the context of globalisation. The topic continues to be a significant economic driver and generates interest among academics, practitioners and society. The chapter translates these issues into a student context, where the emphasis is on thinking critically. Unfortunately, organisations that operate across borders soon realise that the business cases they develop for home markets do not always lead to success in another market. Cross-border business is further complicated by the heterogeneity of markets with differing contexts and customer tastes, and by the nature and scale of competitors. The national competitiveness work of Porter's diamond and MNEs using Bartlett and Ghoshal's Integration/responsiveness framework will help managers perform a systematic analysis of competitiveness. By building on these issues, this chapter seeks to assess a wide variety of organisational and environmental factors that impact structures, markets, products and services.

5.6 End of chapter self-reflection questions

1. Why is globalisation so attractive to the CEO?
2. Using Porter's diamond, identify the concept of locational advantages?
3. What has been the contribution of the Bartlett and Ghoshal Integration/responsiveness framework to practitioners?
4. What is the effect of polarisation during the strategic planning process?
5. What are the key drivers for the growth of the micro-national?

References

Bartlett, C. A., & Ghoshal, S. (1987). Managing across borders: New organizational responses. *Sloan Management Review*, 29(1), 43–53.
Bond, C., & J. O'Byrne, D. (2014). Challenges and conceptions of s: An investigation into models of global change and their relationship with business practice. *Cross Cultural Management*, 21(1), 23–38.
Dobbs, R., Ramaswamy, S., Stephenson, E., & Viguerie, S. P. (2014). Management intuition of the next 50 Years, *McKinsey Quarterly* September 2014. Available at: http://www.mckinsey.com/business-functions/strategy-and-corporate-finance/our-insights/management-intuition-for-the-next-50-years
Dögl, C., & Holtbrügge, D. (2010). Competitive advantage of German renewable energy firms in Russia: An empirical study based on Porter's diamond. *Journal for East European Management Studies*, 11(1), 34–58.
Friedman, T. L. (2005). *The world is flat: A brief history of the twenty-first century*. Macmillan. Available at : https://www.amazon.com/World-Flat-History-Twenty-first-Century/dp/0374292884
Gaudin, S. (2015) Facebook wants to blur lines between reality and virtual reality. Available at: http://www.computerworld.com/article/2902303/facebook-wants-to-blur-lines-between-reality-and-virtual-reality.html

Ghoshal, S. (1987). Global strategy: An organizing framework. *Strategic Management Journal*, *8*(5), 425–440.

Ketels, C. (2016). *Review of Competitiveness Frameworks*. Dublin, Ireland: National Competitiveness Council.

MacIntosh, R., Maclean, D., Stacey, R., & Griffin, D. (2013). *Complexity and organization: Readings and conversations*. London: Routledge.

Martin, I., Chirosa, L. J., Olmo, J., Carreras, D., & Sola, J. (2013). Bibliometric study (1922–2009) on rugby articles in research journals. *South African Journal for Research in Sport, Physical Education and Recreation*, *35*(1), 105–119.

McKinsey (2010) Available at: http://www.mckinsey.com/business-functions/strategy-and-corporate-finance/our-insights/the-global-grid

Meyer, K. E., & Su, Y. S. (2015). Integration and responsiveness in subsidiaries in emerging economies. *Journal of World Business*, *50*(1), 149–158.

Morgan, G. (2016). Dates set for 2016–17 HSBC World Rugby Sevens Series. Available at: http://www.worldrugby.org/sevens-series/news/163532?lang=en

Phillips, P., & Moutinho, L. (2014). Critical review of strategic planning research in hospitality and tourism. *Annals of Tourism Research*, *48*, 96–120.

Porter, M. E. (1990). The competitive advantage of nations. *Harvard Business Review*, *68*(2), 73–93.

Prahalad, C. K., & Doz, Y.L. (1987). *The multinational mission: Balancing local demands and global vision*. New York: Simon and Schuster.

Samuel, A. (2016) Why the sharing economy isn't such a boon for the little guy. Available at: https://blogs.wsj.com/experts/2015/10/15/why-the-sharing-economy-isnt-such-a-boon-for-the-little-guy/

Stokes, K., Clarence, E., Anderson, L., & Rinne, A. (2014). *Making sense of the UK collaborative economy*. London: NESTA.

World Rugby. (n.d.) Available at: http://www.worldrugby.org/sevens/how-to-play

6 Creating value in a global context

6.1 Learning objectives

After completing this chapter you will:

- be able to introduce innovation models that can impact on value and discuss the multiple facets related to the creation of value and value-based management
- be able to emphasise the links between the creation of value and ongoing marketing shifts as well as the area of measurability in marketing
- be able to reflect upon the concept of shareholder value and its relationship with stakeholder theory
- appreciate the complexity of creating value in the new economy
- appreciate that institutional logic requires companies to be more than money-making machines; they are also meant to be vessels for providing societal purpose.

6.2 Introduction

This chapter delves into intertwining topics relating to the subject of value in a global context. New models of innovation that relate to value are discussed. The perspective of value-based management is dissected and then associated with the metamorphosis of marketing as well as marketing measurement itself. Finally, key issues connected with shareholder value and the stakeholder theory are presented.

6.3 Key academic theory

The solution to a stochastic differential equation for new products and services has over time become more and more complicated and multifaceted. Nowadays consumers are being exposed to new influences including social signals, communications, word of mouth and demand-side economies of scale. Diffusion modelling, the marketing field that defines the lifecycle of innovations, has had to adapt rapidly to be able to model and describe such influences.

Peres, Muller and Mahajan (2010) relay their theory on the modelling of influences across and between brands and markets. In a single market, network externalities, social networks, take-offs and technology generations are the focus, while in cross markets, the differences in growth spanning countries is a greater topic of conversation, as are influences and the effects of competition on growth.

Their review suggests the diffusion framework needs to evolve into the market if it is to continue to be considered as a state-of the-art paradigm with the sole purpose of market evolution. It must be able to successfully focus on interpersonal communications in order to surround and hold within the following definition: *Innovation diffusion is the process of the market penetration of new products and services that is driven by social influences, which include all interdependencies among consumers that affect various market players with or without their explicit knowledge.*

Although diffusion modelling has been extensively researched over the past four decades, the author believes there is much more value in this field of study with regard to incorporating current market trends, including the advancements in emerging economies, online social networks and web-based services.

Nowadays consumers still seem dissatisfied even though they have a wider variety of services and products than ever before. Companies specifically invest in producing a greater variety of services and products for consumers but find themselves in a position where they are no more conspicuous than their competitors. The dominant requirements for a successful manager these days are creating and sustaining value creation and growth.

The interaction between consumer and business is fast becoming the hub of value creation. The market finds itself becoming the forum for chatter regarding customer interaction, firms and consumer communities. Within these conversations value creation is realised through a better understanding of risk-benefits, transparency and access, which lead the way to the next practice in value creation.

Customer value, as a concept, is now increasingly appearing in the marketing and strategy literature. It is generally considered that this adds a competitive advantage to the long-term success of any business organisation. And so the concept has had great importance attached to it. Khalifa (2004) compiled a report on the complexity and richness of the concept of customer value. The report reviews and enhances the current available written works on the subject, which includes the configuration of three complementary models, namely: customer value dynamics, customer value in exchange and customer value build-up. Putting thought into the concept of customer value is an invaluable tool when considering the design of a new service.

Nowadays, markets are undergoing a rapid pace of change. A need has been acknowledged by the move towards the modern information economy and this has been the main driver of change in this field. There then comes the question of how this information economy evolution will impact the field. We need to note this metamorphosis and consider how much the changes are down to boundaries, distinctions and divisions and how the practice will be changed in each market. Once complete, it could be that all the old divisions and distinctions are completely dissolved and in the creation of the new ones, there will be an obvious uncertainty. Marketing is being redesigned from the inside out (Berthon & Hulbert 2003).

In the world there is still more emphasis placed on marketing activities in companies. If the marketing department can evaluate the effectiveness of its own activities, it increases the trust of all departments in the company. And it is possible to better plan company investments, to create profit and to invest further. The future of marketing departments is mainly based on their ability to evaluate activities and to demonstrate their own importance in the company. This is a reason to develop an interest in the topic, which deals with measurement of marketing effectiveness. Solcansky and Simberova (2010) deal with marketing effectiveness, point to its importance for company activities and show the most necessary methods for measurement of marketing effectiveness and suggest benefits.

Current literature on mergers leads us to the conclusion that the relationship between merging firms and shareholder gains is dependent for its existence on the ability of the two to work together without problems or conflict.

The advancement and justification in the management literature of stakeholder theory is based upon its ability to serve as a means to pursue the aim of descriptive accuracy and a lack of false consciousness in the normative validity.

120 *Globalisation*

These aspects of the theory, although connected to each other, are quite recognisably different from each other; they produce divergent results and different evidence emerges along with each implication. Donaldson and Preston (1995) critique all aspects of an integrated theory and report how the important contributions relate to each other. They come to the conclusion that all aspects of the stakeholder theory create a mutually supportive unit in a desirable action that creates the base of the theory, which – including the modern theory of property rights – is fundamental.

As shown in Figure 6.1, Companies need to "fight with systems" making sure they link a comprehensive innovation strategy with the existing innovation processes as this will enable structures and successfully allow underlying culture to provide a more supportive base for mind-sets and behaviours that will drive successful innovation.

Innovation is a system-level problem and because of this, widespread change can be wholly ineffective. Instead, leaders should try to boost the ability to drive growth by simultaneously directing innovation strategically, monitor it intensively, pursue it vigorously and nurture it carefully. If an organisation can realise the need to take idea fragments and process them, with the intention of turning them into robust and useful innovations, then this should be encouraged. The alternative is to sit on these innovations and end up with a list of possibilities that are never realised, creating considerable organisational disdain. It is not necessary to create an entire department fully committed to this but at least there should be some visible form of criteria set to judge any such suggestions or ideas to be acted upon.

The definition of innovation is "something that creates value." This is only achievable if the problem to be solved actually matters. Executives commonly think that for innovation to flourish, all boundaries and restraints need to be removed in order for all ideas to be encouraged. Creativity and constraints appear to go hand in hand. Any problem arising can be as diverse as a lack of employee engagement to breaking into new markets.

The requirement for creative ideas, without creating boundaries for resources

There tends to be a trend towards companies preferring to invest in the prolonging of current projects rather than investing in something with the potential to create the business of the future. This may be down to the company having not set enough provisions to be able to invest in both options and therefore if the current projects are working well, less will be invested in future projects at any given time. There is great value in pushing for newer, fresher ideas, encouraging the innovation that will lead to greater experimentation and valuable breakthroughs. But this requires the time to acquire the logical connection points within any organisation.

> Companies make two standard mistakes. Some are so driven to sell the relevant products to increase their market share and others get ensnared by the excitement and drive of making things, particularly new creations. Both these approaches are dangerous in making the business a success. The issue with the second point is that it can lead to too much internal focus. It is critical that companies do not become so fixated on their R&D agendas that they forget about their loyal customer base, the market they are competing in and their current competition. They may be recognised as R&D pioneers but this can be to the detriment of a more important capability – that of sustaining their current trends in performance and therefore managing to maintain their independence.

Figure 6.1 Corporate mistakes

6.4 New models for innovation

There are numerous models available that ensure short-term security with long-term rewards. The traditional venture capital process embodies these features. Corporations would do best to model their internal efforts on the approach adopted by independent groups. Crucially though, an often neglected point is that a tolerance of failure requires the rethinking of how projects are chosen and funded, not just the provision for compensation schemes. The principle reason that failure is not tolerated is simply that decision makers cannot jeopardise the future funding of any projects. The simple fact is that research and exploration would fare much better when evaluating high-risk projects if simple "truth-telling" was compulsory. There are a number of ways to address this issue, from outside experts being brought in to evaluate any new project to venture groups who, given a certain argument, will create an alternative position for the sake of exploring possible failure.

Focusing on products instead of markets

Exciting new products can certainly garner much excitement upon release but in fact it is often the services that come with the product that sell the product to the customer.

Definition of market share

Market share is the name given to consumers' preferred product over all other products available. The higher the market share, the greater the profit and sales, leading to less effort being required to sell in higher numbers and a tougher time for competitors in having their products recognised. This also means that the leader makes more profit in an expanding market as the product continues to sell. But this also requires the market leader to find a way to expand the market to ensure continued success. Being successful is not however, to take over the market completely, as gaining 100 per cent of the market share can lead to risks associated with market actions. Changes in fashion and developments and advancements in products will impact the company hugely. Generally, companies should decide the market share they require to create maximum profit.

Focus on customer share, not market share, to grow a business

If there is a need to grow a business, then the focus must be on identifying the prospects, converting the leads into viable options and paying customers. If this is the case then consideration needs to be given to changing the focus, simply because creating growth by attracting new customers is the most difficult, riskiest, least efficient and least profitable way for a company to grow. While it might seem like the best option, this can be a costly, time consuming endeavour that does not pay dividends. It is a known fact that people will only buy from certain businesses once they know, trust and like the company and its products and services. And yet it seems that this loyalty breeds complacency within the company. The assumption is that existing customers will continue to purchase the same product from the company, when in fact, if marketed correctly, the business could sell other products alongside the original requirement. However, this seems not to be the case and companies tend not to proactively market all their products and services to existing customers, instead wasting huge sums of money marketing their products and services to new clients. This means that they are wasting huge amounts of effort and resources attempting to grow their business when they already have a client base that is under-utilised.

> Traditional strategic thinking argues that greater market share equals greater profit. But bigger is not necessarily better; in many cases, it can actually be worse. As most companies use it, market share can be misleading and even a dangerous measure. The definition of market share, however, is strongly correlated with financial performance and value creation.
>
> - Think beyond the current business offerings
> - The company's weighted average relative market share (MS)
> - Apply the value-creation test
> - Not all growth is good, in fact, some growth actually destroys value.

Figure 6.2 Market share hints

Value can be created for any company by four processes, as shown in Figure 6.2: innovation processes, regulatory and social processes, operations management processes and customer relationship management processes. Within each of these four processes there are many transactions that create value. Mid-level management are involved in the monitoring and strategising of the value creation necessary at this stage, termed the "ploy for value creation." Leading focus here should be to improve asset utilisation or cost structure within the organisation. At this stage, the focus is on strategising to create the best productivity available. Meanwhile value creation is the strategy formulation adapted by the executive senior management as their contribution for the purpose of value creation. Their focus should be on the expansion of revenue opportunities available when they enter a new market or launch a new product or the focus should be on the business diversification strategies.

Sales are not the cause of value – how you conduct your business is what creates value

Successful companies with healthy revenue growth have been known to decline in enterprise value. How can this be possible? It is simply that increasing sales alone does not always translate into value. How you conduct your business is what matters when it comes to value, and this includes the markets you are involved in and the business you serve. Sales are obviously important but profitability and revenue are also important factors. One other relevant necessity is that the enterprise value of the company is not simply based on previous performance, and this factor is a constant reminder for investors in the public market. Previous performance does not guarantee any company the continuation of delivery for any prospective acquirer; simply because the company plans to invest their assets can also be attributed to the value.

Growth just for the sake of it

Conventional wisdom suggests that businesses must expand or they will not prosper and will eventually cease to exist. This is not the case, however, as in every industry there are companies that prosper without expansion. These companies are generally owned and run by people who want to be their own boss. But on the subject of creating enterprise value,

> Where does the profit zone sit in the current economic climate? Will there be a shift in the future? The profit zone is the area of your economics, societal and human neighbourhood where you can earn profit through attention to value delivery.
> As a manager, you were taught the art of pursuing market share while simultaneously ensuring that growth automatically follows, placing you on a direct route to business success.

Figure 6.3 Is market share dead?

the "grow or die" conventional theory is correct. Growth just for the sake of it, however, is not enough.

Many companies fall into the trap of growing revenue by throwing money and resources into current markets. This may seem like a smart move, a safe and familiar move, but in fact it is actually a high-risk strategy. Markets today can often be rapidly superseded by new markets, and this is especially noted in the technology industry. Businesses do not have the luxury of ignoring these new markets as this is where the growth of tomorrow will come from.

Too many companies do not manage to reach their set targets for growth, revenue and profitability. These targets are more achievable when a clear growth strategy has been planned out by any organisation and there is a strong execution infrastructure (see Figure 6.3).

Initiating the process to successfully identify workable strategies

- Grow the core business
- Grow by segmenting the customer base
- Grow simultaneous opportunities.

These are three growth strategies identified and used by senior management. It is recommended that the process should begin with a focus on growth potential in the core business and the growth potential and other opportunities related to the creation of innovative value propositions.

The high level of cross-department collaboration required can be challenging at times for some organisations. This is certainly the case for businesses with inflexible vertical structures. These structures cause problems for employees in responding and adapting to any particular customer service requirements or requests. The ability to deliver a superior level of customer value needs to be maintained by an uninterrupted flow within the organisation. The breaking down of barriers allowing the flow of service and the continuity of quality is essential as a first step to providing the company's strategic capabilities.

A balanced perspective encompassing the needs of stakeholders and major organisational processes must be developed and maintained in order to assure internal operations, employee development and provide value to customers.

Trends and developments in society – social values, consumer behaviour, competitive structures, business ecosystems, social media and social networks, technology, sustainability – force us to put more effort into rethinking whether market share can be used as a predictor of profitability.

Strategy nugget

The Profit Zone – how strategic business design will lead you to tomorrow's profits

MARKET SHARE IS DEAD

The number one problem in business today is profitability. Where will you be allowed to make a profit in your industry? Where is the profit zone today? Where will it be tomorrow?

The profit zone is the area of your economic neighbourhood where you are allowed to earn a profit. To reach and operate in the profit zone is the goal of every company.

You've been told how to get there. "Get high market share and the profit will follow." "Get high growth and your profits will expand." As a manager, you were schooled in how the pursuit of market share and growth automatically places you on a direct route to business success.

However, these formerly direct roads have become mazes riddled with traps, wrong turns and dead ends. Many large companies, after taking the turn towards market share and volume growth, have only hit a profitless wall.

Market share was the grand old metric, the guiding light, the compass of the product-centric age. Companies focused on improving their product and building economies of scale.

The new focus on profit, not just market share, can lead to dramatic rebounds in value. As you think about your own business, ask yourself: Am I managing for market share or for profit? Is the market share I own profitable and alive, or is it profitless and dead? There are countless businesses with high market share but low profitability and low shareholder value.

In a broad cross-section of high market share situations, the right economic response has been: "So what?"

Companies force us to think harder about, or to completely rethink market share as a predictor of profitability.

AM I MANAGING FOR VOLUME GROWTH OR VALUE GROWTH?

"Be in high-growth markets." In the old economic order, in the age of market share, volume growth was a guarantor of success. Growth was what we were taught to pursue. It created higher profits for all, including market share laggards.

Today, no-profit zones are everywhere, and they are growing. The map of the economy is covered with more and larger patches of unprofitability. No-profit zones come in various forms. They can be a part of the value chain (e.g. distribution in computing); they can be a customer segment, they can be an entire industry, they can be an individual customer or they can be entire business models (e.g. hub-and-spoke airlines, or integrated steel mills).

No-profit zones are the black holes of the business universe. Paradoxically, the devout pursuit of market share may be the single greatest creator of no-profit zones in the economy. The vigorous pursuit of market share and the rise in customer power have driven profit from many activities and products, and even from entire industries. More and more no-profit zones have been created. Many companies still continue to pursue a market share and volume growth strategy, trying to get an even bigger piece of a pie that is losing all its value. Market share leadership in a no-profit zone, or high market share with the wrong business design, is more of a curse than a blessing.

GROWTH, WITH THE WRONG BUSINESS DESIGN, DESTROYS VALUE FASTER

There are three curses of growth. First, high growth with a bad business design destroys value fast. Growth is attractive, but growth carries high risk, especially when the business design is wrong. Second, besides being riskier, high growth is much harder to manage. The euphoria of being in a high-growth environment blocks out the reality that growth creates a much higher management challenge. Managing in a downturn is hard work, but managing high growth intelligently is much harder. You're tempted to overbuild capacity, add infrastructure, headcount, lots of fixed costs. Then when the growth waters recede, you're stuck in a no-profit zone with lots of resources and lots of red ink. It's a great way to destroy shareholder value. Businesses do it all the time.

The third curse of growth arises when a business grows by stretching its business design to serve customers that the business design was not intended to serve. To make up for the mismatch, the company is forced to lower prices or expand its scope into areas where it is not operationally efficient. Both of these actions depress profitability. Once again, the end result is a no-profit zone.

No-profit zones are emerging every day. Activities that were once valuable turn profitless. Value migrates towards activities that are more important to customers – activities where profit is possible. Yesterday's profit zones are becoming, with increasing frequency, today's no-profit zones. The single biggest problem in business is staying with your previously successful business model – one year too long.

Where is the profit? In yesterday's world, the answer was: with the player who has the highest market share. In today's world the answer is: with the player who has the best business model, a model designed for customer relevance and high profitability.

Thinking about profitability isn't easy, for several reasons. First, the profit zone, the arena in which high profit is possible, keeps changing and keeps moving. The customer doesn't stand still, and the business design must respond. Second, there are many ways that high profit happens – twenty-two different models that explain and quantify the mechanism by which profit occurs. Third, most organisations use two or three of these profit models. Understanding which ones to apply in which circumstances requires careful thought and considerable organisational persistence.

In this new economic order, characterised not by equilibrium but by fluidity, customers and profit zones always shift. To reinvent its business design and stay a step ahead of these shifts, a company must move beyond product-centric thinking to a customer-centric approach. Market share thinking must yield to a profit-centric approach. The ideas behind customer-centric and profit-centric thinking are critical to success in the new world of business.

Source: *The Profit Zone*, by Adrian J. Slywotzky and David J. Morrison with Bob Andelman.

No-Profit Zones
The two more valuable ideas in the old economic order, market share and growth, have become the two most sensitive ideas in the new order. To apply these ideas appropriately (and safely), you must understand the rise of no-profit zones in the economy.
For over two decades now, the advances in innovation relating to business design and industrial technology, the constant rise in global competition and massive improvements in information technology have changed the current playing fields beyond recognition.

Figure 6.4 Am I managing for volume growth or value growth?

6.5 What is value-based management?

Figure 6.4 explains that in the past few years we have seen an abundance of new management approaches designed to improve organisational performance, including quality management, empowerment, flat organisations, team building, reengineering, continuous improvement, Kaizen and so on. While many have succeeded, many have also failed. More often than not, the cause of the failure was down to unclear or unrealistic performance targets that were not properly aligned with the goal of creating value. When done successfully, an unambiguous metric of value can be created on which an entire organisation can be built.

Value-based management (VBM) can be simply explained as a partnership between the current management processes and a value creation mindset, both being necessary to turn the mindset into reality. Either one on its own is insufficient without the other, but together they are a possible powerhouse of sustained impact. Moving over to a value mindset can create a huge impact.

Management processes

Moving forward with a value-based mindset and creating or finding value drivers is only half the battle. Processes must be integrated by managers to cement the mindset within the daily activities of the staff. Line managers must be able to embrace the value-based thinking as the way forward for decision making. For value-based management to work it must be fully integrated into every decision made by every employee in the organisation. If VBM is introduced at the same time as incorporating the reengineering of planning processes, then it doesn't need to become a bureaucratic time sink.

VBM can force a company to change from a traditional approach and embrace the change in new systems. Specifically, performance measurement can be shifted from being accounting driven to management driven. At the same time creating a performance measurement system can be straightforward for any company willing to understand the key value drivers and who has set their short- and long-term targets. Financial indicators are only based on previous records, by which time it might already be too late to correct any discrepancies. Market share or sales trends can be used as simple early indicators or there are the more sophisticated pointers such as the results of consumer shadowing.

As we find new ways to impress our customers with instant information services, the convenience for them to now shop around for the best deals and better prices is now part of everyday life. This ensures that those who plan to stay ahead in the market must be willing to match price reductions or risk losing customers. This added pressure to reduce prices and/or add extra incentives to buy creates no-profit zones.

Today, no-profit zones are everywhere and they are growing. The map of the economy is covered with more and larger patches of unprofitability. Paradoxically, the devout pursuit of market share may be the single greatest creator of no-profit zones in the economy.

Figure 6.5 New forces

"Infobesity": should marketers go on a data diet?

There are big decisions to be made following the digitalisation of our culture. For some, the sky is the limit and marketers can store virtually limitless volumes of data about their customers or audiences; it is not too large a leap to take data-driven insights on to intelligent actions.

However, some marketing professionals find themselves drowning in data, and they are in danger of suffering from "infobesity" – being weighed down with the sheer amount of data they have gathered.

Innovative leadership has become even more important in the twenty-first century environment. There has been a radical change from the twentieth-century paradigm, where the concentration was focused on efficiency and market share as the profit drivers. Market share is dead, so much so that within certain boundaries, a company with the majority market share can be less profitable than those businesses in the same market with less market share (see Figure 6.6). Reinvention is the key to innovative business, especially now, in the information age. To understand market share you need to identify "profit zones" and "no-profit zones." The success to sustained business requires companies to spend their time doing business in the profit zones and not committing any company resources to no-profit zones. Figure 6.5 explains the added pressures needed to stay ahead in the market and the issues these can cause. Innovation demands high consciousness and attentive leadership. The largest shift that businesses are going through in current times, is to leave behind the urge to assess performance purely in terms of the bottom line. Instead, a more holistic approach is being adopted, with certain large tech companies such as Apple, Google and Microsoft concluding that their actions have huge consequences for the rest of the social environment. Business tycoons such as Warren Buffett, Bill Gates and Patrice Motsepe are also aware that philanthropy is not simply a charitable act, but is also an investment in the future. Ambitious business leaders with the insight to understand that they need to expand their workforce with innovators, understand that the triple bottom line is an important step and not just a tick-box exercise; it is rather a focus that commands returns on philanthropic or CSR investments. It requires high consciousness to understand and include this all-encompassing approach.

Why good companies go bad

This common business phenomenon can also be one of the most baffling. This happens when large successful companies are faced with changes in their environments and do not adapt or

---

All too often, the vigorous pursuit of market share is done at the expense of business design innovation. Market share leadership in a no-profit zone, or high market share with the wrong business design, is more of a curse than a blessing.

There are three factors to consider when discussing growth. Firstly, high growth without a guaranteed business design will eat into profits and destroy value at a phenomenal rate. Second, besides being riskier, high growth is much harder to manage. The euphoria of being in a high-growth environment blocks out the reality that growth creates a much higher management challenge.

Figure 6.6 Curses of growth

128 *Globalisation*

respond effectively. They are left unable to compete in the market when others appear with new technologies, strategies or products, and have no option but to sit back and watch their profits plummet, then their best employees leave and their stock valuation dips (Figure 6.7 explains). Some companies do manage to recover after this painful experience but many do not.

The problem is not simply the inability to react in time, but is the inability to take the appropriate necessary action. Many reasons can account for this problem, from sheer incompetence to managerial ignorance or stubbornness, but the most common issue is a condition called active inertia. This is usually associated with a lack of action to counterbalance the shift in trend. Active inertia is a company's lack of initiative when a change is necessary but the company persists with the established pattern of behaviour, even when there is a dramatic environmental shift. They stick with the models that produced results in the past and in doing so they simply free-fall to disaster.

Inertia is such a common problem that it is important to recognise the symptoms and sources. After all, if managers see that lack of action is the problem they may conclude that action is the best defence. But if they note that their action is not helping to turn around the problem they may want to inspect their assumptions before acting. Once they can correctly identify the problem, they will garner a clearer insight as to what actually needs to be done and, just as importantly, what may hold them back. This will significantly reduce their odds against failure and ultimate ruin.

The hidden competitive curve

There is a hidden curve tracking the competition shifts in any industry. Figure 6.8 discusses the re-inventor companies; high performers will see the changes and adapt accordingly, by

---

Managing in an economy slump can be difficult, but managing high growth sensibly and productively is much harder. You're tempted to overbuild capacity, add infrastructure, headcount, lots of fixed costs. Then when the period of maximum growth is over, the company is left to struggle in a no-profit zone.

The third curse of growth arises when a business grows by stretching its business design to serve customers that the business design was not intended to serve. Once again, the end result is a no-profit zone.

Value migrates towards activities that are more important to customers – activities where profit is possible. Yesterday's profit zones are becoming, with increasing frequency, today's no-profit zones.

Figure 6.7 Managing in a downturn

The investment community is also down-grading the "old order" market share stocks and reallocating its investments to the "new order" re-inventor companies. Systematically the companies capable of adapting and reinventing their business design will be the ones that can establish a profit zone for themselves.

Where is the profit? In an era gone by it was simply: with the company owning the highest market share. In today's world, the answer is: with the player who has the best business model, a model designed for customer relevance and high profitability.

Figure 6.8 Re-inventor companies

> The ever-changing profit zone can be baffling and confusing and increasingly elusive as requirements and demand continue to evolve. Customer demands change and evolve rapidly and the business design must find a way to keep up in order to proceed with a profit margin, or even better, it must anticipate the needs and wants of the customer in advance. In this new economic order, characterised not by equilibrium but by fluidity, customers and profit zones always shift.

Figure 6.9 Profitability

creating the next basis of competition within their industry, even if they are still currently exploiting the existing businesses that have not yet seen the height of their sales capabilities.

The hidden talent curve

Companies often fail to focus on the developments and retention of what is called serious talent, people with the capabilities and the desire to drive new business growth. This is definitely the case with businesses that are doing well but have yet to hit their peak. Sometimes the decision is taken that the companies' operations could be leaner, learning this from the initial learning curve, and meaner, because of pressure to increase margins and profit. The mistake is to reduce investment in talent and headcount, resulting in the loss of the people who can help them reinvent the business each time the market shifts.

Moving the edge of the organisation to the centre

All employees, especially frontline employees, managers and even far flung research teams play an important role in detecting the shifts in the market. But then it is the high performers who find a way to bring their points to the strategy making process.

6.6 Marketing metamorphosis

We are on the cusp of a marketing renaissance. Just like past industry-shifting advancements, the transition from print to digital and the invention of mobile make this a period of thrilling innovation. The explosion of social networking and real-time technologies, and the emergence of big data are all adding to what is now a revolution in the post-traditional advertising world.

Consumers are more demanding, smarter and more empowered than ever before – why? (See Figure 6.9.) Social networking and the Internet have changed the world as we know it. This has created paradigm shifts where brands become publishers and consumers turn into influencers, creating content that can be shared with the minimum amount of effort. Consumers digest information with an enormous appetite and at a rapid pace, taking on board thoughtful and relevant content which then requires the elite brands to rethink their marketing strategies in order to accommodate.

Every interaction with a customer is of vital importance in the complex digital world we live in now. In order to cash in on the benefits, marketers must find a convincing way to reinvent themselves over and over again to ensure that every interaction hits the mark and is impactful. To add perspective, according to research, 90 per cent of the world's data did not exist two years ago. Every single day the amount increases due to the ever expanding YouTube, Tweets, Pinterest sites and search engine sharing on the web. If harnessed properly, the phenomenal amount of data out there can change the way marketers perform forever.

People and brands have become completely transparent. Mobile and social media paved the way for the future and now dawns the age of big data that demolishes the loose practices that have been a way of life for marketers for so long (see Figure 6.10). Consumers are ready to embrace real-time, interactive material and content, and they do have the expectation of brands being able to connect to them immediately and deliver a personal response. Customers are more demanding and any less is simply not acceptable. Understanding the value and measure of the content available to consumers across every digital channel, incorporating the mobile and social enables brands to connect with the consumers on never before seen, personal levels. Companies cannot relate to themselves as apart from society or amoral anymore. They must accept that a moral dimension is now a necessary part of the decision-making process. Many companies now find themselves focusing on scrutinising the company ethics and values for the purpose of strengthening organisational functioning, market position and risk management.

Many companies, maybe even as much as two thirds, appear to include their ethics in a category under the umbrella of risk management. Managers tend to relate the corporate values as a way to prevent misconduct with the legal, reputational and financial risks. This comes under the ethics umbrella because companies want to avoid high-profile mistakes and billion-pound losses.

One crucial point, which is now a fairly normal practice that must be recognised, is that companies in today's environment are not just allowed to succeed on their own terms; companies must now adhere to higher standards, they must not only return financial results but they are also expected to behave in an ethically correct manner. This is a given in today's markets.

Where companies tend to develop departmental and divisional supporting metrics, it has been suggested that cross-functional metrics, based on a value delivery system, would be far more productive. These should be implemented to specific roles and tasks within any relevant delivery system.

In this age of head spinning change, we are tempted to look at individuals as just "likes" or as "decimal points that add up to the big data."

Figure 6.10 Cross-functional metrics

One side
Shareholder value is a much hyped phrase, and inevitably invites questions about other stakeholders. . .

- Internally it is measured by "economic profits" which can also be known as economic value added.
- EP measures the future cash flow.
- Shareholder value is a long-term measure. . .? Is it?
- It takes into account the return that shareholders expect from you and so focuses on exceeding their expectations (the cost of equity).

Figure 6.11 Shareholder value – two-sided coin. . .

Strategy nugget

What good are shareholders?

After the results are posted, the shareholders complain, with some justification, about the executives who award themselves huge increases when their results are at best mediocre. Generally the company board members are stuck in an awkward position, as they are required to act on this as the disciplinarian whereas evidence suggests they are generally classed as friendly advisers (see Figure 6.11).

Markets provide liquidity. Owning shares that can easily change hands, with transparent prices, reassures business partners and lenders. This situation can encourage mergers. It gives early investors and employees options and the ability to sell their company shares. It offers early investors who can possibly enable the company's cash flow, a way to realise their investments later. It encourages capitalism. But a market that is made up mostly of short-term investors presents its own problems, and in the past few years these short-term investors have been creating problems. This issue is taking over the stock market. Previously, the New York Stock Exchange could boast average holding periods of seven years. It is currently six months. This trend can be seen similarly in markets across the globe. A more recent development is that these high-frequency traders, whose holding periods are sometimes as short as milliseconds, are now responsible for up to 70 per cent of the daily movement and volume on the NYSE.

The adversarial approach to pay adopted in most countries has created a situation where executives behave in a way that focuses on making money at the expense or lack of regard for ethics. Just 60 years ago households owned over 90 per cent of market shares of corporations. Currently, this number sits closer to 50 per cent of domestically owned shares now being acquired by the institutions themselves. On top of this, overseas owners and hedge funds raise that further to almost 70 per cent. Increased institutional ownership has transformed the equity market world.

Taking too much heed of shareholders' needs and wants can be very damaging for them. The evidence is mounting to back this thought (Figure 6.12 explains). Rosabeth Moss Kanter's (2011) "How Great Companies Think Differently", shows that companies who have the most success at maximising shareholder value over prolonged periods of time are those who focus their goals on specifics other than shareholder value. Customers and employees are generally far more clued in to and aware of long-term commitment to the company than the shareholders, and ethics, tradition and professional standards are often more successful at constraining behaviour than incentives. The facts are simple – it is not that managers and boards don't know what's best, it is simply that a group of short-time shareholders will most definitely not know better. And any relevant governance system using this as a means of

---

- Forget the focus on shareholders – EPS
- Shareholder value is mostly a meaningless concept to most employees, customers and society.
- Shareholder value never creates passion and human involvement.
- There has to be more to life than making your numbers…
- We have to find ways to give people meaning well beyond just money.

Figure 6.12 The other side of the stakeholder value two-sided coin…

survival or assurance that corporations perform, is certainly doomed to failure. This current stakeholder capitalism is recognition that the shareholders of today don't quite manage to make shareholder capitalism work.

Strategy nugget

The different approaches of shareholder and stakeholder value

Many of the most significant value providers for organisations these days are difficult to find, express, measure and recognise and they remain elusive.

These difficult to achieve elements can be captured or traced if a company is smart enough to take the stakeholder approach to their business rather than sticking with the more traditional and standard shareholder view of the business world.

Implementing the stakeholder view, there is a clarity about how resources can be utilised more successfully to achieve value creation with the ability to last a long time. This is certainly a bold approach to adopt, and breaks away from the more traditional shareholder view. This leads to the ability to observe two contrasting approaches:

There are normally several characteristics that prove a shareholder's approach:

- The concentration of focus tends to be narrow, as the drive related to numbers and other quantifiable things is where the importance is placed.
- Dramatic reactions to valuations, mergers or redundancies.
- The focus is financial when related to performance evaluations, with little regard for the importance of the intangible drivers that are necessary for the company to succeed.
- Value sources tend to come from isolated systems, with little coherence.
- A slow response rate to change, and a reluctance to see the advantage in change.
- Management implementing a "quick fix" solution too quickly without understanding that this makes the situation worse in the long run.
- Employees who "think outside the box" to create value may be seen as too extreme and direct.
- The constant push is for bigger earnings and profit.
- There is a long established approach to company growth.
- The success of a business is the reward created for shareholders.

Unlike shareholders, who are only interested in their gains, stakeholders tend to think about the entire success. This can include:

- Visionary competitive thinking with long-term sustainability.
- Quantifiable overall view of the organisation.
- Performance evaluations in relation to operations and strategic issues.
- Consistent and powerful values used for the purpose of ethical or ideological integrity that extends far enough to include external stakeholders.
- An open door policy towards suggestions for innovation and new ideas.
- The ability to resist implementing a fast and easy solution, which may not actually be such, leading to further problems later on.
- Those employees able to create value being rewarded with promotion or career advancement within the company.
- The primary focus is on adding value, the understanding of what value is being added.

- The awareness of the importance of growth through relationships, workers' knowledge, and the competitive market, while focusing on the opportunities to grow the business on the basis of the company's core competencies.
- Creating business success for all engaged parties, not just shareholders.

An effective way of shifting from shareholder value to stakeholder value is to establish or indicate the drivers that create the value for all your stakeholders. This mindset must spread through the entire organisation from the ground up, resulting in people questioning their actions to ensure they are mindful of their own impact towards value creation.

A mistake commonly made in relation to the value creation theme, is to allow the metrics to take over all logical thought. Value creation is not the same and should not be confused with value-based metrics. These are understood and accepted whereas the more important sources, such as ethical behaviour, innovation, leadership and knowledge are less likely to be easily quantifiable.

There is a constant battle to create and sustain value creation because it is impossible to see into the future and so many of the important issues surrounding value creation are almost impossible to measure. However, one place to start is to utilise the human resource capital, as this creates the single most important driver. The importance of this is paramount when you have people who can think laterally to allow you to be innovative and create services or features that show your company as the most attractive to customers.

What unites all stakeholders is the people, they represent the fluid dynamics that initiate and encompass value creation in the era of stakeholder value; this is not just about shareholders. There is no acknowledgement of the word "measurement." People are not managed here, they are led or allowed to lead. There is no such thing as human resources, it is a people department. A contract with employees should be based on mutual respect, genuine interest in their ideas and input to the company, and their ability to develop within their given roles.

Enlightening value maximisation

Value maximisation is not a strategy or a vision, it is not even a purpose – it is the organisation scorecard. People must be given enough structure so they can understand and let themselves be guided by maximising value to stand a chance to achieve it. These people must be on board and ready to embrace the vision or strategy with regard to the fact that it connects with human passion and desire. Short-term profit maximisation is a recipe for disaster. It destroys value unless the stakeholder theory can interject and play a vital role. We have learned from theorists the best ways to lead participants and managers in an organisation to be more creative and think more generally about how their policies relate to all important components of the company. This has to be all encompassing and include employees, customers, suppliers, communities and not just be about the finances.

Enlightening stakeholder theory

Enlightening stakeholder theory is simple. It exploits all that the stakeholder theorists have to offer by way of audits and processes to evaluate and measure a company's management of its relationships with all important factions. Enlightening stakeholder theory adds specification to the point that the objective function of the firm is to maximise total long-term market value. Precisely, this means that any changes in the total long-term market value is measured by the company's scorecard.

Individual focuses on:	Companies focus on:
• Value in my life • Personal productivity • "Solution assembly" • Family, friends and community • Passion partnership • Emotional authenticity	• Growth • Profitability • Shareholder worth • Earnings per share (EPS) • "Customers"

Figure 6.13 The parallel lines test

Institutional logic requires companies to be more than money-making machines; they are also meant to be vessels for providing societal purpose by supplying people who work in them with a meaningful livelihood (see Figure 6.13). If this is the case, then the value that a company creates should not just be measured in terms of short-term profits or the paycheques associated with this, but also in terms of how sustainable conditions allow the company to prosper over a long period of time.

It is not enough just to look at the organisational processes to extract economic value; successful companies create frameworks that use human and societal values as their decision-making criteria: they live by the rule that they have a purpose which involves meeting the stakeholders' needs in many ways, by producing goods and services with the intention of improving the lives of users; by providing jobs and therefore enhancing the workers lives; by ensuring financial viability which, in turn, provides resources for innovation, improvements and returns to investors; by developing and encouraging strong networks of business partners and suppliers.

A common purpose

Purpose and values are at the centre of any organisations' identity, not simply the products they provide, although they can guide people to find or create or invent new products to serve society.

Successful companies establish something greater than transactions to provide meaning and purpose, and while pronouncing a broader purpose than simply making money they can create a new source for innovation. Informal, shape-changing and self-organising temporary networks have more flexibility and can create connections between resources and/or people, more quickly. This then means that people can be held accountable in many different dimensions, simultaneously, by overseeing multiple projects and using networks to provide resources for all the projects, at times skipping the decision-making hierarchy altogether.

Many companies include the "provide world-class service" mantra in their mission statements. They have well-planned business strategies and competent marketing strategies. But where is the customer service strategy? Does it feature as strongly in their mission statement or is it no more than a bullet point? (See Figure 6.14.)

To build a strong customer-driven service platform these companies must have employee satisfaction data; they must collect and manage the right customer, they must collect call monitoring information and employee and customer survey results along with daily internal metrics, and then use a number of different advanced predictive modelling and analytics to bring all this information together to track and predict the success of the marketing and business efforts (see Figure 6.15).

From Company-Driven Metrics:

- Cost per lead (CPL)
- Cost per click (CPC)
- Customer behaviour Maps (Recency)
- Visual Customer Maps
- Return on Ad spend (ROAS)
- The Drilling Down Method
- Life Cycle Metrics
- Mapping Visitor Conversion
- CRM Analytics: Micro vs Macro
- Customer Model: Recent Repeaters
- Keyword Effectiveness Index (KEI) (SEO)
- Share if Needs Models Marketing Performance

...to Consumer-Driven Intermediate Measures

- Cost per *involved* reader/viewer/listener
- Cost per *earned attention*
- Cost per *touch*
- Cost per *touching*

Figure 6.14 Shifts in metrics

The four key types of data necessary for a robust customer-driven platform are:

- Employee feedback data
- Customer feedback data
- Operational daily metrics
- Behavioural monitoring data

These sets of data may not be linked so it can be difficult for a company to understand how the different aspects of the overall operation affect each other and the overall output of the company. The reality is that the four different data points reflect effective "arms" that can be pushed or pulled in any certain direction to affect marketing or business efforts.

Return on humanity and other metrics

Cash flow is a major concern for project accounting, and needs to be considered when net present value is raised and income from operations curves. However, normally the "how big is the return?" question is asked before the "How does this suit our company values?" question. How does it apply to humanitarian systems? This question can be broken down into two parts: 1) how can we convert this from money to social gains?, and 2) how can we then monetise the social gains to convince finance driven agencies that they should invest in humanitarian work?

Companies should look at using metrics such as:

- Return on Humanity metrics (ROH)
- Social Return on Investment (SROI)

> The conversation these days is all about metrics. Even with it being a hot topic it still seems to come with confusion over how to create meaningful metrics. It would appear that a high percentage of managers do not understand it. The easy part is finding things to measure; it becomes more complicated when locating the correct thing to measure. How does a company decide what is the right thing to measure? Simply put, the things that make the company a success are what should be measured. If you are clear about what makes your company successful – delivering value to the stakeholders – then the obvious conclusion is that the company should concentrate on stakeholder value-driven metrics.
>
> Stakeholder Metrics
>
> - Engagement Metrics
> - Change Management
> - Expectations Management
> - Humanity of the Project
> - Share of Needs Models
> - Memetics Research
> - Engagement Index (e.g. Involvement and interaction and intimacy and influence)
> - Transparency Index
> - (True) Relationship Index

Figure 6.15 The only acceptable metric is a stakeholder value-driven metric

There should be a focus on organisational behaviour and values (including drive and partnering, value consciousness and transparency). REDF combines financial and social returns: this includes performance measure and relates it to an "efforts to output" ratio that can be analysed across enterprises (Roberts Enterprise Development Fund – REDF – was formed with a mandate to launch and grow social enterprises; see http://redf.org/). This looks like an institutional metric. ROH analyses four factors: benchmarking, social return on investment, financial sustainability and sales. The benchmarking is related to programme comparison with other options to solve the same issue. The social return benefits society and the financial sustainability requires sufficient customer support with the intention to financially break even. Sales is a paid strategy with a pound volume and customers-served ratio (see Figure 6.16).

Customer engagement index

This is not the same as the customer satisfaction index. It is a step ahead, when the customer is happy and/or content with the product, and they themselves become the marketing manager for the product. While computing customer engagement the factors that need to be considered include purchase behaviour, frequency of interaction, product involvement, extent of referrals, and strength of information shared. This calculation does not have a standard model. Most companies will design their own, using the category in question to base it on, but most companies agree that customer engagement is based around the following factors:

- Customer Behaviour
- Metrics
- Social Media

Creating value in a global context 137

- ROInsight
- ROInvolvement
- ROExperience
- ROEmotion
- ROEngagement
- ROIntegrity
- ROEthos

Figure 6.16 ROI becomes...

The metric can be focused on certain groups of customers to encourage their participation with the company. It can also be used to manipulate effectiveness of various targets and goals that have been set around customer engagement and retention. These web-based strategies can be created to increase customer engagement and be specifically designed to target certain individual customers.

Towards a new understanding of people

New thinking processes are required in order to shift towards a "connected experience economy." The long-held assumption is that consumers are compliant recipients of information. It has always been assumed that consumers are merely the receivers of a brand story, in a push-driven marketing model – this label in itself is narrow and problematic. The customer is simply considered to be a target for returning feedback and impressions.

This needs to change and companies must develop a much more dynamic understanding of their audience. Customers have long since lost their passiveness and must be viewed in a different light. They are compliant helpers, willing to engage in a dialogue with the brand. People will pass on their experiences with products and services and from there other people get ideas or become interested. This is why we need a better understanding of this channel of communication, the language and the frames of references. People must be viewed on their own terms. The consumer must be put in the centre of the experience in order to change. Static models showing the consumer surrounded by media are no longer the best way to focus on a connected and switched on consumer.

Product and brand change: These now give people the ability to live their lives and get their stories out there. The issue is more important and consuming than any brand, and so the new goal must be set for the marketing of the change. The need is now to get the customer to take in and contain the product in their stories, and while there, develop the brand further.

Intelligent platform and measurement system change: To look at the product with a different view requires the understanding of what is a meaningful experience. The approach required must embrace art and science along with technology and understands the experience. This approach must be acquired from many different sources but at its core it should uphold the value of human intelligence and interpretive skills in order to get the desired outcome that would result in actionable models that can have a profound effect on initiatives and business models.

We need to use measurement models that recognise and appreciate the reality of marketing and commerce. This is known as "Return on Experience" (RoX) (see Figure 6.16). We build on the old approaches and add a new way of thinking about it in order to measure and optimise the meaningful experiences. RoX makes an effort to create a model of overall return of investment with the intention of building an "experience led" brand, in fact the goal is to prescribe connected experiences to join the customer and company.

The "Return on Experience" model is made up of three parts:

- Brand and Marketing ROI: a whole formed by parts to measure and assess the return on experience initiatives.
- Return on Media and Channels: cross-media analytics combined with next generation marketing provide a very detailed picture of channel impact.
- Optimisation of the Experience: the measurement framework with the ability to measure and assess, that can be interrogated for insight.

Brand and marketing ROI: the primary part of the model focuses on ROI of the brand and marketing itself. The model evaluates return and efficiency at the corporate level. Marketshare, cost/benefit and scorecard are some examples of ROI analyses.

Return on media and channels: the second part of the model focuses on media and channels. Current developments in media mix modelling have very sophisticated algorithms to measure the effects of quantity of cross-media effects within the marketing field.

Today, many people can experience several hundred "touch-points" through many different media channels.

Brands often get their story across through blended media – the analytics tools can help produce a more accurate return. The predictive forecasting is a major advancement and this can now show cross-channel assist rates or impacts, while accommodating the integration of traditional media and digital media. This approach allows markets to continually calibrate and measure marketing investments and create incremental ROI.

Optimisation and assessment of experience: The current techniques in place used by marketers just cannot efficiently cover the spectrum and range of human behaviour, however the breakthrough in information processing and sensor technology require rapidly evolving behaviour within organisations in order to optimise these experiences. To start with, better sources of data are required along with better ways to extract relevant information.

Sensory technology, as developments continue to be made, for the first time now has communication on its side. Consumer products, offices, retail spaces and homes, now all have the ability to communicate, which also then provides huge levels of current data on a scale never before seen. This data can be useful as a stand-alone or in correlation with other qualitative and quantitative sources, which then produces an invaluable business intelligence. Information processing, combined with the advances in consumer intelligence platforms paves the way for this information to become real business value. Marketers gain advantage for the more dynamic and efficient consumer understanding as they garner greater depth and detail from the information gathered and of the changing world around them.

We have now changed, and evolved into a new way of marketing, now based firmly on communication. To survive and thrive in this new era requires that techniques and methods connect efficiently and effectively. In order for you to achieve the best possible return from any investment, you must assemble and arrange the resources, while being perfectly aware that this is not just about you.

To ensure that an acceptable mode of experience is being created, there must be a way to measure the seamless merging of art, science, technology and story together so the end result can look more extensively at experience, by using intelligent platform sources of numerous data types. Human interpretive skills and intelligence also play a part in creating actionable models that affect initiatives and business metrics.

> The new drive in marketing nowadays is giving it the ability to improve and enhance customers' lives. It is called meaningful marketing or marketing with meaning. Economic and social forces are colliding to fuel the staying power of meaningful marketing.

Figure 6.17 Does meaningful marketing have a future?

6.7 The secret of meaningful marketing

How do brands do it? How do they manage to persuade the consumer that one product over another can provide a more meaningful experience than that of its competitors. Without substance, the conversation about meaning is meaningless. There is no point in persevering with a message if it cannot deliver, because it won't stand up to scrutiny. Brand managers should be advised to ask what value can be added to a person's life and then decide how to deliver that. Another valuable hint is to allocate the role of "hero" to the customer and not the brand (see Figure 6.17).

It is now expected that a brand should enhance and improve quality of life, it should benefit wellbeing, communities and society in general. Figure 6.18 shows who is affected and Figure 6.19 shows how this can work. This mindset requires five mental shifts that companies need to buy in to: from people to citizens, individuals to communities, products to outcomes, systems buildings, functional brands to becoming transformational agents and from just talking to building relationships. Meaningful marketing connects brands with the encouraging mission to improve people's quality of life. This will have a positive impact on all aspects of life, from the environment, to societies and communities, and to how successful the individual's quality of life is. The traditional marketing model that advises us to consume more is under threat. Studies show that material consumption and economic gains do not make us any happier, nor do they encourage a sense of wellbeing for us as individuals or societies.

It appears to be a relatively new concept that brands should concern themselves with our personal lives and wellbeing, but this new phenomenon is increasing as consumers demand that brands enhance and transform our lives by encompassing issues that we think are important. For marketers, a radically new approach is needed that can reconnect brands to people, therefore enhancing their status as "meaningful," and this will, in turn, increase the wellbeing of individuals, communities, the environment and society by allowing all to flourish.

Evidence suggests that meaningful brands create strong brand equity and positive business results. The Havas Meaningful Brands Index tracks over 130,000 people on 300 brands over 23 markets, and reveals that the top ten brands in the Index outperform all others and show greater growth in both brand value growth and market capitalisation. The brands that have the "meaningful" badge systematically enjoy greater consumer preferences, loyalties and advocacy as people have a strong bond and attachment because their perception is that these brands add meaning to their lives. This occurs in all markets and industries.

IT and consumer brands allow us to be more skilled, smarter and make our lives easier, while forging social connections.

Retail brands have the reputation of contributing greatly to our economic wellbeing by helping us create our own wellbeing by producing affordable products alongside a convenient and enjoyable shopping experience. The contemporary design and affordable prices of IKEA allow us to live a more economical and environmentally friendly life. IKEA has mastered the art of creating meaningful connections with its customers on an intellectual, economic, emotional and organisational level. It is no surprise that IKEA ranks highly in the Meaningful Brands Index.

The Brazilian energy brand Petrobras is another company that ranks highly on the Meaningful Brands Index. Petrobras's score is far higher than most FMCG brands and retailers. Petrobras set about forging quality interactions with Brazilians whilst encouraging national pride. For instance, when Petrobras announced their next project, a pre-salt exploration project, they also launched the Bandera Viva campaign. This campaign centred around an interactive space made up of 25,000 photos of anonymous Brazilians, who uploaded their photo and their personal challenge for the future. This allowed Petrobras to understand what challenges faced the Brazilian people and to respond with social, environmental and cultural initiatives that would contribute to Brazil's wellbeing. This type of initiative strengthens the bond between consumers and brands, which gives Petrobras the role of key reference for Brazilians.

Strategy nugget

How to become a meaningful brand?

Meaningful is a mindset, not a marketing issue. There are five key "mental shifts" that companies and brands need to believe in and act on to start reconnecting.

1. FROM PEOPLE TO CITIZENS

To understand our new demands and values, we must start thinking of people as citizens, not just consumers. For brands to become meaningful, they have to really care about people in "human terms." We want companies and brands to listen to us, share our values, and our vision of the world.

Brands must make a commitment to their customers, not make promises they don't keep. They must consider the role of an enabling entity that has the ability to encourage people to achieve their personal goals. What is important is how the brand's existence can motivate people to enhance their lives. For this transformation to take place the vital points are listening to the important issues and understanding how to supply a product that is capable of improving people's lives and getting to know them and understanding which concrete areas of human wellbeing each brand can better leverage.

2. FROM PRODUCTS TO OUTCOME

Nowadays, people require much more than simply a product, a promise and a fairytale story. People require brands to have a more positive effect on their lives and their communities. What people seek in brands are outcomes, rather than products. People expect brands to lead and help them achieve greater outcomes and create new lifestyles more consistent with their real needs, values and context.

3. MAKING THE TRANSITION FROM SEGMENTED GROUP AND INDIVIDUALS TO SYSTEMS AND COMMUNITIES

Community, society and the environment are the context in which we all live and interact. Enhancing the wellbeing of individuals enhances the wellbeing of the communities we belong to. When a large social challenge is addressed the end result is that millions of people's lives are improved and enhanced because these are all interdependent and related segments of a much larger interconnected systems that cannot be ignored.

The Unilever Sustainable Living Plan is a very good example of how a company makes the system work better and enhances people's lives responsibly. For instance, Lifebuoy disinfectant soap provides affordable and accessible hygiene for millions of people. In India, it has prevented millions of children from dying of diarrhoea. Unilever's marketing efforts focused on an ambitious five-year campaign to educate children, their families and communities, to adopt a simple healthy habit of washing their hands daily. By the end of 2005, they reached 18,000 villages, and sales of Lifebuoy soap grew by 20 per cent in 2003–04, and it is now India's most popular soap. It is therefore not surprising that Unilever is one of the most important and meaningful brands in India as it has helped and continues to help transform lives and society in general.

4. THE ABILITY TO BECOME A TRANSFORMATIONAL AGENT FROM THE FOUNDATIONS OF APPARITIONAL FUNCTIONALITY

Brands with a meaningful entity can be transformational; they can transform our lives and our societies for the better; they can provide us with the products, services and tools, and engaging experiences to help people become better. Products and communications are just the means to help us live better. Meaningful brands' purpose is to help you become "a better you." They make commitments and help us become better. Nobody can make us healthier unless we decide to become healthier and adopt better nutritional and physical habits. People achieve outcomes; brands act as our "coach." Most organisations need to transform and reinvent themselves to deliver on this mindset. Traditional organisations have been designed and grown to produce and sell more. It is not a surprise therefore that a number of the more worthwhile and meaningful brands on the planet have undergone a transformation to revolutionise their markets.

5. FROM TALKING TO BUILDING RELATIONSHIPS: TALK, THINK, TRUST

Not many people can create change just by talking. Communications are a powerful means to bring about necessary change on the path to improving our lives. Productive communication requires more than just the company to talk about it. To restore trust and reconnect with citizens, brands must start listening to citizens' demands and start to fuel dialogue about their consumers' important issues (*talk*), open up to new perspectives and shared thinking with citizens and other stakeholders as a move towards a shared purpose (*think*), while in the background, but equally as important, strengthen the relationship with them in order to gain their *trust*. It is through this approach that brands can start reconnecting with people and become meaningful to them.

- Company
- Shareholders
- Employees
- Customers
- Community
- Society

Figure 6.18 Profit sharing – the performance marketing model of the future

```
Action Perception
Value created
(MS) Success= 3(npz,f,m,cfm,cds)+----------
Insight Resources consumed
No-profit zones
Fluidity
Measurement
Cross-functional metrics
Consumer-driven solutions
```

Figure 6.19 The formula for (MS) success

6.8 Chapter summary

The chapter introduces a number of topics related to the concept of value. Models of innovation that influence the creation of value are put forward. The orientation towards value-based management is analysed and then analytically presented with changes in marketing practice as well as methods and tools of marketing measurement. Finally, key issues behind the important and key concepts of shareholder value and stakeholder theory are also discussed.

6.9 End of chapter self-reflection questions

1. What do you understand by the term Value-Based-Management? How can Value-Based-Management enhance organisational performance?
2. Discuss a few ideas about Marketing Metamorphosis and Marketing Renaissance.
3. Why is the transition from shareholder value to stakeholder value so important in today's marketplace?
4. In the sense of analysing value, what is the Parallel Lines Test?

References

Berthon, P., & Hulbert, J.M. (2003). Marketing in metamorphosis: Breaking boundaries. *Business Horizons*, *46*(3), 31–40.
Bloget, H. (2013). Enough with this obsession with stock prices – it's ruining America. *Business Insider* (e-publication)
Donaldson, T., & Preston, L. E. (1995). The stakeholder theory of the corporation: Concepts, evidence and implications. *Academy of Management Review*, *20*(1), 65–91.
Kanter, R. M. (2011) How great companies think differently. *Harvard Business Review*, November.
Khalifa, A. S. (2004). Customer value: A review of recent literature and an integrative configuration. *Management Decision*, *42*(5), 645–666.
Peres, R., Muller, E., & Mahajan, V. (2010). Innovation diffusion and new product growth models: A critical review and research directions. *International Journal of Research in Marketing*, *27*(2), 91–106.
Slywotzky, A. J., & Morrison, D. J., with Andelman, B. (1997) *The profit zone: How strategic business design will lead you to tomorrow's profits*. Corporate Decisions Inc., by arrangement with Times Books, a division of Random House, Inc. [Previous edition published 1998 by Wiley & Sons Ltd.]
Solcansky, M., & Simberova, I. (2010). Measurement of marketing effectiveness. *Economics and Management*, *15*, 755–759.

7 Emerging economies

7.1 Learning objectives

After completing this chapter you will:

- appreciate the political, economic and regulatory forces which shape emerging economies
- be able to understand the different challenges facing BRICS and MINT economies
- appreciate the concept of institutional voids
- be able to identify appropriate differences of the structure of business in emerging economies
- appreciate the concept of growth traps for emerging economies
- understand the nuances of strategic planning in emerging economies

Strategy nugget

Emerging countries

CEOs of emerging economies firms face the duality of increasing competition from more nimble start-ups and from mature MNEs. Basic questions for the CEO to consider include (1) What should drive the strategy of emerging economy firms in the international business arena?, and (2) What determines the success and failure of emerging economy firms? Academia has a role to play, but with the preference of scholars to perform research in developed environments, together with their differing origins, cultures and stakeholder expectations, such research may not be appropriate to gain competitive advantage. Crittenden and Crittenden (2010) note the fragility of the global economy from the perspective of emerging countries and proffer 20 broad research questions, which can be categorised in eight areas:

> *When does an emerging country become an emerged country?*
>
> *What is the direction push with respect to foreign direct investment?*
>
> *What are the salient demographic trends?*
>
> *What will be the impact of technology adoption?*
>
> *What will be the impact of natural resources and sustainability?*
>
> *What will be the impact of political and legal unease?*
>
> *What will determine the selection of market entry?*
>
> *What will be the impacts of institutional voids within emerging economies?*

144 *Globalisation*

Each question provides some guidance for future research, and the selection of research methodology can range from qualitative to quantitative approaches. From a practitioner perspective the answers to each question can help in the strategy formulation and implementation processes.

Questions

1 What do you believe are the most important top three areas?
2 When does an emerging country become an emerged country?

7.2 Introduction

Emerging economies have gained prominence again, and the development of each economy depends in part on its origins. The transition economies of the former Soviet Union, Eastern Europe and East Asia are markedly different from the traditional developing countries in Africa, Latin America and the Middle East. The former group is categorised by a shift from a centrally planned to a market economy resulting in increased privatisation, changing role of the state, and legal and institutional reforms.

An emerging economy will usually exhibit the following:

- Progressing towards developed status;
- Higher annual growth rate, measured using gross domestic product (GDP);
- A wide variety of economic sectors experiencing growth, including services as well as manufacturing exports.

In contrast to developed economies, emerging economies are noted for their rapid economic development and industrialisation, which makes them attractive for export, foreign direct investment and for production and manufacturing bases. Finance lies at the heart of economic development, but capital markets are usually in the early phase of development. Financiers find exchange rates volatile, with less liquid trading, and inflation can also be a problem. A lack of professional service firms can create information asymmetries that can be exploited by mature service firms. The prohibitively high costs of monitoring worsen this situation.

The emerging economies outlook (Figure 7.1) is at a crossroads. Three forces are currently driving markets; failing oil prices, and a rise in the US dollar and slowdown in emerging markets. A central feature of emerging economies has been the growth since the

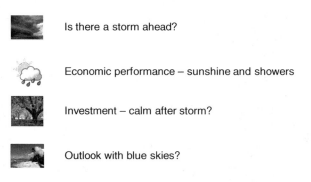

Figure 7.1 Emerging economies outlook

financial crisis of 2008. Yet, at the time of writing low oil prices, which have collapsed from around $110 a barrel, are creating problems for oil-rich emerging economies. According to the *Economist* (2 Jan, 2016) Saudi Arabia needs a barrel of oil to fetch around $85 to finance public spending and around $60 to keep its current account in balance. But with a barrel of oil falling below $40 Saudi Arabia are having to use their (ample) foreign-exchange reserves. The Saudi oil conglomerate, Saudi Aramco, worth an estimated $2 to $3 trillion is seeking an IPO. The fees generated for bankers are expected to be in excess of $1billion.

Such low oil prices are affecting the public finances of Russia and Nigeria too. Russia is one of the world's largest oil producers, and pushed up interest rates to 17% to support the weakened rouble and a dependency on oil and gas. According to the International Monetary Fund, the fall in oil prices has "decimated" Nigerian government revenues and slashed the country's GDP growth from 6.3% in 2014 to an estimated 2.7% the following year. Nigeria now faces substantial challenges as the economy has to operate with cut-price oil prices which will put at risk its objectives of reducing unemployment and poverty.

This chapter considers the dramatically changing landscape (see Figure 7.2), the structure of emerging economies and the role of strategic management. Fifteen years or so after the term BRIC was first used, we shall reconsider the hype of the BRICS and some of the opportunities presented by the MINT economies and outline why and how new markets demand new maps for success. The infrastructure of emerging markets is also reviewed with the predominance of state-controlled companies and family-run businesses, which can lead to the primary object not being solely profit.

7.3 A changing world

Historically, major North American and European MNEs have enjoyed their longest and strongest run of rising profitability in the post-war era thanks to an environment that supported robust revenue growth cost-efficiencies (Dobbs, Koller & Ramaswamy, 2015). Despite, the cyclical turbulent markets the path has been upwards, but the future is beginning to look less rosy. The prominent positions of western MNEs were attributed to scale, global presence and falling costs. But western business models can be ill-suited

Figure 7.2 Changing landscape

146 *Globalisation*

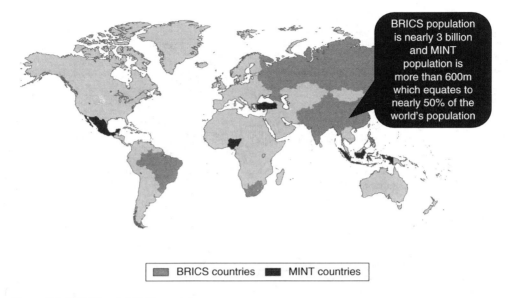

Figure 7.3 BRICS and MINT countries

to the emerging markets. In Chapter 5, reference was made to falling GDP growth and costs bottoming out. These cost drivers are disappearing, and talented ambitious professionals in emerging markets no longer have to move to the West. Organisations in China, India and Brazil are becoming MNEs themselves with the ability to pay attractive remuneration. This has intensified the global war for talent. Figures 7.4 and 7.5 illustrate the economic performance of G8 and G5 countries for the period 2010–16. The data tell a compelling story.

Looking at the banking sector provides some evidence of the shift in balance of power. In 2015, the top four largest banks in the world were all Chinese with the largest, Beijing-based Industrial and Commercial Bank of China, generating $166 billion in sales, $44 billion in profit, $43.32 trillion in assets and $278 billion in market value. But in 2016,

G8 Countries	GDP* 2010 %	Unemployment rate* %	GDP** 2016 %	Unemployment rate** %
Britain	2.8	7.7 Sept	2.2	4.9 Jun
Canada	3.4	7.9 Oct	0.9	7.0 Aug
France	1.8	10.0 Sept	1.4	10.3 Jul
Germany	3.9	7.5 Oct	1.7	6.1 Aug
Italy	1.0	8.3 Sept	0.8	11.4 Jul
Japan	4.4	5.0 Sept	0.8	3.0 Jul
Russia	2.7	6.6 Sept	(0.6)	5.3 Jul
USA	3.1	9.6 Oct	1.2	4.9 Aug

Figure 7.4 2010–2016 upturn?

*Economist poll or Economist Intelligence Unit estimate/forecast.
Source: *The Economist*, 20-26 November 2010.
**Economist poll or Economist Intelligence Unit estimate/forecast.
Source: *The Economist*, 17-23 September 2016.

G5 Countries	GDP* 2010 %	Unemployment rate* 2016 %	GDP** 2016 %	Unemployment rate** 2016 %
Brazil	8.8	6.2 Sept	(3.8)	11.6 Jul
China	9.6	9.6 2009	6.7	4.1 Qtr2
India	8.8	10.7 2009	7.1	4.9 2013
Mexico	7.6	5.7 Sept	2.5	3.8 Jul
South Africa	3.0	25.3 Qtr 3	0.6	26.6 Qtr 2

Figure 7.5 Emerging economies 2010–2016 downturn?
*Economist poll or Economist Intelligence Unit estimate/forecast.
Source: *The Economist*, 20-26 November 2010.
**Economist poll or Economist Intelligence Unit estimate/forecast.
Source: *The Economist*, 17-23 September 2016.

Wells Fargo & Co and JP Morgan Chase & Co entered the top four positions. Table 7.1 provides a summary of the world's ten largest banks. Despite the varying metrics that can be used to rank banks using Tier 1 capital, and relbanks.com using market capitalisation, the overall trend is clear. HSBC was the largest bank in the world in 2008 and is now ranked 8th by Forbes.

The largest Chinese banks are reluctant to have operations in every corner of the world servicing all business sectors. Instead, they would rather focus on growing sustainable business operations. Banks using new technologies no longer have to have a physical presence everywhere to operate globally. Now that the conventional business model is changing, there is now clearly a need to rethink the impact of emerging markets within the banking sector. In terms of business models, bankers need to reassess how work is done, the degree of digitisation, pricing and new product development and how staff (with emphasis on investment bankers) get rewarded. Scaling back operations and introducing cost savings in themselves will lead to sustaining growth. Operating across continents will involve forming relationships with consumers within a business environment of megatrends that are reshaping the world. But caution is warranted, as IMF Chief Economist Maurice Obstfeld stated that growth in emerging economies could slow down for the fifth straight year. Some pertinent questions are posed in Figure 7.6.

Table 7.1 Top ten largest banks in the world by market capitalisation

Bank	Country	Market Capitalisation US$bn (March 2016)
Wells Fargo	US	254.19
ICBC	China	226.55
JP Morgan Chase	US	217.79
China Construction Bank	China	155.97
Agriculture Bank of China	China	155.04
Bank of China	China	144.16
Bank of America	US	142.39
HSBC Holdings	UK	128.91
Citigroup	US	126.74
Commonwealth Bank of Australia	Australia	99.69

Source: Relbanks.com, 11 March 2016.

> - Consider these questions now.
>   - (I) Global trade has continued to slow since 2008. Why?
>   - (II) Emerging economies are slowing down. Why?
>   - (III) What's happened to China?

Figure 7.6 Some questions to consider

BRICS

The growth of the BRIC economies has been well documented in the business press. A multitude of organisations have sought to reap high returns in new markets. However, the difficult regulatory and economic environments have not always led to high returns. For example, the retail industry is replete with examples of successful firms that could not repeat their success in an emerging market. Success does not always solely relate to first mover advantage. Today's winners make the right moves at the right times. Arguably, the window of opportunity is declining, as the GDP figures have fallen. Brazil currently has negative GDP growth and the Russian economy is stagnating. After reaching an all-time GDP growth of 11.4 per cent in 2010, the Indian GDP figure is now 5.3 per cent. China's GDP growth has fallen from just under 12 per cent in 2010 to 7.3 per cent. This chapter considers the challenges organisations face when operating in emerging economies. This point is in stark contrast to the more open, more stable growth opportunities being marketed at the start of the third millennium.

Even as recently as five years ago, the BRICs – Brazil, Russia, India, China – were poised to disrupt the world economy. China had grown used to double digit growth rates. However, as discussed in Chapter 5, this has now slipped. In addition to falling oil prices, Russia is facing fallout from the conflict in Ukraine. Despite hosting the World Cup and Olympics Games Brazil is suffering a severe economic and political crisis, and now has an inflation rate just under 10 per cent, a five-year unemployment rate of 7.5 per cent, and calls for the impeachment of its President who recently began her second term of office. India is the largest democracy in the world, but reforms are required if the country is to reach long-term potential growth. To illustrate this, for India's GDP to grow at 8 per cent, agriculture needs to grow at least 4 per cent, but an alarming rural distress is putting this goal at risk. Another way of trying to access impact is to consider the economies of China and India, who are at different stages of their lifecycles. China ($7 trillion) is slowing down and its economy is three and half times larger than India's ($2.2 trillion). But with China's GDP growth at 7 per cent this adds $490 billion to global growth compared to the GDP growth of 7 per cent for India adding $140 billion.

Originally, the BRICs did not contain a representative from Africa. In 2011, South Africa, the second largest economy in Africa, joined the BRIC economies, so the acronym became BRICS. Although, South Africa's size, population and economy are much smaller than its counterparts it does possess huge potential. Its gold, diamonds, platinum and improving infrastructure make it attractive for investment. In addition, Africa with its 1 billion population and a growing middle class makes it a target for cash-rich governments of individual investors. More specifically, South Africa possesses market opportunities within its borders and can act as a gateway to the rest of the continent. Yet, the economic statistics of South Africa paint a picture with a contracting GDP of -1.3 per cent and an unemployment rate of 25.5 per cent. The figure of -1.3 per cent is the lowest since the 2009 recession, despite growth in categories such as financial services, construction and transport, manufacturing, and mining, although agriculture has shrunk.

POD

Wipro

Wipro Ltd (NYSE: WIT) is a global Indian information technology, consulting and outsourcing company with 170,000+ workforce serving clients in 175+ cities across six continents. The company posted revenues of $7.7 billion for the financial year ended 31 Mar 2016.

Wipro helps customers do business better by leveraging our industry-wide experience, deep technology expertise, comprehensive portfolio of services and vertically aligned business model. Our 55+ dedicated emerging technologies "Centers of Excellence" enable us to harness the latest technology for delivering business capability to our clients.

Wipro is globally recognised for its innovative approach towards delivering business value and its commitment to sustainability. Wipro champions optimised utilisation of natural resources, capital and talent. Today we are a trusted partner of choice for global businesses looking to "differentiate at the front" and "standardise at the core" through technology interventions.

In today's world, organisations will have to rapidly reengineer themselves and be more responsive to changing customer needs. Wipro is well positioned to be a partner and co-innovator to businesses in their transformation journey, identify new growth opportunities and facilitate their foray into new sectors and markets.

The boundaryless global marketplace makes it imperative that CEOs within emerging economies that seek to compete worldwide understand the phenomena of their competitive space. Tight labour markets make it harder for emerging economy firms to fill job vacancies. The effects are not only significant to maintaining the status quo, which can be temporary fixes, but do not address the long-term viability of the firm. The smart firms need to be creative in their talent strategy. The global Indian information technology company Wipro launched Mission 10X in 2007 to address the challenges of employability in engineering education. The initiative has spread to 1,200 engineering colleges across 25 Indian states. Mission 10X consists of an industry–academia interface, which helps in faculty recruitment; faculty development programmes; workshops for students; and sponsorship for faculty to study for PhDs.

MINT

The MINT countries of Mexico, Indonesia, Nigeria and Turkey possess the potential for significant growth. They have locational advantages – Mexico is near to North America and well connected with South America; Indonesia is located in South-East Asia and has strong connections with China; Nigeria with its size and proximity to African markets makes it a potential hub for Africa; Turkey's position makes it a good conduit for the West and East, as it sits on two continents. Three of them (Mexico, Indonesia and Nigeria) are commodity producers of goods made for resale. Each MINT country has a large population with a significant youth element (see Table 7.2).

Nevertheless, while acknowledging the potential, poor infrastructure and societal problems still exist. Mexico has a National Infrastructure programme within the sectors of energy, tourism, water, health, communications and urban development, receiving $596bn. President Enrique Peña Nieto remains focused on implementing his structural reform agenda, but corruption and crime impede progress. According to the Indonesia Chamber of Commerce and Industry, Indonesian logistical costs are higher than those of its neighbours, with costs being 17 per cent of a company's total expenditure. In peer

Table 7.2 Examples of leading MINT companies

Company	Sector	Country
America Movil, Formento Economico Mexicano, SAB (FEMSA)	FEMSA is a Mexican Multinational beverage and retail company.	Mexico
Bank Central Asia, Astral International	PT Bank Central Asia Tbk (BCA) is Indonesia's largest lender by market value and the second largest bank by assets.	Indonesia
Dangote group (Aliko Dangote – net worth $17.7bn)	Dangote Group is one of Africa's leading industrial conglomerates, with interests in everything from cement to food.	Nigeria
Turkish airlines	Turkish Airlines is the national flag carrier airline of Turkey. Turkish Airlines has been named the "Best Airline in Europe" for the sixth year in a row by Skytrax.	Turkey

countries the corresponding figure is below 10 per cent. The archipelagic geography is not supported by an appropriate sea transport system. This creates inflationary pressures on domestic goods, and can make exports cheaper than local goods. A lack of financial resources requires the private sector to get involved. Nigeria with its systemic problems in infrastructure and unstable energy supply can be a burden for businesses too. Problems with corruption, a weak civil service and the slow pace of reform exacerbate the frustrations of doing business. Nigerian investors look to President Muhammadu Buhari and his administration to address some of these persistent challenges. The Turkish economy has been a source of inspiration to other emerging markets (World Bank, 2014). Mexico and Turkey having a GDP per capita in excess of US$10,000, suggests that both economies are comfortably middle class. Yet the Turkish economy has slowed down. Despite considerable improvements in their infrastructure with skyscrapers and super-fast trains, too low investment and, according to PwC the professional service firm, widespread corruption are hampering the ease with which business is conducted. The latter point appears to be a problem in the other three MINT economies. Societal problems among the MINTs are widely documented, with poverty and corruption at the root of their problems, which may be hindering economic development.

Institutional voids

In summarising the picture of BRICS, MINTS or other emerging "economic" nations, infrastructures are problematic. The previous sections focused on particular aspects, but the concept of institutional voids considers the quality of institutions and infrastructures. The "cookie cutter" approach to international trade does not work. The term "institutional voids," coined by Khanna and Palepu (2013), refers to the absence of intermediaries such as market research firms and credit card systems to connect buyers and sellers. The term also explains the broader market ecosystems, which MNEs and local/national enterprises are dependent on and which can lead to underperformance. These can include capital markets, product markets and labour markets. A well-cited example is the Coca-Cola company, who found that their beverages in India were sold "warm," due to power cuts on hot days. Coca-Cola responded by building solar power coolers in conjunction with local refrigeration companies. A business model that is successful in a home market may not be replicated in an emerging market. Like Coca-Cola, there may need to be a differentiated model in the new market. New processes not only have to be different but they must be innovative to overcome infrastructure challenges.

The Global Competitive Index (GCI) (World Economic Forum, 2015) assesses the competitive landscape of 140 economies, providing insight into the drivers of productivity and prosperity. In the 2015–2016 report, Pillar 1: Institutions, BRICS are ranked as follows: Brazil 121st, Russia 100th, India 60th, China 51st, South Africa 38th, and MINTs are as follows: Mexico 109th, Indonesia 55th, Nigeria 124th and Turkey 75th.

The GCI report informs the reader that the first pillar institutional environment considers the legal and administrative framework within which individuals, firms and governments interact to create wealth. The rankings of both the BRICS and MINT countries illustrate the level of institutional voids that potentially exists. When entering an emerging market the CEO in some instances may need to adapt to fresh challenges and discover that success is much harder and may take longer than thought at the outset.

Growth traps of emerging economies

As noted throughout this chapter, businesses in emerging countries start off with rapid growth, which is in part due to the industrialisation effect. However, after this initial growth it becomes difficult to sustain rapid growth. Either economic development plateaus or the growth rates fall below what is needed to allow significant numbers of the population to reap the benefits of middle-income to high-income status. Governments tend to focus on institutional reforms, and economic and social policy. The actual strategic management of indigenous firms is left to market forces. Organisations that are significant tend to have gained first mover advantage, possess a significant market share and be popular within their home market. As firms from overseas see a potentially attractive market, their experience and resources enable them to grab market share from the dominant indigenous firm. As the indigenous firms seek to move up or down the value chain to move away from basic manufacturing or towards the customer, the battle becomes harder.

Ultimately, to be successful indigenous firms in emerging economies must concentrate upon the development of a sustainable strategy. The crux of such a strategy should focus upon capabilities that will provide competitive advantages over the MNEs. These capabilities can be built or bought. In the past, automotive companies such as Toyota and Honda built capabilities to enhance the value-added of their value chain. But today's globalisation with its modular value chains can present opportunities for buying in capabilities. The merger and acquisition route remains attractive, but Asian companies, like their western counterparts, have mixed experiences. A well-cited example is that of the Mexican company CEMEX, which was founded in 1906 and evolved from a small, privately owned cement-focused firm to a publicly traded company employing more than 50,000 and generating sales in excess of US$15bn. Prior to its international expansion, CEMEX spent US$1bn on acquisitions to solidify its position at home, and management developed a set of core competencies that would underpin its strong operational capabilities based on engineering and IT. Since making a national presence in 1976 by becoming Mexico's market leader with its acquisition of Cementos Guardalajara, CEMEX has grown year on year by overseas acquisitions in Spain, Venezuela, USA, Colombia, the Philippines, the Caribbean, Egypt, UK and Australia.

POD

Barbados tourism

For non-oil emerging economies tourism is a major contributor to GDP. The Caribbean is no exception. Barbados is the most easterly of the Caribbean islands, and its humid climate contributes to it being a tourist destination. Barbados' sun, sand and sea have become an attractive destination for wealthy tourists. The period June to November is the wet season and December to May is predominantly dry. Barbados is densely populated with approximately 276,000 inhabitants living on 166 square miles. The gross domestic product (GDP) per capita is US$14,497, which is almost twice that for the rest of Latin America and the Caribbean (UN, 2010). According to the Barbados Statistical Service in 2015, 591,872 stay-over arrivals were recorded.

The direct contribution of travel and tourism to GDP is expected to be 14.2 per cent, rising by 3.4 per cent to 14.8 per cent in 2021 (World Travel Tourism Council [WTTC], 2011). Barbados ranks 10th out of 181 countries in terms of relative importance to travel and tourism, and 133rd out of 181 in terms of growth forecasts (WTTC, 2011). The direct contribution of travel and tourism to employment is 14.6 per cent of total employment. Barbados is predominantly a service sector economy, which accounts for more than 82 per cent of GDP.

The main constraints affecting the competitiveness of tourism in Barbados include: lack of economy of scale, high cost of production/service, high landed cost of raw material together with a lack of overarching tourism policy framework. The last decade has seen several attempts to kick-start the tourism strategic planning process. A tourism green paper was developed in 2001 to guide tourism planning over the short to medium term. The completion of a tourism master plan is mentioned in the National Strategic Plan of Barbados, 2005–2025. Both political parties, Barbados Labour Party (BLP) and the Democratic Labour Party (DLP) referred to completion of a tourism master plan as a key objective in their political manifestos in 2008. A discussion document entitled White Paper for the Development of Tourism in Barbados was published in November 2010. The resulting white paper acts as a statement of Government's policy on tourism development over the medium to long term. This formed the basis of the Tourism Master Plan for Barbados, which was eventually published in 2014. The Barbados Tourism Master Plan 2014–2023 comprised six separate reports:

 i) The Master Plan – 183 pages
 ii) The Environment – 135 pages
 iii) People and Organisations – 177 pages
 iv) Our visitors and the Barbados visitor economy – 238 pages
 v) Services, Infrastructure and Products –Part I 284 pages & Part II 330 pages
 vi) Cultural Heritage and Attractions – Part I & Part II

7.4 The structure of traditional businesses in emerging economies

Family firms

The largest companies in the western economy are usually structured with a broad array of shareholders. Björnberg, Elstrodt, and Pandit (2014) state that less than one-third of the companies on the S&P 500 remain founder- and family-owned businesses. Observations in emerging economies are very different. Approximately 60 per cent of privately owned firms with revenues in excess of $1bn are owned by founders or families in 2010. McKinsey forecast another 4,000 firms hitting the $1bn turnover figure, representing nearly 40 per cent of the world's large enterprises in 2025, up from approximately 15 per cent in 2010. Yet, the vast majority of family business oriented research focuses on developed economies. This limits a full understanding of family firms. The oldest independent family firm in the world is the Japanese Hoshi Ruyokan, which has remained in the Hoshi dynasty for 1,300 years. Forty-six generations of the family have owned and managed the business, which is a small inn that prides itself on the service it provides.

As western family businesses expand and move away from their entrepreneurial origins, they face governance and performance challenges. The founder may have a certain style of making decisions and running the business, which can work in the formative stages. However, problems can occur due to inadequate governance, poor talent management, and reluctant heirs. Both Marriott and Hilton Hotels found difficulties in ensuring that their business continues to operate as family-owned. The Portuguese government had to rescue Banco Espirito Santo, when the great-grandson of its founder resigned after financial improprieties. The Italian Fiat auto group run by the heirs of Gianni Agnelli, quickly went through five CEOs and three chairmen in two years. Only 30 per cent of family businesses last into the second generation; 12 per cent are viable into the third (Fernandez-Araoz, Iqbal, & Ritter, 2015a). The authors outline a three-phase disciplined succession process – discussion and commitment by the shareholders; candidate selection; integration and development of the successor. Yet, it is important not to lose the "family gravity," this being what makes them special (Fernandez-Araoz, Iqbal, & Ritter, 2015). Samsung created the role of "Chief Customer Officer" for the son of the boss, Lee Kun-hee. Another family member proposed a "family learning and development centre" to prepare the next generation of the Lee Family.

The Centre for Family Business at the University of St Gallen compiles in cooperation with EY Global Family Business Centre of Excellence the Global Family Index, the 500 largest family-owned companies in the world. Retail and wholesale companies make up 18 per cent, closely followed by diversified industrial products (17 per cent) and consumer products (15 per cent). The top three firms listed are Wal-Mart Stores (revenue US$476b); Volkswagen (US$261.6b); and Berkshire Hathaway (US$182.2b). The split between private and public sector is 48 per cent and 52 per cent respectively. With Europe accounting for 50 per cent and North America 24 per cent, emerging countries have a smaller impact than one might imagine.

State-owned enterprises

China: Investors in emerging markets have to consider their exposure to state enterprises, which are typically defined as companies that are wholly or partially owned or operated by a government. Traditionally such investors would feel that a state enterprise may have objectives beyond economic with its lower returns. In China the average return on assets for a SOE was nearly half (4.6 per cent) compared with private businesses (9.1 per cent).

State enterprises can be found in both public and private sectors, with a preponderance of public sectors operating in financial, energy, telecommunications and utilities. These sectors are crucial to economic development, so they attract the attention of governments. China's communist background led to state enterprises with the government holding sizeable investments in large institutions such as China Construction Bank, Bank of China, China Mobile, and Industrial and Commercial Bank of China Ltd. Although the current economic slowdown together with the privileged access to loans have led to calls for outright privatisation, such enterprises play a dominant role.

Another issue is whether SOEs will be allowed to fail, which occurred in the late 1990s. If weak SOEs are kept alive, in addition to bailouts they will require cheap credit. This issue has significant implications for global companies operating in emerging countries and would-be investors who need to decide how to invest/support in the Chinese economy. China has approximately 150,000 SOEs and a partial privatisation is required. The Chinese government wishes to pursue a mixed ownership in key sectors such as electricity, oil, gas, telecommunications, military equipment and civil aviation. The financing can include FDI via joint ventures, restructuring, mergers and acquisition and offshore financing.

Africa: Many African economies place SOEs at the centre of their development strategies. The 1990s were a period of privatisations and structural reform programmes. In some instances, SOEs are seen as a partial remedy to market failure and to remove some of the barriers to growth. The private sector can provide a further mechanism to fuel the financing of economic development, and provide two additional benefits. First, more effective SOEs enable governments to redirect monies previously used to subsidise SOEs to use in other essential purposes. Second, the involvement of the private sector can improve salient management activities. Balbuena (2014) concludes her review of state-owned enterprises in South Africa by reminding the reader that governments are the cornerstones of implementing an SOE reform. But in a South African context the broader issues of political governance require particular attention to ensure that proposed reforms are achievable within current political and resource constraints and matched to cultural and legal environment. Among African countries the stage of reform is variable with South Africa and Mozambique being relatively sophisticated.

7.5 Emerging market multinational corporations (EMNCs)

EMNCs pose significant threats to their developed counterparts. The earlier sections of this chapter explored several examples drawn from the BRICS and MINT economies. In recent years, EMNCs have been the focus of substantial attention from both academics and practitioner-oriented press.

1) Bimbo – Mexico (bimbobakeriesusa.com)

After entering the US market in 1996, Bimbo, a Mexican company, eventually challenged and overhauled the established Sara Lee in the bread business by looking for the Achilles heel of the market leader. Strategy execution and attention to operational detail positioned the Mexican upstart ahead of the dominant Sara Lee. By 2010, Bimbo announced that it had acquired the North American Fresh Bakery business of the Sara Lee Corporation. Bimbo's success could be attributed to buying US brands to gain scale, and then introducing its name through its buns and tortillas together with their cuddly bear symbol.

- Mission – Delicious and nutritious baked goods and snacks in the hands of all.
- Our vision – In 2020 we transform the baking industry and expand our global leadership to better serve more consumers.
- Our purpose – Building a sustainable, highly productive and deeply humane company
- Our beliefs – We value the person; we are one community; we compete to win; we act with integrity; we get results; we are sharp operators; we transcend and endure.

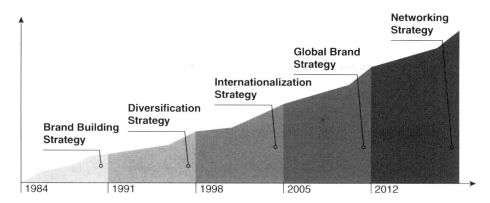

Figure 7.7 Haier strategy 1984–2012
Source: Haier. Available at http://www.haier.net/en/about_haier/haier_strategy/

2) Haier – China (Haier.net)

The Chinese appliance manufacturer Haier deployed a niche strategy focusing on college students looking for compact refrigerators. Since its origins in 1984, Haier has evolved through five stages: brand building strategy, diversification strategy, internationalisation strategy, global brand strategy, and network strategy.

Led by CEO and Board Chairman Zhang Ruimin, Haier enters Networking Strategy Stage in 2013. Lashed by the impact of the Internet traditional economic models are undertaking dramatic changes. Priority of Haier in the future is producing products to meet the personalised demands of the consumers.

3) Suzlon – India

In 1995, Suzlon operating as a textile firm got tired of high costs, and an erratic and inefficient electrical network. Mr Tuishi Tanti, the founder, looked into wind power as an alternative. Suzlon started to develop its own wind-power generators with no prior expertise and realised the enormous potential in the alternative energy market. The textile business was sold in 2001, and the business is now exclusively devoted to the development of wind farms.

Suzlon is now a leading wind turbine manufacturer with a global presence across 19 countries in six continents. The company's value system is "The foundation of our organisation is built on strong values that help us in achieving our vision. These values ensure that we stay true to everything we do."

7.6 Chapter summary

This chapter reiterates that organisations from emerging economies are gaining greater prominence in global business. Despite being latecomers to the international marketplace, emerging economy businesses are able not only to survive but also to prosper. The CEO should be aware of the dangers of grouping countries or cultures. Such an approach can be detrimental to the understanding of the economic situation of each country, and can affect

156 *Globalisation*

the development of long-term and solid business relationships. The chapter considers the changing world and uses the BRICS and MINT economies to illustrate these differences. The slowdown of the BRICS with Brazil and Russia in recession, China slowing down and India still of interest to global investors clearly demonstrates that growth is a short-term concept. While China still has tremendous economic power, its slowdown has affected the global economy. The MINTs are a more recent group of countries which possess large populations, and while there are opportunities many commentators are becoming disillusioned with MINTs too. They each have specific problems but political instability and slowing economic growth are prevalent.

The western world dominance of firms structured with a broad array of shareholders and its associated strategy theories is now being challenged. The presence of family firms and state-owned enterprises shows that strategy needs to be developed in these changing environments too. The chapter ends by showing a variety of successful EMNCs.

7.7 End of chapter self-reflection questions

1. Why did the BRICS, which all seem at one time to embody the economic dynamism, fail?
2. Do you think that the MINT countries will ultimately live up to the hype? What are the key issues which should be addressed?
3. Explain the salient difference between an EMNC and a western MNE?
4. What are the strengths and weaknesses of a state-owned enterprise? Can you illustrate your thoughts with some specific examples?
5. To what extent are emerging markets different from western ones? Justify your thoughts with some practical examples.

References

Balbuena, S. S. (2014). State-owned enterprises in Southern Africa. OECD Corporate Government Working Papers, No.13.

Björnberg, A., Elstrodt, H-P., & Vivek Pandit, V. (2014). The family-business factor in emerging markets. McKinsey Quarterly, December.

Crittenden, V. L., & Crittenden, W. F. (2010). Strategic management in emerging economies: A research agenda. *Organizations and Markets in Emerging Economies*, 1(1), 9–23.

Dobbs, R., Koller, T., & Ramaswamy, S. (2015). The big idea. *Harvard Business Review*, 93(10), 48.

Fernandez-Araoz, C., Iqbal, S., & Ritter, J. (2015). Leadership lessons from Great family businesses. *Harvard Business Review*, 96(4), 83–97.

Khanna, T., & Palepu, K. (2013). *Winning in emerging markets: A road map for strategy and execution.* Cambridge, MA: Harvard Business Press.

World Bank. (2014). *Turkey's transitions: Integration, inclusion, institutions.* Washington, DC: World Bank.

World Economic Forum. (2015). Global competitiveness report 2015–2016. Available at: http://reports.weforum.org/global-competitiveness-report-2015-2016/

Part 3
Contemporary themes

8 Strategic agility and design

8.1 Learning objectives

After completing this chapter you will:

- be able to gain a holistic appreciation of strategic agility and design
- be able to go behind problem areas in defining an effective strategy
- be able to further explore the concept of strategic agility and sense and respond models
- be able to cover and introduce many relevant areas associated with the important issue of organisational design
- be able to introduce novel conceptualisations like betapreneurship and management with meaning.

8.2 Introduction

This chapter dissects strategy problems and raises issues about corporate identity. It defines a number of orientations, roles and responsibilities. It also introduces the concept of strategic agility. A large element of the chapter is dedicated to organisational design. A new look at human resources management is brought in as well as betapreneurship and the need for disruption in the organisation. Sense and Respond Models are also covered as well as the emphasis on management with meaning.

8.3 Key academic theory

Stakeholder theory is a useful framework for analysing the behavioural aspects of the project management process, particularly the complicated process of project management. Projects can be beset by the agenda of various stakeholders within the organisational structure. When this occurs, the implementation of a strong project stakeholder management strategy is necessary to increase the likelihood of success. Stakeholder theory serves as the theoretical underpinning of a case analysis undertaken by Sutterfield, Friday-Stroud and Shivers-Blackwell (2006), which identifies the potential causes of project failure.

Project management lessons learned from the failure and a project stakeholder management strategy framework are presented to facilitate better decision making on the part of project managers to increase the likelihood of successful project management outcomes.

It has been found that strategic managers use very sophisticated tactics when implementing strategic plans but the downside to this is the indiscriminate way in which they use them, which can limit their effectiveness.

An organisational theory that claims there is no best way to organise a corporation or lead a company is bound by situational constraints, which include the manager's need for consultation and the ability to act where necessary; this theory was developed by Nutt (1989) in order to select valuable tactics used by practitioners. Fifty situations of strategic planning were tested: the success rate was 94 per cent when the recommended implementation tactic was enforced but only 29 per cent successful when other tactics were put in place. This suggests that implementing the framework will almost guarantee a higher success rate when implementing a strategic plan.

Disruptions in strategy usually require a business model update. However, as time goes by, efficient firms evolve their business models as a matter of course, resulting in increased stability but also creating rigidity. This can be resolved by implementing three meta-capabilities in order to resume some level of flexibility and agility within the business. These three necessary tools are resource fluidity, leadership unity and strategic sensitivity. Doz and Kosonen's article (2010) investigates the underlying factors and issues with these capabilities. Their detailed research involved a number of companies who were in the process of re-designing their business models. They suggested a number of solid leadership actions that would allow them to introduce the meta-capabilities that would have the ability to speed up the regeneration and renewal in order to transform the business models. The argument can be organised by stating the three main characteristics of the strategic agility framework which was mentioned in their earlier writings, and create comparable actions within leadership, all capable of further improving the quality and extent to which a company can renew their business models.

The sense and respond model of unpredictable, discontinuous change, the adaptive enterprise design, allows organisations to implement a new management tool, resulting in the achievement of competitive advantage, which is a stark incentive in any market where there is unpredictable, constant change. When trying to successfully implement the model a radically different form of governance is required, adaptive behaviour must become normal, and companies must be able to transform their business to conform to new information symbols. The important factor is that corporations must learn the new concept of governance, "context and co-ordination."

Huber (1990) lays out his theory showing the results that decision-aiding technology and computer-assisted communication have on the decision-making process, design of the organisation and the intelligence used by the organisation. There are many controversial areas covered in this theory that are in need of critical empirical investigation. Huber's article is based on the changes in organisational design that are directly related to technology where the timelines and quality enhance intelligence and decision making, as opposed to those that have a negative impact on the production of goods and services.

8.4 The problem with strategy – strategy as a wicked problem

Many corporations have superseded the annual top-down planning ritual, using macro-economics forecasts, with new, far more sophisticated processes. They organise planning meetings often, crunch huge amounts of consumer data and use competency modelling and other such techniques to develop strategy. This is an improvement based on the customer and is capability-focused, allowing organisations to change their strategies with ease, although they often still miss the mark.

Organisations have a knack of ignoring one critical issue: they are unable to develop more and more complex environments in which to successfully operate. The result of this is that enterprises cannot cope with issues that arise because the strategic planning processes are not equipped to deal with them. Many CEOs admit that they cannot resolve issues that arise simply by gathering additional data, defining issues and solving problems. The planning ideas do not produce new ideas. Wicked issues stand alone, because they cannot be defined within traditional processes. A wicked problem has countless causes, is difficult to define and does not come with only one correct answer. Wicked problems arise when companies have to deal with constant and unparalleled challenges. They occur in social contexts: the bigger the issues between stakeholders, the more the problem can be defined as wicked. The social complexities of wicked problems provide as many issues as the technical difficulties that arise, resulting in a situation where they are difficult to manage. Each solution thrown at a wicked problem is a one-shot effort, there is no opportunity for trial and error and so every solution matters hugely.

The problem arises with many stakeholders having many different values and priorities. A wicked problem arises without precedent, and previous knowledge and experience do not assist with each situation. Each wicked problem could be the result of an ordinary, self-contained problem mingled with the wicked effect, but these problems may not come from one source.

Companies must manage the strategic wickedness by involving stakeholders in growing and developing future outlines for new strategies. The intention should be to create a shared understanding of any problems and issues and use collaboration and joint commitment to resolve them. These situations can also be exploited to strengthen collective intelligence, reduce the force of the groupthink and cognitive bias and enable the group to tackle the problems in a more effective manner than individuals. The more stakeholders involved in the planning process adds complexity but generally increases the potential for creativity.

Companies are of the impression that customers and shareholders are critical stakeholders but employees are even more important. Their commitment and knowledge can often play a huge role in developing new innovative strategies.

8.5 Defining the corporate

When companies find themselves with wicked problems to deal with, they must try many strategies in order to adhere to the original sense of purpose. Mission statements lay the foundations of strategy but in such a fast-paced world as we are encountering now, the scope of activities, statement of purpose and concepts of the business may change much more frequently than at any time in the past. The company identity is usually a more enduring statement on intent.

Any organisation's identity consists of values, aspirations and competencies: What is important to the company? What does this company achieve better than other companies? How does this company measure its successes? For example, in 2007 Campbell Soup sold the Godiva business. This decision was not based on the financial performance of Godiva, as this is a profitable company supplying a premium chocolate brand; rather it was based on the fact that Campbell's values, aspirations and competencies are focused on simplicity of nutrition and Godiva chocolates simply do not fit in with that image.

The premium chocolate category was at the time experiencing strong growth and although Godiva was thriving within the market, it did not fit within Campbell's image of simple family meals. An agreement was reached and Godiva was sold to Yildiz Holdings for $850 million (see Figure 8.1). Sticking with its identity, rather than possible profit margins, Campbell sold Godiva quickly and effortlessly. In the current world of Newtonian order, where relationships

162 *Contemporary themes*

are clear between cause and effect, companies are in a position to judge what strategies they wish to pursue. In the wicked environment with complex possibilities, companies do not know if their strategies are appropriate or what consequences may come of them. It would be wise then to forget conventional options and instead experiment with a number of feasible strategies, even before it is clear what the outcome may be.

The "feed-forward" orientation

Planning systems are designed based on feedback, plans are compared with results and corrective actions are implemented as a result. Feedback is a powerful source of learning but has limited relevance in the wicked environment. Feedback allows companies to streamline their strategies whereas wicked problems demand that executives invent new and novel solutions.

Companies have already returned to the original business school model to find a way to address the emerging factors and changes; two factors have come to light as being critical if one expects future corporate success:

1) the speed necessary to adapt to threats and opportunities
2) an in-built flexibility to allow for speedy responses.

It is expected that the top performance indicators will remain unchanged but there will be a significant increase in others. There appears to be a major shift from quantitative to qualitative measures as performance indicators. After economic downturns the norm is for companies to concentrate on their core business. There is also a trend to swap to a more decentralised

---

Nearly half of all strategies fail broadly or simply don't deliver.

Figure 8.1 Reality #1

Some of the realities

The normal is that there is no normal any more. Business issues have shifted from discrete problems to holistic messes – requiring holistic, networked, collaborative approaches to resolve. We cannot use the past to predict the future (Moore's law now applies to our business environment). Creative disruption is becoming a constant.

Figure 8.2 Strategy today is gridlocked by a growing overload of strategic disruptors

---

- Flexible decentralised empowered networks within a structure of strategic intent
- Learning through immersive experiences, scenarios and rapid prototyping
- Acceptance of uncertainty with intuition as a valid contributor to clarity
- Strategic sense-making beyond operational problem-solving
- Uncoupling "winning" from the need for a solution
- Engagement with complexity

Figure 8.3 Dilemma management

organisation in order to connect and respond to customers in a quick and flexible way (see Figure 8.2). Where change is more prevalent and rapid, global innovation management is the key to success – particularly for companies trying to survive in a mature market. Future market leaders will need to have significant entrepreneurial skills and with that comes the agility to execute quick decision making – this is a critical factor as this skill has never been so important as it will be in the future (see Figure 8.3).

8.6 What is Agile?

- Manifested through practices
- Guided by principles
- Defined by values
- Mindset

Sense and respond systems

As most disruptive technologies have a huge impact on enterprise, the sense and respond system plays a critical role in lessening the impact this will have on companies in the foreseeable future. The data explosion will, no doubt, bring an added complication to the management of information for the majority of companies. As the volume of data and speed at which a company can function increase, the requirement for a response to take place instantaneously becomes much more critical. However, the act of moving forward in terms of performance and the cost of technology are making the achievement of this a real possibility, realising that the "sense and respond" pattern is becoming an achievable goal for many companies in many scenarios.

With data being so readily available we now have the ability to command and improve the outcome within the business venture. But there must be a link between the data and the insight to fully harness the potential of the outcome. This is a crucial first step to building a comprehensive sense and respond system. With the initial mapping complete, then advanced analytical technologies will define the sophistication level, accuracy and speed that would simply not have been possible before. The driving forces behind this requirement for sense and respond systems are as follows:

- *The capacity to gain an accurate understanding improves the company's standing and puts it in a more favourable position for those who can embrace it* – the potential to provide a never before known ability to create effectiveness and efficiency.
- *The need to make optimal and rapid decisions becomes vital* – in the coming decade the ability and requirement to make such decisions will allow the sense and respond action to show its true potential, delighting customers and closing deals.
- *The need for effectiveness in a complex value ecosystem* – as many ecosystems grow more complex, effectiveness is imperative for the operation to become a success. The overwhelming volume of data flowing through the ecosystems can complicate the operations with the agility and speed required to make it a success.
- *The growing demand for Agile enterprises* – the future operations will require speed and agility simply not found in traditional companies. Sense and respond systems will be introduced as a fundamental part of systems engagement for the future.
- *Actionable insight becomes a critical part* – for now, companies struggle to find actionable insight. Currently data is delivered in useful packages but these packages do not

always have the type of insight that action can be taken from. This harnessing of insight will become critical in the future, to drive the growth agenda and realise the potential to enable differentiation into the next generation through experiences.

- *Control real time data flows in order to improve insight and decision-making outcomes* – if the ability to tap into the internet and any relevant social ecosystem can be realised, these two are prime examples of real time data flow.
- *Expansion of the cycle of organisational activity* – a great number of companies delete or summarise the historical data on their analytical journey, collecting data from the past. The shift from previous to future requires a rapidity and insight and the ability to examine data autonomously, using sophisticated tools and business intelligence in order to discover deeper insights and make intuitive predictions in order to effectively and efficiently store large amounts of data.
- *Develop automated feedback control systems* – in the past it was assumed that there were certain jobs that only humans could do. As we now see, computers are taking over these tasks and the work is becoming automated as are the closed-loop systems. These systems have the ability to leverage insight and knowledge to automate the action required. Sense and respond systems can be shown as automated close-loop systems.
- *Instrument* – sense and respond will be greatly enhanced with the Internet of Things. The use of instruments and sensors will allow companies to engage in immediate access to data that can then be usefully relied upon to produce the required results. Companies should seek to enable the mechanism to allow access and benefit.
- *Elimination of data silos* – the current pace of technology has required companies to use organisational and data silos. Sense and respond can effectively respond to this belief that all parts of the data are intimately connected and explicable only by reference to the whole. A key tactic in a sense and respond programme is to eliminate these silos.

Making the entrepreneurial dream a profitable reality

Creative entrepreneurs often struggle with the concept of turning their idea into a profitable business concept. These creative minds are brilliant at inventing the concepts that have the ability to transform the market, but all too often the missing link in this process is the business or strategic mind to embrace and follow through on the idea to create a profitable business.

There has been a rise recently in what has been called "Betapreneurs" (Beta – interactively adapting and constantly changing). Betapreneurs are known for spreading their knowledge base and skills over many projects and initiatives rather than just one goal. Obviously, not all their ideas will be successful, but the concept is that there will be more flexibility and fewer overheads at the start-up and continuation of these projects.

Agile mindset: controlling the chaos

In recent times a large number of organisations have introduced the use of "Agile" practices to deliver their technology solutions. Agile has adapted and grown over the years, starting as a software development, and now being used in a wide range of projects in many organisational environments. Agile is primarily used based on the principles of reducing risk and delivering value to a project. But the incremental and iterative approach can create many challenges to managers and is often misunderstood.

At face value, Agile can be a daunting prospect as it disregards the traditional project management steps, which follow a linear design process from start to finish and leaves very

Strategic agility and design 165

- Compass Metric
- Strategic Iteration
- Self-Organised Learning Environments (SOLE)
- Connected Collaboration
- "Radical Management" – Steven Denning
- People Agility, Change Agility, Results Agility

Figure 8.4 And... some new terms emerging

little adjustment to the path that it follows. Agile repeats cycles of a project, repeating the parts of a project in smaller sections. Agile takes steps forward in the project and pauses to check the small amount completed has been correctly managed and delivered and fixes any issues there and then, and then proceeds to the next step. This can sometimes feel like chaos.

The Agile way of working presents many opportunities and challenges to change managers, business leaders and the end user, in fact anyone who is used to working with a more traditional method. Agile works successfully when the key project people can adapt and effectively proceed with an unpredictable, wild ride.

Agile is not a concept that can be adopted half-heartedly. It is about "being" agile, not "adopting" agile. The project has to be completely immersed in "agile" to have any chance of being a success.

Many organisations have, in the past, tried to adopt an agile practice in isolation. These companies struggle to grasp the concept correctly and can end up looking for amendments at the wrong points in the process, and while trying to make an effective contribution, they can miss out on crucial flexible approaches made available to them through the market conditions necessary for a modern business.

The agile mindset leads to cultural changes in any business when properly adopted though the processes and practices (see Figure 8.4).

8.7 The lost art of organisational design

The topic of effective organisational design goes far beyond disciplinary lines. This means it is not taught effectively in business schools. And this leads to a lack of decent research in the area, which means that nobody in any organisation dares to touch it, except top managers. You need to understand business models in order to design an effective organisation – this includes leadership, accounting, information technology, organisational behaviour and business models.

Over the past few years thought leaders and writers have created a huge number of buzzwords to help managers freshen the think-tank of an organisation. There is constant talk of networked organisations, virtual organisations, learning, boundary-less, wiki and starfish organisations, to name but a few.

But reading these works results in frustration. The vast majority of writings on this subject are limited to certain types of organisations, or utopian society; it can be shallow, in that the advice offered has no theoretical underpinning. Those who write about the utopia generally balk at the rigidity of the nature of hierarchy and enthusiastically praise the virtues of "organisations with no structure." The networks, self-organising work and empowered employees, according to them, will amazingly dispel command-and-control organisations. Another range of books and related articles offer design choices and list detailed pros and cons. But again these analyses are largely unfulfilling. Statements of Considerations and trade-offs do not manage to provide any sense of direction. When the chapter is finished there is no clear path for an organisation to take; there may be plenty of choices, but no explanation for the decision and no theoretical underpinning is available.

Considerations for organisational design

Organisational design is not valued or important in itself but is useful in achieving an aim. And that aim is to create and sustain an organisation that is capable of achieving long-term success in a complex and dynamic world.

It is important to remember the following:

- There is more to an organisation that just its design – you need to create a cohesive whole, including values, leadership and processes in order to bring the design to life.
- There is no clear and single correct design for an organisation, but it is advantageous for any design process to be based on strong design principles.
- Organisational design is a constantly evolving, repetitive process. This can be confusing if the principles are not set out clearly and assumptions are not explicitly laid out.
- This initial design may not last long, as you venture further into the project you will learn more about different design options and that learning curves are inevitable.

What is the benefit of finding another way to build and govern organisations? By dividing an organisation into functions, departments and sub-sections, you are actually hindering work-flow, building territories and driving out new initiatives and entrepreneurial thinking, however, this is exactly what companies have done for years.

Companies today are hung up on Tayloristic thinking and assume divisions between functions is the best way to work. Taylor's plan of separating execution from thinking, assuming that those who co-ordinate and control should be located in a different location from where the actual work is carried out, have created phenomenal misalignment with today's success factors.

However, the alternative has not been that clear either, until recent times. The knowledge of how to inspire Tayloristic organisations to change into post-Tayloristic organisations has been scarce. If the current standard is to be left behind due to obsolete thinking, two things need to change. There need to be new systemic models and new mental models. These need to be built strong enough to govern in the twenty-first century and be robust enough to transform organisations through this.

The fundamental problem is not that people are not smart enough to work with the accelerated dynamics that we see today but simply that the organisations are not designed to work with the capabilities of the humans who work within them. The Tayloristic model cannot cope these days and organisations who insist on persevering with this, are, quite simply, doomed to failure.

Visualising alternative organisations – as seen by Henry Mintzberg

Organisations as "pyramids and chains"

- Process chains within the hierarchy can strengthen the vertical chain.
- This layout can sustain the centralisation and support the management.

Organisations as "hubs"

- Hubs are the point of focus: it is the hub that attracts and moves people.
- The hub is less interested or focused on sequential activities, it mostly concentrates on its own purpose.

Organisations as "networks"

- Some organisations do not have a focal point or "centre."
- These organisations use free interaction and work in any direction via collaborative relationships.
- This type of organisation does not follow a standard structure but does apply other rules in order to function successfully.
- This organisation is not necessarily focused on specific activities or managers.

What can an organisation expect to accomplish when putting this into practice?

Semco's Survival Manual is a prime example of what can be accomplished. This is the company's sole set of principles, and claims that "Semco does not use a formal organisational chart. Only the respect of others turns someone into a leader. When it is absolutely necessary to sketch the structure of some part of the company, we always do it in pencil and dispense with it as soon as possible."

Other Betacodex pioneers, Handelsbanken and Guardian Industries, also do not have a standard organisational chart, and work with only three levels of hierarchy. As these companies have stated, hierarchy doesn't matter and three levels is enough, regardless of the size of the company.

Typical phases within an organisational evolution: according to systems thinking

Organisations have much in common with living organisms, according to cybernetics. Just as organisms evolve throughout the different stages with their lives, organisations evolve, change and adapt during their existence.

In most cases, organisations begin with a small cohort of people. This is the "pioneering phase" in which the company relies on entrepreneurial skills, autonomy, informality and decision-making. This pioneer stage appears chaotic.

However, these skills in abundance are what make the organisation thrive and grow, sometimes at an incredibly rapid rate. As this happens, new rules and tasks arise. There is a need to become more professional, employ more specialists, design a more formal structure, standardise systems and processes and plan for the future. This is the "differentiation stage." It is basically conforming and designing. The hierarchy, departmentalisation and functions are created and defined. The decision-making appears more streamlined and centralised and most importantly the rules of the organisation replace the improvisation and freedom of the early days. This may be much less stressful for many as order takes over from the initial chaos, but it does show a maturing phase that loses the impetuousness of quick, almost frantic, decision making of the early days which some thrive on and find the most "fun" in.

This happens over again with organisations and from there many organisations find themselves forever more in the Tayloristic paradigm. Very few organisations ever make it to the other side and come out into what is known as the "integration phase." This integration relies on a company having the ability to apply the thinking that turns a large organisation into smaller integrated mini-companies that can apply independence and decision making of their own.

8.8 Ways to empower the organisation

Hierarchical organisation charts disguise the view that employees take orders from "the boss" or the hierarchy. Hierarchies have a way of making you think that each employee looks "up" to the boss. It does not encourage a stance of looking "out" to the future. This limits the potential of any company or organisation to serve the market (see Figure 8.5).

Visionary organisations, however, make far better use of the pull from the outside to energise, organise and stabilise their adaptive network of cells. That way, these organisations are mastering the art of using the differing interests of the market forces such as investors, legislation and customers to arrange and manage their network of cells.

There are, of course, different ways to organise for empowerment and these differing typologies can and do exist in combinations.

- Profit centre networks
- Cross-organisational value creation networking between independent cells
- Project orientated or multi-project organisations with established project teams and temporary centres instead of the standard permanent profit centres.

Creating and integrating a cell structure design is imperative to the success of the organisation. Building an organisation without command and control and little to no hierarchy, is virtually impossible.

Key learnings with a Brazilian packaging company

- The concept of "shifts as teams," the previously predominant way, would be completely abolished within the plant in favour of newly created production cells which would be formed around the existing production lines. This would result in no more shift leadership staff.
- Previously almost half the employees would have spent their time working in support functions such as internal logistics, maintenance and quality. These teams would be dissolved and the staff would be integrated into mini-plant teams. With the exception of the plant managers, all staff including previous supervisors would need to become team members within the cells, depending on their areas of expertise and preferences.
- Salaries would remain unchanged but job titles would change or be completely abolished depending on the severity of the changes.
- Each mini-plant would take on sole responsibility for its business including maintenance, staffing, quality, planning and production. They would be empowered to self-manage, acquiring the necessary services from their surrounding support services. They would also be expected to challenge support teams for continuous improvement. They may elect a spokesperson and have direct contact with the plant manager for progress reports.
- The mini-plant must be able to support and organise its own workload, instead of the old regime where they were managed by their supervisors. In order to accomplish this successfully, a new strategy would need to be invented to display client orders, shift-changing performance and cell co-ordination in order to alleviate any conflict that may arise from these changes.

```
Companies talk about

• Growth
• Profit
• Shareholder value
• Customers

Individuals talk about

• Their own personal needs
• Their families and friends
• Their community
• The world they live in
• Emotion...
```

Figure 8.5 Companies vs. individuals

Mini case study

In 2014, the *Wall Street Journal* reported that companies were beginning to move away from the traditional HR department.

At times it can feel like the HR department is a burden, but living without one can have major challenges too.

LRN Corp. restructured a number of years back. This is a company that advised and helped companies to develop ethics and compliance programmes. Through this process the 250-employee business formally put an end to current department names and job titles. They also abolished their human resource department.

"We wanted to force the people issues into the middle of the business," said David Greenberg, Los Angeles-based LRN's executive vice president.

If a company decides to implement a flat management structure and distribute more accountability to their employees they often find themselves taking aim at human resources. Executives claim that an HR department suffocates innovation and hampers development with their ineffective and inefficient processes and policies. Meanwhile a thriving HR software industry has allowed the automation or outsourcing of the HR department and its related functions of recruitment and payroll to become simpler than ever.

Some employees find the lack of an HR department impacts how the company is run, especially with the basic HR roles such as pay issues or employee disputes. LRN and other companies say they are learning as they go.

The 11-year old landscaping company, Ruppert Landscape Inc., an SME with 900 employees, has never created an HR department. Instead, managers are tasked with renewing contracts, training new employees and hunting down graduate talent, all the while ensuring that clients' requirements are met.

CEO Craig Ruppert advised that a decentralised structure encourages accountability and autonomy among leaders in the company, which is based in Laytonsville, MD, and supplies to markets from Atlanta to Philadelphia. He estimates that his managers spend around 5 per cent of their time on human resource related matters.

"I just have a hard time understanding how somebody in an office two or four states away can do a better job solving an employee problem than someone who has a vested interest in the employee," Mr Rupper said.

Interpersonal issues or problems must be handled and resolved differently when there is no HR to mediate. The Toronto-based marketing agency, Klick Health, which focuses on health care, has disbanded their human resources department and implemented two "concierges." They now rely on employees with customer services experience who have been given the job of creating what CEO Leerom Segal calls a "frictionless" work experience for employees.

For the concierges, this means a range of chores requiring anything from career-development to mentoring sessions.

When team members dislike each other or managers don't gel with their employees, the expectation is that they will figure it out without Mr Segal's intervention. "We ask senior leaders to recognise any potential chemistry issues early on," he said, "and move people to different teams if those issues can't be resolved quickly."

8.9 It is time to move away from the traditional human resource department

Most people can recount a horror story about their HR department. They are considered at best a "necessary evil" and at worst a dark malevolent force which uses red tape and outdated, nonsensical rules to prevent progress and curb change.

Times are changing: what organisations need for human resource departments in the twenty-first century

The current and historic role of a human resources department is to make companies grow by finding the right people for their jobs. There has been little change to this role since its inception back in the nineteenth century when the primary purpose was to protect women and girls in the industrial environments in which they found themselves for the first time. The department has since evolved into other areas including recruitment, attendance and compensation. Training, organisational behaviour and selection assessment were introduced in the late 1960s and over the last decades the title has mostly changed from Personnel to Human Resources, with little impact.

It is normal practice these days for business leaders to describe the HR department as uncreative, reactive and ignorant of the basic business protocols. This is based on the perception that HR departments spend their time measuring and focusing on projects or incentives that add nothing to the value of their organisation.

An HR department that wastes its time focusing on simple projects that have no value for the rest of the company does not in any way help an organisation increase its profits or expand its operation. Despite this, many HR departments relentlessly pursue these ridiculous goals in order to have something productive to report on at leadership meetings.

Despite efforts to improve its reputation as a trustworthy pocket in an organisation, the introduction of the HR Business Partner title has not proved that HR is anything more than a cost centre. The problem lies with the lack of hands-on business experience. To add to their issues, some HR departments are plagued with inaccuracies in their data, leading to a rather inconsequential side-step for the beleaguered department rather than any significant or appropriate move forward.

True business partners

If HR professionals want to be seen as true business partners then they must portray themselves as a business person who specialises in HR and not an HR professional who can advise in business. It would be advisable for such an individual to complete a secondment in a business unit to achieve the required perspective and training.

A successful HR business partner must grasp the concept of business and how it works to be able to hold their own in the business world and talk competently about the subject. If this skill is mastered you can earn your seat at the table, once you prove your worth with measured and proven impact. This will also come with the trust and respect of your leaders.

HR needs to focus on the following six critical areas in order to make an impact on today's economy:

Align and design organisational purpose

The majority of organisations plough on without any clear purpose, despite the evidence proving how important this is. To date, many companies still cannot state their purpose and why they continue to exist. Most employees consider their wages as their main reason to work for the organisation.

Recruit for excellence

The most disappointing thing is to interview for a company that seems to represent your values, but fails once you become an employee. Misperceptions and false marketing are the main reasons that employee/company relationships fail. An Employee Value Proposition (EVP) showing the values and culture of the organisation should be created and instilled in the organisation in order to prove your worth. If employees are not revelling in the EVP then you could find yourself misleading prospective candidates.

Every organisation should hire employees who are passionate about the aims of the company. What you portray to your candidates will shape their experience and reflect what kind of organisation you want them to think they are coming to. When you project enthusiasm and positivity in the interview stages you are more likely to get employees who understand what the company stands for and show the same passion and commitment.

The creation of organisational alignment

It has been known for some departments such as HR and other service providers to celebrate certain achievements and objectives even when the company is failing. While supporting and encouraging successes in the workplace is to be commended for building morale, it is ridiculous to expect small achievements to be celebrated if overall success is not assured.

In order to build and sustain a successful organisation, a team effort is required across the board. All areas must be achieving goals and targets. This is not to say that some departments cannot work harder or shine brighter at certain times, but as a whole, those high-performing departments must also look to the poorer performers in times of need to sustain success overall.

The entire workforce must think "organisation first" throughout all processes and objectives. The organisation has to be supported all the way, by each and every employee. Incorporating reward and recognition schemes, for long- and short-term goals, will tie employees to the organisation's mission and purpose and will help merge the entire organisation cohesively.

Ensure measurement of the important things

Good measurements are essential to the success of the organisation. How can you improve your organisation without controlling and understanding any improvements made, based on implementing controlled measures?

There are a few important questions that need to be answered in order for each department to understand if they are measuring effectively:

172 *Contemporary themes*

- Are our customers, business and employees happy?
- Are we contributing successfully from every level of the organisation?
- Are we managing our effectiveness and impact?
- Is the measured information helping to improve our success as an organisation?

Now is the time for HR to evolve in order to provide better service to any successful organisations for generations to come. The organisations that adapt and introduce the new agenda will prosper by attracting the best talent. Those that are not willing or able to make the change may suffer.

All innovation is divergent

Companies required to, or aspiring to, enhance their innovation must develop new skills on top of the already present flow of convergent, implementation projects. These skills must be connected to their pre-project networking, development model pluralism and project convergence.

1) Mechanisms of transition must be refined from divergent technical ideas to actual focused projects.
2) They must create space for individual creativity to flourish, and there must be a mechanism to allow networking idea exploration.
3) Finally, it should be emphasised that the need to build knowledge around time-focused projects must be managed and adapted to the level of innovation and technological complexities.

Preconditions for innovation require personal perseverance and divergent idea generation

Ideas that have new functions, products and solutions are the essential starting point for any innovative development. These require nurturing by their innovators before any formal project can be established. The term "innovator" refers to researchers or developers in a certain field who are consistently generating proposals and designs and are therefore more advanced than inventors. This title is understood to be used for a unique technical invention with very little practical use.

For innovators to thrive and become successful it is of paramount importance that their managers defend their ideas and technical solutions against cost-cutting measures or conservatism.

8.10 Betapreneurship means seeing failure as a learning curve

One of the good points about betapreneurship is the empowering nature it encourages in people and businesses to implement change by embracing the collaboration and adopting the "redesign and rethink" culture.

It is imperative that this positive thinking is uppermost in purpose-driven organisations. 3M introduced its 15 per cent "time to think" programme, and because of such a scheme many great innovations and initiatives have been produced. Google's 20% programme invited in-house entrepreneurial thinking and encourages this type of collaboration.

It is critical for organisations to encourage disruptive innovation to thrive, because it is the people-led alliances that will fuel the drive of successful organisations in the future.

Strategy nugget

"Betapreneurship" promotes growth

It has become clear as we venture further into the twenty-first century that fresh approaches are urgently needed in order to speed up and stabilise sustainable global economic growth and advance human welfare through job creation. As such, there needs to be a way to stimulate innovation from an early stage, and foster a culture of entrepreneurship.

Cultivating entrepreneurship

Creative learning needs to come from a process of trial and error – this is the critical part of learning how to be a successful betapreneur, this is how betapreneurs operate.

Innovation is not solely applied for start-ups. Large companies encourage new ideas by employing "intrepreneurs" (entrepreneurs who work within the company) in order to not only compete but to stay ahead of the pack when it comes to new ideas and innovations.

Google's 20% programme encourages an entrepreneurial environment by allowing employees to work on their own chosen projects one day a week. It is, therefore, not surprising that they are in receipt of over 1,000 job applications per day. This is also noted in their interest and investment in a wide variety of start-ups, including Facebook in 2007.

Innovation is key

The entire Finnish economy suffered when Nokia's problems started. The outcome for Nokia was clear, innovation was the key to turning things around. The Finnish government then created Alto University to devise a way of integrating engineering with creativity. This resulted in the business accelerator "start-up sauna" which was founded in 2010 by a group of students inspired after visiting MIT (Massachusetts Institute of Technology).

The sauna's unique environment provides a work space, offers networking opportunities, entrepreneurial coaching and in general acts as a catalystic platform for new innovations and inspirational start-up ideas. There is the opportunity to take part in global study trips in order to stimulate entrepreneurship, proving that funding is not the only requirement but that we are required to shift mindsets. There is also an emergence of empathy – not just a need to make money but a desire to battle social challenges and find satisfactory solutions.

Disrupt your organisation

Leading brands are well aware of the value of causing a disturbance in their sector before having disruption forced upon them. The survival of a company depends on its entrepreneurial teaching and creativity and its ability to innovate through teaching, creating thriving new companies instead of relying on current providers.

It is critical that SMEs understand the need to adjust and acclimatise to the disruption that technology brings. At the beginning of the process, an idea, an innovation that may sound completely ridiculous can end up making excellent business sense. Failures will always be a part of finding the road to success, and betapreneurs are fully aware that the disruption they may cause within the organisation, along with their ideas and innovations, will initially be met with ridicule and contempt, followed by blank refusal, and even violent opposition, but perseverance will bring acceptance when the case has been investigated and proved to be worthwhile.

Ensuring people are given what they actually want

Gap analysis is a simple way to make sure people are actually getting what they want, the need to find a company who can supply something for the people who are looking for it. Many times creative entrepreneurs struggle with the ability to provide the "idea" with a reality and create a profitable business out of it. Often the missing link appears once the creative idea has been conceived but there is no strategy or business to implement it.

Connecting people with their wish list

A nicer way to see creative entrepreneurship being a profitable entity is to use gap analysis to connect people with what they want and deliver precisely that product to them.

"Betapreneurs"

Betapreneurship is carving a new path to investments. Where it was previously accepted that companies would look for venture capitalists to part with huge sums of money to back a project, betapreneurs allow a large number of small investments to be made, making up the same total but creating a lot less risk for the investor. With this strategy many more small projects can be undertaken and run alongside each other with minimal cost involvement. The more ideas and initiatives on the go at one time will result in more being tried and tested in the market place. This trend can grow freely, especially if financial markets remain relatively unstable and investment budgets are hard to come by.

A more pleasant way to analyse creative entrepreneurship is by simple gap analysis. Connect people with what they really want. Look to find a niche in the market and partner up with a company that can supply the desired concept and deliver to the end. Although it sounds simple enough, providing people with something they want or didn't know they needed, advertising agencies and management consultants spend huge amounts of time and effort trying to find solutions to these problems. What they are missing is on-the-ground insight. They should not rely on "user research" but base their work on actual experiences. Trendy agencies have a hold on the market but the needs and opportunities for young dynamic and creative entrepreneurs are greater, as they are where the new insight is found!

Creating the connector

The advice given to cultural and creative entrepreneurs is simple – find a business partner who excels in strategy and apply the beta concept, embrace your projects the beta way. Look at the links and try to envisage being the connection between people and projects. You may have the experience, skillset or knowledge that bigger companies don't yet have. Take your ideas and make them concepts, they will continue to grow and develop as long as you have a customer base.

Betapreneurship – Europe

The EU now acknowledges entrepreneurship as a career in order to encourage start-up companies to contribute and create innovation in the European job markets. Betapreneurs are the future of the twenty-first century, the professionals who create the process of experimenting with various methods of doing something until the best possible scenario is found to be most successful and then follow through to make innovation successful. Self-reliance and resilience are paramount in this while the company endeavours to craft the future. As things stand right now, only 30 per cent of Europe's entrepreneurs are women, but the prediction is that by 2020 two thirds of graduates will be female and this will obviously change the face of entrepreneurship.

8.11 Meaningful management

Management matters, the decisions that are made by any management, whether good or bad, affect most people attached to any company or employer. Management is an essential part of life – without it nothing would be achieved and so management determines quality of life for most people in society.

If the management is not efficient and effective then most people will be miserable for most of their working lives, but this doesn't just affect the employees, it can affect anyone who has any contact with this company. If management is right for its time and works well, most people will live fulfilled lives.

Currently, we mostly suffer from management that is wrong for its time. The management that we have now is dysfunctional. For far too long, people have just assumed that this situation is "the way things are done" and this will continue, no matter what. The current approach to management is aimed at making money and is seen as the only viable modus operandi. This is fact, as any efforts to improve management never result in any permanent improvements.

Redesign is essential

As things currently stand, any effort to improve and restructure management fails, because management is suffering from a dysfunction, not a malfunction. Repairing a malfunction can cause things to get back on track and improve the function of the organisation. A dysfunctional organisation is beyond this, repair is not the answer, and a more radical change is required.

What is required is not "better" management of the same type but quite simply a different style of management. The good news is, we now know what makes up this different management. It comprises of different ways of organisation, different goals, different values and ways of communicating. It is better not only for employees and employers but for all concerned with the prosperity of the company, including the shareholders and in fact the organisation itself. Companies who operate in such a manner are phenomenally profitable.

A great awakening

Implementing change in any management style requires a great awakening. Are the leaders and managers today ready for such a huge step? Do they have it in them to recondition themselves to think differently and introduce the paradigm shifts necessary for actual change to occur? Do they have the foresight to envisage the prosperity that results from such a monumental change?

People all over the world are beginning to wake up to the realisation of this, not better management, but different management. People are realising that maybe the way things have always been, the way they have always been *told* it has been, is not necessarily the way it has to be. There is more to this, another way, a tried and tested way, readily available to them if they can just make the adjustments. There is a glimpse of recognition and a growing realisation that traditional management does not have all the answers and we can simply liberate ourselves by doing things differently.

The emerging process of societal change has played a huge part in the shift in management, where the structures we currently live with can be improved and enhanced in order to improve and enhance our lives.

Strategy nugget

Meaningful Managing

In considering Steve Jobs' management skills you may come to the conclusion that he is a bit of an anomaly. The leadership style he adopted could be admired or criticised, but never replicated. There is no framework that fits him: orthodox management and Steve Jobs were polar opposites.

Theories on institutional management have always focused on his style because he was exceptional at planning and directing the specific area that has been unclear to management: creating meaning for both employees and customers.

People were at the centre of Steve Job's ideology. This does not mean he gave in to demands nor does it suggest he created a fun environment where ideas started at the bottom and worked their way up. His approach was not to listen to users' suggestions but to propose his ideas to them. Jobs' leadership style was an often harsh, top-down approach. He was often the protagonist at his own product launches.

"Managing by meaning" is understanding the human element, the emotional, rational or cultural dimension that makes up humanity and it is those qualities that make Apple so unique. When you create a meaning for people to embrace they appreciate it. It is widely known that people do not buy Apple products purely for their functionality or utility; we can even look past certain limiting factors within each Apple product, yet embrace the identity and design. The important factor for Jobs was not simply designing something beautiful but also creating new meaning for his customers.

Jobs had a way to incentivise and add meaning to his workers. It is a well-known fact that Apple's employees were encouraged to work hard to meet deadlines for visionary projects, the end result being the satisfaction of Jobs himself. There was a fanatical drive, a sense of mission. Apple proved their worth by being the company that enhanced and improved people's lives, they left their mark because they were bold and strove to "think different."

Academics and experts come to the conclusion that this approach was purely down to Steve Jobs' unique personality. He fitted the role of "guru" so well and was an exemplary role model. He found such prolific success because institutional management has its roots firmly in social sciences, analytics and engineering. While Jobs showed that he did not consider these unworthy, he attached more meaning to certain other unfathomable areas such as humanity and culture, an area that business schools cannot claim to have mastered.

8.12 Chapter summary

This chapter has as its main remit the coverage of key issues and concepts like the failure of strategy and strategic plans, corporate identity, the new normal environment, strategic agility, organisational design and new corporate formats, organisational disruption, the new role of people management, betapreneurship, sense and respond models, systems thinking, strategic experimentation, strategic cadence and management with meaning.

8.13 End of chapter self-reflection questions

1. Comment on the reasons behind the failure of strategic plans.
2. Apart from the content of this chapter, what other attributes do you think are fundamental to triggering a level of strategic ability?
3. Discuss new formats of organisational design that we anticipate as being prominent in the future.
4. Dissect and analyse the concept of betapreneurship.
5. What attributes of Steve Jobs management style made Apple such as a success?

References

Denning, S. (2011). Busting bureaucracy with radical management, *Management Innovation Exchange*. Available at: http://www.managementexchange.com/blog/busting-bureaucracy-radical-management

Doz, Y. L., & Kosonen, M. (2010). Embedding strategic agility: A leadership agenda for accelerating business model renewal. *Long Range Planning, 43*(2–3), 370–382.

Huber, G. P. (1990). A theory of the effects of advanced information technologies on organizational design, intelligence, and decision making. *Academic Management Review, 15*(1), 47–71.

Mintzberg, H. (1994). The fall and rise of strategic planning. *Harvard Business Review*. Available at: https://hbr.org/1994/01/the-fall-and-rise-of-strategic-planning

Nutt, P. C. (1989). Selecting tactics to implement strategic plans. *Strategic Management Journal, 10*(2), 145–161.

Sutterfield, J. S., Friday-Stroud, S., & Shivers-Blackwell, S. L. (2006). A case study of project and stakeholder management failures: Lessons Learned. *Project Management Journal, 37*(5), 26–35.

Verganti, R. (2011). Steve Jobs and management by meaning. *Harvard Business Review*. Available at: https://hbr.org/2011/10/steve-jobs-and-management-by-m

9 Business ethics

9.1 Learning objectives

After completing this chapter you will:

- appreciate the influence of ethics on business and society
- be able to consider the dilemma of ethical behaviour
- appreciate the trends in ethics
- understand some key issues of ethical decision-making
- understand what is meant by the term ethical value.

9.2 Introduction

Business ethics now shapes leadership behaviour and corporate culture. Adopting ethical practices can enhance trustworthiness among stakeholders. To illustrate this point, the Institute of Business Ethics (2016) refers to 96 per cent of FTSE-listed companies deploying a code of ethics. CEOs appear to be driving down the business ethics mindset deep into their organisations with changes being made to organisational structure and processes. But CEOs ought to be aware of any public perception of greenwashing. Mechanisms such as hotels who stress their green credentials by allowing guests to sleep on the same sheets and reuse towels, but then do very little to save energy and water, are now quickly seen as a story with no sincerity. Energy companies too are often guilty of using the term "green technology," which attempts to overcome unethical aspects of their business, such as oil spills. Any efforts to

- Rethinking values in the post-crisis world.
- Companies must have conscience.
- Companies being corporate citizens have a moral imperative.
- No justification for "immoral actions".
- Teleological approach creates more problems than it solves.
- Money matters less, what you do with it matters more!

Figure 9.1 Ethics

acquire values rather than solely being results-driven ought to be prioritised. Ethics requires a basic change in values and conscience (see Figure 9.1).

Ethical behaviour is increasingly important to organisational success in today's business environment, but the quantitative assessment of a qualitative process raises a number of appropriate questions. Can it really be done? We have witnessed CEOs asking this question, as well as: How does my company demonstrate the value that ethics provides? CEOs know that it is something that they should do (increasing numbers of stakeholders demand it), but they have a paucity of readily available tools to measure it (the value) meaningfully. This chapter will explore this fascinating dilemma, and will consider the opportunities of corporate social performance. Admittedly, it is not possible to evaluate social accountability as easily as financial performance. The different approaches in measuring corporate social performance will be briefly explored from the perspectives both of academics and practitioners.

We can end this introduction in a positive manner, by considering the shift in consciousness with some organisations such as Kingfisher, with its net positive strategy. In its annual report Kingfisher, a UK home improvement company with 1,000 stores and growing omnichannel operations across 10 European countries, revealed its goal to be a truly sustainable company. Management have set themselves 53 targets to help them get there. The targets include: innovation; energy; timber; communities; people; suppliers and partners; environment. There are currently more than 1,100 B-corp businesses in 37 countries, the majority being small and privately owned. B-corps are for-profit companies that seek to meet rigorous standards of social and environmental performance, accountability and transparency. The Brazilian fragrance and toiletries maker, Natura, became the largest and first plc to gain B-corp sustainability certification.

Strategy nugget

Ethical value

Business people ought to take the moral high road, as ethical behaviour has proven to be profitable in the long run. But as the business landscape continues to change, what are the implications for ethical value? The CEO together with members of the management team and colleagues need to drive the process of protecting, nurturing and enhancing ethical value. How should this be performed? What experiences have organisations learned from their ethics and compliance journey?

How do we measure ethical value? Can it truly be measured? Rates of return can be measured, however CSR measures are difficult. The ultimate answer is to have a balanced approach.

The FTSE4Good Index measures against standards (PartyGaming is a member, which in itself is an interesting issue) and ethical indices in use (a 2010 study by SustainAbility identified 108 tools and a 2013 report by Corporate Citizenship identified more than 250 global and local schemes).

Corporate social performance

Keeping track of the good that the private sector delivers to communities, employees and consumers is a laudable goal. Conceptually, the metric of corporate social performance can measure this good. But, as previously highlighted, it is not possible to evaluate social accountability as easily as financial performance. How does a manager rate an organisation as a good corporate citizen?

The attributes of corporate social performance (CSP) are such that institutional investors and customers can compare firms' performances, which would provide a move towards a more socially conscious market. Early proclaimers were of the opinion that any investments in CSR would lead to costs being greater than social benefits. Nevertheless, to provide a coherent view of a firm's social performance, it is just as important to monitor its activities as the financial consequences resulting from them. These outcomes impact stakeholders, who have not been focused on sufficiently in past research. It is crucial to find a consistent basis to measure CSP in order to advance academic studies as well as provide a guideline for business to monitor ethical progress.

There are currently two main approaches to measure CSP (Wood, 2010). One is normative, which is to say that it includes a predisposition of the ideal ethical behaviour for a business, while the other is a structural framework geared towards documenting different aspects of CSP. Normative CSP is often considered more philosophical. The model by Carroll (1979), for example, presents first and foremost a "should be" approach to discretionary, ethical, legal and economic responsibility. Wood (2010) criticises this framework for its focus on the manager's perspective. It does not incorporate research about the relationship of business and society. The consequences of corporate actions are crucial to evaluate social performance beyond mere policies.

While such a theoretical concept allows a better understanding of CSP and its processes, it does not give concrete ways to measure ethical behaviour in a manner that is relevant in a corporate context. When analysing different studies in approaching CSP, Beurden and Gössling (2008) have identified three main categories through which performance is assessed: Social disclosure, corporate action and corporate reputation. Disclosure can be evaluated through public content analysis, however even available data is not necessarily complete or accurate. Corporate action is reflected in surveys as well as concrete CSR initiatives. The latter might be affected by subjectivity, as many charitable actions are image oriented and may not provide the same positive impact that the publicity suggests. Lastly, studies also focus on corporate reputation based on rating agencies. While this gives an idea of public opinion, it does not necessarily reflect the actual consequences of the business's CSP. Even in these seemingly unified categories, measurements are inconsistent and make comparability difficult.

It is now much less a question of whether social accountability affects financial outcomes, but rather how it does so specifically (Searcy, 2011). While expenditures and profits are easily calculated, measuring ethical behaviour encounters more difficulties. Current research is starting to address these obstacles and provide a broader approach to monitoring social responsibility instead of focusing only on the financial relationships in the process.

An overview of the current research shows that there is further need to investigate the nature of CSP, its specific impact and measurability. It requires a consistent framework to build upon for future research. It is crucial to consider studies across different fields and incorporate multidimensional approaches. External forces, such as the lack of corporate transparency, will always limit research opportunities. However, the pressure on companies to comply with social expectations beyond legal regulations and to disclose information about their practices is continuously rising and might provide a more extensive overview in the future.

Questions

1 What do you understand by the term ethical value?
2 How do we measure ethical value? Can it truly be measured?

9.3 Ethical behaviour

Ethics should be based upon value drivers, but what is right or wrong varies by culture. Individuals face ethical dilemmas which continually test their personal ethics and values. The CEO can attempt to shape the structural variables to influence ethics, reward-allocation systems, management behaviour and human resource management systems. When developed effectively, ambiguity and uncertainty are reduced and can help to shape healthy ethical culture. Figure 9.2 emphasises five views of ethical behaviour.

Utilitarian view

The utilitarian approach seeks to make the most good for the most people, but can become dubious when an unethical decision could have the effect of creating the most good (e.g. corporate espionage). The need for an effective ethical framework is essential if one wishes to properly analyse the moral dimensions of a situation. Benefits include the identification of key themes, questions which collectively can be used as a basis for making informed and defensible decisions. Obviously, there are no silver bullets but the cautious ethical decision-maker can critically synthesise the options. As mentioned previously, the academic literature advocates a variety of foundation bases. The breadth and depth of the subject is both appealing and dangerous.

Justice view

The justice view looks at the impartiality of treatment of the individual according to legal rules and regulations. As the business environment becomes more complex, inappropriate contracts can lead to exploitation and oppression. Norms about what is considered ethical depend on how individuals define acceptable behaviour. When viewed from organisational scientist and legal scholar perspectives, justice and fairness need not necessarily be the same thing. Justice can be likened to protecting the weak from the strong (i.e. adherence to law), and is much broader than fairness. Fairness, on the other hand, is judged by moral integrity (reaction).

Moral-rights view

Respecting and protecting individual liberties, privileges and rights are evident within a modern society. If one assumes that a decent society protects rights and management is not operating in a pursuit of overzealous personal gain, then the moral-rights view can prevail. The boundaries of human rights can be blurred, but the case for moral-rights is improving. Individuals are not to be manipulated in terms of not being able to tell the truth, having the right to privacy and being safe in the workplace.

- Utilitarian view
- Justice view
- Moral-rights view
- Individualism view
- The business – society relationship

Figure 9.2 Ethical behaviour

Individualism view

When formulating strategy an often-forgotten consideration is how this decision promotes the long-term self-interests of the individual. The CEO and their management teams must accept that the primary commitment of employees is by default to long-term self-interests. At the individual level, dilemmas may be created by supervisory behaviour, peer group pressure, policy statements and written rules. Choices are also affected by belief systems, cultural norms and constructed through interactions.

Several arguments are put forward to explain why organisations should place attention on ethical behaviour. Matthews and Gandel (2015) introduce the five biggest scandals of 2015. During 2015 four corporate scandals (see Figure 9.3) that surfaced included:

Volkswagen emissions scandal: When the news broke in September 2015, VW admitted that it had used software to trick the Environmental Protection Agency's emissions testers into thinking that their cars were more environmentally friendly. VW lost $20bn in market value, as analysts worried about compensation claims from aggrieved customers. In addition to reputational damage to VW, the company has had to set aside more than $18bn. Many customers have declared that they will take the compensation on offer and then acquire a vehicle from another manufacturer.

FIFA corruption scandal: FIFA had been embroiled in corruption rumours for several years. High ranking officials were suspected of taking bribes for granting broadcasting rights for matches and hosting rights for the World Cup. Qatar were given hosting rights, despite a limited football history and little football infrastructure. Moreover, the summer temperatures of Qatar potentially in excess of 50°C make playing football rather arduous. The FBI indictment of seven FIFA officials was a coup. Sixteen more were added and collectively they face 92 counts under the US criminal code, including racketeering, conspiracy, fraud, wire fraud, money laundering and obstructing justice. The sums of money involved are well over US$200m in bribes and kickbacks. Blue chip sponsors such as Coca-Cola and McDonald's were instrumental in driving changes by dismissing senior executives.

Toshiba accounting scandal: The 140-year old Japanese conglomerate Toshiba overstated its earnings by nearly $2bn over seven years. Somewhat perturbing, Toshiba had created a corporate culture in which management decisions could not be challenged. Employees were pressured into inappropriate accounting practices by understating costs in financial statements. Inventory was also improperly valued. Half of the board resigned and more external replacements were to be brought into the company. The country's president made changes to corporate governance. Publicly traded companies now need to have at least two external independent directors on the board. Other unexpected consequences were Japan's $1.3 trillion government pension investment fund suing Toshiba for losses, due to the more than 40 per cent fall in share price.

Turing Pharmaceutical and Martin Shkreli: As part of its strategy Turing increased the price of a drug used to treat HIV by nearly 5,500 per cent from $13.50 to $750 per pill. This alone brings into question the aspect of ethical behaviour by its CEO. But the CEO was

- VW
- FIFA corruption
- Toshiba accounting scandal
- Turing Pharmaceutical

Figure 9.3 Scandals

quoted as saying that the price hike could have been higher, as his primary duty was to make profits for shareholders. However, in a separate matter the CEO was arrested for operating a Ponzi-type scheme. Prosecutors were investigating the behaviour of the CEO, who was accused of using the funds of a former company, Retrophin, to pay off investors, which was deemed to be fraudulent.

Collectively, the behaviour of senior executives within the four organisations reinforces the dangers of a capitalist society, where the sole pursuit of profit is a threat to a sustainable economy.

The Oxford English dictionary defines "ethical" as "related to moral principles or the branch of knowledge dealing with these." The emphasis is on the word "moral," which is concerned with the principles of right and wrong behaviour and the goodness or badness of human character. The Institute of Business Ethics UK, defines business ethics as "the application of ethical values, such as integrity, fairness, respect and openness to business behaviour" (Chartered Institute of Management Accountants, 2008).

Common examples of bad behaviour include: deception, pollution, and poor treatment of employees. Momentum grows, as interest in the way organisations behave, especially if badly, gains more newspaper column inches. While good business behaviour is also worth understanding, it gets less attention in the media. Examples include: providing employment, improvements in standards of living, contributing to society, and working with charities. The organisational climate should motivate moral corporate behaviour. How this is done within firms varies considerably, and can be affected by legislation. Although companies are institutionalising ethics, ethical infractions continue unceasingly. Arguably, individuals require not only the intellect but also the will to do the right thing in the face of temptation. The Corporate Bribery Act 2010 is a piece of legislation put in place to update and enhance UK law on bribery.

Points of the act include:

- The Act deals only with bribery and not other forms of white collar crime.
- The organisation may be liable for failing to prevent a person from bribing on your organisation's behalf but only if that person performs services for you in business. It is very unlikely therefore that the organisation will be liable for the actions of someone who is a supplier.
- There is a full defence if the organisation can demonstrate that they had adequate procedures in place to prevent bribery. But there is no need to put bribery prevention procedures in place if there is no risk of bribery.
- Hospitality is not prohibited by the Act.
- Facilitation payments are bribes under the Act just as they were under the old law.

The ethical individual chooses the moral course of action regardless of personal sacrifice. Determining how and why the individual acts ethically has been contemplated by many writers. A key feature of this chapter is that firms need to possess a conscience, realise that there is role for corporate citizenship and have a moral imperative. The latter causes mayhem in the media. Individuals and companies seek to minimise their tax liabilities through effective tax planning. This can involve depending upon advice of leading tax experts, who can operate within the law and be tax compliant. However, there is growing unrest over the grey area between compliant behaviour and tax avoidance. Despite being legitimate, tax avoidance is not illegal (tax evasion is), but it is now felt that this is not operating within the spirit of the law. Specifically, questions are being asked as to whether this behaviour is ethical.

184 *Contemporary themes*

Armitage (2016) writes about Ernst & Young's (EY) presence as auditor and tax adviser to Google, Apple, Facebook and Amazon, which makes it by far the most prevalent accountant in the current tax controversy. Unfortunately, each of these multinationals have come under major fire for avoiding taxes. This places EY in the limelight of public criticism in the maelstrom of tax avoidance. The settlement between Google and the UK tax authorities to pay £130m in back taxes in the UK was widely criticised as being too lenient. The mood was not helped by the actions of a senior Google executive: the President of Google's European, Middle East and African region when quizzed by the UK Public Accounts Committee was unsure what his basic salary was. He was even unable to provide a ballpark figure. Starbucks has faced much criticism for its tax avoidance strategy too. Tax campaigners were strident in wanting to ensure that UK profits were not being diverted elsewhere. The scandal erupted in 2012 and it was only in 2015 that the company scrapped its complex tax structures and paid a significant amount of UK tax, more than £8m tax on its pre-tax profits of more than £34.2m.

The rush of ethical behaviour by prominent individuals with regard to their tax affairs and hidden wealth has gained media scrutiny and the so called "Panama Papers" clearly indicate the scale of the issue. The Panama leaks, consisting of 11.5m files from the database of the world's fourth largest offshore law firm, have led investigators to many heads of government and their families.

POD

Donald Trump

The US Presidential results proved to be another surprise result. Much like Brexit, the bookmakers made the wrong call. Opinion polls had Clinton ahead of Trump by approximately four percentage points. Despite Clinton wining the popular vote 48 per cent to 47 per cent, and against all the odds and predictions, Donald J. Trump obtained 290 votes against Hillary Clinton's 232. The Republicans are now in the White House, control the Senate and the House of Representatives. What was surprising was that throughout Trump's campaign he was mired in scandals and gaffes. But he was still able to strike a chord with the electorate. Despite Clinton being accompanied by ex-President Bill Clinton and having celebrity endorsements from Beyoncé, Jay Z, Jon Bon Jovi, and Katy Perry, Trump was victorious. The voter revolt against the Democrats has created a new political space in the USA, and the repercussions of a Trump Presidency vowing to make the USA great again will be very interesting.

9.4 Trends in ethics

Linking business outcomes (economic) with society's needs (societal) is a complex issue. Some perspectives of ethical issues now include:

Sustainability

The fastest-growing cause for shareholders is sustainability (Serafeim, 2016). Being proactive with investor activism can help improve a company's sustainability in addition to performance. Sustainability has moved on from sole preoccupation with waste management. Now with so many solutions available, often with low costs, firms have commenced their sustainability journey. For the SME sustainability can begin with a waste management strategy. For the larger corporate it continues to climb the ladder, with the CEO being fully engaged. Unilever's CEO has seen his company ranked the world's most sustainable company for six

- Until recently, most businesses assumed that being green and making money were mutually exclusive.

- Making products more ecologically friendly was seen as a cost, not an opportunity.

- Leading organisations recognise that sustainability and growth can go hand-in-hand.

- Unfortunately, too many organisations look at green products through a features and benefits lens.

Figure 9.4 Sustainability is a differentiator

straight years in a survey conducted by Globescan and SustainAbility. Sustainability is a differentiator (see Figure 9.4).

In today's business environment "sustainability" is top of the agenda for CEOs globally. In the Accenture (2013) study, which includes insights from more than 1,000 CEOs across 103 countries and 27 industries, headlines include:

- Ninety-three percent of CEOs believe that sustainability will be important to the future success of their business.
- CEOs' perceptions of the importance of sustainability vary by industry.
- CEOs see consumers and governments as increasingly influential with their approach to sustainability.
- CEOs are increasingly market-focused in their motivations to invest in sustainability.
- CEOs feel uncomfortable that the global economy is not on track to meet the future challenges of a growing population.
- CEOs feel that businesses can do more to address sustainability challenges.

So, it is now a matter of not if, but how, CEOs should manage sustainable activities through their management teams and employees. Figure 9.5 refers to some of the potential of sustainability. Business as *unusual*: sustainability, in every possible meaning of the word, is the only way forward.

- Social networks are changing sustainability reporting and stakeholder engagement.

- The integration of social media and sustainability is creating new business opportunities.

- The confluence of social media and sustainability is supercharging business performance in three core sustainability functions:
    - Reporting and compliance
    - Stakeholder engagement
    - Operational efficiency

Figure 9.5 Sustainability 2.0

Education

The concept of business ethics continues to evolve from being an oxymoron to becoming a strategic management issue. This advancement has implications for companies and business and management education. Free market systems are underpinned by honesty, but the threat of malfeasance does hamper investors' trust. The ethics education task force established by the AACSB board of directors sees the need to strengthen management education. Their report in 2004 urges and encourages administrators and faculty to contemplate their current approaches to ethics education and to explore methods in enhancing the curriculum with emphasis on the design, delivery and evaluation of business ethics.

A hotly debated issue is whether ethics can be taught. Nearly two and a half centuries ago, Socrates pronounced that ethics could indeed be taught. Nevertheless, business schools today in general struggle to teach the subject meaningfully, when arguably the need is at its greatest. Opinions do vary on how ethics should be part of the business school curriculum, in terms of embedded topics across different modules or as a standalone module (Floyd, Xu, Atkins, & Caldwell, 2013; Slocum, Rohlfer, & Gonzalez-Canton, 2014; Wart, Baker, & Ni, 2014). This dilemma is pronounced by Floyd, Xu, Atkins, and Caldwell (2013) who advocate standalone units that use case studies for enhancing the soft skills of decision-making and handling of ethical issues. Alternatively, Slocum, Rohlfer, and Gonzalez-Canton, (2014) recommend small-scale insertions in the teaching delivery of ethics in both standalone or integrated ethics curricula.

Our experiences are that there ought to be some acknowledgement that ethics should be fully integrated into the curriculum, rather than a mere bolt-on. Incentives have to be built into managerial processes to allow for leaders to "do things right", so this needs to be adequately covered in business schools. Business and management students require education in more than the generic areas of, say, marketing, accounting, business and management. Immersion needs to include ethical concepts too with leaders being responsible for creating an ethical climate. Controls should exist concerning the corporate regulatory environment and internal control. A variety of programmes may support enhancing strategic thinking on developing effective processes. The rigor of such programmes will depend in part upon the current trends that prevail in industry sectors. Ethical education needs to be impactful and new pedagogical provisions built around technology should be the drivers. Stanford University presents their sustainability 3.0 agenda (see Figure 9.6).

- The purpose of sustainability 3.0 was to identify and map a **shared and actionable vision for sustainability at Stanford** over the next 5 to 10 years, building on the first initiative on environment and sustainability that launched in October 2003 and the formalisation of Sustainable Stanford that started in 2007. the effects of both initiatives are palpable. the university is now at the implementation phase of sustainability becoming a **core value on campus**, to be further evidenced through **teaching, research, and action**.

Figure 9.6 Sustainability 3.0 Stanford University

Unfortunately, the status of business ethics education has been designated by researchers as "the common practice in business schools of marginalising ethics by scattering ethics topics superficially and incoherently across the curriculum" (Swanson & Fisher, 2008, p. 1). Floyd, Xu, Atkins, and Caldwell (2013) consider the status of business ethics education and deploy a survey to provide results, which include making five recommendations:

- Rethink current policies within business schools, such as offering ethics courses earlier in the curriculum.
- Enhance scope from solely considering a publication-related ethical issues to addressing issues deemed important by deans, ethics experts and students.
- Business schools should create a more effective culture of academic integrity.
- Students should be given greater opportunities to apply ethical principles.
- Subject matter experts and faculty who teach and conduct research in business ethics should expand their research.

The Harvard Business School oath is an exemplification of the response within the business school sector. A group of Class of 2009 Graduates of Harvard Business School, convened initially by Maxwell Anderson, created an oath. The group aspires that the Oath will: a) make a difference in the lives of MBAs who take the oath; b) challenge other MBAs to work with a higher professional standard, whether they sign the oath or not; and c) create a public conversation in the press about professionalising and improving management. As a broader group of MBA students, graduates and advisors, the oath is their way of laying out the principles of what an MBA ought to stand for.

Corporate social responsibility

Social commentators' expectations have led to a blurring of the boundaries between the public and private sectors. Nelson (2004) reported that the increased financial muscle and activism of institutional investors together with regulations have responded to the spate of corporate ethics scandals and governance crises. This now calls for better corporate governance, and greater corporate accountability, transparency and legitimacy. So much that is written suggests that organisations should make deliberate choices that embrace CSR practices. Consciously, following this direction of travel provides answers to crucial questions that reinforces its importance.

Why is CSR important?

- What is the relationship between business and society?
- There is a market for morality – if markets are changing, business schools need to change and internalise CSR practices.
- Students have broader choices about where they end up working.
- Can we monetise the values within companies?
- Great companies of tomorrow will have shared values – affecting the mainstream of strategy.
- Too important to leave to government to sort out. Government is incapable and needs a strong regulatory environment.
- MBAs need to consider triple bottom line – profits, environmental and social performance.

188 *Contemporary themes*

Nevertheless, if all organisations were adopting CSR practices, we would not have to consider the alternatives. Merely restricting CSR to philanthropic issues can create a negative impact within the organisation. Other negative connotations include:

Why is CSR unimportant?

- CSR has become an industry, and is a growing phenomenon.
- Business education is not about business ethics and CSR, but the role of business schools in society.
- Businesses should be judged by what they do rather than what they say.
- Modern version of CSR – doing well by doing good.
- Businesses are under pressure to create shareholder value.
- CSR is an intensely confused concept.
- CSR is really good management, which leads to higher profits and good social outcomes.
- BP was recognised for being socially responsible, but look what occurred.

To conclude, some key trends and issues are provided in Figure 9.7.

POD

Coca-Cola Enterprises

In their 2015/2016 Corporate Social Responsibility and Sustainability Report, The Chairman and CEO of Coca-Cola Enterprises (CCE), John F. Brock in his foreword stated:

"When we started our sustainability journey in 2006 very few companies, including CCE, had adopted measurable sustainability targets. Now – 10 years on – we have a well-established sustainability plan with stretch goals designed to address business-critical social and environmental issues.

CCE has an important role to play in promoting sustainability across the beverage industry and our value chain. Our CRS report reinforces our commitment to being a sustainability leader in our sector.

1. Viewing CSR in a broader and more systemic context
2. The enabling role of government
3. The relative efficacy of regulatory and voluntary approaches to CSR issues
4. Exploring the linkages, and often inconsistencies, between a company's CSR, corporate governance and public policy positions
5. Developing a more strategic and integrated "value proposition" for CSR at the level of the firm
6. The leadership role of CEO's and boards of directors
7. The potential of collective CEO action
8. The role of the financial sector in redefining risk, opportunity and fiduciary responsibility
9. The role of the media as watchdog, endorser and multiplier
10. Measuring the impact and effectiveness of CSR and partnerships
11. Scaling-up the impact of partnerships

Figure 9.7 Key trends and issues in CSR

It is clear that sustainability is not something which can be seen as separate to business strategy, or as optional. We must continue making long-term sustainable decisions, which support wider society and the environment in partnership with our customers, our employees and our shareowners."

Coca-Cola Enterprises build their CSR practices around six matters: Wellbeing; climate change; resource scarcity; sustainable sourcing; water; employment and diversity.

Source: Coca-Cola (2016) Reflections on a ten year in sustainability Available at: https://www.cokecce.com/news-and-events/blogs/reflections-on-a-10-year-journey-in-sustainability

Compliance

Organisations are increasing their actions towards ethics and compliance. With every new corporate scandal, stakeholders invariably call for more moral responsibility within firms. Stakeholders are soon able to distinguish between those companies with real commitment from those simply giving lip service. Ultimately, the CEO at some stage needs to "put their money where their mouth is" to ensure staff resources are assigned to the compliance activity. To some people compliance is a focus on following the rules and regulations, whereas ethics seeks to encourage behaviour beyond just following rules and regulations. The financial industry is a classic example often cited of individuals following rules and regulations but whose behaviour remains unethical. Nevertheless, compliance is becoming more prevalent in discussions being held within organisations. As the firm expands its global footprint, compliance issues increase in magnitude and complexity, which leads to an increase in newly hired staff. Organisations are looking to strengthen their compliance teams with permanent graduate level appointments. Individuals work across all business areas and contribute on compliance related matters. They may also take the lead in driving the compliance programme including policies, education and monitoring plans.

Continued changes in regulation demand evolution of compliance procedures. An effective ethics and compliance programme costs money, but if successful the return can be favourable (Volkov, 2015). Thomson Reuters define compliance management

> as a holistic, connected methodology designed to protect and enhance business value by fostering a regulatory risk-aware culture. A prerequisite for any effective compliance management program is the training of employees on the laws, regulations and policies that apply to their job responsibilities.
>
> (Thomson Reuters, n.d.)

In practice, caveats are noted. Weber and Wasieleski (2013) detect more comprehensive ethics and compliance programmes and initiatives to reflect growing concerns, but stress that the command-and-control approaches are not fool proof.

9.5 Ethics in decision-making (EiDM)

Understanding the process of making ethical decisions is a good step in making better choices. When the objective is to avoid making unethical decisions, the connection between ethics and decision-making is climactic. Academic studies utilise a descriptive philosophical or theological lens and examine a myriad of disciplines including business and management

(Lehnert, Park, & Singh, 2015). Powers and Vogel (1980) identify six factors underlying moral reasoning: moral imagination; moral identification and ordering; moral evaluation; tolerating moral disagreement and ambiguity; integrating managerial competence with moral competence; moral obligation. Rest (1986) is accredited with developing the most widely used model of moral behaviour. By starting with the construct of moral action, Rest worked backwards and deduced that ethical action is the outcome of four psychological sub-processes: moral sensitivity (recognition of ethical issue); moral judgment (what is right and wrong); moral focus (motivation to deliver); moral character (overcome distractors and develop tactics and strategies).

There is a large body of literature focusing on the various approaches (Craft, 2013). Lehnert, Park, and Singh (2015) synthesise and examine trends based on four dependent variables, awareness, behaviour, judgment, and intention and the associated independent variables relating to individual, organisational and moral intensity factors. In their conclusion, despite decades of investigation, there is not a clear understanding of their impact in the context of ethical decision-making.

The following section considers a framework that draws from and consolidates observations from some appealing research (Barr, Campbell & Dando, 2011).

EiDM in action

Four key elements of EiDM:

Context

Context and culture were found to be rigorous reasoning, the ability to apply decisions, and reflection and feedback. Context and culture permeates through all the other three elements. Decision-making is not performed in a vacuum, so taking unbiased actions will be challenging. The array of macro and personal contextual and cultural factors both conscious and unconscious will interact on an individual's judgment and reasoning, and the propensity to act on it.

RIGOROUS REASONING AT THE POINT OF DECISION-MAKING

Consistency is a key component when evaluating any elements of an ethics programme. An experienced team can be more skilled in filtering the contextual and cultural factors that might influence any given situation. Corporate values can act as a dominant filter. This requires two drivers, continuous improvement campaign and mechanisms for explicit knowledge to pervade the firm.

ABILITY TO APPLY DECISIONS

Factors such as self-preservation, fear, ignorance and real or perceived pressure from stakeholders or senior management can create difficulties in applying the right decision. The ability of individuals to feel well supported in doing the right thing is a vital element. This was one of the strongest messages noted during the Barr, Campbell and Dando (2011) study. A common remark is: "My managers often say they know the right thing to do, but then doubt it is the choice senior leaders really want to hear."

Table 9.1 Ethics in action

Title	Author/Organisation	Methodology	Findings
Corporate Governance and Business Integrity, 2015	OECD	Survey findings based on 88 responses from companies and almost 40 interviews with mainly private sector companies.	Corporate leadership is taking business integrity more seriously. 80% of surveyed companies were strongly involved in the design and implementation of the company's integrity policy.
Managing Responsible Business, 2015 Edition	Chartered Global Management	2,500 Chartered Global Management Accountant and CIMA students	Most critical areas were security of information (94%); safety and security in workplace (91%), discrimination (81%), conflicts of interest (81%), and bribery (80%).
Ethics at Work, 2015	Institute of Business Ethics	Face-to-face (Britain – 674 full-time respondents) and online (France, Germany, Italy and Spain – 750 full and part-time respondents per country) Employees surveyed in Britain, France, Germany, Italy and Spain.	Proportion who said honesty is practised "always/frequently" varied between Britain (81%), Germany (63%), France (66%), Italy (73%), and Spain (77%).
The State of Ethics in Large Companies, 2015	Ethics and Compliance Initiative, USA	Companies with more than 90,000 employees.	Large companies obtain impressive results when investing in ethics and compliance. Each key area of ethical performance – pressure to compromise ethical standards, observation of misconduct, reporting of violations and retaliation for reporting improves in large companies with a strong ethics culture. One-third observed misconduct in large companies with effective ethics programmes, as opposed to almost 51% among all large companies and more than 62% for large companies that do not have effective E&C programmes.
Global Trust Barometer, 2016	Elderman	Surveyed more than 33,000 respondents aged 18 and over, across 28 countries.	90% of respondents stated that their organisation has an anti-corruption programmes in place.
Anti-Corruption survey, 2015	Dow Jones State of Anti-Corruption	259 responses from compliance professionals worldwide to an online survey.	69% reported that they were confident about their organisation's due diligence information and processing.

(continued)

Table 9.1 (continued)

Title	Author/Organisation	Methodology	Findings
EU Speak Up Benchmark, 2015	Cercle d'Éthique des Affaires (CEA) of France, Forética of Spain, and the Institute of Business Ethics (IBE), UK.	75 responses received from representatives of both listed and non-listed companies.	93% of participants have speak up arrangements in place. 72% did permit anonymous reporting, but this differed considerably between countries (for example amongst UK companies this figure rises to 93%, whereas amongst Spanish firms, it falls to 31%).
UK Whistleblowing Report, 2015	The Public Concern at Work (PCAW)	1,876 individual contacts made in 2014.	78% of whistleblowers who contacted PCAW raise their concerns with their employer prior to contacting PCAW. Top issues were financial malpractice (18%) followed by ethical concerns (17%). Interestingly, 22% were from the education sector.
Attitudes of British Public to Business Ethics, 2015	Forum for Private Business	2,000 British adults, with the sample weighted to be representative of all adults in Great Britain aged 18+.	Findings show a crisis of trust in big business. 78% of the sample agreed that big businesses are likely to prioritise profits over high ethical standards. 74% of the sample agreed that the majority of big businesses have no concern for small business owners in the UK.
Overarching view on the results of Ethics Survey studies, 2015	Institute of Business Ethics		The global business ethics landscape seems to be moving in a positive direction.

REFLECTION AND FEEDBACK

Implanting ethical decision-making throughout the organisation is important. Reflection enables decision-makers to challenge their own thinking and use them constructively to inform future decisions. Some decisions can lead to intended and unintended consequences, and the organisation needs to learn from its actions.

This chapter concludes by summarising a number of pieces of research highlighted by the Institute of Business Ethics (see Table 9.1).

9.6 Chapter summary

This chapter considers the theoretical and practical benefits of business ethics to both business and society. Consideration of the role education plays in the early dissemination of ethical practice is articulated throughout the chapter. Trends in ethics are considered with the aim of reminding the reader of the breadth of the term "ethics," with the term "corporate social responsibility" being only one facet. The relationship between ethics and trust may appear tenuous at times, but abuses of ethics resulting in unethical behaviour are highly undesirable. Examples are provided to illustrate the variety of such abuses. There is a positive depiction of ethics, as examples are provided of what various organisations are doing. Honesty, genuine concern for customers, and strong ethics and values will be rewarded. Understanding the process of making ethical decisions is a good step in making better choices. When the objective is to avoid making unethical decisions, the connection between ethics and decision-making is climactic. The chapter ends with a reflective piece by summarising some research highlighted by the Institute of Business Ethics.

9.7 End of chapter self-reflection questions

1. How is business ethics shaping business and society?
2. How have the four corporate scandals mentioned in the chapter reminded us about the dangers of a capitalist society?
3. What role can business schools perform in educating students about business ethics?
4. What are the key facets of ethical decision-making?
5. What do you understand by the 1970 economist Milton Friedman's statement "the business of business is business"?

References

Accenture (2013). The UN global compact: Accenture CEO study on sustainability. Available at: https://www.accenture.com/us-en/insight-un-global-compact-ceo-study-sustainability

Armitage, J. (2016). Ernst &Young: Accountancy giant advises Google, Apple, Facebook and Amazon on tax affairs. Available at: http://www.independent.co.uk/news/business/news/ernst-young-accountancy-giant-advises-google-apple-facebook-and-amazon-on-tax-affairs-a6837906.html

Barr, D., Campbell, C., & Dando, N. (2011). Ethics in decision-making. Institute of Business Ethics. Available at: https://www.ibe.org.uk/userassets/pubsummaries/eidm_overview.pdf

Beurden, P. van, & Gössling, T. (2008). The worth of values: A literature review on the relation between corporate social and financial performance. *Journal of Business Ethics*, 82(2), 407–424.

Carroll, A. B. (1979). A three-dimensional conceptual model of corporate performance. *Academy of Management Review*, 4(4), 497–505.

Chartered Institute of Management Accountants (2008) Managing responsible business. Available at: http://www.cimaglobal.com/Research--Insight/Managing-responsible-business--a-global-survey-on-business-ethics/

Coca-Cola (2016) Reflections on a 10-year journey in sustainability. Available at: https://www.coke cce.com/news-and-events/blogs/reflections-on-a-10-year-journey-in-sustainability

Craft, J. L. (2013). A review of the empirical ethical decision-making literature: 2004–2011. *Journal of Business Ethics*, *117*(2), 221–259.

Floyd, L. A., Xu, F., Atkins, R., & Caldwell, C. (2013). Ethical outcomes and business ethics: Toward improving business ethics education. *Journal of Business Ethics*, *117*(4), 753–776.

Matthews, C., & Gandel, S. (2015). The 5 biggest corporate scandals of 2015. Available at: http://fortune.com/2015/12/27/biggest-corporate-scandals-2015/

Nelson, J. (2004). Leadership, accountability, and partnership: Critical trends and issues in corporate social responsibility." Report of the CSR Initiative Launch Event. Corporate Social Responsibility Initiative, Report No. 1. Cambridge, MA: John F. Kennedy School of Government, Harvard University. Available at: https://www.hks.harvard.edu/m-rcbg/CSRI/publications/report_1_Launch%20Summary%20Report.pdf

Institute of Business Ethics (2016) Survey on Business Ethics 2015. Business Ethics Briefing, Issue 51, Feb. Available at: http://www.acoi.ie/download/Surveys%20on%20Business%20Ethics%202015.pdf

Lehnert, K., Park, Y. H., & Singh, N. (2015). Research note and review of the empirical ethical decision-making literature: Boundary conditions and extensions. *Journal of Business Ethics*, *129*(1), 195–219.

Powers, C. W., & Vogel, D. (1980). *Ethics in the education of business managers*. Hastings-on-Hudson, NY: Hastings Center.

Rest, J. R. (1986). *Moral development: Advances in research and theory*. Boston: Praeger.

Searcy, C. (2012). Corporate sustainability performance measurement systems: A review and research agenda. *Journal of Business Ethics*, *107*(3), 239–253.

Serafeim, G. (2016). The fastest growing cause for shareholders is sustainability. Harvard Business Review. Available at https://hbr.org/2016/07/the-fastest-growing-cause-for-shareholders-is-sustainability

Slocum, A., Rohlfer, S., & Gonzalez-Canton, C. (2014). Teaching business ethics through strategically integrated micro-insertions. *Journal of Business Ethics*, *125*(1), 45–58.

Swanson, D. L., & Fisher, D. G. (2008). *Advancing business ethics education*. Charlotte, NC: IAP.

Thomson Reuters (n.d.) Available at: https://risk.thomsonreuters.com/en/risk-solutions/compliance-management.html

Volkov, M. (2015). Top 5 ethics and compliance trends for 2015. Available at: http://blog.volkovlaw.com/2015/01/top-5-ethics-compliance-trends-2015/

Wart, M. V., Baker, W., & Ni, A. (2014). Using a faculty survey to kick-start an ethics curriculum upgrade. *Journal of Business Ethics*, *122*(4), 571–585.

Weber, J., & Wasieleski, D. M. (2013). Corporate ethics and compliance programs: A report, analysis and critique. *Journal of Business Ethics*, *112*(4), 609–626.

Wood, D. J. (2010). Measuring corporate social performance: A review. *International Journal of Management Reviews*, *12*(1), 50–84.

10 Digital strategy

10.1 Learning objectives

After completing this chapter you will:

- appreciate the influence of digital strategy on the economy
- appreciate the evolution of e-business strategy
- be aware that the game changing challenge of digital business requires evolution, together with the adaptation of prior insight and theory
- understand what firms need to do to cope with the dynamic, unstable and unpredictable digital environment
- be aware of the influence of social media, niche social networks and Internet of Things.

10.2 Introduction

Digital disruption caused by the duality of technology and new business models is here to stay. The CEO and their organisation realise the need for change, and seek to take advantage of available opportunities. Traditional competitive dynamics were slow and presented less risk. Now the velocity of change and higher stakes make it imperative that the CEO no longer clings to out of date business models. A prime example is the impact of WhatsApp, which disrupted the $100bn global text messaging market. Their business model appears to be allowing consumers to send messages to each other free of charge via smartphones. Both WhatsApp

- Transformation of industries
- Eliminate time and distance boundaries
- Collaboration
- Customer and supplier relationships
- New organisational forms
- Social connections and participation
    - Social media, mobility, and power
    - Innovation (crowd sourcing)

Figure 10.1 The impact of the Internet

196 *Contemporary themes*

and Instagram owned by Facebook are continually looking for ways to enhance their business model. With Facebook losing its lustre for millennials, it's beginning to lose its appeal for online marketing campaigns. WhatsApp is seeking to create revenue from connecting businesses with customers via chats and calls. Instagram has enhanced its algorithm to show content of interest based on engagement, which improves the user experience.

The Internet has impacted the business world (see Figure 10.1). The digital world has transformed how products and services are bought and sold. Despite digital strategies being available to all and in itself having little inherent value, through the use of appropriate concepts, models and frameworks competitive advantage is attainable. This chapter will consider these latter issues closely and outline how firms can better fit and apply their digital strategies. This feature is noteworthy as for the first five decades, the concept of strategy was designed for traditional bricks-and-mortar firms (see Chapter 1). The extant strategic management literature proposes the competitive positioning works of Porter (1980), and the RBV work of Grant (1991) which ignores the dominant role of the Internet. Borderless boundaries and geographical scope make it exigent to enhance agility, flexibility, efficiencies and effectiveness. Management need to be continually finding new ways of delighting their customers in the ever-changing digital environment. Issues such as the digital divide, privacy of data and information overload make it harder for marketers (see Figure 10.2).

10.3 E-Business strategy reflection

Background

The emergence of e-business strategy as a taught subject in colleges and universities throughout the world has not been matched by rigorous academic research. Of note is the dropping of the letter e in front of the word business and the increasing use of the term digital strategy. The salient relationships are depicted in Figure 10.3, which were considered more than a decade ago.

Modern organisations are under increasing pressure from stakeholders to find new ways to compete effectively in dynamic markets and changing customer preferences (Phillips & Wright, 2009). Consequently, organisations have sought structures and technologies that improve flexibility through the use of e-business strategy. Consistent with Nadkarni and Narayanan (2007), the following sections consider the importance of flexibility in fast-changing

- The digital divide:
    - Socioeconomic, education, generational, attitudinal, etc.
    - Generation Y
    - Solutions: government, social enterprise, innovation, collaboration
- Privacy of data
    - National regulations
    - Personal vs. business data
- Information overload
    - Collecting data vs. application of knowledge

Figure 10.2 The impact of the Internet: issues

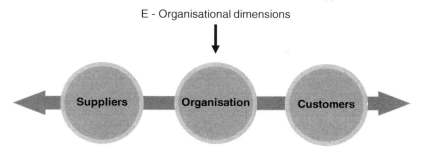

Figure 10.3 Changing business relationships

business environments. Dunford, Cuganesan, Grant, Palmer, Beaumont, and Steele (2013) reaffirm the concept of flexibility as ubiquitous and a rationale for organisational change. Organisations are finding that their ability to respond to unpredicted changes in the market is becoming a key factor in survival. The ability to adjust e-business processes to customer preferences (flexibility) has become a necessity for online systems. Despite the interest in e-business flexibility the academic literature has not kept pace with industrial developments.

During the earlier commercial phases of the Internet, a plethora of e-business models were advocated, prompting management to search for the best model (Phillips, 2003). Differences between an e-business model and an e-business strategy are noteworthy for any organisation (Margretta, 2002). Now firms adopt e-business processes as one of the mechanisms for creating competitive advantage (Verdú-Jover, Alós-Simó, & Gómez-Gras, 2014). E-business models tend to ignore competition and organisational dynamics. Yet competitiveness is more of an issue, particularly as information-age technologies become more available and accessible to competitors. Increasing competition forces commercial organisations to diversify into new markets and operate in multiple sectors. These threats make the creation of alliances with suppliers/competitors a useful response. However, implementation can become problematic due to issues surrounding system interoperability, process interoperability, and conflicting organisational and sometimes national cultures. Global commercial organisations face threats from smaller, more nimble organisations that possess network-centric operations. Beidleman and Ray (1998) contend that financial services firms are increasingly caught up in the flexibility revolution. Supporting this assertion Adolf and Hooda (1997) refer to the new business model of banking as achieving a level of organisational agility and responsiveness that permits continuous pursuit of new opportunities as they emerge in this fast-changing market.

There has been significant managerial interest in the opportunities available to use e-business solutions to create competitive advantage. As stated by Swaminathan and Tayur (2003), e-business can be defined as a business process that uses the Internet or other electronic media as a conduit to fulfil business transactions. However, a critical assumption is that e-business encompasses e-commerce, and goes far beyond e-commerce to include the application of information technologies for internal business processes as well as the activities which a company engages in during its communications with suppliers and customers (Phillips, 2003). These internal activities can include functional activities, such as marketing, accounting, human resource, and operations.

As organisations embrace the Internet, one of the burning issues management face is that of getting people to work differently in organisations that are changing shape. E-business organisations need to have a combination of inside–out and a range of competencies.

Contemporary themes

Wang (2000) asserts that e-business should be viewed less as a phenomenon of purely online business and more as a challenge of organisation redesign. Phillips (2003) points out that organisations looking to implement an e-business strategy must align themselves internally with the demands that the dynamic environment imposes on strategic behaviour. A good example of this is that despite making a significant investment in their e-business strategies and IT, some managers remain unclear about how to adapt their organisation. Advancements in technology create the opportunities for new forms of arranging work, such as collapsing boundaries between suppliers, customers and competition. Management need to identify the key attributes and processes that are a pre-requisite for competitive advantage. According to Neilson, Pasternack and Visco (2000), the evolution to e-organisation takes place along seven key dimensions—organisational structure, leadership, people and culture, coherence, knowledge, alliances and governance (see Figure 10.4).

Organisations are increasingly facing the challenge of e-business, that is, the use of Internet tools to support their business processes (Cagliano, Caniato, & Spina, 2003). Strategic business units are finding that their ability to respond to unpredicted changes in the market is becoming a key factor in survival. Consistent with Dreyer and Gronhaug (2004), flexibility relates to an organisation's capacity to change or exploit external opportunities, and is an important competence.

The dramatic growth in the number of companies that use the Internet to bring about competitive advantage prompts many questions for the strategist. The concept of e-business strategy addresses the issue of how the Internet can reshape companies and provide competitive advantage (Cagliano et al., 2003). Phillips (2003) believes that success is dependent upon management being open-minded to understanding and deriving real value from the Internet. Bremser and Chung (2005) state that constant change in the environment means continually evolving strategies, new products, and new processes to adopt. Lumpkin and Dess (2004) explore several ways that firms are using the Internet to add value, and highlight four value-adding activities – search, evaluation, problem-solving and transaction. Krell and Gale (2005) observe that much of the discussion of e-business either fails to address strategic issues or addresses only the limited topic of strategies for electronic markets.

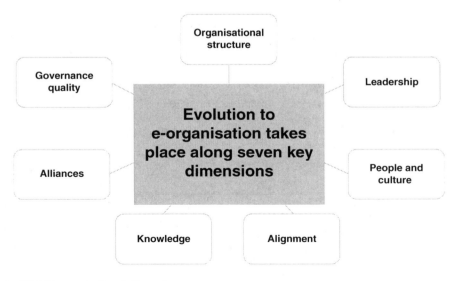

Figure 10.4 E-organisational dimensions

Stroud (1998) points out that the benefits the Internet can deliver will not materialise unless a company adapts its structure and processes. Yet very few theoretical frameworks truly help practising e-business managers understand and craft a winning strategy (Brunn, Jensen, & Skovgaard, 2002). Willcocks and Plant (2001), who were searching for B2C e-business initiatives for common paths and practices, note two themes. First, the movement towards online is an evolutionary process for bricks-and-mortar companies. Second, planning and flexibility in a turbulent market and technology environment is a goal for the strategist.

Now that the Internet presents a source of innovative opportunities, calls to rethink the diffusion of traditional strategy formulation with new approaches are in vogue. According to Porter (2001) the greatest impact of the Internet is its ability to reconfigure traditional industries. Porter (2001) asserts that his five forces framework (Porter, 1980) can be used in an e-business environment. The following five underlying forces can determine e-business industry attractiveness: threat of substitute product/service, bargaining of suppliers, barriers to entry, bargaining power of buyers and rivalry among existing competitors.

Some debate still remains about the merits of the Internet. For example, in contrast to Porter (2001), Tapscott (2001) is of the opinion that the networking effects alter the competitive dynamics of different industries, and facilitate a shift from those organisations that vertically and virtually integrate. Interestingly, Kim et al. (2004) report that strategies that integrate elements of cost leadership and differentiation will out-perform cost leadership or differentiation strategies. Strategies that incorporate an integrating dimension should be an objective rather than the adoption of a Porter's stuck in the middle strategy, which suggests no clear strategic focus.

An increasing number of authors propose models for the management of organisational change as firms migrate along the digitisation path. Sharma (2004) presents a change management model for e-business that involves three phases: people; processes and technology; and customers, suppliers and other value chain partners. Earl (2000) advocates a six-stage evolutionary model of e-business implementation. To help managers move from traditional to e-business, Hackbarth and Kettinger (2000) propose a methodology that charts the path to effective digital business strategy. Their four-stage methodology makes use of SWOT analysis and each stage has its own activities, tasks and outputs. Gardner and Ash (2003) emphasise the non-linear and emergent nature of the necessary changes and consider corporate intent and strategy, application of the business models and the role of an agent or moderator. Ash and Burn (2003) propose a model of transformation for guiding organisations through the successful implementation of their e-business strategy. Their case findings demonstrate the integration of technologies, the differentiation of business models, and the demonstration of value-adding in products and services along the customer and supplier chains. Krell and Gale (2005) postulate another model which could assist addressing technology, business processes, strategy, and organisation change issues.

During more recent times considerable research effort has focused on e-business modelling technologies and its multidimensional applications. Lipitakis and Phillips (2016) highlight that the traditional business modelling research, belonging to the organisational management field and forced by the increasingly extendable evolving e-market opportunities, has been gradually redirected to the e-business modelling research of e-business technologies and their applications (Brynjolfsson & Hitt, 2003; Rust & Kannan, 2003; Zilman, 2005–2012; Yunus, Moingeon, & Lehmann-Ortega, 2010). Although several researchers and practitioners are using various business models, there is a comparative lack of theoretical understanding and knowledge of suitable tools in the area of e-business modelling. Research efforts have been directed to the study of the transformation of the traditional business models to e-business, the investigation of the impact of e-business on traditional business practices, the exploitation of opportunities enabled by e-business technological innovations and related business modelling complex applications, including Internet business models, business models on the web, business models in e-commerce and generally business models for e-markets (Koellinger, 2008). E-business can be defined as any process that a business organisation conducts over information technology or computer-mediated networks, including various activities that businesses may conduct over the web, containing the concept of e-commerce and applications of information technologies for business processes, commercial and functional activities, such as finance, marketing, human resource management and operations (Zhang & Gai, 2005).

Digital strategy

Due to the new normal environment (e.g. post financial recession, rise of social media and investments in digital business processes) organisations need to evolve. The two-way communication flow empowers a new set of more active consumers. Being digital is no longer merely part of the enterprise – it should be now fully integrated into business processes. The rapid increase of channels and messages raises the profile of all firms.

CEOs are now transforming their businesses via digital strategies and rethinking online relationships (see Figure 10.5). This evolution can be illustrated by the Russell Reynolds Associates annual survey. They surveyed more than 2,000 C-level executives on the impact, structure, barriers and enablers of digital technologies across 15 industries. Predictably, media, telecom and consumer services were the highest ranked, and asset wealth and industrial were at the bottom. Grossman (2016) suggests that there are three levers that organisations can pull to keep pace: catalysing roles by bringing in new people; fostering a culture of making data-based decisions; building digital technology into the lifeblood of the organisation. Those organisations that fail to address these three areas will get left behind.

The information systems community has successfully pushed for the creation of a digital business strategy that raises IT strategy from the functional to the corporate level. Many firms still focus on organisational learning and knowledge as dominant themes but there has been limited response to applying these to the digital era. The game changing challenge of digital business requires evolution, together with the adaptation of prior insight and theory. Digitisation gives the strategist a new avenue to pursue. The digital challenge creates emerging perspectives and future avenues for competitive advantage. The revolution in changing relationships between the firm and customers has driven firms to operate outside of their comfort zones. The days of mass products being sold to mass audiences are evaporating. Firms with decent products and strong marketing campaigns are realising that this does not automatically translate to competitive advantage. This is partly due to the changing roles and behaviours of consumers with customer-centric thinking being positioned at the heart of the

- Proximity and frequency of contact
- Similarity
- Self-presentation
- Reciprocity and self-disclosure
- Consistency

Figure 10.5 What we know about online relationships

more adaptive firm. Competition now means that everyone is trying to differentiate thorough service and customer solutions. However, CEOs now find themselves being challenged by prior thinking and developing new insights on the interface between customers and the modern organisation.

Bharadwaj, El Sawy, Pavlou and Venkatraman (2013) present a comprehensive framework to define the next generation of digital strategy insights. They include: scope of digital business strategy; scale of digital business strategy; speed of decision-making; and sources of value creation and capture. Arguably, digital strategies should play a pivotal role in operationalising each key theme, or face becoming irrelevant at the strategic decision-making level. This transfunctional process becomes more influential than the marketing function per se with digital strategy itself being the strategy (Bharadwaj et al., 2013). This defies the traditional insight that says the creation of a digital business strategy is the new task solely of senior managers, who should no longer be creating a top down general business strategy that gets supported and implemented by functional strategies such as IT and marketing. With IT gaining prominence by fusing products, services and business functions to enhance business performance, strategic marketing needs to move away from its functional and myopic lens. This is far from the first time that strategic marketing has been urged to "develop closer linkages across functional groupings" (Rudd & Morgan, 2003, p.163). So we here note both the opportunity for strategic marketing and that there is a degree of urgency to redress the balance by incorporating its perspective of consumer co-creation of value, communicated by means of social media, away from internal IT infrastructure and processes.

Success in a digital environment is not solely about technology. Kane, Palmer, Phillips, Kiron and Buckley (2015) identify strategy as the key driver in the digital arena. Those firms that are unwilling to take risks are unlikely to thrive and are likely to lose talent, as employees at all stages of their careers wish to work for firms that embrace digital processes. Kane et al. (2015) raise the following highlights:

- Digital strategy drives digital maturity
- Power of a digital transformation strategy lies in its scope and objectives
- Maturing digital firms build skills to realise the strategy
- Employees want to work for digital leaders
- Taking risks becomes a cultural norm
- Digital agenda is led from the top.

10.4 Organisational flexibility

Organisational flexibility is the degree to which an organisation possesses a variety of actual and potential procedures to improve the controllability of the organisation and environment (Palanisamy, 2005). Phillips and Wright (2009) stress that the processes underlying flexibility are multidimensional, with prior research adopting differing perspectives, such as economic (Klein, 1984), organisational (Jennings & Seaman, 1994), operational (Newman, Hanna, & Maffei, 1993) and strategic (Sanchez, 1995). More holistic and strategic approaches now supersede the traditional approaches of flexibility. Ozer (2002) highlights the importance of considering a holistic view by presenting various sources of flexibility, such as technology, human resources, operations, marketing, finance and management. With the inclination for the consumer to purchase goods and services via the Internet, the universality of mobile devices has exacerbated the need for flexibility. With fixed-PC access to the Internet still

- Private and public sector organisations are finding that their ability to respond to unpredicted changes in their marketplace (agility) is becoming a key factor in survival.
- The ability to adjust e-business processes to customer preferences (flexibility) has become a prerequisite in online systems.

Figure 10.6 Agility and flexibility

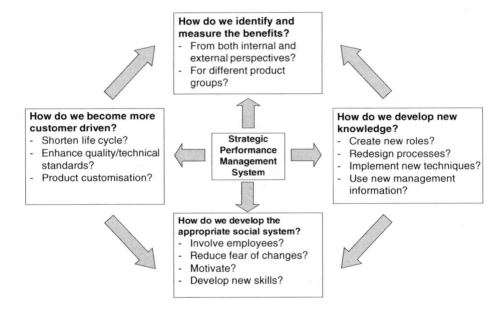

Figure 10.7 E-procurement: strategic performance measurement system

important, markets and individuals prefer mobile access. For example, in Africa the fixed-PC dominance was quickly altered to a predominance of mobile phones. Such changing business dynamics and disruptive technological shifts augment the need for flexibility (see Figure 10.6).

Nevertheless, many firms do not retain the flexibility to adopt e-business activities to constantly changing business imperatives (Bauer, Němcová, & Dvořák, 2010). Organisations of all sizes realise the need for flexible structures when implementing their e-business strategy. Ultimately, the resource capability of an organisation together with capacity for exploitation determine the level of flexibility firms may exercise in uncertain environments (Fredericks, 2005). Flexibility ought to pervade e-business supply chains, which link partners with the goal of reducing transaction costs. Inadvertently, this may harm supply chain flexibility and reinforces the call for offer flexibility and partner flexibility (Gosain, Malhotra, & El Sawy, 2004). The former relates to the ability to support changes in offer characteristics, and the latter the ability to modify linkages to partners with different partners.

Modern supply chains still have to cope with unexpected changes in supply or demand and advancements in technology and automation, shrinking global markets and environmental pressure. E-procurement systems are now able to incorporate a strategic performance measurement system (see Figure 10.7). These must work effectively with opportunities presented in new emerging economies and shifts in demand patterns. Appreciating the granularities of operations, goals and deadlines is crucial, so that alignment is maintained with the business strategy. Resilience of supply chains is enhanced when there is strong collaboration with suppliers. Yet much still needs to be done, as stated by Moscoso and Lago (2016), who voice concern that supply chain flexibility needs further improvements. Some of the supply chain management challenges are:

- Higher product and components complexity
- More customisation and product (offering) variety
- More pressure on prices and discounts
- Increased demand uncertainty
- Labour costs increase in developing countries
- Specialisation and global competition of suppliers
- Increasing commodity and exchange-rate volatility
- Increased regulations on trade and product responsibility.

POD

Information technology

Information technology and a new generation of devices, such as iPads, games consoles, set-top boxes and smartphones are changing how sport, entertainment and fashion are consumed and distributed. These devices provide new ways for audiences to connect and watch sport, entertainment and fashion. During the economic slowdown and in tough competitive markets, advertisers and event organisers need to create new and cost-effective experiences.

Interestingly, these experiences need to take into consideration that consumption patterns can differ by key segments. Men tend to participate in online fan clubs or community groups and are more focused on information and interested in data. Women tend to enjoy the social media aspect and older consumers are increasingly turning to social media. Overall, the distinction of TV and Internet is blurring and the consumer is now getting far greater choice and better quality experience than was thought possible even a couple of years ago.

Organisations such as Sky illustrate the ability to continue enhancing products and services to keep pace with changing consumer behaviour. Consumers want convenience and the ability to watch programmes when they choose. Sky Go allows consumers to watch their favourite sport, entertainment or fashion programmes live in the UK and Ireland, on the move or on demand on an Android smartphone, iPhone, iPad, laptop or Xbox 360.

In addition to technology reducing the cost to reach multiple market segments, opportunities exist for advertisers and event organisers to create engaging new experiences. Consumption has changed from a one-way static model to a two-way interactive communication process, in which audiences are more involved. Facebook, Twitter, YouTube and blogs provide a voice for fans to interact with other fans and provides commercial opportunities for sports organisations.

10.5 Social media

Social media is not a strategy. It is one of the communication tools available. It is a great and potentially personal tool, but does not stop there. Friends, fans and followers influence consumers' purchasing decisions in ever more sophisticated ways. In the first decade of the twenty-first century, new media technologies for social networking such as Facebook, MySpace, Twitter and YouTube began to transform the social, political and informational practices of both the individual and institutions across the globe. Today's social networks are not solely about websites; they are more about experiences. Social networking sites can grow rapidly and can die. Recently the site Friends Reunited, which was launched in 2000, and acquired by the broadcaster ITV for £175m in 2005 announced its closure. Its ten million registered users had failed to engage with the website. At its peak more than 23 million users were revisiting old pals and former adversaries. However, despite changes in ownership, the business was unable to cover its costs and firms such as Facebook became the way to make contact. Figure 10.8 summarises some of the impacts of social media.

The News Corp under the leadership of Rupert Murdoch paid US$580m in 2005 for MySpace and sold the company for US$35m in 2011. At its peak MySpace attracted 75.9m monthly unique visitors and it went head to head with Facebook for users and advertising dollars. Unfortunately, MySpace's demise was in part due to its failure to innovate its design aspect at the necessary pace. The MySpace approach allowed the user to control and design their profiles. Facebook soon realised that users were more interested in communicating with friends and family members rather than the technical aspects of the experience. Hence, users migrated to Facebook en masse. The inability to innovate occurs in bricks and clicks too. Thus, social media is not a strategy in itself, but merely one of the communication tools available. It is a powerful and potentially personal tool, but needs to keep evolving. Social media can be an enabler and an accelerator of existing core capabilities, values, attributes and plans. It can even be a catalyst for change. But it cannot magically create what does not exist. Figure 10.9 shows the shifts taking place.

- One of the central tenets of recording consumer behaviour is the acknowledgment that social media has disrupted traditional relationships.
- Consumer decision-making is no longer solely based on price; online customer reviews are now part of the consideration set when deciding which hotels to include in the shortlist.
- Customers are changing their behaviour faster than organisations can evolve.
- Organisations now need to cope with digitally empowered customers.
- 93% of hotel guests are influenced by reviews.
- Innovative businesses have come to realise that smart mobile applications are the way to optimise and extract data analytics for competitive advantage.

Figure 10.8 The social media situation

Digital strategy 205

MORE.......		LESS........
New social tools and services	———	Privacy
Content	———	Single destination websites
Collaboration	———	Desired exclusivity
Machine intelligence	———	Real relationships
Social connections	———	Direct only marketing

Figure 10.9 Social media trending

Niche social networks

First mover advantage has been obtained through the use of social media, but as social media moves towards being a commodity, firms need to work harder to be distinct online. So content alone is insufficient. Mechanisms need to be incorporated that will organise and filter content. The Internet is in danger of becoming too generic with the dominance of the mega social network brands. Individuals are now looking for specific networks where they can connect with specific audiences with similar interests. Small is arguably the new Big, as social media is becoming increasingly personalised. Internet users are increasingly seeking connections and content that filters out the "noise" and want to focus on those online conversations that truly matter to them. From a marketer's perspective a highly targeted audience of, say, 1,000 is preferable to a fragmented audience of 1m.

Individuals appear to be getting bored of Facebook and Instagram. Fewer people are spending time on mainstream social media apps. Research by SimilarWeb, which analyses time spent on Facebook, Instagram, Twitter and Snapchat, observed that Instragram had the largest fall in global usage, down 23.7 per cent year-on-year. Facebook was the most used and Twitter was the least used social networking app. In addition to some of the earlier alternatives to Facebook (see Figure 10.10), there is a proliferation of niche social network sites such as Periscope, Telegram, Whisper and Yik Yak, which allow people to chat anonymously in closed environments.

LinkedIn
Twitter
Pinterest
Instagram
Tumblr
Myspace
Tagged

Figure 10.10 Facebook alternatives

10.6 Internet of Things

Projections suggest that by 2020, an estimated 50bn devices will be connected to the Internet (DHL & Cisco, 2015). One third will be via computers, smartphones, tablets and TVs. The remaining two-thirds will be "things," including sensors, actuators and other technological innovations that enable firms to compete more effectively. Despite the term Internet of Things (IOT) being coined by Kevin Ashton in 1999, its true potential has yet to be explored. The relatively new era of IOT refers to the interconnection of everyday objects, which are equipped with ubiquitous intelligence. This network of physical objects or "things" embedded with software, electronics, and sensors enables the collection and exchange of data. The IOT is not a single piece of technology but incorporates several developments that collectively provide capabilities to act as a conduit between the physical and virtual worlds.

Radio frequency identification (RFID) is a core technology that consists of wireless use of electromagnetic fields to transfer data to automatically identify and track tags attached to objects. The tags contain electronically stored information which can be deployed in a strategic manner. In the retail industry, radio frequency identification (RFID) is being rolled out among more supermarket and other retail stores and can result in reducing stock levels by more than 90 per cent and shortening the time it takes to check stock. The RFID market includes cards, labels, fobs, and other factors for both passive and active RFID. Other sectors and uses include: healthcare and medical; passenger travel; distribution of products by land, sea and air; animals and farming; leisure and sport; manufacturing; security. Benefits can accrue across the value chain and can help reduce cycle time, provide clarity, streamline core supply chain processes and assist retailers to capture data and use data management software to identify customer buying patterns.

From a strategic perspective IOT can enable the firm to improve performance, reduce costs, create new revenue streams and new innovative products/services. Hence firms need to capitalise on IOT and implement strategies to capitalise on the opportunities. Yet there are criticisms of IOT:

- Ethical decision-making;
- Security – threat of cyber-attacks, for example, the most common sensor, RFID, has weak security;
- Privacy – the prevalence of big data enables firms to establish patterns of individual behaviour;
- Identity;
- Environment impact;
- Autonomy and control;
- Social control.

To conclude, Figure 10.11 reaffirms that social media is not a strategy.

> On its own Social Media is not a Strategy. It is merely one of the communication tools available. But it can make great things happen quickly.

Figure 10.11 Social media is not a strategy

10.7 Chapter review

This chapter aims to contextualise and clarify some of the major digital strategy issues, and discuss and illustrate strategic considerations and their operational application. Covering key topics such as reflection on e-business strategy and modern digital strategies, the reader is able to appreciate the importance of business models. Organisational flexibility is included to illustrate one of the salient competencies required. As organisations complete their first round of major investments in digital strategies, key questions re-emerge. Lessons must be learned from prior IT investments and their problems; digital strategy is a much broader concept. It's not about what is spent, it's the firm's ability to harness the available technologies to gain competitive advantage. The well-known social media firms are prime examples of this. This necessitates a continual rethink of functions and processes. Human involvement is pivotal, and individuals need to be led in new environments.

10.8 End of chapter self-reflection questions

1. What are the key components of a digital strategy?
2. Do you believe that digital is now more than a set of technologies?
3. What are the strengths and weaknesses of a social media firm? Illustrate your thoughts with some specific examples.
4. To what extent are emerging markets' social media firms different from their western counterparts? Justify your thoughts with some practical examples.
5. What steps can the CEO take to enhance organisational flexibility?

References

Adolf, R., & Hooda, R. (1997). Customer-centric technology. *Banking Strategies*, 73(Nov–Dec), 39–48.
Ash, C. G., & Burn, J. M. (2003). A model of e-business transformation. *Information Technology and Organizations: Issues, Challenges, Solutions*, Vol. 1 (2003) and Vol 2., 266–269.
Bauer, O., Němcová, Z., & Dvořák, J. (2010). E-commerce and its impact on customer strategy. *Economics & Management*, 15, 397–407.
Beidleman, C., & Ray, M. (1998). The agility revolution. In J. W. Cortada, & J. A. Woods, (Eds.), *The quality yearbook*. New York: McGraw-Hill.
Bharadwaj, A., El Sawy, O.A., Pavlou, P.A., & Venkatraman, N.V. (2013). Digital business strategy: Toward a next generation of insights. *MIS Quarterly*, 37(2), 471–482.
Bremser, W. G., & Chung, Q. B. (2005). A framework for performance measurement in the e-business environment. *Electronic Commerce Research and Applications*, 4(Dec), 395–412.
Brunn, P., Jensen, M., & Skovgaard, J. (2002). E-marketplaces: Crafting a winning strategy. *European Management Journal*, 20(June), 286–298.
Brynjolfsson, E., & Hitt, L. M. (2003). Computing Productivity: Firm-Level Evidence. Working paper no. 4210–01. Cambridge, MA: MIT Sloan School of Management.
Cagliano, R., Caniato, F., & Spina, G. (2003). E-business strategy: How companies are shaping their supply chain through the Internet. *International Journal of Operations Production Management*, 23(Oct), 1142–1162.
DHL and Cisco (2015). Internet of Things will deliver $1.9 trillion boost to supply chain and logistics operations. Online at: https://newsroom.cisco.com/press-release-content?articleId=1621819
Dreyer, B., & Gronhaug, K. (2004). Uncertainty, flexibility, and sustained competitive advantage. *Journal of Business Research*, 57, 484–494.
Dunford, R., Cuganesan, S., Grant, D., Palmer, I., Beaumont, R., & Steele, C. (2013). "Flexibility" as the rationale for organizational change: a discourse perspective. *Journal of Organizational Change Management*, 26(1), 83–97.

Earl, M. J. (2000). Evolving the e-business. *Business Strategy Review, 11*(Summer), 33–38.

Fredericks, E. (2005). Infusing flexibility into business-to-business firms: A contingency theory and resource-based view perspective and practical limitations. *Industrial Marketing Management, 34*(Aug), 555–565.

Gardner, S., & Ash, C. G. (2003). ICT-enabled organizations: A model for change management. *Logistics Information Management, 16*, 18–24.

Gosain, S., Malhotra, A., & El Sawy, O. A. (2004). Coordinating for flexibility in e-business supply chains. *Journal of Management Information Systems, 21*(3), 7–45.

Grant, R. M. (1991). The resource-based theory of competitive advantage: Implications for strategy formulation. *California Management Review, 33*(3), 114–135.

Grossman, R. (2016) The industries that are being disrupted the most by digital. Harvard Business Review. Available at: https://hbr.org/2016/03/the-industries-that-are-being-disrupted-the-most-by-digital

Hackbarth, G., & Kettinger, W. J. (2000) Building an e-business strategy. *Information Systems Management, 17*(Summer), 78–93.

Jennings, D. F., & Seaman, S. L. (1994). High and low levels of organisational adaptation: An empirical analysis of strategy, structure and performance. *Strategic Management Journal, 15*, 459–475.

Kane, G. C., Palmer, D., Phillips, A. N., Kiron, D., & Buckley, N. (2015) Strategy, not technology, drives digital transformation. MIT Sloan Management Review and Deloitte. Available at: http://sloanreview.mit.edu/projects/strategy-drives-digital-transformation/

Kim. E., Nam, D. I., & Stimpert, J. L. (2004). The applicability of Porter's generic strategies in the digital age: Assumptions, conjectures, and suggestions. *Journal of Management, 30*(Oct), 569–589.

Klein, B. H. (1984). *Prices, wages and business cycles: A dynamic theory*. New York: Pergamon.

Koellinger, P. (2008). The relationship between technology, innovation and firm performance-empirical evidence from e-business in Europe. *Research Policy, 37*, 1317–1328.

Krell, T., & Gale, J. (2005). E-business migration: A process model. *Journal of Organizational Change Management, 18*, 117–131.

Lipitakis, A., & Phillips, P. (2016). On e-business strategy planning and performance: A comparative study of the UK and Greece. *Technology Analysis & Strategic Management, 28*(3), 266–289.

Lumpkin, G.T., & Dess, G. G. (2004). E-business strategies and internet business models: How the internet adds value. *Organizational Dynamics, 33*(May), 161–173.

Margretta, J. (2002). Why business models matter. *Harvard Business Review*, (May), 86–92.

Moscoso, P. G., & Lago, A. (2016). Investing in supply chain flexibility: A design framework. *Journal of Advanced Management Science, 4*(3), 271–275.

Nadkarni, S., & Narayanan, V. K. (2007). Strategic schemas, strategic flexibility, and firm performance: The moderating role of industry clockspeed. *Strategic Management Journal, 13*, 19–34.

Neilson, G. L., Pasternack, B. A., & Visco, A. J. (2000). Up (e)organization! A seven-dimensional model for the centerless enterprise. *Strategy and Business*, (January), 52–57.

Newman, W.R., Hanna, M., & Maffei, M. J. (1993). Dealing with the uncertainties of manufacturing: Flexibility, buffers and integration. *International Journal of Operations Production Management, 13*, 19–34.

Ozer, M. (2002). The role of flexibility in online business. *Business Horizons, 45*(Jan–Feb), 61–69.

Palanisamy, R. (2005). Strategic information systems planning model for building flexibility and success. *Industrial Management & Data Systems, 105*(1), 63–81.

Phillips, P. A. (2003). *E-business strategy: Text and cases*. Maidenhead, England: McGraw-Hill.

Phillips, P. A., & Wright, C. (2009). E-business's impact on organizational flexibility. *Journal of Business Research, 62*(11), 1071–1080.

Porter, M. E. (1980). *Competitive strategy*. New York: Free Press.

Porter, M. E. (2001). Strategy and the internet. *Harvard Business Review*, (March), 63–77.

Rudd, J. M., & Morgan, R. (2003). Editorial-marketing strategy: A history of the next decade. *Journal of Strategic Marketing, 11*(3), 161–164.

Rust, R. T., & Kannan, P. K. (2003). E-service: A new paradigm for business in the electronic environment. *Communications of the ACM, 46*(6), 36–42.

Sanchez, R. (1995). Strategic flexibility in product competition. *Strategic Management Journal*, *16*(Summer), 135–159.
Sharma, S. A. (2004). Change management framework for e-business solutions. In: M. Singh, D. Waddell, (Eds.), *E-business innovation and change management*. Hershey, PA: Ideal Group Inc.
Stroud, D. (1998). *Internet strategies: A corporate guide to exploiting the Internet*. Basingstoke: MacMillan.
Swaminathan, J. M., & Tayur, S. R. (2003). Models for supply chains in e-business. *Management Science*, *49*(10), 1387–1406.
Tapscott, D. (2001). Rethinking strategy in a networked world (or why Michael Porter is wrong about the internet). *Strategy and Business*, 26(Third Quarter).
Verdú-Jover, A. J., Alós-Simó, L., & Gómez-Gras, J. M. (2014). Strategic Flexibility in e-Business Adapters and e-Business Start-ups. In *Handbook of Strategic e-Business Management* (pp. 139–155). Berlin/Heidelberg: Springer.
Wang, S. (2000). Managing the organisational aspects of electronic commerce. *Human Systems Management*, *19*, 49–59.
Willcocks, L.P., & Plant, R. (2001). Pathways to e-business leadership: Getting from bricks to clicks. *MIT Sloan Management Review*, *42*(Spring), 50–59.
Yunus, M., B. Moingeon, & L. Lehmann-Ortega. (2010). Building social business models: Lessons from the Grameen experience. *Long Range Planning*, *43*(2–3), 308–325.
Zhang, G., & Gai, J. (2005). Strategic choice for being e-business. In *Proceedings of the 7th international conference on Electronic commerce* (pp. 184–187). New York: ACM.
Zilman, M. P. (2005–2012). Academic and scholar engines and sources: An internet miniguide annotated link compilation. Virtual Private Library, 1–67. http://virtualprivatelibrary.blogspot.co.uk/Scholar.pdf.

11 Small and medium-sized enterprises

Paul Phillips and Simon Raby

11.1 Learning objectives

After completing this chapter, you will:

- learn about the economic impact of small and medium-sized enterprises (SMEs)
- become conscious to the factors that influence strategy formulation and execution in SMEs
- understand how strategy relates to broader issues central to SME growth
- comprehend the role that strategy plays in the management of people in SMEs
- recognise how SMEs are viewed and strategically compete in global markets.

11.2 Introduction

Small and medium-sized enterprises (SMEs) are highly important and influential organisational forms. In the UK, SMEs make up 99.3 per cent of the 5.4 million private sector businesses, and employ 60 per cent of the UK workforce. Together, SMEs account for £1.8 trillion of UK business transactions, representing 47 per cent of all private sector gross domestic product. The importance of SMEs to the UK and global economy is greater than their sheer number, with these organisations helping to improve productivity through innovation, competition and job creation (ERC, 2016). Because of this, unlocking the potential of SMEs is a key agenda item on the policy table of many governments. During the Global Financial Crisis (GFC), the one consistent message was that of growth achieved by SMEs.

What might be surprising to note is that four fifths[1] of SMEs do not employ any labour; they are organisations that represent the interests of the self-employed. The prevalence of non-employing' enterprises has increased dramatically since the turn of the century. Non-employing enterprises now account for nine out of every ten businesses that have commenced trading since 2000.[2] The predominant industries in the UK, by SME business population, are construction (20 per cent), professional, scientific and technical activities (15 per cent) which includes the likes of software and consultancy firms, wholesale and retail, trade and repair (10 per cent). SMEs are least likely to be found in the mining and quarrying sector (1 per cent). When calculated on revenue generation the wholesale and retail trade and repair sector is most dominant, accounting for a third of all revenues from the SME sector (BIS, 2015), a trend that may well be enhanced by the increasing power of the gig economy.

SMEs operate in a rapidly changing and fast-paced competitive environment. This is an environment characterised by fashions that change at break-neck speeds, with increasing levels of global competition, and new forms of technology that need to be understood and integrated to existing business models. For SMEs to thrive in this new world they need to understand how to apply strategy concepts and tools to position themselves and carve out a competitive space. Whether it be for survival or growth, leaders and managers of SMEs need to find ways to respond to the uncertainty, turmoil and competitive pressures that they face on a daily basis. Whilst crisis management might well be appropriate at a given moment (Berman, Gordon, & Sussman, 1997), it is essential that leaders of SMEs effectively manage the present whilst charting a course for the future (Beckford, 2015). Managing this strategic duality forms a key thesis throughout this book.

The application of strategy to an SME context presents a number of challenges. Although the strategy literature is rich in content, much of it has been developed with the larger organisation in mind. Developing our understanding as to how SMEs differ from larger organisations will help to consider the options SMEs have and the choices they can take to achieve competitive advantage. Internal and external factors influence the ability of SMEs to take onboard the ideas contained within larger firm theory. Arguably, poor strategy practices (and management practices more generally) are reasons for the high number of business exits. It will require an awareness of the factors that shape the way we develop and implement strategy in an SME context to ensure that we, as future leaders in business, can move beyond uncertainty and achieve enduring success, individually and organisationally. What we can be certain of is that we are now living in a world where small is the new big!

Strategy nugget

Exploring the winning strategies of Canadian SMEs

SMEs play a vital role in the Canadian Economy. Of the 1.17 million businesses operating across Canada, 97.9 per cent are "small" (0–99 employees) and 1.8 per cent are "medium" (100–499).[3] SMEs employ the majority of private sector labour, with seven out of ten (70.5 per cent) employees working for a small enterprise and two out of ten working for a medium business. SMEs are responsible for creating the majority of jobs, with 87.7 per cent of all job creation being attributable to SMEs.[4] In terms of growth, when measured by revenue high growth firms (HGFs) make up between 4.2 per cent (accommodation and food services industries) and at most 11.7 per cent (construction industries) of the business population. When measured by employment, the lows (2 per cent for accommodation and food services industries) and highs (5.5 per cent for construction industries) become more conservative.

Our awareness of the strategies and management practices that Canadian SMEs use to achieve growth and success has been supported by research carried out by the Business Development Bank of Canada (BDC). In the autumn of 2015, BDC published a report that presented the results of a survey conducted with 1,015 SME leaders across Canada. This study, entitled: "SMEs and growth: challenges and winning strategies", set out to identify those SMEs pursuing a growth strategy, the barriers experienced to its successful implementation, and the common approaches used to overcome these barriers. The research finds that four out of ten SMEs are pursuing a growth strategy. This leaves the majority (60 per cent) having experienced weak or negative growth during the past three years. The reasons cited by leaders within the report for this sluggish growth included: rising operating costs (64 per cent), difficulties in hiring and retaining qualified personnel (55 per cent) and external competition (48 per cent).

The report goes on to identify the "winning strategies" that were reported by leaders to have promoted the growth of their SMEs, as follows:

1 *Customers*: understand your customers and place them at the heart of your plans
2 *Employees*: build and develop your talent base and a competent management team
3 *Innovation*: innovate in products, services, processes and markets
4 *Investment*: invest in the latest technologies.

The report cited the importance placed by growth-oriented SMEs on the investment in a skilled management team, and the need for SMEs to create a focus on their strategic growth plans:

> Better planning can also provide a significant boost, with the largest SMEs far more likely to do strategic and growth planning than the smallest ones. . . strategic and growth planning can pay off in a clearer vision, coordinated action and better results.
> (Pierre Cleroux, VP Research and Chief Economist at BDC)

Re-written based on the report "SMEs and growth: challenges and winning strategies" published in October 2015.

https://www.bdc.ca/EN/Documents/analysis_research/challenges-winning-strategies.pdf

11.3 Factors that influence strategy in SMEs

As identified above, much of the research on strategy has focused on large firm contexts. This would not be problematic if it weren't for the fact that smaller enterprises are not "little big businesses" (Welsh & White, 1981); they have their own unique contexts. Here we will examine the factors that influence strategy formation and execution in SMEs.

At their core, strategic management theories are aligned with models of growth (e.g., Penrose, 1952), and there is an inherent assumption that the strategies of SMEs should be growth-oriented, that is, SMEs will always get bigger. However, it is now recognised that growth is not predictable, and the majority of firms do not grow or aspire to grow (Wright & Stigliani, 2013), at least not on a continuous basis (Storey, 2011). To make such an assumption would be, to use Storey's term, a "one-way bet." Between five and ten per cent of all firms could be considered, at any given moment, to be experiencing "high growth" (Anyadike-Danes & Hart, 2016). Because of this, it is likely that the majority of SMEs are operating in a survival mode, employing competitive strategies characterised by tactical short-term changes in response to presenting business needs.

The strategic approach of SMEs is influenced by a number of factors unique to a smaller enterprise context, and the challenges these provide and the response that SMEs can take is highlighted in Table 11.1. These factors create what Cunningham and Harney (2012) refer to as "strategic tensions" (p. 536). These tensions can challenge small firms in their ability to implement strategic management practice across managerial, organisational and environmental levels. However, while strategy in SMEs may be considered as more emergent (e.g., Harney & Dundon, 2006) one should not presume that decision-making is purely accidental. Whilst it is true that smaller enterprises do have more limited access to a ready supply of plentiful resources, they must acquire and deploy resources efficiently like any other organisation. Indeed, smaller enterprises may even have some advantages over their larger counterparts. When small, management structures, practices and processes can remain simple and nimble, allowing decisions to be expedited and changes in direction to be quickly navigated. Leaders of SMEs are able to formulate, execute and witness the impact of their strategic decisions on organisational performance.

More often the reason for the limited evidence of a particular approach taken to strategy is a reflection of the ownership and leadership profile of the SME. It is recognised that the skills and knowledge (e.g., education, learning, attitudes, prior experience and propensity to network) of individual business owners is central to understanding how and why entrepreneurs make the decisions they do (e.g., Leitch, Hill, & Neergaard, 2010; Storey, 2011; Wright & Stigliani, 2013). One should also recognise that the rationale for growth can vary by stakeholder group (Gibb, 2000). For instance, an entrepreneur's focus on "profit maximisation" or "lifestyle" does not sit comfortably with the attention that policy makers place on employment growth. Through a policy lens there could be a danger that big firms are viewed as "beautiful" and slow growth in employment is associated with poor performance (Leitch et al., 2010).

Table 11.1 Factors that influence the formation and execution of strategy in SMEs

Qualities	Strategic challenge	Strategic response – examples
Liability of newness (e.g. Stinchcombe & March, 1965)	When young, firms lack a reputation/brand in the marketplace (e.g. reputational capital).	Focus on "word of mouth" and informal networks. Emphasise "personal touch" and excellence in customer service.
Liability of smallness (e.g. Welsh & White, 1981)	When small, firms suffer from a scarcity of resources (e.g. financial, physical, human and technological capital).	Bootstrap developments, making commitments at time of need (e.g. Timmons, Spinelli, & Tan, 1994). Develop strategic alliances to provide access to capital (Bretherton & Chaston, 2005).
Ownership (e.g. Goss, 1991)	Founders can employ different control strategies, and these will influence employee investment and involvement in strategic thinking.	"Fraternal" approaches provide employees with a degree of autonomy and input to decision-making, whilst "sweating" views employees as a resource to be exploited.
Leader personality/style (e.g. Mintzberg, 1973; Miles et al., 1978)	Leaders will have varying personalities, and these can influence their view of risk, change and innovation.	Some leaders are visionary and take risks, invest in innovation and seek to anticipate change, whilst others are more cautious and calculating.
Informality (e.g. Marlow et al., 2010)	As the firm grows, leaders need to consider the level of structure and process they implement.	More simplified hierarchies can lead to simpler lines of communication and expedited decision-making.
Supply chain relationships (e.g. Rainnie, 2016)	The nature of inter-organisational relationships may vary between the firm and its customers and suppliers.	Rainnie's (1989) typology proposes four modes of small firm operation, each indicating the level of influence a customer or supplier has on the firm's operations.
Competitive environment (e.g. Covin and Slevin, 1989; D'Amboise & Muldowney, 1988; Dean et al., 1998)	SMEs can be vulnerable to market shifts and changes and need to respond to environmental conditions, seeking out advantage through profitable strategies and niches.	For hostile environments, SMEs can employ an organic structure, entrepreneurial and forward-looking strategic profile. For benign environments, SMEs can employ mechanistic structures, conservative strategic profiles focused on refining existing business models.

11.4 What is strategy anyway?

Strategy as a cross-cutting and multidisciplinary endeavour

The development of effective strategy processes within SMEs can be costly and challenging, and are often presumed to curb entrepreneurship and innovation. Strategic management refers to the mechanisms that can provide opportunities for competitive advantage, but can naively be reduced to the writing of a formal plan (Mazzarol, 2001). A key feature of strategy is often growth, however growth is often narrowly defined by researchers and policy makers as an outcome, an increase in size (e.g., in revenue, employees etc.). This overlooks the fact that for competitive advantage to be achieved SMEs, and organisations more generally, need to develop and orient their capabilities and resources. This requires leaders and those working with and for SMEs to understand the strategy *process* and its interaction with other variables.

A team of academics in the UK have developed a research model – Promoting Sustainable Performance (PSP)[5] – to investigate the determinants of sustainable growth for SMEs. One of the outputs of this programme is the identification of a set of capabilities that leaders of higher growth SMEs were developing and employing to strategically grow their enterprises (see Gilman, Raby, & Turpin, 2012).[6] These findings offer a unique insight into the world of the small enterprise owner and leader, and the issues that need to be attended to. The ten capabilities are detailed in Table 11.2 and can be explored through a short video cartoon.[7]

Table 11.2 The "BIG Ten" capabilities of growing SMEs

'BIG Ten' capability	Summary of attribute
FOUNDATIONAL – change and transformation	
Transformer	Anticipating change and managing transition
PILOT – the role of a '*Strategic Steward*'	
Enthusiast	Passion and energy, with purpose
Strategist	Executable vision and strategy
Integrator	Value, relevance and relationships
PEOPLE – the role of a '*People Patron*'	
Delegator	Structures that afford accountability
Engager	Involving, developing, motivating and rewarding
Sponge	Learning and exploiting knowledge
PROCESS – the role of a '*Relentless Renovator*'	
Innovator	Idea generation and activation
Calculator	Measuring, tracking and adjusting course
Systemiser	Refining processes and systems

Source: Copyright Business Improvement and Growth (BIG) Associates Ltd. Reproduced with kind permission.

These capabilities help us to develop an awareness of the broader issues central to SME growth, and their interaction with strategy. Focus on one aspect at your peril! Within the research, those SMEs that demonstrated an awareness of, and were taking action across a range of these capabilities were achieving higher and more sustained levels of growth. Each of these ten capabilities was explored in greater detail by the research team in partnership with business leaders across the South of England. Hosted by the digital radio show *The Business Bunker* the research team led a "BIG Insights" discussion on the essence of each capability and the way in which they could be applied in an SME context.[8] The next section focuses on one of these capabilities – The Strategist – and draws on an interview conducted by one of the authors and Dr Brian Harney, an expert in SME strategy from Dublin City University Business School.

Exploring the essence of "good" strategy[9]

The Strategist (see the "BIG Ten" capabilities outlined in Table 11.2) refers to the importance of developing a clear vision and strategy for the firm's future and sharing and embedding this throughout the firm (Gilman, Raby, & Turpin, 2012). Yet, Gilman et al.'s (2012) research shows that there is limited presence of formal strategy processes in SMEs. Typically half of all SMEs surveyed reported not having a business strategy or plan. On closer inspection, when speaking with the business owner personally, the researchers found that only 10 per cent of those initially reporting existence of a strategy could provide evidence. So that's only 1 out of 20 SMEs!

When looking for strategy, then, what exactly is one trying to find? Ideally, there should be some form of physical evidence, some paperwork, as well as evidence of strategic conversations. Do employees understand the direction and trajectory of the organisation? What effort is dedicated to strategic thinking, working "on" not just "in" the business? Why is this so important? Well, the collective evidence tells us that strategy holds the strongest relationship with organisational growth (Davidsson, Achtenhagen, & Naldi, 2005). SMEs ought to be no exception. Unfortunately, few SMEs get it right. Reactive decision-making is the norm and this often leads to ineffective and inefficient resource usage, with effort expended on fulfilling the needs of today, rather than building for tomorrow.

Emergent or deliberate?

Two eminent thinkers that were considered in earlier chapters, Michael Porter and Henry Mintzberg, provide two perspectives for the SME (Moore, 2011). The Porterian view considers strategy as a competitive position. This perspective argues that organisations can only achieve success if they establish a unique position in the marketplace, and sustain it. This can either be on the basis of a premium or differentiated service or quality offering or alternatively on the basis of a low cost or no-frills strategy. These are what Porter labels "generic strategies." In making such decisions Porter emphasises that strategy resides in activities and at its heart "*is choosing what not to do*"(Magretta, 2011). This is pertinent for the SME, as we explored earlier how they possess scarce resources and need to focus their energy and attention.

Henry Mintzberg, Professor of Management Studies at McGill University in Montreal, views strategy in multiple ways, as one or all of the 5Ps, namely: a plan (where are we now and where are we going?); a ploy (disrupting, dissuading or discouraging others); a pattern (something that emerges from past behaviour); a position (where you are in relation to your environment/context); a perspective (something that emerges from the way individuals in organisations think). This form of emergent strategy is mainly the choice for entrepreneurs, who have an idea of where to end up, but not how they will get from A to B.

The difference that is typically picked up is that Porter's approach appears more deliberate, planned and rigid, whereas Mintzberg's approach appears more emergent, allowing for learning and change.

A game of roulette or black jack?

Professor David Storey, OBE, uses an analogy to explain how entrepreneurs and leaders of SMEs typically run their businesses. He equates the building of a business to the game of roulette; you place your bets, and you hope everything lands as it should. This type of game relies on optimism, chance and the depth of the business owner's pockets (Storey, 2011). Those business owners with deep pockets can effectively stay in the game for longer, whilst others may exit early on, whether this is a conscious decision, or not.

The simple point to take from this is that Storey challenges whether we are in control of our own destiny and that of the enterprises we seek to build. Can we really believe that we can predict what will happen in our environment? The answer to this is of course a resounding "no," although we can get better interpreting signals and cut though the noise (Silver, 2013). We do therefore have choices, about how we interpret information, which opportunities we take (i.e. where we place our chips) and which we don't (i.e. when we choose to fold). What this moves us to is that "good" strategy is more than a simple gamble.

Unpacking the ingredients of "good" strategy

So strategy is important. Those organisations that are strategic in their approach to doing business outperform those that are not. So what is "good" strategy? How do we know when we are being strategic? Rumelt (2013) distinguides between "good" and "bad" strategy, with good strategy being "a comprehensive response to an important challenge" (Rumelt, 2012, p. 16), and must meet four strategic management challenges:

1. *Orientation*: in essence this is your *purpose* and *vision*. What problem are you trying to solve? What was the burning reason why you established the business? What do you want to achieve?
2. *Relevance*: What is your value proposition? What value do you deliver beyond others? What interest do your customers have in you?
3. *Trade-off*: What is your core competence? Where do you excel? What is the essence of success? Are you fully exploiting what you are capable of?
4. *Execution challenge:* How do you translate your vision into something that is actionable? How do you know you are doing well?

The fourth challenge, that of execution, is one often given the least amount of time. Envisioning exercises are widespread in organisations, and strategy is more than a set of post-it notes or a document. It is the ongoing commitment to spending time having strategic conversations, appreciating that strategy formation and execution are two sides of the same coin (Martin, 2015). The process of exploring, shaping and defining takes place with others. It is not safe to assume that everyone in the organisation knows what you are aiming to achieve. Fundamentally, strategy is about *articulating* how you are going to get from where you are now (the reality) to where you want to get to (the vision), while staying true to your purpose (the reason why you exist) and your values (what's important to you).

POD

Tourists learn Greek and get local discounts

The best way to learn a new language is to speak with the locals. Seeing a business opportunity here, a Greek entrepreneur has set up a new innovative SME that rewards both tourists and local enterprise.

"Glossopolis is a travel platform that connects tourists with local business through the Greek language," said Athina Pitta, who founded the company in 2013.

By completing different online courses the Athens-based SME offers tourists discounts at bars, restaurants, hotels and other local services. This helps tourists prepare for their holiday, save some extra cash and boost the Greek economy.

"We support local businesses by giving them income from abroad in a win-win situation," added Athina.

To help get Glossopolis off the ground, Athina participated in the Erasmus for Entrepreneurs programme where she ended up gaining invaluable experience in Brussels.

"I worked at the European Forum of Technical and Vocational Education and Training (EfVET), it was a very good step to learn how to promote your business to other countries," said Athina.

"I met other entrepreneurs and that was a huge inspiration because I saw innovative business models that helped me find solutions to complicated problems."

Glossopolis has since seen growth in both staff and revenue. Athina now has five employees, attracts travellers from 118 different counties and is hoping to expand to France and Spain.

"I believe young entrepreneurs in Greece have chances," said Athina. "We have the internet and we speak languages – we can find our customers abroad."

Source: http://ec.europa.eu/small-business/success-stories/2016/may/index_en.htm

11.5 What role do people play?

People are a source of sustained competitive advantage. The Resource-Based View (RBV) (Barney, 1991) introduced the notion that competitive advantage could be achieved (and sustained) through a firm-level strategy that involves the development of unique, hard-to-copy resources and capabilities. This view is now positioned as offering potential balance to the strategy literature, with the appraisal of internal strengths and weaknesses (i.e. knowledge & relationships) being seen as just as important as the assessment of external opportunities and threats in a firm's product market (Boxall & Purcell, 2003) during strategy formulation and execution. At the heart of the RBV is the attention given by firms to the development of a unique combination of human and social capital (Sirmon & Hitt, 2003), that allows for heterogeneity when set against competitors. However, how might this be achieved? This is where the discipline of Human Resource Management (HRM) plays a central role.

If HRM refers to the various approaches we can take towards managing people, strategic HRM refers to the process of linking the management of human resources to the competitive strategy of the firm, with the aim of improving organisational performance (Bratton, 2007) and developing sustained competitive advantage (Legge, 1995, 2005; Storey, 2007). At the heart of this debate is the identification of those HR practices that firms can use to effectively recruit, develop, reward and retain employees. Over the past two decades HR researchers have presented various theories, models and views. The "best practice" or "best fit" approach proposes that there is a universal system that can outperform all others (in essence, a "one-size fits all" approach). The "contingency" perspective suggests that optimal HR practices and systems "are relative to the circumstances of the firm" (Wood, 1999, p. 368).

Some commentators have even suggested that the universal and contingency approaches can be synthesised, with firms selecting "what works" for their specific context from a common set of overarching HR policies and practices (Boxall & Purcell, 2003). Appelbaum, Bailey, Berg, & Kalleberg's (2000) seminal AMO framework is an example of this approach, with people performance, and superior organisational performance, being an outcome of three practice bundles: practices that promote employee ability (A), motivation (M), and the opportunity to participate or contribute (O). What we now know, however is that HRM is a matter of "it depends" when it comes to smaller enterprises, with leaders choosing to take a "configurational" or "pick and mix" approach to HRM. At the heart of this approach is the recognition that formation and implementation of HRM, like strategy, is influenced by a range of contextual factors, both internal and external to the firm. Some factors to be aware of are captured in Table 11.3.

Table 11.3 Factors that influence HRM formulation and implementation in SMEs

Factor	HRM tensions
National and cultural context (e.g. Gilman & Raby, 2013)	The country that an SME operates within can influence policy and cultural aspects to which the firm must respond.
Sector (e.g. Ram, 1994)	The need for HRM practice can vary by industry sector, and can limit opportunities for the mobility of workers.
Presence of strategy (e.g. Harney & Dundon, 2007)	SMEs have a greater propensity for "crisis management," and this responsive mode may take precedence over longer-term investments in people management practices.
Implementation (e.g. Bowen & Ostroff, 2004)	The implementation of HRM in SMEs is more likely to occur at a line management level, than a centralised function. This can create nuance in the approach taken.
Leaders orientation (e.g. Heneman et al., 2000)	HRM can find its way to the bottom of the list of presenting issues that the leaders need to deal with and remain as an aspect that "I will deal with when I have the time."
Skills (e.g. Gilman & Edwards, 2008)	Leaders of SMEs are more likely to be trained and hold experience of other functional areas.
Costs (e.g. Sung & Ashton, 2005)	Studies show that the costs of implementing more sophisticated human resource practices can be prohibitive to SMEs and can result in a "zero-sum" game at best.

POD

On the road towards the electric car revolution

In the coming years electric cars will be the driving force of the automotive market, but before that happens Europe will need to establish a network of charging stations.

From its headquarters in Bratislava, GreenWay established the most comprehensive network of electric vehicle charging stations in Slovakia, and now the SME has set their sights further afield.

"Our aim is to create an ecosystem for electrical mobility in all of Eastern Europe," said Peter Badik, co-founder.

In 2015 GreenWay finished constructing Slovakia's network of 20 charging stations and are on the cusp of expanding into Poland, where a network is almost non-existent.

"In the Netherlands you have around 300 fast-charging stations, in Poland whose population is four times bigger, you have six," said Peter. "We want to be the company that accelerates coverage for the whole country."

GreenWay's fast-charging stations are strategically located to enable users to make longer journeys across Europe's growing electric mobility network.

"The biggest argument against buying electric vehicles [EV] is that you can't travel long distances," said Peter. "But if you provide coverage across whole countries then you break that barrier."

Establishing a network before a significant amount of users exist is a costly investment. Fortunately for Slovak EV users, the European Commission's trans-European transport network (TEN-T) aims to close gaps between transport networks and provided GreenWay with funding to help achieve their goal.

"The support of the European Commission gives us a certain competitive edge and a security for a young sector that is already moving forward," said Peter.

Source: http://ec.europa.eu/small-business/success-stories/2016/september/index_en.htm

11.6 The contribution of SMEs to economic activity

SMEs are normally defined as enterprises that maintain revenues, assets or the number of employees below certain thresholds. Most major economies have varying definitions. These range from no definitions in the USA where, for tax reporting purposes, the Internal Revenue Service separates small from large and mid-sized enterprises. Small enterprises are companies and self-employed individuals such as freelancers and contractors with assets of $10 million or less, and large businesses are those with over $10 million in assets. The following section considers the EU, Chinese, and ASEAN SME contexts.

The EU context

SMEs are defined in the EU by staff headcount and either revenue or balance sheet total value. Table 11.4 illustrates the ceiling figures. Defining what an SME is has helped the EU government target these organisations with specific support programmes. The European Commission policy in relation to SMEs is mainly concentrated in five priority areas (European Commission, 2017b):

- Creating a business-friendly environment
- Promoting entrepreneurship
- Improving access to new markets and internationalisation
- Facilitating access to finance
- Supporting SME Competitiveness and Innovation

Smaller enterprises are prevalent in all countries, and their growth and success impact the economy considerably. So it is not surprising that SMEs are a major focus of EU policy. According to the EU, SMEs represent 99 per cent of all businesses. In the past five years, SMEs have created the bulk (85 per cent) of new jobs and account for the majority of private sector employment in the EU (Eurofound, 2016). These grand statistics often cover up the heterogeneity in SME performance, with eight million job losses experienced in two particular sectors, namely manufacturing and construction (European Centre for the Development of Vocational Training, 2016). Growth has been experienced in professional (legal, accounting and engineering activities) and admin (employment, security, travel and building maintenance) services.

Eurofound (2016) assert that SME job creation should be supported by:

- A favourable business environment, with effective institutional administration
- Effective public support structures
- Sound infrastructure, with access to external finance
- Motivation of the owner-manager to grow the business and to take some level of risk.

SMEs represent an essential source of economic growth and sustainable development. This is pertinent for the financial and wellbeing for any economy. The ability to provide a vehicle for socio-economic empowerment should not be underestimated. All countries need growth businesses; it is no good placing emphasis on start-ups without a strategy for supporting scale-up enterprises. SMEs present the majority of job opportunities in low income countries and can aid development challenges. These include sustainability and service delivery which can yield economic prosperity. In a report by the London Stock Exchange, the high growth potential of EU SMEs and their future for European economic growth and job creation were stressed.

The "1000 companies to Inspire Europe report 2016" identifies 1,000 SMEs (see Table 11.5), together with the sectors and trends that will shape the future of EU economies. These sectors include technology, food and drink, manufacturing and engineering, consumer services, and professional services. The 1,000 SMEs were selected from across all 28 EU countries.

Table 11.4 EU definition for micro, small and medium enterprises

Company category	Staff headcount	Turnover	Balance sheet
Medium-sized	< 250	≤ € 50 m	≤ € 43 m
Small	< 50	≤ € 10 m	≤ € 10 m
Micro	< 10	≤ € 2 m	≤ € 2 m

Source: European Commission, 2017a.

Table 11.5 The 1,000 companies to Inspire Europe report 2016

Sector	Firms
Technology Disruptive innovation drives success in a sector where non-traditional competitors and markets are constantly emerging to challenge established leaders and turn their business models upside down… and unicorns are appearing with increasing frequency in European cities.	*BlaBlaCar* – Ride sharing (France). Shift towards a shared economy. World's leading long-distance ridesharing platform operating in 22 countries and 30m users. *Fractus* – Wireless antennae (Spain). It is a world leader in the research and design of optimised antennae for wireless devices, and has licensed its technology to manufacturers across the world – Europe, the US and Asia. *Accedo* – Video user experience (Sweden). While the company knows that linear television will not go away – indeed 95 per cent of television is still watched the "old way" – it is now clear that more viewers are switching to an on-demand viewing experience. Habits are changing at a rapid pace, and with that, so are the demands of the market. The results of this are likely to be dramatic, and to the benefit of Accedo.
Food and drink The pleasures of eating and drinking are not only woven inextricably into Europe's social and cultural fabric – they're vital to its economic success. The sector generates a huge variety of produce to feed consumers' taste for tradition and appetite for adventure, both in the EU and beyond.	*Balticovo* – Eggs producer (Latvia). With almost 45 years of experience in the egg industry, modern production facilities and an annual egg production of 600 million, exporting to 18 countries around the world, Balticovo have become not only a leader within the field, but have market-leading expertise. *Loux* – Soft drinks (Greece). Loux's commitment to its customers has helped it capture over a quarter of the market of "refreshments with flavour" – no mean feat given the dominance of multinational soft drink brands across Europe. Today the brand is supported by 450 representatives across Greece, and is available in 20 countries worldwide. *Grosbusch* – Fruit importer (Luxembourg). Recent challenges, meanwhile, have arisen more from internal structure organisation and business planning – where being a family-run business can pose its own challenges. "But we've managed to structure and plan the business to the smallest detail now," says Goy. By 2020, Marcel Grosbusch & Fils hopes to employ over 250 people. "The next few years will be an exciting time for us. We'll be focusing even more on the German and French markets in order to develop."
Manufacturing and Engineering In a sector still feeling the effects of the economic crisis, the companies that succeed are those that embrace innovation, invest in new technologies and explore new models for business and fundraising.	*DESMI* – Manufacturer of pumps and systems (Denmark). DESMI has enjoyed a compound annual growth rate of 11 per cent in the past few years – despite the recent turbulent period. Henrik puts much of this success down to the firm's decision, in 2005, to globalise the company. "We decided on a strategy for growth through globalisation and we also decided to establish a production facility in China, in order to increase competitiveness and to be close to the marine market in Asia." *Eurotex* – Ladies' garment manufacturers (Romania). The company manufactures 400,000 garments per month and now works with many of the biggest high street brands, including

(continued)

Table 11.5 (continued)

Sector	Firms
	the likes of Zara and Mango, to help design and deliver new lines of clothing where cheaper Asian production is too slow to meet the fashion industry's fast-moving demands.
Consumer Services	
What do we want? When do we want it? In the case of European consumers, the answer is often intangible products and services, consumed at the same time as they are produced. As European industry has declined, the service sector has increased in importance – a trend that is showing no sign of going away.	*Continuum Attractions* – Visitor attractions (UK). Continuum Attractions does something few companies dare to do: it puts its employees first, and customers second. And given that it is in the business of making fun – literally, through its operations of theme parks and museums across the United Kingdom – this becomes even more intriguing. *Dentix* – Healthcare (Spain). In 2011, Dentix launched with just seven clinics in Madrid. The company then went big – very big. By the close of 2015, it had dentistry clinics not just in Spain, but in Italy, Colombia and Mexico. Revenue soared from just €3m in its first year to €270m last year, an increase of 9,000 per cent.
Professional Services	
Professional services companies face the challenges of pricing pressures, regulatory changes and increasing competition. But those that allow their business models to evolve while maintaining an unwavering focus on cost management and enthusiasm for innovation have found a winning formula.	*Flow Traders* – Financial technology (Netherlands). "We focus strongly on our team-driven culture," says Dennis Dijkstra, CEO of the company. "We build on three components, namely excellence in pricing ETPs, developing cutting edge proprietary technology and a strong risk management focus." *Ozogroup* – Business services (Malta). "While other European countries were suffering from recession, we had a steady growth," says Mario Muscat. "Instead, manpower has always been our biggest obstacle. With Malta having the lowest unemployment rate in Europe, it's always hard to find the right people for the job in an economy where the best talent is already taken."

Source: London Stock Exchange, 2016.

The Chinese SME context

China, being a command economy, is very different from the western world's mixed economies. Arguably, Chinese SMEs are unique, making the western world's general assumptions of strategic management of limited use. Starting from a definitional standpoint, quantitative and qualitative characteristics are both used. The first dimension of SMEs' quantitative characters include revenue, number of employees, and asset size. However, there is no universal criteria among non-European countries, with the economic and labour market contexts influencing a given country's answers to the question "How big is a small enterprise?" The second dimension of qualitative characteristics includes ownership, control and scope of operations.

From a methodological standpoint, Europe and China are similar, with both using number of employees, annual revenues and asset value. The Chinese government, like Europe, uses a dual dimension system to identify SMEs, and classifies them into five types with corresponding quantitative criteria respectively. If an organisation meets any one of the standards in its industry (see Table 11.6), they can be identified as an SME. A major difference is that the scales used for Chinese SMEs are much larger in comparison to European standards. In

Table 11.6 Chinese SME definitional characteristics

Industry	Number of Employees	Annual Revenues (Million China Yuan)	Overall Assets (Million China Yuan)
Manufacture	2000	300	400
Construction	3000	300	400
Wholesale & Retail	500	150	No requirement
Transportation	3000	300	No requirement
Hotel & Restaurant	800	150	No requirement

Note: 1 Chinese Yuan is approximately £0.10

Sources: Adapted from Liu (2008).

China, an SME does not have to be an independent company and the country has a large and relatively cheap labour force.

In 2013, there were more than 50 million SMEs in China, contributing 55 per cent to GDP and employing 75 per cent of the workforce. In comparison with other countries, Chinese SMEs have their unique internal and external environments. The high staff turnover rate (three times higher than average level of the other East Asia countries) is another concern for Chinese SMEs, with researchers indicating the lower HRM ability and inappropriate performance measurement system as two of the most crucial factors that contribute to this effect (Wang, & Wang, 2012).

Apart from above internal issues, there is a variety of external environmental factors that also influence Chinese SMEs' development. Some researchers state that because of the discrimination by the Chinese banking system, Chinese SMEs place more emphasis on cash flow management than their western counterparts (Zhao, 2012; Shan, 2012). Wan (2012) points out that most of the Chinese SMEs define sales and marketing as their strategic priorities because of large scale and intense homogeneous competition in all industries. Tang (2011) urges that with the acceleration of globalisation, Chinese SMEs need to set targets for institutionalisation, and internationalisation.

The ASEAN

The Association of Southeast Asian Nations (ASEAN) was established on 8 August 1967. The member states of the association are Brunei Darussalam, Cambodia, Indonesia, Lao PDR, Malaysia, Myanmar, Philippines, Singapore, Thailand and Vietnam. The ASEAN Secretariat is based in Jakarta, Indonesia and with the recent creation of the ASEAN Economic Community (AEC) the 600m population has new momentum.

At the heart of these economic drivers will be micro, small and medium enterprises (MSMEs). Their dominance is well illustrated in terms of number of establishments (between 88.8 per cent and 99.9 per cent) and share of employment (between 51.7 per cent and 97.2 per cent). Indonesia has the largest share of number of establishments and total employment. Interestingly, Thailand has the largest share of total exports.

AEC will lead to movement of goods, services, investment, capital and skilled labour and attract investment opportunities. It is also anticipated that investment will come from multinational enterprise or from ASEAN's own indigenous large-scale enterprises. A competitive environment requires local firms to enhance their productivity in order to integrate with regional/global value chains, then create mechanisms to proactively explore and take opportunities. For the first five years of trading, ASEAN MSMEs need to seamlessly integrate with the AEC and regional value chains and for their proceeding years of growth become globally competitive, innovative, inclusive and resilient. A two-pronged approach (competitive pathway and inclusive pathway) will try to ensure that global competitiveness and social inclusion can be realised simultaneously.

ASEAN acknowledges the diversity of MSNEs across its region and the complexity of issues and challenges. These are all central themes of this textbook, which reinforce the strategically relevant topics discussed in each chapter. From an international perspective, the ambivalent nature of small enterprise owners to strategy is risky. Actions need to be coordinated and flowing steps are used to serve as a guide.

11.7 Chapter summary

The application of strategy in SMEs presents a number of challenges. The lexicon of strategy needs to be refined for the SME context. The economic driver is important, as the health of an economy is strengthened by a vibrant mix of SMEs. High performing SMEs brings a number of benefits to a variety of stakeholders. This chapter also considers the often-neglected area of strategy formulation and implementation within SMEs. Intense competition requires more effective strategies, but this requires a clear internationalisation process. Examples are given which look at successful EU firms in the sectors of technology, food and drink, manufacturing and engineering and consumer services. Collectively, this will help to reinforce the differences in managing a SME in a developed and emerging economy. Using a broad sample of SMEs we outline the salient strategic management issues, and provide some frameworks that could be used to help effective strategy decision-making.

11.8 End of chapter self-reflection questions

1 Why is SME growth of such interest to government around the world?
2 What do you believe are the key characteristics of strategically oriented SMEs?
3 Why are effective strategy processes so scarce in SMEs?
4 What level of importance is placed on taking a strategic approach to managing people in SMEs?
5 What challenges do you see the ASEAN having with its proposed single market?

Notes

1 Of the total UK SME population, only 1.3m SMEs employ people (Rhodes, 2016).
2 The UK business population has grown by 1.9 million since the year 2000 (Rhodes, 2016).
3 Source: Statistics Canada, Business Register, 2016.
4 Source: Statistics Canada, *Labour Force Survey* (LFS), 2016.
5 PSP utilizes a mixed method approach to understanding SME growth. Data is collected and synthesized through quantitative and qualitative instruments (e.g. surveys, personal interviews, detailed case studies and focus groups) with leaders and SMEs. The research model is guided by a multidisciplinary team of researchers at Kent Business School, University of Kent representing a wide range of business and management disciplines.
6 Contact simon@big-associates.com to obtain a full copy.
7 Navigate to "BIG Ten" at www.time2thinkbig.com.
8 To listen to a short podcast on "The Strategist" navigate to: http://www.kentbusinessradio.co.uk.
9 This section draws on a blog that was originally published on the "BIG blog" on the University of Kent's Business School website: www.kent.ac.uk/kbs.

References

Anyadike-Danes, M., & Hart, M. (2016). *Spatial Incidence of High Growth Firms*, Enterprise Research Insights Paper Series, February 2016.

Appelbaum, E., Bailey, T., Berg, P., & Kalleberg, A. L. (2000). *Manufacturing Advantage: Why High-Performance Work Systems Pay Off.* New York: Ithaca.

Balbuena, S. S. (2014). *State-owned Enterprises in Southern Africa.* OECD Corporate Government Working Papers No.13.

Barney, J. (1991). Special theory forum: The Resource-Based Model of the firm – Origins, implications, and prospects. *Journal of Management, 17*(1), 97.

BDC (2015). *SMEs and Growth: Challenges and Winning Strategies*, October 2015, downloaded from: www.bdc.ca.

Beckford, J. (2015). The Intelligent Organization: Realising the Value of Information. Aningdon, UK, & New York: Routledge.

Berman, J., Gordon, D., & Sussman, G. (1997). A study to determine the benefits small business firms derive from sophisticated planning versus less sophisticated types of planning. *The Journal of Business & Economic Studies, 3*(3), 1–11.

BIS (Department of Business Innovation & Skills) (2015). Online at: https://www.gov.uk/government/uploads/system/uploads/attachment_data/file/467443/bpe_2015_statistical_release.pdf

Björnberg, A., Elstrodt, H-P., & Vivek Pandit, V. (2014). The family-business factor in emerging markets, *McKinsey Quarterly*, December.

Bowen, D. E., & Ostroff, C. (2004). Understanding HRM-firm performance linkages: The role of the "strength" of the HRM system. *Academy of Management Review, 29*(2), 203–221.

Boxall, P., & Purcell, J. (2003). *Strategy and Human Resource Management.* Basingstoke: Palgrave Macmillan.

Bratton, J. (2007). Strategic human resource management. In: J. Bratton, & J. Gold, (Eds.), *Human Resource Management: Theory and Practice.* 4th ed. Hampshire: Palgrave Macmillan.

Bretherton, P., & Chaston, I. (2005). Resource dependency and SME strategy: An empirical study. *Journal of Small Business and Enterprise Development, 12*(2), 274–289.

Covin, J. G., & Slevin, D. P. (1989). Strategic management of small firms in hostile and benign environments. *Strategic Management Journal, 10*(1), 75–87.

Crittenden, V. L. & Crittenden, W. F. (2010). Strategic management in emerging economies: A research agenda. *Organisations and Markets in Emerging Economies, 1*(1), 9–23.

Cunningham, J., & Harney, B. (2012). *Strategy and Strategists.* Oxford: Oxford University Press.

D'Amboise, G., & Muldowney, M. (1988). Management theory for small business: Attempts and requirements. *Academy of Management Journal, 13*(2), 226–240.

Davidsson, P., Achtenhagen, L., & Naldi, L. (2005). Research on small firm growth: A review. Working paper. Brisbane: Brisbane Graduate School of Business, Queensland University of Technology.

Dean, T., Brown, R., & Bamford, C. (1998). Differences in large and small firm responses to environmental context: Strategic implications. *Strategic Management Journal, 19*(8), 709–728.

Dobbs, R., Koller, T., & Ramaswamy, S. (2015). The Big Idea. *Harvard Business Review, 93*(10).

ERC (2016). Boosting UK productivity with SME growth. Available at: enterpriseresearch.ac.uk.

Eurofound (2016). ERM annual report: Job creation in SMEs. Luxembourg: Publications office of the European Union.

European Centre for the Development of Vocational Training (2016). *European Sectoral Trends: The Next Decade.* doi:10.2801/25967.

European Commission (2017a). *What is an SME?* Available at: https://ec.europa.eu

European Commission (2017b). Entrepreneurship and small and medium-sized enterprises (SMEs): What the EU does for SMEs. Available at: https://ec.europa.eu.

Fernandez-Araoz, C., Iqbal, S., & Ritter, J. (2015). Leadership lessons from great family businesses. *Harvard Business Review, 96*(4), 83–97.

Gibb, A. A. (2000) Small and medium enterprise development: Borrowing from elsewhere? *Journal of Small Business and Enterprise Development, 7*(3), 199–211.

Gilman, M., & Edwards, P. (2008). Testing a framework of the organisation of small firms. *International Small Business Journal*, *26*(5), 531–558.

Gilman, M., & Raby, S. (2013). National context as a predictor of high-performance work system effectiveness in small-to-medium-sized enterprises (SMEs): A UK–French comparative analysis. *International Journal of Human Resource Management*, *24*(2), 372–390.

Gilman, M., Raby, S., & Turpin, J. (2012). *The "BIG Ten" characteristics of success*. The Centre for Employment, Competitiveness and Growth, University of Kent.

Goss, D. (1991). *Small Business and Society*. London: Routledge.

Harney, B. (2012). Book review and commentary: Good strategy/bad strategy, *Irish Journal of Management*, *31*(2), 126–131.

Harney, B., & Dundon, T. (2006). Capturing complexity: Developing an integrated approach to analysing HRM in SMEs. *Human Resource Management Journal*, *16*(1), 48–73.

Harney, B., & Dundon, T. (2007). An emergent theory of HRM: A theoretical and empirical exploration of determinants of HRM among Irish small-to medium-sized enterprises (SMEs). *Advances in Industrial and Labor Relations*, *15*, 109–159.

Heneman, R. L., Tansky, J. W., & Camp, S. M. (2000). Human resource management practices in small and medium-sized enterprises: Unanswered questions and future research perspectives. *Entrepreneurship: Theory & Practice*, *25*(1), 11.

Khanna, T., & Palepu, K. (2013). *Winning in emerging markets: A road map for strategy and execution*. Harvard Business Press.

Legge, K. (1995). *Human resource management: Rhetorics and realities*. Basingstoke: Macmillan Press Ltd.

Legge, K. (2005). Human resource management: Rhetoric and realities anniversary edition. Basingstoke: Palgrave Macmillan.

Leitch, C., Hill, F., & Neergaard, H. (2010). Entrepreneurial and business growth and the quest for a "comprehensive theory": Tilting at windmills? *Entrepreneurship Theory and Practice*, *34*(2), 249–260.

Liu, X. (2008). SME development in China: A policy perspective on SME industrial clustering, in H. Lim, (Ed.), *SME in Asia and Globalization*, pp. 37–68. ERIA Research Project Report 2007–5. Available at: www.eria.org.

London Stock Exchange (2006). *The 1000 Companies to Inspire Europe*. Available at: http://www.lseg.com.

Magretta, J. (2011). *Jim Collins, Meet Michael Porter*. Harvard Business Review, December 15.

Marlow, S., & Patton, D. (1993). Managing the employment relationship in the smaller firm: Possibilities for human resource management. *International Small Business Journal*, *11*(4), 57–64.

Marlow, S., Taylor, S., & Thompson, A. (2010). Informality and formality in medium-sized companies: Contestation and synchronization. *British Journal of Management*, *21*(4), 954–966.

Martin, R. (2015). Stop distinguishing between execution and strategy, *Harvard Business Review*, March *13*, 2013.

Mazzarol, T. (2001). Do formal business plans really matter? An exploratory study of small business owners in Australia. *Small Enterprise Research*, *9*(1), 32–45.

Moore, K. (2011). *Porter or Mintzberg: Whose View of Strategy Is the Most Relevant Today?* Forbes Magazine. Available at: http://www.forbes.com.

Miles, R. E., Snow, C. C., Meyer, A. D., & Coleman, H. (1978). Organizational strategy, structure and process. *The Academy of Management Review*, *3*(3), 546–562.

Mintzberg, H. (1973). *The Nature of Managerial Work*. New York: Harper & Row.

Penrose, E. T. (1952). Biological analogies in the theory of the firm. *American Economic Review*, *42*(5), 804.

Rainnie, A. (2016). *Industrial Relations in Small Firms: Small Isn't Beautiful*. London: Routledge.

Ram, M. (1994). *Managing to Survive: Working Lives in Small Firms*. Oxford, UK: Blackwell.

Rhodes, C. (2016). *Business Statistics*. House of Commons Library Briefing Paper, Number 065152, 23 November 2016.

Rumelt, R. (2012). *Good Strategy/Bad Strategy: The Difference and Why It Matters*. New York: Profile Books.
Shan, Y.F. (2012). The study on development of micro-loan companies of China: The situation, difficulties and countermeasures. Shandong University of Finance and Economic.
Shenhar, A.J., & Dvir, D. (1996). Toward a typological theory of project management. *Research Policy*, *25*, 607–632.
Silver, N. (2013). *The Signal and the Noise: The Art of Prediction*. New York: Penguin.
Sirmon, D. G., & Hitt, M. A. (2003). Managing resources: Linking unique resources, management, and wealth creation in family firms. *Entrepreneurship: Theory & Practice*, *27*(4), 339–358.
Stinchcombe, A. L., & March, J. G. (1965). Social structure and organizations. *Advances in Strategic Management*, *17*, 229–259.
Storey, D. J. (2011). Optimism and chance: The elephants in the entrepreneurship room. *International Small Business Journal*, *29*(4), 303–321.
Storey, J. (2007). *Human Resource Management: A Critical Text*. 3rd edn. London: Thomson.
Sung, J., & Ashton, D. (2005). Achieving best practice in your business: High performance work practices: Linking strategy and skills to performance outcomes. London: Department of Trade and Industry.
Tang, Y. K. (2011). Influence of networking on the internationalization of SMEs: Evidence from internationalized Chinese firms. *International Small Business Journal*, *29*(4), 374–398.
Timmons, J. A., Spinelli, S., & Tan, Y. (1994). *New Venture Creation: Entrepreneurship for the 21st Century* (*Vol. 4*). Burr Ridge, IL: Irwin.
Wan T. (2012). The characteristics of Chinese SMEs' finance management. *Journal of Tianjin Manager College*, *5*(5), 26–29.
Wang S. Y., & Wang L. (2012). The attributions of high turnover rate in the Chinese high technology SMEs. *Economic Tribune*, *1*(1), 166–176.
Welsh, J. A., & White, J. F. (1981). A small business is not a little big business. *Harvard Business Review*, *59*(4), 18–27.
Wignaraja, G, & Dumaua-Cabauatan, M. (2016). Go back to basics to help ASEAN SMEs benefit from AEC. Available at: http://blogs.adb.org/
Wood, S. (1999). Human resource management and performance. *International Journal of Management Reviews*, *1*(4), 367.
World Bank (2014). Turkey's transitions: integration, inclusion, institutions. Washington, DC., USA.
Wright, M., & Stigliani, I. (2013). Entrepreneurship and growth. *International Small Business Journal*, *1*(31), 5–26.
Zhao G. (2012). Reflections on the promotion of SME loaning platform construction in Chinese commercial banks. *Economic Problems*, *20*(2), 60–62.

12 Strategic performance measurement

12.1 Learning objectives

After completing this chapter you will:

- understand the problems of over-reliance on financial oriented performance measures
- be cognisant with the role of strategic performance measurement within organisations
- be able to describe the various approaches and types of performance measurement systems
- appreciate the influence of the marketing dashboard and its influence on strategy
- be able to describe the difference between private and public sector oriented performance measurement.

12.2 Introduction

A core tenet of this textbook has been the need for the CEO to improve performance. Given the role of stakeholders, the journey needs to be measured in terms of performance. Substantial resources continue to be invested in performance measurement systems. Surprisingly, despite the substantial resources invested, the intended benefits often fail to accrue. Performance measurement brings a number of behavioural and outcome benefits to practitioners, but communication flaws can be damaging. Effective performance measurement requires management to arrange work and establish decision-making processes together with the communication of renewal strategies (Sainaghi, Phillips, & Zavarrone, 2017). The relationship between strategy and performance is pivotal and motivation of employees at all levels is another enabler. Ideally, performance measurement should be integrated with overall business strategy and include a comprehensive array of measures, which should include financial and non-financial metrics. Thus, performance measurement remains one of the most critical activities for those concerned with the strategic planning and management of tourism. Figure 12.1 outlines some of the shortcomings.

Nevertheless, making performance measurement research both rigorous and relevant and helping decision-makers implement better decisions remain a challenge. Practice is theoretically interdisciplinary, where no single discipline can provide a complete explanation and the cross-border locations of organisations make the context phenomenologically complex. In short, the new normal continues to change, so given the precarious state of many firms, alignment of PMS and strategy is a high priority (Sainaghi, Phillips, & Zavarrone, 2017). During tough economic times, aggressively reducing the cost base is insufficient. Chief executive officers must do things more effectively. This can involve the creation of new business

Strategic performance measurement 229

- Overly focused on the past
- Overly focused on the short-term
- Overly focused on a financial performance
- Overflow of information
- Information not available in time
- Easy to manipulate
- Too aggregate
- Imprecise, often provides erroneous information

Figure 12.1 Shortcomings of performance measurement

- A contingency approach can also improve economic performance, as measurement gaps between the firm's strategic priorities and management practices are minimised.

Figure 12.2 Contingency approach

models and reducing complexity. Measuring business performance is a key requirement of any organisation. The differing perspectives due in part to the multidisciplinary focus such as accounting, finance, economics, strategy, marketing and operations make the phenomenon that more complex. Contingency approach is highly relevant (see Figure 12.2).

After more than three decades, the performance management revolution continues to gather pace with advocates of performance measurement systems (PMS) arguing that they can lead to superior firm performance. However, drivers of PMS usage at the managerial level do not always coincide with drivers at the firm level, and this can lead to a constraining effect on organisations. A significant transformation within organisations during the last decade has been the adoption of strategic performance measurement systems (SPMS), which are a subset of PMS (Bisbe & Malagueno, 2012). SPMS can aid strategy implementation and the strategy (re)formulation process. Nevertheless, despite the growing number of publications on organisations' PMS, consensus on implementation remains elusive. Moreover, SPMS need to be flexible and dynamic to ensure strategic alignment of salient processes. This chapter will provide an overview of the salient performance measurement literature and insight to allow the reader to think critically about the design and implementation of SPMS.

POD

G4S strategy, performance and risk

G4S is the world's leading global, integrated security company specialising in the delivery of security and related services to customers across six continents.

Our strategy addresses the positive, long-term demand for our services and we differentiate the G4S brand through our values and by investing in our customers, our people and our services.

We build valuable, long-term relationships with our customers by combining a deep understanding of their businesses with our expertise in designing and delivering industry-leading, innovative services that protect and create value for their organisations.

Our strategic priorities are: investing in people, customers, service innovation and growth, operational and service excellence and disciplined financial management.

One of the strengths of our strategy is that there are multiple sources of value organic opportunities to drive revenue growth and opportunities to improve PBITA margins through productivity improvements and portfolio management.

Source: http://www.g4s.com/en/Who-we-are

12.3 Performance blind spots

Given the surfeit of measures, CEOs still suffer from their inability to measure everything that matters. If the performance measures ignore a critical area for corporate success, the business could be at risk. From a slightly differing perspective, some organisations are unable to answer some rather fundamental questions:

- What does success look like?
- What are the processes we must get right?
- What does failure look like?
- What must we not do?

Sometimes bad decision-making can be a consequence of an over-reliance on intuition. Such biases are worrying and even more so, if the strong voice has a negative combination of experience and ability. Another area often forgotten is that of leading indicators. Accounting indicators are backward looking and being historic focus on past events. Analysts know that CEOs sometimes withhold information in their annual reports, which can lead to an incomplete view of opportunity and risk. A dominant asset class is that of intangible assets, including intellectual, social and brand capitals. If handled poorly this can lead to a significant gap between a company's balance sheet value and market capitalisation.

Financial performance tends to be measured over the short term and induce short term "fixes." So, the link between business and production process systems and financial systems are lag indicators (see Figure 12.3), whereas, strategic management/marketing are forward

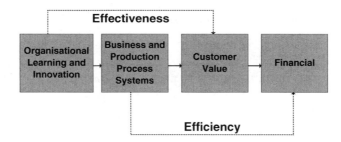

Figure 12.3 Relationship between lead and lag indicators

looking and seek long-term fixes. Customer value is a good indicator, as changes in customer buying behaviour can be spotted prior to the production of the monthly management reports. But, observing such touchpoints needs new forms of marketing measurement too. What is clearly accepted, if not actually practised by many is the idea that financial measures alone are sufficient to manage the firm. They are necessary, but not enough as they may not capture all of a company's strategic objectives.

Strategy nugget

Managing strategic performance in 3-dimensions (based on paper by Phillips and Parry, 2004)

INTRODUCTION

A measurement diversity approach can enhance economic performance, as managers place emphasis on a broad set of financial and non-financial performance measures (e.g. Lingle & Schiemann, 1996). A contingency approach can also improve economic performance, as measurement gaps between the firm's strategic priorities and measurement practices are minimised (e.g. Langfield-Smith, 1997). Nevertheless, despite frameworks emerging, such as the balanced scorecard (Kaplan & Norton, 1996), that extend organisational perspectives beyond traditional financial measures, many organisations still fail to identify, analyse and act on the non-financial measures (Ittner, Larcker, & Randall, 2003).

This developmental paper outlines a tested strategic performance system (see Phillips, 1999) that utilises a 3-dimensional perspective to leverage competitive advantages at three levels of activity. The *SPS: 3-D* model encourages hoteliers to enhance their strategic planning processes, translating these into improved business results and removing blocks to organisational learning – across all aspects of performance.

CURRENT CHALLENGES FOR THE HOTEL SECTOR

There is a rich variety of performance initiatives and debates taking place within the hospitality sector. Currently, favourites include the Balanced Scorecard (Kaplan & Norton, 1996) and Six Sigma (Linderman, Schroeder, Zaheer, & Choo, 2003), whilst leading industry figures and academics continue to question the suitability of current approaches to hospitality performance metrics (Demetriadi, 2002).

Perennial concerns focus on:

- too many measures existing
- measures not relating to strategy
- measures being results-biased and not telling managers how the results were achieved and how they got there
- reward-system not being aligned to performance measures and measures not supporting team-based management structure.

Some hotel organisations are currently investing significant resources in BSC and Six Sigma performance initiatives. Despite there being evidence of documented successes, our research has shown that current thinking is still constraining the breakthrough in performance that the sector needs. The *SPS: 3-D* model is designed to assist hotel organisations, at different stages of their performance initiatives and at different levels of operation, to address critical strategic issues – whether evolutionary or revolutionary advances are sought. Further, the model can help organisations address some of the following common problems.

SOME HOTEL ORGANISATIONS ARE NOW LOOKING FOR THE NEXT
BREAKTHROUGH IN RESULTS USING BSC

First-generation BSC products are, primarily, marketed as control tools for managers with the "red, yellow, green" reporting of achievement of targets – green indicating a job well done, yellow meaning scope for improvement and red needing immediate attention.

To get breakthrough results, however, hotel organisations need to replace simplistic causality between the four perspectives of financial, customer, internal business processes, and innovation and learning. Second-generation BSC initiatives need to be able to identify cause-and-effect relationships of strategic management with performance management – translating these into operational tactics.

Some hotel organisations have failed to derive tangible benefits throughout the organisation – at the strategic, business and operational levels.

For those organisations that are trying to grapple with the implementation of strategic initiatives, such as BSC and Six Sigma, we believe that problems do not necessarily reside in the technical aspect of the initiatives, per se. Success will come from two critical perspectives: first, by integrating the multiple perspectives of staff at the strategic, business and operational levels into a consolidated view of the Critical Success Factors. Second, by rising to the challenge of focusing on the best measures of organisational effectiveness instead of relying on issues that are relatively easy to measure.

SOME HOTEL ORGANISATIONS ARE PLACING TOO MUCH RELIANCE ON
TRADITIONAL QUANTITATIVE INDICATORS.

Traditional indicators such as RevPAR have been used extensively by practitioners, consultants and the academic community to assess hotel performance. Notwithstanding the usefulness of RevPAR for benchmarking hotel performance, the inherent pitfalls in the RevPAR performance indicator make it a poor proxy for the complex hospitality sector.

Recently, practitioners (Slattery, 2002; Younes & Kett, 2003) and academics (Enz, Canina, & Walsh, 2001) have expressed the danger of an over-reliance on RevPAR. Slattery has stated that the gap between the concept of RevPAR and RevPAR statistics has become too wide to be ignored. Younes and Kett advocate the new concept of GOPPAR, which reflects the total underlying operating profit of a hotel, while Enz et al. assert, with supporting evidence, that the commonly used average measures of ADR, RevPAR and occupancy may be insufficient to see what the "typical" hotel's performance is really like.

Managing in 3-dimensions

BACKGROUND

Building upon Phillips' (1999) multidimensional performance measurement systems for hotels, as the overall framework, the *SPS: 3-D* model (see Figure 12.4) comprises three levels, with each containing a core section and two enveloping "environmental hemispheres" – addressing Market Environment and Strategic Philosophy. The Input and Output arrows are placed at the critical interfaces between the Market Environment governing hotel market segments and the Strategic Philosophy of critical stakeholders demonstrating the organisation's current state.

The *SPS: 3-D* model takes the view that there is a strong link between strategic orientation (strategic philosophy) and performance (metrics) with the mediating variables (market environment) affecting the dynamics of this relationship. Our research, over the last five years, has shown that performance measures used by best practice organisations reflect this relationship – hotel organisations have been found to be no exception.

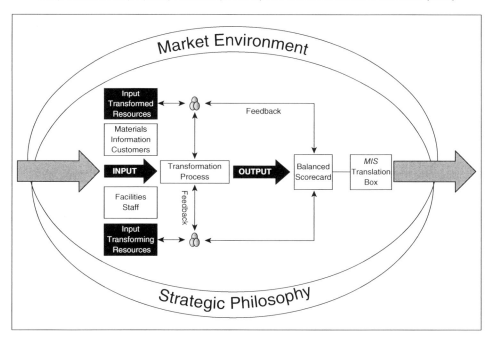

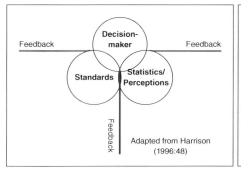

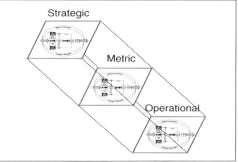

Figure 12.4 Managing strategic performance in 3-dimensions

CORE SECTION

The model encourages hoteliers to recognise the criticality of blending transforming resources (e.g. facilities and staff) with transformed resources (e.g. food and beverages, information and customers) in this phase (Slack, Chambers, & Johnston, 1998). This distinction ensures that a realistic interpretation of inputs is considered and fed into the operational strategy, at each level, for example, the degree to which a hotel brand needs to be proactive, in light of decisions being taken by different customer segments.

All inputs are fed into the hotel organisation's internal transformation. These core activities relate to the critical drivers of value within hotel organisations – the property, brand, IT and management. Continual improvement and organisational learning is incorporated into the *SPS: 3-D* model, through the use of three feedback filtering loops.

TRIPLE-FILTER FEEDBACK

The triple-filter feedback is used by Harrison (1996) to focus on Decision-makers, Standards and Statistics / Perceptions, enabling users to address a variety of conceptual issues, neglected by traditional models. The "decision-maker" feedback filter enables users to incorporate the interaction of a hierarchy of players (e.g. decision-influencers and decision-takers, etc.) into the dynamics of practical decision-making process, while dealing with operational concerns (e.g. dominant logic and company politics).

The "standards" feedback filter reflects the pervasiveness of statutory guidelines, company policies, etc., and enables accepted norms to be tested. For example, many hotel companies still budget 4 per cent p.a. for maintenance "capex," despite recent evidence suggesting that this rule of thumb measure falls well short of market requirements.

Many organisational practices assume that managers have accurate perceptions of their organisations' market environment and strategic philosophy. Mezias and Starbuck (2003) show that most managers have markedly different perceptions and that some have inaccurate perceptions. Hence, the "statistics / perceptions" overlap of the feedback filter ensures the robustness of the information captured by managers and the appropriateness of its measurement – whether it be qualitative or quantitative.

OUTPUTS

The outputs of the transformation processes are fed into the hotel organisation's performance initiative, such as the BSC or Six Sigma. The translation box recognises the likely need for the core metrics to be fed into the organisation's proprietary management information system (MIS).

CONCLUSION

Recent hospitality sector performance confirms that traditional performance measurements are not providing the accuracy or richness required by decision-makers. Emerging measures hold out rich promise but cannot yet deliver the level of confidence required for organisations to commit to them.

This paper seeks to bridge this gap and to demonstrate how the SPS: 3-D Model can integrate trusted approaches to performance measurement with the insights that come from new techniques, whilst taking different perspectives, in order to open up new vistas on future potential.

12.4 Performance measurement systems

After more than three decades, the performance management revolution continues to gather pace with advocates of performance measurement systems (PMS) arguing that they can lead to superior firm performance (De Geuser, Mooraj, & Oyon, 2009; Evans, 2004; Hoque & James, 2000; Lingle & Schiemann, 1996; Van der Stede, Chow, & Lin, 2006). However, drivers of PMS usage at the managerial level do not always coincide with drivers at the firm level (Wiersma, 2009). Consequently, with such a dichotomy, prior research demonstrates that PMS can have both an enabling and constraining effect on organisations (Fried, 2010).

Enabling effects can include: measuring intangible and tangible performance (Kaplan & Norton, 1996), facilitating decision-making and influencing employee behaviour (Sprinkle, 2003), alignment with strategy (Chenhall, 2008; Ittner, Larcker, & Randall, 2003; Kaplan & Norton, 1992), strategic learning (Chenhall, 2005; Fried, 2010; Kaplan & Norton, 1996), communicating information horizontally and vertically (Chenhall, 2003). Speklé and Verbeeten (2014) are of the opinion, on the other hand, that constraining effects include: coercive expert systems (Ahrens & Chapman, 2004; Wouters & Wilderom, 2008), and needing to shape and control strategy (Robins & Baden-Fuller, 2010). Also, the literature refers to "dual role of controls" (Tessier & Otley, 2012) of PMS, which depicts the classical distinction between the decision-facilitating and decision-influencing roles (Ahrens & Chapman, 2004). The former relates to the provision of useful information to guide decision-making, and the latter considers the role of incentives. In addition, PMS are crucial to the resource orchestration processes and many firms have deployed enormous amounts of capital, time and effort developing and implementing such systems (Koufteros, Verghese, & Lucianetti, 2014). In light of this, settling these key debates may be particularly helpful for the advancement of PMS theory and practice.

These observations require further research efforts to provide definitional and analytical understanding of PMS. During the last decade, the strategic performance measurement system (SPMS) has had a significant transformation effect within organisations (Bisbe & Malagueno, 2012), which are a subset of PMS. SPMS can aid strategy implementation (Kaplan & Norton, 1996) and the strategy (re)formulation process (Bisbe & Malagueno, 2012; Gimbert, Bisbe, & Mendoza, 2010). Despite the growing number of publications on organisations' PMS, consensus on implementation remains elusive (Marinho & Cagnin, 2014). In the new normal environment together with increasing global competition, examining how organisational strategy in uncertainty conditions influences the design of effective SPMS remains useful. Kolehmainen (2010) asserts that SPMS need to be flexible and dynamic to ensure strategic alignment of salient processes. Unfortunately, much prior research on dynamic SPMS was originally conceptual in nature (Kennerley & Neely, 2002). Moreover, subsequent research cast doubt on the success of SPMS in dynamic environments (Bisbe & Malagueno, 2012).

For example, SMEs dominate the business landscape, but the focus of many research studies has been on the larger organisation. As Franco and Haase (2015) state, the SME liability of smallness represents an inherent disadvantage, as they only have access to limited resources. Moreover, the literature and research on PMS in the SME environment is scarce and lacks new approaches (Chalmeta, Palomero, & Matilla, 2012). Research evidence suggests that western theories focusing on organisations and their environments are likely to suffer from a weak fit (Boyacigiller & Adler, 1991; Kiggundu, Jørgensen, & Hafsi, 1983) in terms of generalisability to a non-western context. Cultural differences may also limit the ability of management to transfer and operationalise some systems and procedures (Jogaratnam & Tse, 2006, p. 455). Thus, the western-centric notion of SPMS needs to be overcome.

12.5 Strategic performance measurement systems approaches

Performance management as a rigorous discipline appears to be in an early state of maturity (Thorpe & Beasley, 2004). In particular, it lacks a suitably grounded framework for the non-linear relationships and management of performance (Smith & Goddard, 2002). Probably the main reason for this unsatisfactory situation is the complex and highly interdisciplinary nature of performance management research, which involves many disciplines of varying states of maturity and methodological practice (Ermolayev & Matzke, 2007). Determining the appropriate measures can be awkward (see Figure 12.5).

Sainaghi, Phillips and Corti (2013) examine performance through the lens of the balanced scorecard. Prior research notes that approaches to performance management have identified the inadequacies of solely relying on quantitative and short-term indicators, and have led to the development of SPMS frameworks, such as: performance pyramids and hierarchies (Dixon, 1990), intangible asset scoreboard (Sveiby, 1997), SMART (Cross & Lynch, 1988), performance prism (Neely, Adams, & Kennerley, 2002), success dimensions (Shenhar & Dvir, 1996) tableaux de bord (Bourguignon, Malleret, & Nørreklit, 2004), and balanced scorecard (Kaplan & Norton, 1996). These frameworks provide a way of capturing financial and non-financial performance measures and the concept of SPMS are becoming increasingly part of contemporary practice (Rigby & Bilodeau, 2011). SPMS operationalise firm strategy with a set of performance measures (Choi, Hecht, & Tayler, 2013), which in today's economic and competitive environment necessitates explicit links between strategy and performance measures. Otherwise problems can result for strategic control (see Figure 12.6).

Hence, performance management frameworks now need to move beyond the mere collection of financial and non-financial measures and seek to identify causal and non-linear links among measures, strategies and outcomes. The performance measurement literature

- Measure causes, not effects
- Look for trends, patterns and structures, not events
- Introduce new measures each time you introduce new goals!
- The measurement must reflect the strategy!
- Develop composite measures if necessary

Figure 12.5 Determining measures

Organisations can experience two primary problems with respect to their choice of performance measures used for strategic control:

- Incorrect measures will lead to attention being placed on the wrong objectives
- Improvements in strategic performance measures may not be linked to the actual goals expected.

Figure 12.6 Primary problems

emphasises the importance of these linkages between strategy and such measures (Otley, 1999; Ittner, Larcker, & Randall, 2003; Chenhall, 2008). Micheli and Manzoni (2010) note that SPMS should possess the following characteristics: integration of long-term strategy and operational goals, evidence of multi-perspective indicators, presence of cause–effect linkages and the inclusion of a sequence of goals-targets-action plans.

Currently, a majority of the SPMS projects are undertaken by organisations applying the BSC. According to Chenhall (2008), a distinctive feature of the BSC is the identification of financial and non-financial measures covering different perspectives, which provides a way of translating strategy into action. Speckbacher, Bischof and Pfeiffer (2003) assert that the BSC evolves and can assist practitioners by providing three different types of PMS: minimum standard, cause-and-effect, and fully developed. The minimum standard combines financial and non-financial measures. The next evolution is the cause-and-effect, which illustrates the salient relationships between strategies and outcomes and now more recently clarifies the objectives, outcomes and connecting incentives for the organisation. This indicates that the BSC can be used in organisations at different stages of their development of PMS, which broadens the appeal of this research to academics and practitioners.

Furthermore, BSC approaches focus on the specific strategies adopted by an organisation, and provide a robust tool to incorporate PM processes. Many approaches exist using the BSC in implementing PM. For example, Speckbacher et al. (2003) identify three classes of implementation in practice including: a mere derivation of KPIs (the most widely seen form in the practice) to the BSC-III that has the fullest contents to support action plans and incentives. Other BSC implementation approaches (Letza 1996; Ahn, 2001; Brewer, 2002; Lohman, Fortuin, & Wouters, 2004; Papalexandris, Ioannou, Prastacos, & Soderquist, 2005) provide integrated methods to combine with existing approaches. Kaplan and Norton (2008) continue to provide further evidence for using the BSC to integrate strategy with operations.

However, a number of criticisms of the BSC approach exist. Tapinos, Dyson and Meadows (2011) employ a large survey of strategy developers to study the effects of using the BSC. They conclude that their results did not support the idea that the BSC was widely used throughout the strategy development process and that the strategy process of users was neither more efficient nor more effective than non-users. Jackson (2006) points out that the BSC adopts a very machine-like view of the organisation. Although claiming to embrace different viewpoints, BSC imposes the same viewpoint on a range of organisational activities and thus tends to stifle creativity. Unfortunately, the BSC lacks effective procedures to integrate the key soft and culture factors into the PM system, and to encourage bi-way communications between the staff and their managers (Liu et al., 2012). Interestingly, Zeng and Luo (2013) raise some limitations of the BSC in a Chinese context and provide some guidance for overcoming limitations. These include overcoming cultural barriers. Moreover, the widely used BSC is too mechanistic and rigid for many SMEs, which are under constant pressure to cope with uncertainty, and innovate their products and services. Despite recent attempts addressing these issues, SPMS can be too complicated to implement for most SMEs that have only limited resources in general. Furthermore the underlying framework of the SPMS for an SME has to be robust, flexible and easy to understand.

12.6 Application of the balanced scorecard

The balanced scorecard complements financial measures of past performance with measures of the drivers of future performance. The objectives and measures of the scorecard are linked to four perspectives: financial, customer, internal business process, and learning and growth. These four perspectives provide the framework for the balanced scorecard (Kaplan & Norton, 1996).

The balanced scorecard (see Figure 12.7) depicts metrics in terms of financial and non-financial measures. These need to be embedded in the information systems for the benefit of all employees. Customer-facing employees must understand the financial consequences of their decision-making. Management must understand the key success drivers of long-term financial success (Kaplan & Norton, 1996). The objectives and the measures for the balanced scorecard are more than just a somewhat ad hoc collection of financial and non-financial performance measures; they are derived form a top-down process driven by the mission and strategy of the firm or of the business unit (Kaplan & Norton, 1996).

Measures typically include the following categories of performance:

- Financial performance (revenues, earnings, return on capital, cash flow)
- Customer value performance (market share, customer satisfaction measures, customer loyalty)
- Internal business process performance (productivity rates, quality measures, timeliness)
- Innovation performance (percent of revenue from new products, employee suggestions, rate of improvement index)
- Employee performance (morale, knowledge, turnover, use of best demonstrated practices).

POD

Strategy-focused organisation, performance blindspots and challenges

Kaplan and Norton (2001) postulated that the BSC can be used to help create the strategy-focused organisation, as the tool has uses beyond performance measurement to strategic management. It is based on a common set of five principles: (i) translate the strategy to operational terms, (ii) align the organisational to the strategy, (iii) make strategy everyone's day job, (iv) make strategy a continual process, (v) mobilise leadership for change.

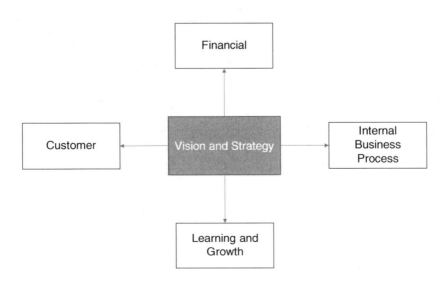

Figure 12.7 Balanced scorecard

Strategic performance measurement 239

However, many organisations possess blindspots and are unable to answer some rather fundamental questions, such as:

- What does success look like?
- What are the processes we must get right?
- What does failure look like?
- What must we not do?

Further real challenges exist in the definition and measurement of organisational performance including:

- Paucity of empirical research to test and validate existing and new frameworks
- Too much focus on being efficient rather than on being effective
- Development of strategic performance measurement approaches, which incorporate a forward perspective.

Strategy maps

The business world is intrinsically non-linear, complex and dynamic, and any insight gained from performance measurement is welcome. The BSC through its traditional perspectives can show diagrammatically how value is created, but it tends to be operations focused (Kaplan & Norton, 2004). To enhance communication and execution, a strategy map (see Figure 12.8) can be deployed. This enhanced link between operational control and strategic alignment will provide a richer picture of the salient elements of the strategy. In addition, the complex

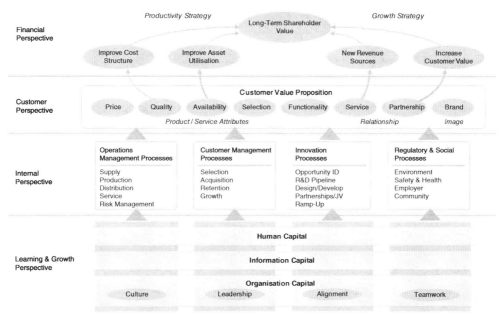

Figure 12.8 The strategy map

cause-and-effect relations can be shown in a sequence, which makes it easier for stakeholders to understand. Strategy maps have been used in service, manufacturing and non-profit making organisations. Kaplan and Norton (2004) identify five "customer value propositions:"

- Product leadership – differentiation strategy, which seeks to reduce the time to market, emphasising product innovation and superior product functionality in serving multiple market segments.
- Customer intimacy – differentiation strategy, which stresses building long-lasting relationships with customers by capturing knowledge about them and their needs.
- Low total cost – cost leadership strategy, which seeks to reduce cost, improve quality and move know-how from top performing units to others.
- System lock-in – generates long-term sustainable value by creating high switching costs for customers.
- Value innovation – selecting a set of attributes and service features that are especially preferred by the larger customer segment, while keeping costs and prices down for such superior performance by under-delivering on features not critical to customer satisfaction.

12.7 Marketing performance

The marketing function requires commitment from throughout the firm. When dealing with customer engagement, there are opportunities to exploit digital data. Despite marketers often arguing that they cannot be too quantitative, due to a fear of analysis paralysis, the general pattern of evolution of marketing metrics appears to be:

- Little awareness of the need for marketing metrics at top executive level
- Seeking the solution exclusively from financial metrics
- Broadening the portfolio with a miscellany of non-financial metrics
- Finding some rationale(s) to reduce the number of metrics to a manageable set of about 25 or less.

The new normal environment (e.g. post financial recession, rise of social media and investments in digital business processes) demands that marketing evolve to remain relevant. The information systems community is calling for the creation of digital business strategy, highly integrated, that raises IT strategy from the functional to the corporate level. With IT gaining prominence by fusing products, services and business functions to enhance business performance, marketing needs to move away from its functional and myopic lens. Changing social practices are raising consumer expectations, especially in tones of engagement, and this is affecting what needs they have that might be served by business.

Marketers need to adapt to this challenge to remain key to their business's success in the digital era. This line of thought does matter, and at some point metrics in use should deliver an accurate depiction of marketing performance.

As marketers typically are not equipped to speak the quantitative language of CEOs, they find that they are able to exercise less and less "clout" in business deliberations. CEOs are starting to play bigger roles in making marketing budgeting decisions. Marketing today is still treated as expense depreciations, with a schedule of one year. By adding data that are not normally part of the balance sheet or P&L statement – such as new customer growth, customer retention rates and share requirements – the impact of marketing efforts can be seen more clearly.

Strategic performance measurement 241

> ...is used as a framework for measuring and reporting corporate performance against:
> - economic / financial parameters
> - social parameters and
> - environmental parameters
>
> i.e. the profit, people and planet approach

Figure 12.9 Triple bottom line

The triple bottom line (see Figure 12.9) is used as a framework for measuring and reporting corporate performance against:

- economic / financial parameters
- social parameters
- environmental parameters

i.e., a profit, people and planet approach. The best managers and the best-run companies in the world all share one thing in common. They consistently deliver superior returns to their shareholders. But beating the market or the industry average is not in itself superior performance. Becoming a value creation leader means posting shareholder returns in the top quartile of industry year after year. This typically requires a doubling of economic profit every three to five years. Is this raising the bar while delivering corresponding higher perceived value experiences to consumers? Some common marketing and finance measures are provided in Figures 12.10 and 12.11 respectively.

A marketing dashboard (see Figure 12.12) is like a "reverse prism" that pulls together a rainbow of data, key performance indicators, graphic analysis, and modelling into a coherent and focused team – in "stormy weather," marketers need to learn to "fly by instrument."

• AL	Other attitudes (i.e. liking)	• LS	Conversion (leads to sales)
• AW	Awareness	• MN	Margin on new products
• BK	Brand product knowledge	• NC	Number of new customers
• CD	Number of complaints	• NP	Number of new products
• CS	Customer satisfaction	• PC	Number of products per customers
• DA	Distribution availability	• PI	Commitment purchase intent
• DC	Per cent discount	• PM	Purchasing on promotion
• DI	Perceived differentiation	• PT	Penetration
• EL	Price sensitivity/elasticity	• QE	Perceived quality/esteem
• GM	Gross margin	• RC	Relevance of consumer
• IP	Image/personality/identity	• RN	Revenue of new products
• LE	Number of leads generated	• RP	Relative price
• LR	Loyalty/retention		

Figure 12.10 Common marketing measures used by board

• AL	Other attitudes (i.e. liking)	• PI	Commitment purchase intent
• BK	Brand product knowledge	• PM	Purchasing on promotion
• DA	Distribution availability	• PT	Penetration
• DC	Per cent discount	• QE	Perceived quality/esteem
• DI	Perceived differentiation	• RC	Relevance of consumer
• IP	Image/personality/identity	• RN	Revenue of new Products
• LE	Number of leads generated	• SL	Salience
• LR	Loyalty/retention	• SP	Marketing spend
• NP	Number of new products	• VO	Share of voice
• PC	Number of products per Customers		

Figure 12.11 Common marketing measures used by finance

Dashboards should have real-time information. Simulations and "what if" tests of different product/service strategies are employed. Users need performance and predictive dashboards to chart what-if analysis. Customised marketing performance dashboards can be used by

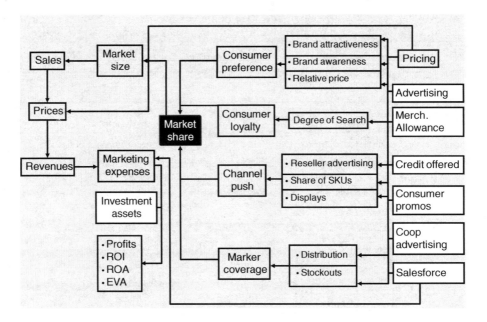

Figure 12.12 Driving performance with the marketing dashboards

sales teams and management to support mobile devices. Traditionally, dashboards have focused on consolidating Key Performance Indicators into a single screen or view. Mobile interfaces do not support the ability to provide this type of information in a single view, thus future management dashboard applications will need to use multiple views for mobile dashboards. With interactive marketing changing quickly, to remain at the forefront of many societal changes, effective marketing dashboards are a high priority.

12.8 Performance measurement in the public sector

Inefficiencies and ineffectiveness of the public sector have led to continued criticisms in many countries. Now, changing demographics and people living longer places greater pressure on the public sector. Essential social drivers such as individualisation, flexibility and the ageing of society will fundamentally change social relations. Patchwork-families, single households, serial partnerships and jobs will replace traditional structures and change how people holiday, with whom and when. So-called flexible jobs sometimes with zero-hour contracts and project oriented engagements will replace traditional full-time jobs. The average age of retirement will be 70. The middle class will slowly drop out of sight and into the networked economy. The gap between those with "lots of time and little money" and those with "no time and lots of money" will get bigger. The changing role of the public sector will need to adjust to cope with this context. The main goal for people in the new millennium is to prevent illness and to avoid the need for recovery. It is not enough anymore to reach a significant age. Fitness of the mind and well-being in terms of the overall quality of one's health is a crucial personal goal. The private sector needs a new mindset (see Figure 12.13).

So, effective measurement of public sector agencies and assessing how they plan to meet current and emerging needs is integral to successful governments. In addition, performance measurement systems enable governments to assess the quality of their resource allocation and determine how best to achieve goals. Departments can understand how well they are meeting government's expectation, and use results as a basis for continued improvement. The government and other stakeholders can use the results to understand the challenges facing government, and current levels of achievement for its population.

In examining the role of performance measurement in the public sector, the application of private sector measurement practices and principles is hardly a novel problem. But the public sector has different barriers and challenges. Government agencies exist to fulfil their charter, so it's more about mission effectiveness. Unfortunately, the mission can change frequently due to media and public pressure. Also the needs of a nation can take priority over existing strategies. Hence it is not static and each department needs to use the appropriate metrics that are measurable and relevant. This will lead to desirable outcomes such as greater transparency.

BBC

The funding of the public sector from taxes, duty etc. makes it exigent that the BBC is seen to be enhancing public value. Drivers include reach, quality, impact and value for money. In terms of performance measurement the cost per household is 40p per day (£145.50 per year).

- A new mindset is required for public sector performance measurement...!

Figure 12.13 A new mindset

For the year ended March 2016, the total licence fee income was £3.7bn. Many consumers argue that the licence fee is outdated and should be scrapped. The BBC's mission is to inform, educate and entertain. The common good of the BBC is set out and reinforced in its Charter and Agreement. It has an intrinsic purpose: to provide programmes that inform and educate and entertain people as individuals. Its instrumental purpose is to deliver external benefits to society through creating a rich culture, promoting debates and building a sense of community via shared experiences.

NHS

The UK NHS continues to lurch from one financial performance challenge to another. For example, at the time of writing the NHS is struggling to meet many of its key performance targets. Unprecedented demand for A&E care, beds and ambulances paints a worrying picture. Hospitals struggle to ensure the A&E four-hour wait is achieved, with only 83 per cent being achieved (target being 95 per cent). With 3.8m people waiting for an operation, which is the highest since 2007, this is a concern. The King's Fund think-tank, an NHS dashboard, provides indicative measures of impact as follows:

Health care-acquired infections – MRSA infection and C. difficile infections are closely monitored.

Workforce – the number of full-time equivalents working in hospital and community health services (excluding GPs) was more than 1.024m.

Waiting times – now there are two official waiting time targets – patients on the waiting list for more than 18 weeks is one. The other is the proportion of patients waiting more than six weeks for a diagnostic test, which has now missed its target (1 per cent) for the past 28 months in a row.

Urgent care – ambulance trusts have been given a target of 8 minutes to respond to an urgent case with no more than 25 per cent outside of the target. Unfortunately, since 2014 the target has been missed. In March 2016 the figure was 33.5 per cent.

Delayed transfer of care – at the end of March 2016 more than 5,700 patients were delayed in hospitals, which despite being an improvement is still historically high.

Collectively the above pose significant problems. The continued deteriorating finances among providers create tremendous difficulties for the NHS in delivering the requisite public services. Three issues high on the agenda of trust financial directors are: delayed transfer of care, four-hour wait times and staff morale.

12.9 Chapter summary

A core tenet of this chapter has been the need for the CEO to be continually improving performance. Given the array and role of stakeholders, the journey needs to be measured in terms of performance, which should be outcome based. Substantial resources continue to be invested in performance measurement systems, but the outcomes are frequently fulfilling financial or social metrics. The chapter draws attention to some blind spots, which can be due to the cognitive representations of the CEO and their management teams. Put simply, bad decision-making can be a consequence of an over-reliance on intuition. Performance measurement systems and their approaches are used to illustrate some of the challenges which need to be considered during the phases of design and implementation. The application of the balanced scorecard considers the more practical issues of strategic performance measurement. The onus is on marketers to demonstrate returns on marketing investment (ROMI) are positive to the firm. However, as corporate budgets get slashed, marketers must learn to restructure their spending without diminishing their brand's presence in several ways. The chapter concludes by looking at performance measurement in the public sector.

12.10 End of chapter self-reflection questions

1 Explain how strategic performance measurement is gaining in popularity.
2 In what ways would you explain the difference between performance measurement in the private and public sector?
3 What are the strengths and weaknesses of the balanced scorecard approach to performance measurement?
4 What do you believe are the core performance measurement challenges of the NHS? Why is the NHS continuing to fail on its key performance targets?
5 What are the benefits of effective performance measurement?

References

Ahn, H. (2001). Applying the balanced scorecard concept: An experience report. *Long Range Planning, 34*, 441–461.
Ahrens, T., & Chapman, C. S. (2004). Accounting for flexibility and efficiency: A field study of management control systems in a restaurant chain. *Contemporary Accounting Research, 21*(2), 271–301.
Bisbe, J., & Malagueno, R. (2012). Using strategic performance measurement systems for strategy formulation: Does it work in dynamic environments? *Management Accounting Research, 23*, 296–311.
Bourguignon, A., Malleret, V., & Nørreklit, H. (2004). The American balanced scorecard versus the French tableau de bord: The ideological dimension. *Management Accounting Research, 15*, 107–134.
Boyacigiller, N. A., & Adler, N. J. (1991). The parochial dinosaur: Organizational science in a global context. *Academy of Management Review, 16*, 262–290.
Brewer, P. (2002). Putting strategy into the balanced scorecard. *Strategic Finance*, 44–52.
Chalmeta, R., Palomero, S., & Matilla, M. (2012). Methodology to develop a performance measurement system in small and medium-sized enterprises. *International Journal Computer Integrated Manufacturing, 25*, 716–740.
Chenhall, R. H. (2003). Management control systems design within its organizational context: Findings from contingency-based research and directions for the future. *Accounting, Organizations and Society, 28*(2), 127–168.
Chenhall, R. H. (2005). Integrative strategic performance measurement systems, strategic alignment of manufacturing, learning and strategic outcomes: An exploratory study. *Accounting, Organizations and Society, 30*(5), 395–422.
Chenhall, R. H. (2008). Accounting for the horizontal organization: A review essay. *Accounting, Organizations and Society, 33*, 517–550.
Choi, J. W., Hecht, G. W., & Tayler, W. B. (2013). Strategy selection, surrogation, and strategic performance measurement systems. *Journal of Accounting Research, 51*, 105–133.
Cross, K. F., & Lynch, R. L. (1988). The "SMART" way to define and sustain success. *National Productivity Review, 8*, 23–33.
De Geuser, F., Mooraj, S., & Oyon, D. (2009). Does the balanced scorecard add value? Empirical evidence on its effect on performance. *European Accounting Review, 18*, 93–122.
Demetriadi, J. (2002). How to measure success? *Hospitality, The Journal of the Hotel & Catering International Management Association*, February, 16–17.
Dixon, J. R. (1990). The new performance challenge: Measuring operations for world-class competition. Homewood, IL: Business One Irwin.

Enz, C. A., Canina, L., & Walsh, K. (2001). Hotel-industry averages: An inaccurate tool for measuring performance. *Cornell Hotel and Restaurant Administration Quarterly*, *42*(6), 22–32.

Ermolayev, V., & Matzke, W. E. (2007). Towards industrial strength business performance management. In *Holonic and Multi-Agent Systems for Manufacturing* (pp. 387–400). Springer Berlin.

Evans, J. R. (2004). An exploratory study of performance measurement systems and relationships with performance results. *Journal of Operations Management*, *22*, 219–232.

Franco, M., & Haase, H. (2015). Interfirm alliances: A taxonomy for SMEs. *Long Range Planning*, *48*(3), 168–181.

Fried, A. (2010). Performance measurement systems and their relation to strategic learning: A case study in a software-developing organization. *Critical Perspectives on Accounting*, *21*, 118–133.

Gimbert, X., Bisbe, J., & Mendoza, X. (2010). The role of performance measurement systems in strategy formulation processes. *Long Range Planning*, *43*, 477–497.

Harrison, M. (1996). *Principles of Operations Management*. Harlow: FT/Prentice Hall.

Hoque, Z., & James, W. (2000). Linking balanced scorecard measures to size and market factors: Impact on organizational performance. *Journal of Management Accounting Research*, *12*, 1–17.

Ittner, C. D., Larcker, D. F., & Meyer, M. W. (2003). Subjectivity and the weighting of performance measures: Evidence from a balanced scorecard. *The Accounting Review*, *78*, 725–758.

Ittner, C. D., Larcker, D. F. & Randall, T. (2003). Performance implications of strategic performance measurement in financial services firms. *Accounting Organisations and Society*, *28*, 715–741.

Jääskeläinen, A., & Laihonen, H. (2014). A strategy framework for performance measurement in the public sector. *Public Money & Management*, *34*(5), 355–362.

Jackson, M. C. (2006). Creative holism: A critical systems approach to complex problem situations. *Systems Research and Behavioural Science*, *23*(5), 647–657.

Jogaratnam, G., & Tse, E. Ching-Yick. (2006). Entrepreneurial orientation and the structuring of organizations: Performance evidence from the Asian hotel industry. *International Journal of Contemporary Hospitality Management*, *18*, 454–468.

Kaplan, R. S., & Norton, D. P. (1996). Using the balanced scorecard as a strategic management system. *Harvard Business Review*, *74*, 75–85.

Kaplan, R. S., & Norton, D. P. (2001). *The strategy-focused organization: How balanced scorecard companies thrive in the new business environment*. Cambridge, MA: Harvard Business Press.

Kaplan, R. S., & Norton, D. P. (2004). Strategy maps: Converting intangible assets into tangible outcomes. Cambridge, MA: *Harvard Business Press*.

Kaplan, R. S., & Norton, D. P. (2005). The balanced scorecard: Measures that drive performance. *Harvard Business Review*, *83*, 172–180.

Kaplan, R. S., & Norton, D. P. (2008). *The execution premium*. Barcelona: Deusto.

Kennerley, M., & Neely, A. (2002). A framework of the factors affecting the evolution of performance measurement systems. *International Journal of Operations & Production Management*, *22*, 1222–1245.

Kiggundu, M. N., Jørgensen, J. J., & Hafsi, T. (1983). Administrative theory and practice in developing countries: A synthesis. *Administrative Science Quarterly*, *28*(1), 66–84.

Kolehmainen, K. (2010). Dynamic strategic performance measurement systems: Balancing empowerment and alignment. *Long Range Planning*, *43*, 527–554.

Koufteros, X., Verghese, A. J., & Lucianetti, L. (2014). The effect of performance measurement systems on firm performance: A cross-sectional and a longitudinal study. *Journal of Operations Management*, *32*(6), 313–336.

Langfield-Smith, K. (1997). Management control systems and strategy: A critical review. *Accounting, Organizations and Society*, *22*(2), 207–232.

Letza, S.R. (1996). The design and implementation of the balanced business scorecard: An analysis of three companies in practice. *Business Process Re-engineering & Management Journal*, *2*, 54–76.

Linderman, K., Schroeder, R. G., Zaheer, S., & Choo, A. S. (2003). Six Sigma: A goal-theoretic perspective, *Journal of Operations Management*, *21*(2), 193–203.

Lingle, J., & Schiemann, W. (1996). From balanced scorecard to strategic gauges: Is measurement worth it? *Management Review, 85*(3), 56–61.

Liu, W. B., Meng, W., Mingers, J., Tang, N., & Wang, W. (2012). Developing a performance management system using soft systems methodology: A Chinese case study. *European Journal Operations Research, 223*(2), 529–540.

Lohman, C., Fortuin, L., & Wouters, M. (2004). Designing a performance measurement system: A case study. *European Journal Operations Research, 156*, 267–286.

Malmi, T. (2001). Balanced scorecards in Finnish companies: A research note. *Management Accounting Research, 12*, 207–220.

Marinho, S. V., & Cagnin, C. (2014). The roles of FTA in improving performance measurement systems to enable alignment between business strategy and operations: Insights from three practical cases. *Futures, 59*, 50–61.

Mezias, J. M., & Starbuck, W. H. (2003). Studying the accuracy of managers' perceptions: A research odyssey. *British Journal of Management, 14*(1), 3–17.

Micheli, P., & Manzoni, J. (2010). Strategic performance measurement: Benefits, limitations and paradoxes. *Long Range Planning, 43*, 465–476.

Neely, A. D., Adams, C., & Kennerley, M. (2002). *The performance prism: The scorecard for measuring and managing business success*. London: Prentice Hall Financial Times.

Otley, D. (1999). Performance management: A framework for management control systems research. *Management Accounting Research, 10*, 363–382.

Papalexandris, A., Ioannou, G., Prastacos, G., & Soderquist, K. E. (2005). An integrated methodology for putting the balanced scorecard into action. *European Management Journal, 23*, 214–227.

Phillips, P. A. (1999). Performance measurement systems and hotels: A new conceptual framework. *International Journal of Hospitality Management, 18*(2), 171–182.

Phillips, P. A., & Parry, B. (2004). *Managing strategic performance in 3-dimensions*. London: BAM.

Rigby, D. K. (2011). *Management tools and trends 2011: An executive's guide*. London: Bain & Company. Available at: http://www.bain.com.

Rigby, D., & Bilodeau, B. (2011). Management tools and trends 2011. London: Bain & Company.

Robins, J., & Baden-Fuller, C. (2010). New editor announcement and introduction to special issue. *Long Range Planning, 43*, 463–464.

Sainaghi, R., Phillips, P., & Corti, V. (2013). Measuring hotel performance: Using a balanced scorecard perspectives' approach. *International Journal of Hospitality Management, 34*, 150–159.

Sainaghi, R., Phillips, P., & Zavarrone, E. (2017). Performance measurement in tourism firms: A content analytical meta-approach. *Tourism Management, 59*, 36–56.

Shenhar, A. J., & Dvir, D. (1996). Toward a typological theory of project management. *Research Policy, 25*, 607–632.

Slack, N., Chambers, S., & Johnston, R. (1998). *Operations Management*, 2nd edition. Harlow: FT/Prentice Hall.

Slattery, P. (2002). Reported RevPAR: Unreliable measures, flawed interpretations and the remedy. *International Journal of Hospitality Management, 21*(2), 135–149.

Smith, P. C., & Goddard, M. (2002). Performance management and operational research: A marriage made in heaven? *Journal of Operations Research Society, 53*, 247–255.

Speckbacher, G., Bischof, J., & Pfeiffer, T. (2003). A descriptive analysis on the implementation of Balanced Scorecards in German-speaking countries. *Management Accounting Research, 14*, 361–388.

Speklé, R. F., & Verbeeten, F. H. (2014). The use of performance measurement systems in the public sector: Effects on performance. *Management Accounting Research, 25*(2), 131–146.

Sprinkle, G. B. (2003). Perspectives on experimental research in managerial accounting. *Accounting, Organizations and Society, 28*, 287–318.

Sveiby, K. E. (1997). The intangible assets monitor. *Journal of Human Resource Costing & Accounting, 2*, 73–97.

Tapinos, E., Dyson, R., & Meadows, M. (2011). Does the Balanced Scorecard make a difference to the strategy development process. *Journal of Operations Research Society, 62*, 888–899.

Tessier, S., & Otley, D. (2012). A conceptual development of Simons' Levers of Control framework. *Management Accounting Research, 23*(3), 171–185.

Thorpe, R., & Beasley, T. (2004). The characteristics of performance management research: Implications and challenges. *International Journal of Productivity and Performance Management, 53*(4), 334–344.

van der Stede, Wim A., Chow, C. W., & Lin, T. W. (2006). Strategy, choice of performance measures, and performance. *Behavioral Research in Accounting, 18*, 185–205.

Wiersma, E. (2009). For which purposes do managers use Balanced Scorecards? An empirical study. *Management Accounting Research, 20*, 239–251.

Wouters, M., & Wilderom, C. (2008). Developing performance-measurement systems as enabling formalization: A longitudinal field study of a logistics department. *Accounting, Organizations and Society, 33*(4), 488–516.

Younes, E., & Kett, R. (2003). GOPPAR, A derivative of RevPAR. *HVS International – London*. March.

Zeng, K., & Luo, X. (2013). The balanced scorecard in China: Does it work? *Business Horizons, 56*, 611–620.

Part 4
Radical/futures themes

13 Strategic thinking

13.1 Learning objectives

After completing this chapter you will:

- be able to take a whole new perspective on strategic thinking
- learn and be exposed to a number of paradigm shifts
- be able to dissect a number of key issues in strategic thinking in management
- be able to analyse many facets that characterise the new "normal" environment, although there will be nothing normal about it!
- be able to ascertain that business cannot be seen as... usual... There is a complete revolution of values, technologies, concepts, trends, structures, core techniques and processes.

13.2 Introduction

The purpose of this chapter is to delve into major paradigm shifts like the age of anxiety, a new revolution in business, a new world and economy, a meaningful economy, finding a purpose and fair finances.

This chapter is intended to dissect a number of key paradigm shifts that have a tremendous influence on management practices in the future. It also contains insights related to the enormous technological pace of change and the way it has an impact on organisations. These are some examples and issues that strongly call for a total renewed view of strategic thinking in management, including a depiction of the "new normal" business environment.

A number of key new concepts are introduced, such as reverse innovation, the age of anxiety, fair finances, evenomics, new business ecosystems, benefit corporations, deglobalisation, emotional engagement, and self-organisation, among others.

The main thrust of the chapter relies on the call for a new thinking organisation!

13.3 Key academic theory

Every aspect of our lives is changing. Society, the economy and our current technology demands are affecting every sector's management needs in organisation. A great amount of thinking is required to cover any eventuality and as this transpires, many management paradigms are being designed and practised each and every day. As time passes we note that most of these paradigms are based on empiricism, where it appears that in practice, they are simply not effective enough and end up being shelved due to their inability to perform, having had little or no theoretical support. Although this practice is acceptable in the short term, while we try to harness the accelerated change that we now live with, it seems a more practical paradigm shift is required.

Murthy (1996) makes a case for this and proposes a shift in the present paradigms. Strategy is sometimes called "strategic planning" and then is used indiscriminately with "long-range" planning. Executives talk frequently about "market strategy" or a "pricing strategy" when they really mean a plan to penetrate a market or to keep prices competitive. Such "strategies" are really major operational decision points that presume an overall corporate or divisional strategy.

Strategy has a very precise meaning, which Tregoe and Zimmerman (1983) define as a framework that guides those choices that determine the nature and direction of an organisation. These "choices" confront an organisation every day. They include choices about an organisation's products or services, the geographical markets and customer groups the organisation serves, the organisation's capabilities of supporting those products and markets, its growth and return, and its allocation of resources.

How these choices are made determines the nature of an organisation. If they are made within the context of a strategic framework, the organisation's direction is clearly under the control of the managers who develop that framework. If these choices are made in the absence of a strategic framework, you abdicate that control and run the risk of having a direction that is uncoordinated and in the hands of whoever is making these choices.

McFadzean (1998) tells how an organisation can improve its creativity by introducing a creative culture within the company. She also discusses the option of group creative problem solving. When creating a creativity continuum, this can present three different technique scenarios – paradigm preserving, paradigm stretching and paradigm breaking. The important part is recognising which technique should be used for which situation. The paradigm preserving techniques have proven to be more acceptable but less innovative, while paradigm breaking gives support to participants wishing to develop completely unique ideas. However, this can create an uncomfortable use procedure and therefore should not be undertaken by a novice. The paper describes six different CPS techniques – two paradigm preserving, two paradigm stretching and two paradigm breaking techniques. Creative problem solving (CPS) and innovation are of critical importance to companies whose goal is to gain flexibility and competitive advantage.

Strategic disruption and the consequential discontinuities usually require business models to be modified to better fit the purpose. But with time, firms with their finger on the pulse will adapt and evolve, introducing increasingly stable business models supplying the necessary rigidity. It can be a much simpler job to resolve the contradiction if there is development of three core meta-capabilities to make an organisation more agile: leadership, strategic sensitivity and resource fluidity.

Doz and Kosonen (2010) take a look at the underlying determinants of these capabilities. They base their findings on research undertaken in twelve companies which were in the process of re-inventing their business models. A proposed repertoire of concrete leadership skills and actions was enabled to accelerate the meta-capabilities in order to renew and transform their business models, in order to best show off the point they are making.

These authors rely on three main dimensions of a strategic agility framework that they had previously presented; they created corresponding vectors within the relevant leadership actions, presenting each as a way to enhance and develop a company's creativity and ability to renew a business model.

As humans search for a meaning to their existence, work holds a central role. The majority of adults spend a great amount of their waking hours in their place of employment, and this, in its entirety, creates a primary source of belonging, identity and purpose. Organisational scholars are finding increased benefit in understanding the factors involved in the contribution of a meaningful work environment, which include job design, organisational mission, interpersonal relationships and cultures. Although unrelated, business ethics scholars have found themselves exploring the concept of a meaningful workplace with moral consequence. This includes management and others, and examining any definable characteristics within the boundaries of meaningful work.

Michaelson et al. (2014) look at the links within the disciplines and present research opportunities and conclusions with regard to the interface of organisational perspectives.

The rationale for the content of this chapter can be expressed as follows. It embarks on a thorough dissection of the key paradigm shifts which are transforming the face of business. The issue of business with a purpose and meaning is also discussed, as well as the age of the multi-sided business and fair finances. We also focus on the need to have permeable organisations and a lot more strategic thinking. Companies and management need more mind-stretching and thought-provoking values, policies and strategies. We also discuss innovative organisational structures ranging from business colonies to holographic organisations. We cover management dilemmas and the need for strategic agility. We dissect issues related to the phenomena of experimentation as the new planning and strategy by discovery. The "umbrella" message relates to a meaningful economy, the dyad values and value, therefore, of the pursuit of meaningful management.

13.4 A reverse innovation

Reverse innovation requires that the dominant logic relied upon by a company can be put aside, the institutionalised thinking that makes every decision and commands every action within the company. This obviously involves major change. It involves changes in the company's organisational structure, restructuring and retraining the sales force and redesigning the product-development and manufacturing methods.

We are talking of a two-part approach: radical change involving an astute leadership. This involves the company setting ambitious goals, by creating a new dynamic organisational structure and introducing new workable design methods that ensure the legacy units survive and thrive under new direction and avert conflict between new and old.

For most multinational companies, globalisation will be the main provider of the profits for many years to come. Ideally, it would be supported by reverse innovation and while still intertwined, encourage companies to continue to develop new ways to do business and branch out into new sectors in which to grow. It is not achievable to get clean-state innovation without introducing the concept of and embracing clean-slate organisational design. It is not possible to re-arrange dominant logic without a change to the structure, employees and hierarchy.

The term "reverse innovation" may be common-place in discussions by multinational companies who are embracing their role in emerging markets, but not everyone realises it is as relatable to a state of mind as much as to a common or best practice.

Beyond taking new innovations, inventions and products, specifically designed for emerging markets and selling them in developing countries, it requires a company to reverse the way they approach innovation. For managers who struggle to move on from the old dominant logic, change can be frightening, but if they are willing to embrace it, it can be enlightening.

Living and leading in a VUCA world

The idea of living in a VUCA world, a world with volatility, uncertainty, complexity and ambiguousness, means preparing to embrace new challenges and increase the pressure (see Figure 13.1). Now the financial crisis is over and growth is picking up, a great number of organisations are experiencing a "new normal" in the business environment. These organisations are now aware that the old way of doing things, and its paradigms have gone.

Rather than tolerating the previous issues and problems, which required analysis, speed and elimination of any such issues, we are now emerging in a new world where dilemmas rule and these require patience, sensible decision-making and the ability to engage with uncertainty.

Therefore, leadership thinkers have been acknowledging the lessons learned and this has directed them to create new paradigms to allow them to survive and thrive in a "perpetual white-water" environment where out-dated ideas of predicting the correct path to take were coming up short, where the chances of highest growth means taking bigger risks in more risky, constantly changing and less familiar markets, where new, powerful and, from time to time, asymmetrical global competitors are emerging from developing economies. It shows the traditional competitors now to be more ruthless in persevering in a slow-growing developed market, where drastic changes are creating a downturn effect on a non-segregated global economy; where the rapid growth of "big data" is a huge threat to decision makers from an overwhelming aspect and where new technologies are rupturing sectors and sometimes entire industries at an ever increasing speed.

It is easy to see how leaders are very much more aware of the effects of VUCA in every decision they make and every challenge that presents itself. Complexity is overridden by "clarity, the deliberate effort to make sense of all the chaos" (Kurup, 2016). When a lack of clarity becomes overwhelming, leaders must depart from convention and set up incremental dividends, thus capturing the concept of "wirearchy" as opposed to "hierarchy" – where social networking in many areas with many other individuals would provide a far superior outcome than it is possible to achieve from just one brilliant idea.

Research in human capabilities and neuroscience is becoming a far more practical science as the world evolves in ever new complexities, and leaders must, in parallel, develop new skills and the power to lead in it.

Sensible decisions are now paramount, more than any previous time in recent history, for many companies, and as the world continues to become an ever smaller place due to the expanding global economy, we find ourselves not that far away from genuine globality involving each and every country where competitors are emerging from everywhere.

- Volatility – rate of change
- Uncertainty – unclear about the present situation and future outcomes
- Complexity – multiplicity of Key Decision Factors
- Ambiguity – lack of clarity about the meaning of an event.

Figure 13.1 It's a VUCA world

> Our age of anxiety is, in great part, the result of trying to cope with the current environment and future society with yesterday's paradigms, concepts, techniques and tools.

Figure 13.2 Age of anxiety

- Social Capital
- Attention Economy
- Consumers in Control: Made of/by/for consumers
- Glocal
- New Business Ecosystems
- Sense and Respond Models
- Evenomics

Figure 13.3 New economy

To lead in a turbulent environment requires the ability to utilise all capabilities bestowed on us as humans. It will require profound intelligence, cognitive, spiritual, social and emotional connections to prevail.

A true VUCA convert is the person who is able to holistically harness leadership. Figures 13.2 and 13.3 provide a summary of the terms "our age of anxiety" and "new economy."

13.5 Deglobalisation redraws the investment map

Divergence between financial markets and economies has become an increasingly important macroeconomic trend that we have seen in the past few years. It reflects the deglobalisation of a worldwide supply chain. While bigger countries with more advanced internal markets will probably thrive, the smaller countries who have not yet succeeded in breaking into the export value chain, may suffer.

The relationship between growth and globalisation can be defined as a very simple relationship: rapid movement of any type of capital across national borders or barriers, rapid increase of trade agreements and loosening of protectionism allows whole industries within countries to trade more freely.

One characteristic of the current globalisation is the understanding that wealth creation can be distributed across national boundaries. At the beginning of industrialisation, we saw raw materials being imported by more industrialised countries to be exported as a finished product. However, the world supply chain is described as one country supplying a raw material to another, as a result of globalisation, which provides the required components in order to sell on to another country where the finished goods will be manufactured for export. In other words, the process of globalisation seems to be slipping into reverse.

Research has been produced that proves contributing factors actually include a net loss for the developed world's share of global value-added exports during 2001–2011 (Japan and the US being hit the hardest) and a net gain by new and emerging markets (mainly China). China has also been internally combining its supply chain, producing a greatly reduced number of imports of partially finished goods for their own domestic production within the same time period.

Put simply, we expect the countries with larger internal markets to fare better than those smaller countries with less efficient systems, which have yet to make a more significant mark in the export value chain.

13.6 The problem of business ecosystems

The strategies for business and commercialisation successes are evolving significantly as we ourselves evolve from an industrial-era to a knowledge-era economy. This transition comes with positive and negative consequences. The old ways are no longer appropriate and consequently, companies must evolve with these changes in order to survive. Fortunately, there are tools available to help with the transition.

The constant change in technology, markets, business models and expectations require companies to evolve and innovate more rapidly than ever before. Technology innovation is not a sufficient factor to achieve growth, profit or success alone. Innovative business models now need to be implemented for success in commercialisation. These business models must accomplish customer satisfaction by creating new paths in which to flourish but also be able to defend against lower costing disruptors.

Older versions of successful-era business models held the competitive edge as the superior position was based on in-house technology designed for specific roles, product excellence, careful management, robust supply chains and scarce resources. This outlook provided a certain security for the industry when resources were scarce and expensive and the unit used to represent real value did not extend to information or relate to the virtual, digital domain. Abundant networking capabilities, innovative software systems with minimal supply chain involvement, and global communities of people used a freely available source code, efficiently and effectively solving problems, and in a time appropriate manner to render the older versions of these business models, at times, completely ineffective at producing business results.

In the knowledge-era the only companies to survive are those who can effectively implement new business models that can successfully address the ever-evolving customer values. Companies new to the market have rapidly evolved their business models that create and provide adequate leverage for current infrastructures in new and interesting ways.

Shifts in users are spreading widely. Facebook has been seen to evolve from its original straight-forward collaboration tool into a phenomenal point of connection for an ever-growing audience. The pervasiveness of the Internet and its availability of data and knowledge to people, have created an information overload. Social networks are a great way to convert huge amounts of data into workable information. When people want to make a purchase decision, they take to social media networks. Social networkers can decide which product will suit them best, from the information, reviews and product details available online. This form of endorsement is hugely powerful and enables huge quantities of data to be made widely available and processed in a short timescale. The understanding that we can control people and information across the worldwide web shifts the power from local enterprise to global networks.

An environmental shift has appeared and has been transitioning virtual worlds and gaming environments. As more people become aware of the existence of these websites, they become the chosen meet-up place for the younger generations logging on. This has displaced shopping malls, coffee houses and street corners. Some companies have recognised this shift and have worked their way in by creating shops in a virtual world. They can offer shopping, movies, hobbies and even educational tools. We are spanning virtual worlds now by creating voice monitoring between avatar owners, virtual shopping experiences which result in goods being delivered to your home, and exporting virtual goods, such as an award you created in a virtual world, delivering it to your door. Hotels have been created in a virtual world where feedback can be collected on designs, services and amenities before actually being built in the real world. Within this virtual work there are realtors for property, casino operators and decorators, all thriving in this new environment. The virtual work displaces the much more passive activities such as television by the introduction of interactivity, entertainment and travel to the forefront. Virtual worlds can produce the transactions that produce real money.

In the new knowledge-era world, competition between any newly created business model is now becoming an important factor in the ability to create business success. Companies must both recognise their competition and choose wisely how they will participate.

In this knowledge-era economy a proposition of value does not necessarily guarantee success. In order to compete effectively in the market, the business model of any company must be better than similar models used by competitors. Small players can amalgamate their efforts and co-create competition against larger businesses. As it is no longer a viable option to state that it is business as usual, new mechanisms need to be examined and introduced in order for a company to be able to keep up with the knowledge-era economy.

13.7 Why a business system?

Business ecosystems create many advantages. They may provide small companies with the proprietary advantage needed to compete with larger companies. They can create an ecosystem that can provide the mechanism to create intricate pockets of excellence across any fields, including research, business and marketing, and technology in various areas and sectors and catapult them into a global competitive force.

Designed on a natural ecosystem, a business ecosystem creates two different market dimensions. First, in a stable business environment, ecosystems provide resistance to invasion. Larger companies resist changing their business models and command their users to adhere to the use of their products, the outcome is that they treat their customers as part of their supply chain. Second, in unstable and dynamic environments these ecosystems provide resilience against change. The rapid and intense innovation that companies can now produce and achieve, hugely contributes to the ability to survive the changes. The dimensions can protect the larger players in a place where they find themselves under increased vulnerability in the dynamic version, whilst allowing newcomers to negotiate an important and effective community to their advantage to undermine the larger adversary.

There are two vitally important roles in a business ecosystem: The Keystone and The Niche player. The keystone is of utmost importance as it provides the central point for the ecosystem. This allows the ecosystem to adapt to any external changes it may face. The keystone is responsible for:

- The overall and final output of the ecosystem
- Monitoring the ability to achieve the goals set out by the ecosystem in an efficient manner
- Stability and resilience of the ecosystem by ensuring that existing members cover the roles of absent members
- Creation of new members in order to maintain on-going growth and value of the ecosystem.

A keystone holds up its responsibilities by ensuring it provides a dominant design that can facilitate collaboration and control collective innovation.

A niche player also plays a vital role within an ecosystem. Niche players are not necessarily small in size or scope. The niche player tends to be a focused player, providing valuable innovation quickly, in any relevant field of expertise to the entire ecosystem, including its collective value proposition. By creating an alliance with each other, mimicking a mutualistic relationship between each contender within the natural ecosystem, niche players create a strong and healthy input to a larger overall cause. Collaboration provides both companies with mutual economic advantages. To assist with the collaboration, the keystone provides the relationship management, technology, skills, processes and intellectual property management.

The goal of any business venture is commercialisation and the relevant ecosystem can help smaller more specialised companies to compete and do well by filling the gaps within their domestic capabilities and facilitate collaboration.

The current knowledge economy is capable of creating great opportunities for offers and current business models. The older industrial-era models now show displacement by newer, more efficient models that allow the inclusion of new companies with an ability to compete in the current markets.

Ecosystems have a great ability to assist companies. Currently, in these recessionary times, a robust ecosystem is paramount in allowing the company to survive, with partnership and growth being of critical importance. These ecosystems provide an efficient partnership for collaboration to support commercialisation. Network clustering and technology transfer remain focused on certain very specific opportunities that can help create a more stable environment. Ecosystems are more effective at filling gaps and addressing change so that superior outcomes can be achieved.

But what is required more than anything else is that businesses simply must find a way to adapt in a world where people are now demanding much more – where profit is not the only important factor. There needs to be a revolution. To rewire your business you need to understand the way your business works to succeed in the consumer revolution. You need to understand today's biggest trends: social media, the mobile web, gamification and real-time have forced companies to rethink how they run their businesses. Consumers are shifting the business landscapes and creating a new digital culture one step at a time (see Figure 13.4).

Networks are now creating an ever-expanding "ecosystem," in which people assume they can have 24-hour broadcast of their lives. But now we need to understand where this behaviour is heading by trying to decipher the importance or significance of it and make sense of what route the social networking and mobile web is taking. In the middle of all this, a new type of consumer is emerging and they're changing the foundations of business. As consumers connect with one another, a complex and vast information network begins to develop and can steer markets, experiences and decisions. It is a huge disruption.

> Business as usual is no longer a worthwhile cause. It places value in the wrong things, finds a way to reward the wrong people and does not behave in an appropriate way for the times. In the current climes, businesses must be able to make sense of new technologies, harness geographical shifts in power, get to grips with generational differences and understand the continued economic crises that we are going through and be sympathetic to the needs of a planet that is being increasingly ravaged.

Figure 13.4 Dear Business as Usual, It's time for a revolution

Rewire the way you run your business to succeed with the new consumer revolution

The end of Business as Usual (see Figure 13.5) explores each aspect of the complex consumer revolution that is changing the future of media, culture and business. As consumers connect to one another, a huge efficient network begins to take shape and creates disruption by steering decisions, experiences and markets.

13.8 Strategic thinking

Strategic thinking is a process that defines the manner in which people think about, assess, view, and create the future for themselves and others. Strategic thinking is an extremely effective and valuable tool. One can apply strategic thinking to arrive at decisions that can be related to your work or personal life.

The definition of strategic thinking is laid out as a thinking process in which an individual or group creates success in any endeavour. When applied to cognitive behaviour, it produces a thought process. When applied to an organisational strategic management process, it requires the application of unique business insights and any given opportunities that arise with the intention of creating a competitive advantage for any organisation. This can be implemented individually or collaboratively depending on the needs, and can be divided or created collaboratively using key people who have the capabilities to steer a company to success. It is sometimes more valuable an experience to proactively create together where individual members can gain insight on other perspectives and other complex issues surrounding the group.

Rethinking business strategies

Nowadays we have a plethora of digital technologies that have the ability to create individual consumption from mass consumption. However, to date, we have largely stuck to the older methods. These technologies have been used to reduce operational costs by automating processes and services, in exchange for a labour substitution and therefore increased profit, and the end result is that more commodities are available to us than ever before.

The current period of economic turmoil may be a sign of yet more dynamic changes in business practices. There is a driving need in both public and private sectors to change the way we do things, enabled by technology, to create new economies, strategies and practices.

Agility, robustness and stability are necessary aspects of business as unusual when faced with such instability. Seely-Brown and Hagel (2008) write that previous business models

---

Your views of the business world will change from its leadership and culture, to customer services, sales and marketing and product development. These critical insights include:

- Growing consumer influence, which smart businesses can use to their advantage.
- Brands redefining digital consumer landscapes after moulding shared experiences, these can be manipulated by astute companies to their advantage.
- Connect with an ever-growing audience through new media focus points between brands, customers and new influences.
- Significantly improve the culture to establish trust significance and influence amongst connected customers.

Figure 13.5 The end of Business as Usual

("Push" models) were designed for their ability to precisely forward plan, but this relies on a stable market, slight variation and basing the findings on past performance.

The newer models ("pull" models) have proven to more accurately reflect the current chaos, with the unpredictability of human nature bringing complexity and uncertainty to the mix. Variability is what people learn to expect. The old push models start to disintegrate as management and measurement, control and command become less effective or predictable. Pull models work efficiently with the understanding and respond effectively to customer demand.

Competitive advantage can often be based on how quickly a company can adapt, how the knowledge flows, and regards human networks rather than focus on the physical assets. The ability of small practice set ups to go up against large established companies with mere basic human capital and a pay-as-you-go infrastructure is fast becoming a reality.

The importance of this is utilising the combined passion and brain power of the employees within the organisation and the customers on the outside. A hierarchical structure may very well have disappeared from the formal organisational chart but they are still a huge part of the power structures and centralised decision making required by the company. This allows the traditional Taylorist carrot and stick model which was produced from the industrialisation process of the late nineteenth century.

As much of the work on twenty-first-century organisations is based on knowledge work rather than the results of the production line, the Taylorist approach to manage and measure becomes far more difficult to perceive in tangible unitary terms. This can also cause demotivation in an otherwise engaged and passionate workforce (a recent YouGov survey showed that UK job satisfaction rates have plummeted to an all-time low). It is, therefore, not surprising that people tend to want to leave organisations in which they feel they have no control or voice.

Customer power should never be underestimated in connection with this model. Zuboff and Maxim (2002) examined the model of businesses where people worked collaboratively towards all goals where mutual benefit was an option. The UK government's plan of "The Big Society" has been described as a frustrating experience for its citizens. There are now also forums and community social networks where people will partake in advice exchange with no reward with the intention of sorting each other's issues. These sites are now more frequently used as they are readily available on search engines and are a vastly preferable option to sitting in an endless queue waiting for a response from a call centre advisor.

The signs are all there that we should expect a dramatic shift commencing in the business world. This appears to be based on the current unpredictability and uncertainty. This is also helped by the change in which technology is used to meet the new demands put on it. Networking technologies, co-ordination and collaboration are all critical to the current revolution.

Mini case study

Crowds: inventing new ways to network

As a result of better networking, there is new and more productive innovation. This comes about by a more diverse range of people creating something new. Companies will survive or crash by showing the stamina and ability to successfully innovate, amd this is especially true in tough times. IBM connected 150,000 people in 104 countries by investing in "Innovation Jam" – this included their own employees, students and business partners. The result was that

IBM invested $100 million over a two-year period to develop the top ten ideas. This idea was mirrored by Dell in a project called "Ideastorm."

It has been shown through studies that companies that can concentrate on high levels of collaboration and community have a much lower staff turnover as a result.

Successful selling depends on building good relationships. The most successful salespeople spend their entire careers building strong networks of business contacts. The quality of any relationship directly results in the success of the salesperson, and therefore produces success within the company.

The biggest challenges are felt by traditional business practices when social tools are introduced. The breakdown of traditional hierarchy, the relinquishing of managerial control, establishing viable governance strategies and building trust – these are the features that keep an organisation on an even keel.

The decision as to which social networking technologies suit each company best is an integral decision that must be made to ensure that the company performs to its fullest potential. But another critical factor for the success of a company is making sure that its employees also actively participate. Richard Dennison of BT confirmed that an organisation plays a huge part in the success or failure of enterprise social networking: "The organisation has the hardest and most critical role of all – they have to create the atmosphere and a space in which people feel free to participate, feel free to express themselves without recrimination and trust that their contributions are being taken in the way that they mean them to be taken."

An asset-less and agile organisation has been predicted by futureologists, but it has become apparent that many large organisations are trying to become asset-less and therefore incredibly agile. There is also a rise of collaborative behaviours including cross enterprise and self-organising with the help of social networking applications. Huge opportunities can be made available by centralising access to tools, for sharing and collaboration.

Finding a purpose

There is a higher purpose to businesses in the twenty-first-century. They must create meaning that evolves further than the tasks they carry out, the work itself and the ability to create profit. They look to find the answers to the greatest problems that matter to society, a Purpose of Significance.

Strategy nugget

How great companies think differently

It is now time for theories and beliefs about business to match up with the way large companies see themselves and their operations in the world today. Financiers and economists have traditionally stuck to the plan that the entire reason they trade is to make a profit. This theory is deeply embedded in the American capitalist system, shapes the behaviour of many great corporations, compelling them to continue taking certain courses of action, whether they are relevant or not. These decisions are based on financial terms.

Institutional logic requires them to be more than simply the instrument that generates the money; it also requires them to portray themselves as vessels able to accomplish societal purposes and enabling people who work for them to sustain meaningful lives. The value that a company creates through this school of thought is not just measured in terms of short-term profits or pay checks but also through the conditions it can sustain by allowing it to grow and develop over time. There are more than just financial returns being delivered by these corporate leaders, they are constructing enduring institutions.

Great companies are now creating frameworks that use decision making criteria as a societal or human value instead of seeing an organisational process as no more than a way to extract economic value. There is a belief that it is their responsibility to meet stakeholders' needs by providing a service or producing the goods that will enhance users' lives. This is achieved by providing jobs that will sustain the quality of life, through the development of networks that provide business partners, suppliers and customers while simultaneously providing financial viability through resources for innovations, improvements and investors' returns.

Institutional logic should be measured with economic logic but is of no less importance. Profit, however, is not the sole end, in fact it is rather a way to ensure that the returns continue. The organisation is no more idealised than the profit-maximising view.

The speed of change is increased by globalisation. The number of competitors available on a global scale provides a greater challenge than ever before. The global economy is highly competitive and places a premium on innovation, thus relying on human motivation, collaboration and imagination. This is further complicated by global mergers and acquisitions, the success of which relies on the effectiveness of the integrated organisation.

Also, the business of seeking public approval or legitimacy by merging social objectives with corporate objectives has become the priority. Multinational companies may have concerns regarding local appropriateness and cultural acceptance; this must be achieved by gaining approval from government authorities and opinion leaders within the confines of the space they operate within. Their employees must be able to both perform within the company and represent the company in the external community.

A common purpose

If the company is considered as a social institution, there will be a buffer against incompatibility and uncertainty, providing a coherent identity. Business mixes change often as a company expands. Large institutions establish something greater than transactions to give them that meaning and purpose.

Globalisation created a situation where companies could detach themselves from one specific area, while creating the requirement that companies must internalise the needs of those societies. Creating coherent institutional values can eradicate this complex issue.

Successful mergers are noteworthy for the special importance they put on values and culture. In 1996, two Swiss pharmaceutical companies merged to form Novartis. Daniel Vasella, the CEO, envisioned the new company's mission to incorporate global meaningfulness and this needed to play a central role in the integration and growth strategy. The dilemma was how to incorporate a tangible experience for the employees that would reflect those values. When the idea of a global day of community service was mentioned – never done in Europe before – Novartis got on board. The company let each country organisation decide how it would best serve local communities, given the interpretation of the two companies' histories and one future going forward. This day is now an annual event for the company and is held on the anniversary of the merger.

Stating values and purpose through service is a common way for great companies to confirm their identity.

June, 2011 saw IBM celebrate its 100th anniversary. They offered a service to the world, with over 300,000 IBM employees signing up to perform 2.6 million hours of service on one global day of service. These people donated access and training to software tools, with many of them having been developed specially for the occasion, to schools, governmental agencies, and non-government organisations. These incentives and projects included training related to anti-bullying and privacy issues delivered to over 100 schools in Germany, a website created and developed for the visually impaired in India, which was then rolled out to over 50 locations, and access granted to women entrepreneurs in the US allowing them access to small business resources. In order to prove IBM's commitment to contributing to society these tools were given away, even though in some cases there was the potential for the software to form the basis for commercial products.

A long-term project

A long-term perspective can be justified when thinking of an organisation as a social institution, justifying a short-term financial sacrifice where the outcome is the ability to achieve enduring corporate purpose over time. Resources are required in order to keep a company profitable, so it is imperative that enough attention is given to financial logic. This said, large companies are willing to sacrifice financial opportunities in the short term if those opportunities do not align with institutional values. It is imperative that values are upheld in order to protect the company's reputation and identity where standards in product quality, manufacturing or customer service are concerned.

Emotional engagement

The transference of institutional values can bring positive emotions to the forefront, can encourage motivation and increase self-regulation and peer regulation.

Robert McDonald, a Procter and Gamble executive, believed that a company's principles, purpose and values are the foundation of its culture, bring out strong emotions within its employees and give a meaning to the company's brand. No more than a month after becoming the CEO of the company in 2010, he had elevated that purpose, improving the lives of consumers all over the world, into a business strategy: to improve more lives in more places more completely.

Mini case study

P&G

In P&G West Africa, each and every employee has a purpose-driven quantitative goal: How many more lives have I improved this year? So P&G West Africa's Baby Care Group created Pampers mobile clinics to attempt to decrease the number of infant deaths. Two nurses and a physician travel around the region in a van, examining babies, teaching post-natal care, and making referrals where necessary for the mothers to receive immunisation shots or further care. This group also registers the women for mVillage, a text messaging service provided to offer hints and tips and questions and answers from health care professionals. At the end of the visit each new mother gets two nappies for their child. The passionate drive for P&G employees to feel like they are making a difference to the lives of these people is a strong one. There is a pride that Pampers sales have sky-rocketed in West Africa and that this region of the world has the fastest growing P&G market.

In organisations which consider themselves social institutions, work is meaningful and takes priority in employees' minds. The compelling nature of this is that it works as a whole, and not just in a select few. It is a typical example of CEOs and their missions, and how they must communicate the company's values and purpose to their employees. Conceiving of the firm: with the long-term perspective in mind, short-term sacrifice of financial goals must become acceptable in the interest of the firm's sustainable success as a social institution.

Strong institutional values can produce strong emotions, inherent motivation and create self or peer regulation. Great companies see their business as hardworking, held in high esteem and respected. This reputation allows the cross-sector collaboration necessary to integrate into global economies. With the formation of public/private sector partnerships, both business and social interests can be considered.

When the focus is placed on social practices, conditions can often generate ideas and experiences that lead to new innovations in products, business models and services.

To clearly and distinctly pronounce a broader purpose, not solely of money making, can develop actions and strategies, it can develop and produce new sources for innovation with the intention of helping people evolve their personal values and corporate desires within their everyday working lives.

Self-organisation

Large powerful companies take for granted their customers' trust and rely heavily on the relationships, not just the structures and rules. These companies are more likely to allow their employees the free will to integrate and co-ordinate their own activities by producing their own work strategies and patterns and creating new ideas.

The logic of the institution requires the mentality that employees are not lazy, money-hungry people who do little or no work, nor are they treated like robots that can produce high-quality performance morning, noon and night. No, these employees are given the power to make their own choices about how hard to work on certain new ideas and concepts and how these may contribute, therefore allowing recourse allocation to not depend solely on budgets and strategies but also on the forward thinking, spontaneous ideas and preferences of staff at all levels.

Pronouncing a clear purpose, not necessarily based on money making, can widen the prospect of new sources of innovation. When people organise themselves, creating new networks and sharing information, new innovations and creations can be the result. Any organisation must encourage the forming of these networks and support them fully. These networks can flourish if they have a volunteering system where individuals create surprisingly innovative ideas that their bosses may not be expecting. Also, these forums are often very good at keeping the good ideas flowing long after the company may have abandoned them.

Self-organising communities generally pack a powerful punch when it comes to change, enabling companies to advance in directions in which they would not normally travel. An employee with no specific orders can facilitate exploration and an entrepreneurial spirit. Indeed, if there had been no self-forming networks, IBM might never have produced two big ideas, green computing and virtualisation. These were among IBM's previous top strategic priorities, to which a web chat of over 140,000 employees contributed over several days.

Fair finances

As it is no longer an acceptable way for companies to hand out huge bonuses to leaders that are massively more than the bonuses the workers can expect, there are new, more acceptable ways for businesses to finance these funds.

POD

The rebellious Scottish brewer BrewDog and its fan-funding programme, the web platform Kickstarter: After describing any would-be project, anyone can be invited to become "backers," meaning that there is an opportunity to co-fund development of the project. This encourages consumers to become investors in the products that they love.

At Mondragon a democratic vote taken within each individual operating company decides the ratio of gnarl manager to executives, and those at the forefront – the ratios vary from 3:1 to 9:1 in the 250 different Mondragon businesses, and the average is 5:1.

POD

The fair move: the trend towards fair value accounting by Nishan Perera

A financial statement is capable of delivering a plethora of information, but in its most basic form it shows a snippet of the company's current financial state. It is a complex picture as it conveys many different assets, liabilities and equity details. These reports constantly evolve to meet the demands of the business world in order to portray a better vision of the workings of the company. With this in mind, the next major change to be examined in corporate financial reporting requires a shift towards the use of fair value accounting. Although the idea of transparency is far from a new concept, its influence is picking up momentum and will continue to do so. Because of this, there will be implications that will need to be considered for how accounting will evolve and how all stakeholders in a company, particularly investors, will analyse firms.

13.9 What is fair value?

Fair value is held in high esteem in the modern business world today. Its definition is simply the acceptable price people would be willing to pay for a valued item. In the current complexities of business, this can be difficult to measure by today's standards, but it has been found to be a much more accurate measurement by way of finding out how much something is worth without reverting to the initial or historical cost.

The "fair move"

To many in the accounting profession this is not exactly reasonable. While this is the way accountancy has been presented for many years, it has been proven to hold no truth in accuracy when a company is presenting its financial reports.

In 2006, FASB issued FAS 157: "Fair value measurement." It does not require that the fair value be applied to specific ideas, but it does clarify how to value items that must be measured as such. In some ways, this can be considered by a predecessor of what is to come and emphasises the importance of fair value measurement. The statement details many aspects surrounding fair value including: fair value measurement, its scope, valuation techniques, initial recognition, fair value hierarchy, disclosures, implementation guidance, transition issues, present-value techniques, background information, basis for conclusions, and reference to other financial standards (Fuglister & Bloom, 2008).

What this means for business in the future

With these numerous changes, the business world will undergo many different adjustments. The very fundamentals of financial reports will change. Financial instruments, whether they are assets or liabilities, will no longer remain at a stagnant value throughout financial periods. Instead, there will be a reflection of the changes in the marker and from there, the true value of the financial instrument will be apparent. The costings in any financial reports, as they are updated, will show more relevance.

Ready or not, here comes fair value

There are a number of points that people should recognise fairly early on, and should understand shortly after that. Accounting is the most fundamentally important part of a company, it is the recorder of all financials within a company and therefore keeps a track of all aspects of the company's productivity.

Fair value accounting requires accountants to constantly evaluate a company's assets and what it owes. There will be the allowance to pay attention to the current market value and put into perspective how this will affect the company's operations, thus also allowing the ability to become more familiar with the standard practice of fair value. However, all corners of an organisation play a part, and fair value implications within accounting affect every part of the operation of a business. Fair value accounting will even influence professors teaching in the best universities in the land. Much thought will be put into fair value by financial analysts where capital budgets are concerned, with regard to how companies deal with everyday finances and how much structure is placed in their debt. There should be much attention to detail given by corporate executives to the fine details of any company operation to be sure of how it will affect the company's financial statements and what part that plays in the long-term success of the company. These are just some examples of how critical job roles will change.

No doubt even more work will be attributed to the transition of fair value accounting. Financial statements will need to be scrutinised in their entirety more than ever before. More issues will come to light causing worry or concern: the ability to acquire an estimate; relying on hypothetical market behaviour can create problems for the future for companies; compliance issues may be raised in respect to company resources; values may fluctuate and could possibly require repeat estimations. As the business world starts to realise its true value in assets, shareholder equity and liabilities, financial statements will be constantly requiring modification. This must be considered as a move towards fairness and good practice within the company for all stakeholders, instead of an undesirable challenge to be dealt with. Anyone who takes the time to read the financial statements should have the foresight to look at more than just the net income. This is the time to delve further into the details of the financial statement and show an understanding into the shift towards fair value. This might be time consuming and tedious at the outset but will prove beneficial in the end as the profitability of the company will be realised.

While it can be debated as to whether this is in fact fair or not, this practice is being introduced now. The FASB have recorded through their financial statements that this is the future. They are being followed by international standards, the IASB are promoting this and reflecting fair value by trying to reflect each other directly. From here on, businesses operating on a worldwide scale will need to understand the workings of fair value accounting and accept how it will affect their business. This change is coming and has the opportunity to alter how business is run for the foreseeable future. Whether ready to embrace it or not, all those in the business world should take heed of the future.

For further information see Johnson (2007).

13.10 Chapter summary

This chapter starts by analysing the critical role of innovation in achieving business effectiveness. We dissect a myriad of strategic discontinuities and the context of living in an uncertain world as well as in an era of a new economy. The chapter also examines the new concept of benefit corporations and the pressing need towards fair finances.

We introduced views regarding the trend in the direction of de-globalisation and emerging business ecosystems. All of these paradigm shifts call for the rethinking of business strategies.

13.11 End of chapter self-reflection questions

1. Select three major paradigm shifts and critically comment on these.
2. Develop an analytical discussion on why it is no longer "business as usual."
3. Why do you think that it is important for a business organisation to find a purpose and to have higher values, well beyond just providing value attached to products and services?
4. Comment on the Age of the Multi-Sided Business Model.
5. What do you understand by the term fair value? How reliable are the market values of Apple, Facebook, Microsoft and Google?

References

Doz, Y. L., & Kosonen., M. (2010). Embedding strategic agility: A leadership agenda for accelerating business model renewal. *Long Range Planning*, *43*(2–3), 370–382.

Fuglister, J., & Bloom, R. (2008). Analysis of SFAS 157, fair value measurements. *The CPA Journal*, *78*(1), 36.

Hagel, J., & Brown, J. (2008). From push to pull: Emerging models for mobilizing resources. *Journal of Service Science*, *1*(1), 93–110.

Johnson, S. (2007). Ready or not, here comes fair value. CFO. Available at: http://ww2.cfo.com/accounting-tax/2007/10/ready-or-not-here-comes-fair-value/

Kurup, S. (2016). VUCA prime: Responses to a volatile world. Available at: https://www.linkedin.com/pulse/vuca-primeresponses-volatile-world-sanjay-kurup/

McFadzean, E. (1998). Enhancing creative thinking within organisations. *Management Decision*, *36*(5), 309–315.

Michaelson, C., Pratt, M. G., Grant, A. M., & Dunn, C. P. (2014). Meaningful work: Connecting business ethics and organization studies. *Journal of Business Ethics*, *121*(1), 77–90.

Murthy, P. N. (1996). Paradigm shift in management. *Systems Research and Behavioural Science*, *13*(4), 457–468.

Tregoe, B., & Zimmerman, J. (1983). Strategic thinking. *Industrial Management & Data Systems*, *83*(7/8), 17–21.

Zuboff, S., & Maxim, J. (2002). *The support economy: Why corporations are failing individuals and the next episode of capitalism.* New York: Viking Penguin.

14 The future of the future

14.1 Learning objectives

After completing this chapter you will:

- be able to highlight the constant emergence of new paradigms in society which impinge hugely on management
- be able to discuss new formats and designs of the future organisation – from shape-shifters to permeable companies; new structures and the age of the multi-sided business perspective and platform; the emergence of future business colonies; the holographic organisation design and the corporate DNA
- be able to dissect why strategic thinking is the strategy's orphan. Also, delve into the reasons why we see so many bad strategies . . .
- top analyse the role of networks and new voices entering into the business ecosystem
- tackle the role of complexity theory in business and strategic ability.

14.2 Introduction

The content of this chapter includes discussions on permeable companies, a new outlook for strategic thinking, the age of the one-sided business, corporate "stretching" and the future of work environments (e.g. business colonies, the holographic organisation, thinking organisation etc.). Critical areas of analysis include dilemma management, strategy agility, experimentation as the new planning, strategy discovery, meaningful management, disruptions and igniters, web 2.0, business strategies, some top technological trends and the value of data. Other important strategic questions are also raised such as, "What will be the next Internet?" and "Is data destroying insight?"

14.3 Key academic theory

These are times of change in every respect. Society, technology and the economy are affecting the management needs of organisations in every sector. A considerable amount of thinking is going on to meet the situation and many management paradigms are being suggested almost every day and are being practised. Most of them are based on empiricism. In practice, they are turning out to be fads and not as effective as they are expected to be, due to very little theoretical support. While all this practice has meaning in the short run, in terms of accelerated change, as now, a paradigm shift seems to be needed. Murthy (1996) argues for this and proposes a shift in the present paradigms.

While the drawing of lines between industry boundaries has never been easy it is indeed becoming more and more difficult in the current economic climate. The fuzzy boundaries between different industries have contributed to such factors as globalisation, deregulation and important breakthroughs in science including the strategic importance of information technology.

This explanation has a valid foundation but has failed to provide the systematic framework that explains why companies invest and engage in the activities that result in a blurring of the surrounding inter-industry boundaries. There also follows the why and how of the boundary-crossing behaviour that garners different results from company to company. Nicholls-Nixon and Jasinski (1995) designed a conceptual model where the behavioural and economic perspectives are successfully integrated in order to combat these issues.

Within the environment

Where there is a volatile environment that shows constant uncertainty and change, there may be some allowance for innovation, the ability for different styles of strategic thinking, instead of the mainstream traditional and conventional strategic planning. Many organisations now embrace the scenario planning tool, committing to the redesign of the strategic planning process and are finding success in this. But scenario planning needs the power of both left- and right-brain thinking. While left-brain thinking reflects the planning ability of the strategy makers, right-brain thinking reflects the thinking aspect of strategy making. Between these factors there exists a relationship that encourages and enhances strategic thinking to the level of "emotional intelligence" of business leaders as considered by Graetz (2002).

Strategic thinking capabilities can be encouraged and enhanced through an organisation, but only emotionally intelligent business leaders with a high degree of emotional intelligence will successfully lead the way.

Ghoshal (2005) makes the case that academic research connected to the organisation and conduct of business and management has specific negative and significant influences when relating to the practice of management. The influences he discusses are related to the time of incorporation, relying on the worldview of managers, while integrating a set of assumptions and ideas that play an important role in management research. Specifically, Ghoshal is intimating that instigating ideology has inspired amoral theories, allowing business schools to release their students from any sense of moral responsibility.

As ethics and morality are inseparable from human intentionality, our dealings with management practice have been based on the assumption that we deny any moral or ethical considerations, thus allowing business studies to become a science.

In the aftermath of the now accepted end of the previous strategic planning approaches, it is now acknowledged that strategic thinking is the problem solver of the future, and the way forward for all work in the strategy field. It has had little attention paid to it before now in any form of the literature, however finding a way to properly describe the process that strategic thinking goes through must prove it produces benefits while creating the worth to be incorporated into the relevant and current planning practices.

Liedtka (1998) addressed some important issues when discussing strategic thinking, placing relevance on five elements: the intent-focused, the incorporation of a systems perspective, the involvement of thinking in time, the intelligently opportunistic approach and the hypothesis driven venture. When put together, each of these adds a superior value which gives organisations the ability to be more adaptable and more successful at doing so. But in order to enhance the planning process by incorporating strategic thinking, it is necessary to acknowledge the three separate areas of the process: programming, management of strategic issues and repertoire-building.

Strategic behaviour is vital for a successful and strong performance within a competitive environment. Therefore the key issue for companies is to design a successful strategy. This requires a number of key aspects under the strategic thinking umbrella, including analysing the strategic environment, realising the vision and future of the company and implementing new strategies and ideas to improve products and services with the intention of being the best in the market. Strategic planning will help advance and enhance any business plan. Many businesses are exceptionally good at strategic planning but there seems to be a void where few companies actually devote the right amount of resources to it, resulting in strategic meltdown and disaster. Companies seem to continue to apply the same strategies, ones that are no longer working for them, yet expect different, successful outcomes. In order to create and establish a successful strategic environment, management and employees must all be on board with the new active strategic decision making that is taking place. However, this proves too much for some companies as they do not have the workforce training programmes in place. Benito-Ostolaza and Sanchis-Llopis's (2015) study proves that training can affect strategic behaviour in any firm. They start with two groups of employees, each with identical qualifications and only train one of the groups. This training entails a process aimed at fostering strategic thinking. This results in one group gaining the ability to significantly increase their strategic decision-making skills, thus proving the originally proposed explanation of the positive impact of training.

Utilising a grounded-theory approach, a study by Mohrman, Tenkasi and Mohrman Jr. (2003) examines a number of companies and the results state that there is a difference in capabilities with the use of social networks to implement the necessary base or core organisational change. This study specifically examines how networks enhance and enable local units to learn and develop new and useful schemata. These skills, behaviours and understandings require the adoption of the relevant organisation-wide planned change.

There needs to be a mix of local learning networks working symbiotically to successfully implement the necessary change. It was noted that organisations that failed to successfully implement the changes relied too heavily on the hierarchical change implementation networks. Where there is a fast paced unit there will be more diverse networks, ranging from strong to weak capabilities, external and internal, spanning all system levels. The connections, when properly implemented, will enhance and encourage the sharing of information, along with allowing new capabilities, with the combination and exchange allowing and enabling localised self-design.

Hagiu and Wright (2015) study the economic sacrifices that organisations must make in order to find themselves in a more advantageous position, either closer to or further away from a multi-sided platform (MSP) depending on and relative to the three traditional alternatives: resellers, input suppliers or vertically integrated firms.

These trade-offs result in a comprehensive discussion concerning the defining features of MSPs. They develop a formal model that focuses solely on the MSP in direct contrast to vertical integration choice, which is then combined into the context of any given professional services. The most critical trade-off then becomes visible where decision-making co-ordination creates spill-overs between professionals (most successfully achieved by a vertical integrated firm) and the requirements to drive unobservable effort by trained professionals and make sure that these same professionals can transform and redesign their decisions to suit their own private information. This is most successfully achieved by an MSP.

Hagiu and Wright include the impact of the base-line trade-off through the nature of available contracts within the MSP and vertically integrated firm, all the while confronting the expected pessimism shown by the professionals who take the decision to join the MSP or vertically integrated firm.

A model was developed by Johannessen (1991) to meet some of the criteria for a holographic-heterarchical organisation. The model is intended to be used as a reference model at the meta level. The primary objective is to design a holographic organisation that can learn, adapt, create, and change in conjunction with rapid changes in the environment.

March (1991) discusses the relationship between the exploitation of old certain ways and new possibilities within organisational learning. There is an examination and explanation of the complications that arise between the two, in particular the allocation of resources between the distribution of the benefits and the costs within space and time, along with the ecological interaction effects.

We find that two situations regarding the use of knowledge within organisations and development are being modelled. Firstly, the organisational code and the mutual learning of members of an organisation and secondly, the competitive advantage garnered from learning in competition for primacy. An argument is developed through the paper, where adaptive processes are more likely to become effective in the short term by refining exploitation more rapidly than exploration, but this will self destruct if kept in place to run to the long term. The paper assesses the possibility that some tried and tested organisational practices can improve on this tendency.

Benner and Tushman (2003) create a circumstance where process management influences both the organisational adaption and technological innovation. The argument is put forward that process management activities, while hugely beneficial for stable organisations to thrive, cannot be relied upon to remain consistent in all situations and indeed can only be truly successful with change and incremental innovation. They also make a strong point towards the necessity that process management activities must be protected from activities set to explore any form of ambidextrous organisational flow where lots of things happen at once, providing the complex contexts for such inconsistencies to harmoniously coexist.

Non-linear behaviour can often be observed in a surprising fashion in complex organisations. While this has been studied by organisation scientists for many years, it is now possible to create new approaches to non-linear interactions using the computational and conceptual tools now available.

Complex adaptive system models have given us a unique way of simplifying the complex. These can be characterised by four main elements: agents with schemata, coevolution to the edge of chaos, system evolution based on recombination and self-organising networks sustained by importing energy. New model types that incorporate all the above elements stand a good chance of moving forward with organisational science by incorporating computational agent based-stimulation with empirical observation.

When dealing with strategic management, if applying complex adaptive system models to the equation, effective adaptive solutions can rapidly evolve. Complex organisations must have the ability to establish and modify the strategic direction in order to effectively implement and evolve their self-organised, improvised solutions.

Managers can alter the landscape for local agents by influencing strategic behaviour and configuring the organisational architecture differently, resulting in agents adapting to the change (Anderson 1999).

272 *Radical/futures themes*

Changes in business models come about when disruption and strategic discontinuities become a normal part of life. Efficient companies will evolve naturally into stable business models, which then become rigid. This can then cause a contradiction where the loss of flexibility creates new issues. Resolving this opposing issue can be simplified by developing and implementing three core meta-capabilities with the effect of making the organisation more robust and agile: fluidity, leadership unity and strategic sensitivity. Doz and Kosonen's (2010) paper reviews the underlying factors which decisively affect the outcome of these capabilities, relying on the research they undertook within 12 companies who were in the process of re-inventing their business models. They created solid leadership actions where meta-capabilities were used to speed up the regeneration and transformation of their business models.

In order to contain the argument, three main aspects of the strategic agility framework can be developed to enhance the corresponding leadership actions, resulting in an enhanced ability to renew and evolve business models.

Additional key academic theory

Zeng and Chen (2003) propose a social dilemma approach to cooperation induction in multi-party alliances. They first establish that managing the inherent tension between cooperation and competition in alliances is essentially a social dilemma, where an individually rational but socially defecting choice may lead to a higher payoff for an individual partner but where, once all partners adopt such a strategy, the alliance will fail. They then develop propositions on how partners can improve their chances for cooperation, and discuss the limitations of the social dilemma approach and its implications for future research.

Maccarone's (2009) paper provides the results of investigation into the approaches to corporate social responsibility (CSR) by companies, and the myriad differences that come to light through explanatory contingent variables. The empirical analysis was produced due to the exploratory nature of the research undertaken and from the objectives carried out. These results then created a mutual relationship between endogenous parameters and contingent variables, i.e. descriptive variable through the CSR approach.

- From economic egoism, walling of separation, secretive business, control economy, display, attention and mentions, to multi-lateral consideration, sharing and collaboration, trust and consumer generation, transparency and cooperation, search and attention economy and the age of reconnection.
- From simple structures, centred devices, interruption, intervention, intrusion, insistence, directing, shouting and ROI investment to meaning, complex platforms, person-centred engagement, connecting, delivering content and ROI involvement.
- From reacting, big promises, explaining linear, separateness and component thinking to interacting, intimate gestures, revealing, non-linear, relatedness and thinking in wholes.
- From task analysis, problem solving, structure creates process, forecasting through data analysis, collecting and sequential models to complex adaptive systems, butterfly effect, self-organising patterns, shapes and structures, foresight through synthesis, perceiving patterns and simultaneous happenings.

Figure 14.1 Paradigm shifts

The results from the empirical analysis raise the issue of industry-specific aspects that can influence management to lean towards making certain decisions. It also showed that the degree of internalisation within a company and the size of the company were context factors, along with a link to the level of integration within the organisation, and a strong value system between the overall competitive strategy and CSR.

The paper gives vital understanding of the diverse behaviours that organisations adopt in regard to CSR issues. There is particular emphasis on empirical findings in relation to a contingent approach, therefore providing a valuable basis relating to cross-country analysis.

Oliver and Holzinger (2008) present a dynamic capabilities framework to explain the effective strategic management of the political environment. They argue that the effectiveness of political strategies will be a function of firms' dynamic political management capabilities and propose four firm-level strategies – proactive, defensive, anticipatory, and reactive – for managing the political environment effectively. They develop propositions to explain how particular dynamic capabilities are associated with the effectiveness of alternative political strategies and conclude with suggestions for future research into effective strategic political management.

14.4 Strategic thinking

Strategic thinking is a process that defines the manner in which people think about, assess, view, and create the future for themselves and others. Strategic thinking is an extremely effective and valuable tool. One can apply strategic thinking to arrive at decisions that can be related to your work or personal life. Strategic thinking is defined as a mental or thinking process applied by an individual in the context of achieving success in a game or other endeavour. As a cognitive activity, it produces thought.

When applied in an organisational strategic management process, strategic thinking involves the generation and application of unique business insights and opportunities intended to create competitive advantage for a firm or organisation. It can be done individually, as well as collaboratively among key people who can positively alter an organisation's future. Group strategic thinking may create more value by enabling a proactive and creative dialogue, where individuals gain other people's perspectives on critical and complex issues. This is regarded as a benefit in highly competitive and fast-changing business landscapes.

14.5 Why the paradigm shift is so difficult in management

Paradigm shifts can be intermittent, sporadic, broken or interrupted. Working with constant effort within existing paradigms causes frustration, not progress. Progress requires scientists to look at the problems in different ways to solve the fundamental issues.

Managers or business schools must embrace the change, whether they wish to or not, because there is a continuous paradigm shift happening in management. It's a shift from company-centric values where the business's priority is to make money for shareholders to the new customer-centric importance of adding value for customers.

Among the many factors driving this shift is the understanding that the new paradigm, when correctly executed, will make much more money for the company than shareholder capitalism. One only has to look at companies such as Apple, Amazon and Costco, which implemented the shift successfully, to see the results. The fact that it is a better environment for those who carry out the work as well as those who benefit from the work enhances the experience.

The shift in management is a shift from shareholder capitalism to customer capitalism where the company must change its priorities to focus on the customer. The shareholder must adapt to this change because the management practices previously used to ensure success for the shareholder are now completely incompatible with the new goal of pleasing the customer.

One issue that science must contend with regarding paradigm shifts is that the shifts appear to hold no common sense. Copernicus's theory of the heliocentric universe proved this to be a serious issue! It was clear that the stars and sun revolved around the earth, obviously!

For so many managers today, the idea that the main purpose of a company to make money for its shareholders is equally clear. The shareholders created the company. They control it and own it. It is only common sense that they would be most interested in making money for themselves. The issue is that anyone who sets foot in the marketplace, who operates on the basis of "value for money" will not part with their money without believing that we are offering them something. They may be willing to do business with us initially, but once they are aware that we are only out to make money for ourselves, at their expense, they cease all business with us as soon as they can.

The idea of a company in business to make money for the shareholders at the expense of the customer was not invented by anyone who had ever spent time in the marketplace or asked customers to part with their money. It was created by money men trying to figure out a way to get rich from a pre-existing set up and adding academics to think it through. They had no thought of the destruction caused by these companies, who devote themselves solely to making money, from making money from bad profits, looking for the get-rich-quick deal that would ruin their reputation and the sustainability of the company, or steering clear of innovation for fear it was too risky an endeavour.

In times gone by, when a few big companies had the lion's share of the spending power and could dictate shopping habits, this theory of focusing purely on making money worked. But with globalisation and the Internet appearing on the horizon to shift the balance of power from the seller to the buyer, companies who focused purely on their net profit began to struggle with their profitability. And so now, the theory of solely making money is obsolete. Producing profits is a by-product of the company's activities, it should not be the goal.

Similarly, the shift from a firm-centric to a customer-centric outlook can cause managers, who perceive themselves as being in control of the workplace and marketplace, many a missed night's sleep! To buy into the new paradigm would be conceding that the customer is in control! Although the company-centric and customer-centric views are both beautifully simple and internally consistent, they differ completely in terms of success and accuracy. The company-centric view, in terms of accuracy, has offered no explanation for the decline in success in invested capital and return on assets for more than forty years and also suggests no forward thinking in an economy where the demand continues to shrink.

In terms of success the boundaries are set between whether the shifts are good for the company and its shareholders, good for those participating in the work, good for those expecting the end product and good for any other parties involved, be that community or societal.

Most of the writing produced in the last century on this subject has focused on three main parts: what is good for those completing the work? What is good for those receiving the work? What is good for the society in which the company operates? However, the decisive

- We cannot solve problems by using the same kind of creative thinking we used when we created them (Albert Einstein)
- Thinking outrageously about learning environments. Outrageous means exceeding all bounds of reasonableness: it means something shocking
- Future thinking

Figure 14.2 Strategic thinking: Strategy's orphan

advantage for the customer-centric view of the company is much better for the company itself, this leading to higher profits for the company and its shareholders. The rest of the success is a bonus. The inexorable shift is in the fact that it makes more money.

Execution has many blind spots. Taking a step back from execution on a regular basis to spend some time examining your business and what you are trying to achieve is just as important as being an execution pro.

Good execution demands good planning. Good execution provides an easy to read rulebook to keep everyone on track. It allows you to understand the maximum effectiveness of the execution you plan to carry out. It keeps the team motivated by the "big picture" while the actual execution provides better leads and bigger profit. Good execution is at the heart of creating a brand with good company culture, coherence, accessibility and is desirable to be a part of. Strategy is about making things simple.

But when many companies reach a plateau and stall, the introduction of strategic planning can help enhance the original vision and take them forward in a new direction or dimension.

14.6 The role of networks in organisational change

Corporate boundaries are becoming fuzzier and fuzzier. New voices are entering all the time in the market, originated from business stakeholders, which might include suppliers, customers, governments and even competitors. Markets are becoming conversations and the new competitive structure is between networks and other corporate networks. This means that companies need to change their organisational design to become more flexible. There are many new formats that help a company to respond to these market shifts – business colonies, self-managing teams, the holographic organisation among others. This is really the start of the true multi-sided business model. This also means that companies need to embark on an organisational stretch.

- Distributed co-creation moves into the mainstream
- Making the network the organisation
- Experimentation and Big Data
- Imagining anything as a service
- The age of the multi-sided business model
- Innovating from the bottom of the pyramid

Figure 14.3 Major trends in new strategic thinking

A few years back, the world's leading manufacturer and designer of office products decided it required a complete organisational overhaul. Product line co-ordination was poor, communication between design teams was lacking and the key people in the business were too remote from the customers to be of any use. The company dealt with this by creating an office-free environment where all parties, designers, architects and customers could come together in a less formal environment and mingle. The space was designed to be visually attractive and conceptually compelling. However, it did not capture the imagination to arouse meaningful innovation or better relations with the customers. A mere four and a half years later the decision was taken to revamp the space again.

This operation has occurred in many organisations where they have responded to organisational changes and operational dysfunction without realising the actual cause. An organisation hampered by slow decision making may decide to decentralise their operations. A company with poor communications or the inability to be flexible may try to break down barriers to prevent business units or functions operate as silos. Yet as smart as these solutions look on paper, they often show little promise of success and so the reorganisation of a company will come around on a fairly regular basis, often with no significant improvement.

One key factor in this is that the boxes and lines of a standard hierarchical organisational chart do not show clearly the many relationships between business units, hierarchies and functions that make up the whole organisation. These critical relationships enhance the workings of any business by defining how work is completed in today's knowledge intensive and increasingly collaborative companies. It is no small surprise then that re-engineering of business processes and total quality management projects, to name just two examples, fail two out of three times due to the ignoring of these invisible but essential networks.

Companies that invest the time and energy into understanding the highly complicated invisible networks and relationships will greatly improve their chance of making a successful organisational change. A decisive network approach to change can help focus on points in the company where relationships may need to increase or reduce and can identify critical points of connectivity that need to be protected or destroyed. A network approach is an ideal way for companies to introduce change and make it a permanent feature by working through influential employees, to concentrate on parts of the network where there is need for expansion or reduction while measuring the effectiveness of major initiatives.

Brokers who integrate fully with a number of different subgroups within an organisation can be particularly influential. "Bridging" relationships between entire networks can position these brokers to knit together many essential networks in order to make their dealings more efficient by means of gathering and disseminating information in a high-touch way. Brokers also tend to be in a better position to understand and communicate what aspects of the business require reorganisation and what would work across subsections, functions and locations. They also have a high level of credibility with staff. If managers can get the brokers on board early in the process they have a much higher success rate with any major cultural shift, implementation of new technology or post-merger integration.

It is far too easy for an organisation to overlook the importance of the broker due to the unique role they play within the company. They may in fact have a smaller number of relationships compared to other influential connectors to whom staff may frequently turn for information or advice. In the situation of a merger for example, it is often the case that a company doesn't know or underestimates the importance of a broker to the merged entity.

Infusing organisational change with network understanding

By taking the time to look at the networks within the company before implementing major changes, companies can learn and understand much more than just who the brokers are within an organisation. When a large pharmaceutical company, for example, reviewed their collaborating networks they realised that the workstation walls were too high and this physical barrier was causing remoteness among groups of staff. Once this was corrected a 50 per cent increase in connectivity was found to be the result along with impromptu meetings and better communication levels among staff.

14.7 Shifting to a matrix structure from brain- and region-centric structures

In 2005 a leading provider of IT-consulting services and outsourcing, with 10,000 staff, over a billion in revenues and over 70 offices world-wide was struggling with its current organisational structure. An increase in the size of the company had made the current systems unworkable and created rigidity in company decisions. Out-dated expertise, technology and solutions were rife within the company and costs were rocketing.

The company bosses were convinced that the organisational focus on individual offices or areas was to blame for these issues and problems. They came to the conclusion that they should move to a client-based matrix, while combining industry-focused practice groups with a sales organisation that focuses mainly on regional focused sales. They convinced themselves this would create a globally integrated business. Many organisations have followed this route, often with mixed results.

In order to be sure that all reorganisation issues were being covered precisely, this company analysed and mapped the networks that the employees relied on in their work. The critical finding of fundamental importance was that a number of key executives, all of them apart from one, a director or vice-president, were the reason for the organisational bottlenecks. Many employees regularly came to these executives for decisions, information or resources but the majority could not get access. Reorganising or shifting a matrix structure without removing the bottlenecks would not solve any of the current issues and almost certainly create disappointment.

The company implemented two important things to relieve these issues. The first crucial point was to implement "expertise locator" technology. This helped employees to find solutions and answer questions quickly and without the need to move requests further up the chain of command. The second point was that management changed the pound threshold on orders so that lower-level employees could make pricing decisions and close deals. As a result of this, the company created a new team, below executive level, that could exercise senior management decisions for costing and defining customer-specific solutions.

One more important finding that came to light was the fact that collaboration between regions was actually fairly strong, where a number of employees serve as "connectors," but was weak overall across regions. Encouraging connections between the central people in each region would help immeasurably to ensure global co-ordination. The applications services leader, one of the largest groups, introduced central players from various other groups in order that they could build a more effective awareness of "who knew what" than would have been possible if the company had taken the usual steps implemented by many matrix reorganisations.

By focusing on removing bottlenecks and connecting relevant employees the company massively accelerated the shift to a matrix organisation, which resulted in it being far more efficient. For example, employee connections with each other between functions increased by 13 percentage points. This then created significantly improved client services, revenue and transfer of best practices.

14.8 Combining dispersed personnel into a single function

Another goal that companies going through the reorganisation process try to achieve is to bring together employees who perform related tasks in different regions of the organisation. Core functions, such as finance, IT, human resources or purchasing are mostly duplicated and have the same processes throughout the company, and consolidation provides economies of scale while also sharing knowledge, expertise and best practices throughout the company globally. Network analysis can reveal opportunities for highlighting best practices and integration by showing global functional networks more transparently. These well-functioning relationships should not be disrupted.

The world's largest engineering consultancy, with more than 5,000 specialists in 36 countries and almost a billion in sales undertook a reorganisation in 2003. Having undertaken many mergers previously, the firm still suffered from a lack of consistent global processes and continued with regions and business units functioning separately. The first step to integrate the entire company was to consolidate the IT function. This was currently divided into six different regional sections, and was to be combined into one global department. This was thought to provide a better service at a lower cost. The key to success would have to be collaboration for all 185 people in 27 offices in 11 countries. This had been sadly lacking until this point with internal customers paying different prices, receiving different services, and software and hardware providing different functionality.

Analysing this network showed that a number of issues wouldn't be solved by creating the desired unity and governance structure – information sharing was limited across a number of geographies because of the previous autonomous structure and the firm's hierarchy. The experts at lower levels were not communicating with their colleagues across the organisation but instead with their superiors, losing vital valuable knowledge. It came as no surprise that network connections clustered round bottlenecks and awareness of certain colleagues' expertise was low. Many employees were now expected to work together in harmony when in fact they had never even exchanged an email let alone met each other.

It was decided that the IT department would support this reorganisation in three ways. It firstly augmented the travel budget in order to facilitate face-to-face meetings, thus improving overall department-wide communication. They also implemented team-building activities, a staff newsletter and staff meetings. Secondly, IT knowledge communities were created for major expertise areas with the intention of encouraging and creating collaboration, sharing knowledge and developing and disseminating best practices globally. And lastly they created project management teams to dispel traditional geographic boundaries and focused them on a few functional initiatives, such as platform standardisation.

Within two years the IT function was operating with true integration and was globally successful. The following network analysis showed huge improvements in connectivity, highlighted the creation of economic value and showed significant time saving across the firm's previous business unit and geographical lines. To date, managers in the organisation still use network analysis as a tool for seeking out opportunities to improve effectiveness through collaboration and communication.

When considering reorganisation, executives should not focus on the formal organisational structure, but instead acknowledge informal communication channels and key staff, the opinion leaders. By understanding the networks the employees use to complete tasks and get work done, these executives can grasp the organisational changes and enhance the process rather than create a headache for all concerned.

Business leaders should be aware of opportunities available to them to transform product offerings into services, as their competitors will probably also be doing the same. A wide and varied new spectrum of services can be offered when new platforms are created to combine with a broader view of the assets, and these include physical and intellectual capital. However, being able to innovate in services requires a fundamentally different mind-set from the one needed when designing products.

14.9 The age of the multi-sided business tool

The multi-sided business tool model can create more value when used through interaction with multiple players instead of the traditional one-on-one information exchange. Advertising is a classic example of how these models work in the media industry. Newspapers, magazines and television impart their content while receiving most of their revenue from a third party, advertisers. Technology is creating other powerful forms of multi-sided business models. For example, in some information businesses, revenue is generated when data is gathered from one set of users and another set of users is charged to use the information services.

As more people move to online services, it becomes more apparent that network services can magnify the value of a multi-sided business model. The "freemium" model is a prime example. Some customers get free services and this cost is covered by those who are willing to pay a premium for special services available. Skype, Pandora and Flickr all use this kind of cross-subsidisation and also demonstrate the leveraging effect of networks. The service is more valuable when there is a bigger quantity of free users. Pandora commands a huge amount of data from its free users and can refine its music recommendations accordingly.

Other companies too, find benefit from their core business being part of a network. For example, Mastercard has built an advisory unit in order to gather information from its core credit card business. It collects data on spending habits and sells this information to other companies who want a better understanding of buying trends.

Of course this does not apply to all companies but for those who think they can benefit, they should start by taking stock of all the data they have amassed, including data flow from customer transactions and look at who might find this information useful.

14.10 Innovating from the bottom of the pyramid

The adoption of technology has been a global phenomenon and the scale of use has been hugely embraced by emerging markets. Research has shown that disruptive business models occur when extreme market conditions combine with technology, such as poor infrastructure, low cost curves for talent, hard-to-access suppliers or customer demand for low prices. As an economic recovery is now showing in some parts of the world, high rates of growth are being recorded and companies who have embraced the new models are emerging as global players, whereas many multinational companies are only now starting to consider these developing markets as a fountain of technology-enabled innovation instead of manufacturing hubs.

Hundreds of companies are now emerging on to the global platform with everything imaginable on offer. These companies are showing the world there is a new type of competitor on

280 *Radical/futures themes*

the scene now. They are challenging the growth plans of the dominant players in the developing markets and also exporting their radical models to existing markets. In response to this the established global companies must create communication channels with local networks of suppliers, entrepreneurs, investors, fast growing businesses and influential people causing disruptions.

14.11 What is a multi-sided platform?

A "multi-sided platform" is a business model pattern. This brings together two or more distinct sets of customers who are co-dependent on each other. These platforms are only useful to one group of customers if the other group is also present. The platform creates value by creating interactions between groups. This multi-sided platform becomes more valuable when it attracts more users. This phenomenon is known as the "network effect." Network effects along with "positive feedback loops" are economic terms that describe the ballooning effect that some companies create to benefit the markets they are involved in.

A business model is the name given to the systems that a company uses to create, deliver and capture value. A business model dictates the short and long-term strategies that a company employs to gain competitive advantage, which then translates to an operating model.

Platform operators do incur costs by serving the full range of customer groups but often there is a purpose in luring one segment with a cheaper value proposition with the aim of luring users in the platform's other areas.

From an executive perspective as regards the operating model, the company organises all functions from services, sales and marketing and support functions, to provide the margins that will be necessary to make the business a success.

The average 30-year old in the US has already worked 11 jobs. In one decade the same average 30-year old will have worked on between two hundred and three hundred projects. Companies are moving towards a fluidity in their operations, the digital networks between buyers and sellers driving this liquefaction more efficiently than ever before.

But the far-reaching effects of our steadily flowing digital business do not end with successfully performing transactions. Now it is beginning to change virtually every aspect of the business process, not only how a business conducts itself but also the duration, importance and permanency of work assignments, the relationships between employer and employee and the organising of principles when talent and work assignments merge.

Stretch is the ability to engage people with a challenge and move them to a level of performance they did not know they were capable by "liberating and energising" them, and raising individual aspiration levels and encouraging people to lift their expectations of themselves and others – to create stretch:

- Establish shared ambition through well-communicated shared goals
- Visible celebrations of success will breed optimism
- Structure around focused, small groups that are specialised and niched, resulting in "the emergence of a collective identity"
- Ensuring that individuals have a clear picture of how their own tasks contribute to the overall performance of the company, and have the ability to create personal meaning and ownership.

Figure 14.4 Stretch

> Rather than workplaces, in the future there will be business colonies. This will be a kind of evolution of our current co-working spaces that we have today. People will come together for the project and once the project is over they move on to another project. Some of these business colonies will be virtual, physical or a combination of both. Business colonies will be structured around particular areas such as nano- tech, games development and IT.

Figure 14.5 Business colonies

The centre of the new work revolution will contain a new kind of business structure that will serve as an organisational magnet for work projects and supply the talent to complete the project. This will be a business colony (see Figure 14.5).

14.12 Business colonies defined

Business colonies are a new kind of organisational structure evolving from the need to match talent with forthcoming work projects. The focus will be based on the static workforce based in a physical location combined with a "virtual" workforce. Some organisations may forgo the overheads of the physical location altogether and form a virtual communications structure completely.

Most business colonies will be focused on a task that suits the expertise of the team. In some instances, large companies will establish their own business colonies in order to expand capabilities without increasing staff numbers and costs. At the helm of the colony will be the project managers who will prove that the colony can successfully carry out experimental projects best performed outside the boundaries of the existing workflow.

Colonies will be allowed to develop their own standard operating procedures in relation to management software, legal structures, payment processes and dispute solving. As time progresses these colonies will be assessed on their ability to complete a task successfully, while showing the efficiency, quality of work and treatment of the talent.

The driving forces

The driving force behind the reality of the business colony is more than the simple fact that they are a good idea. In fact, it is being driven more by the logical step in evolution to combine emerging culture with technology and governmental systems.

This results in companies looking for a way to negate the costs of adding more staff and the resulting costs. Project-based work is the logical option. The technology available now is making it easier to match talent with pending work assignments.

Colonies: when it works and when it doesn't

Not all organisational situations would benefit from a "colonised" workforce. Here are some instances where a business colony does not make good business sense:

- **High accountability positions** – Any task involving money or personnel records, or any senior management positions should be performed by a loyal member of the workforce.
- **Sensitive issues or trade secrets** – where a project involves sensitive issues or the company's trade secrets, it is necessary to keep this task within the confines of trusted employees.

- **Deep-rooted knowledge work** – A project that requires the full understanding of the company's history, culture and methodologies would not be a successful place for a colony.
- **Customer-facing jobs** – Most customer-facing jobs require a solid, dependable and static workforce; this situation would not lend itself well to a colony.

While not every situation is suitable for project work, it appears that managers across the globe are willing to undertake this challenge and experiment with what will and will not work in this area.

There is good sense in aligning yourself only with projects that suit your skillset and expertise. There is a higher rate of success and the work is more meaningful when reputation is at stake. Although these tasks or projects may have tight deadlines, staff will find greater purpose when they are able to pick their own projects and giving them the ability to choose the way they are completed provides greater purpose.

The business colony, when adding up all the positives of purpose, meaning, freedom, stability and flexibility, brings a number of powerfully compelling reasons to switch. When a project is created within a colony, taking logical steps to manage it, the first task must be to assess the size and scale of the project and break it down into sizeable chunks of manageable workload. The project's budget must also be taken into consideration. Once these tasks have been suitably organised and a timetable for completion has been agreed, the work projects can then be divided up and assigned to those who will complete them.

Reputation

Reputation is everything in a business colony environment. People with exemplary reputations will be the ones at the top of the list for being called on for each new project that arises. New people arriving at the colony will need to prove themselves as capable and successful in order to increase their chances of becoming a project manager in the future.

Some projects may escalate and expand much faster than anticipated, in which case a referral system may be necessary to use social networking to its full advantage to bring other expertise into the area.

An online reputation is built up of many parts. It can be the standard profiles and professional bios that create interest but the entire picture, including photos and pictures, conversations, data sets and reference points, helps build the entire impression that a future investor will use to assess your overall abilities.

Evolution

Co-working spaces are a logical choice for business colonies. Mostly these colonies consist of a variety of talent with the ability to take on extra tasks. Although colonies may form in many different ways, some will form because of their speciality pool to complete relevant tasks. Some may be private colonies sustained by large companies, others will be non-profit colonies.

With time, educational facilities will start to transform themselves into educational colonies with a selection of internal colonies designed to provide students with practical work experience alongside their studies. Moving away from the "tenured faculty," educational colonies will require "teaching entities" which will match the teaching requirements of the curriculum on a project by project basis.

The business environment is perpetually being challenged to provide more from less. Any company which cannot find more efficient ways to do things most probably will not survive. As is standard, the highest cost on any company balance sheet is the labour. Business colonies exist to provide the matching of labour to the projects for an exact duration. This can simply provide the best value for money and improve overall efficiency.

Business colonies should not be a way for companies to take advantage of cheap labour although some will try. Instead, the future era of skill shortages will enable talented people to benefit by demanding high rates for their unique expertise.

With time, people will not relate to the hiring and firing of today's business world. As we embrace the concept of the business colony, business as we know it today will cease to exist.

14.13 Management dilemmas

All entrepreneurs face the same kind of management issues, and the choices they have to make can provide them with success or disaster. All businesses are concerned with productivity: what can we be most productive with and where does that place us in the market. These entrepreneurs or business people must find a niche in the market that makes them stand out from the rest. The style of the organisation is the driving force behind success. There are multiple dilemmas to be faced when dealing with the topics of style and productivity.

1) **Product or service** – This seems an easy choice to make but the implications of picking one over the other can have big consequences.
2) **Support or lead** – the choice between being a front runner in the market or supporting other larger companies from the back, the possibilities for both are endless.
3) **Innovate or conserve** – The importance of innovation is great, focusing on new applications and markets moving forward. But the profit from this is still in the future and there is also a lot to be said for maximising your current business. If there is no investment, the time may come when business declines and if there is no new innovation to take the place of the current systems, the company may find itself in trouble. However, investment and innovation may take over and this could cost the company its current successful methods of productivity.
4) **External or internal focus** – There are people who watch the markets and can move into each niche and expand successfully to garner the best possible profit. These flexible first-movers are ready to jump when necessary. Some have built up their own ideas by perceiving information differently. This dilemma is current in organisations – it appears that sales and marketers are more externally driven while administration and IT tend to lean towards in-house streamlining.
5) **Own product or leverage on third-parties** – Does the company create and manufacture on site? Or does the company thrive on leverage from a third party? Both these types of company are successful although the latter does better with the emergence of the internet marketplace.
6) **Cooperate or compete** – This is more apparent where companies who value teamwork will also set personal targets for their staff. This works best when proportionately balanced.
7) **Consumer or company** – This is the least important of the dilemmas for a manager, if the context has already been set. This is however, of critical importance to an entrepreneur who wishes to attract a small clientele, instead of driving thousands of demanding consumers to the business.

- Flexible decentralised, empowered networks within a structure of strategic intent
- Learning through immersive experiences, scenarios and rapid prototyping
- Acceptance of uncertainty with intuition as a valid contributor to clarity
- Strategic sense-making beyond operational problem-solving
- Uncoupling "winning" from the need for a solution
- Engagement with complexity.

Figure 14.6 Dilemma management

How organisations learn to regenerate strategy is the key issue today. But they also need the speed and manner of identifying future changes.
Moving without inertia from strategic insight, to execution and back, to strategic insight. That is the essence of Strategic Agility. The ultimate strategy. It requires sensing and responding to change at the edges of an organisation.

Figure 14.7 Strategic agility

14.14 Participatory change, participatory economy

Strategic agility is the thing that organisations need to mobilise operations to capitalise on opportunities, even with time pressure and incomplete data. Organisations need strategic agility for taking risks and maximising on opportunities in uncertain circumstances. Organisations recognise that great opportunities cannot be planned and therefore rely on strategic agility to achieve long-term goals. Senior leaders must comprehend the value in exploring opportunities in an uncertain world, in order to enhance strategic agility.

It is a wise move for organisations with strategic agility, not to over commit to just one vision. These organisations are aware that plans can often go wrong. They have the ability to compete, grow, change their plans and prosper. Similarly, the ability to work around obstacles instead of being worn down by problems is a sign of strategic agility. Strategic agility is a vital part of every organisation's business plan. Leaders must know their current environment and have the ability to change agendas and execute plans in order to enhance the strategic ability of an organisation. In order to understand the basic skills of a proactive execution, the leadership team must be able to mobilise people around new ideas in order to create active and worthwhile coalitions. This requires them to create and work with the political common sense to adhere to the fundamental principles that allow them to engage employees and move forward with the capacity to sustain the momentum of the project. It is therefore a successful leader that can embrace strategic agility and enhance the leadership skills of key players.

14.15 Chapter summary

This chapter deals with the future of the future by bringing in novel paradigmatic approaches in the conceptualisation of strategic thinking. With this focus in mind, we cover and dissect important new issues like the multi-sided business, the emergence of business colonies, the organisation, dilemma management and strategic agility.

14.16 End of chapter self-reflection questions

1 Why do you think that the huge number of paradigm shifts are not properly assessed and responded to by management?
2 Discuss some ideas about the "fabric" of a bad management strategy.
3 Comment on the role of multi-sided platforms and multi-sided businesses in the future.
4 How do you see the evolution of the concept of business colonies in terms of organisational working patterns?
5 Why do you feel that there are so many bad strategies in practice?

References

Anderson, P. (1999). Perspective: Complexity theory and organization science. *Organization Science*, *10*(3), 216–232.
Benito-Ostolaza, J. M., Brañas-Garza, P., Hernández, P., & Sanchis-Llopis, J.A. (2015). Strategic behaviour in Schelling dynamics: Theory and experimental evidence. *Journal of Behavioral and Experimental Economics*, *57*, 134–147.
Benner, M. J., & Tushman, M. L. (2003). Exploitation, exploration, and process Management: The productivity dilemma revisited. *Academy of Management Review*, *28*(2), 238–256.
Doz, Y. L., & Kosonen, M. (2010). Embedding strategic agility: A leadership agenda for accelerating business model renewal. *Long Range Planning*, *43*(2–3), 370–382.
Ghoshal, S. (2005). Bad management theories are destroying good management practices. *Academy of Management Learning and Education*, *4*(1), 75–91.
Graetz, F. (2002). Strategic thinking versus strategic planning: Towards understanding the complementarities. *Management Decision*, *40*(5), 456–462.
Hagiu, A., & Wright, J. (2015). Multi-sided Platforms. *International Journal of Industrial Organization*, *43*, 162–174.
Johannessen, J.-A. (1991). The holographic organization: A design model. *Cybernetics and Systems: An International Journal*, *22*(1), 41–55.
Liedtka, J. M. (1998). Strategic thinking: Can it be taught? *Long Range Planning*, *31*(1), 120–129.
Maccarrone, P. (2009). Factors influencing the attitude towards corporate social responsibility: Some empirical evidence from Italy. *Corporate Governance*, *9*(2), pp. 103–119.
March, J. G. (1991). Exploration and exploitation in organizational learning. *Organization Science*, *2*(1), 71–87.
Mohrman, S. A., Tenkasi, R.V., & Mohrman Jr. A. M. (2003). The role of networks in fundamental organizational change: A grounded analysis. *Journal of Applied Behavioural Science*, *39*(3), 301–323.
Murthy, P. N. (1996). Paradigm shift in management. *Systems Research*, *13*(4), 457–468.
Nicholls-Nixon, C. L., & Jasinski, D. (1995). The blurring of industry boundaries: An explanatory model applied to telecommunications. *Industrial and Corporate Change*, *4*(4), 755–768.
Oliver, C., & Holzinger, I. (2008). The effectiveness of strategic political management: A dynamic capabilities framework. *Academy of Management Review*, *33*(2), 496–520.
Zeng, M., & Chen, X-P. (2003). Achieving cooperation in multiparty alliances: A social dilemma approach to partnership management. *Academy of Management Review*, *28*(4), 587–605.

Further reading

Battram, A. (2002) *Navigating complexity: The essential guide to complexity theory in business and management*. London: Spiro Press.

Caldart, A. A., & Ricart J. E. (2004). corporate strategy revisited: A view from complexity theory. *European Management Review*, *1*(1), 96–104.
Casti, J. L. (2014). *Complexification: Explaining a paradoxical world through the science of surprise*. New York: HarperCollins.
Hout, T. M. (1999). Books in Review: Are Managers Obsolete? *Harvard Business Review*, *77*(2), 161–168.
Okes, D. (2003). Complexity theory simplifies choices. *Quality Progress*, *36*(7), 35–38.
Olsen, E. E., Eoyang, G. H., Beckhard, R., & Vaill. P. (2001). *Facilitating organization change: Lessons from complexity science*. San Francisco: Pfeiffer.
Sherman, H. J., & Schultz, R. (1998). *Open boundaries: Creating business innovation through complexity*. Reading, MA: Perseus Books.
Waldrop, M. (1992). *Complexity: The emerging science at the edge of order and chaos*. New York: Simon and Schuster.

Index

3M 172
"1000 Companies to Inspire Europe report 2016" 220, 221–222

A.T. Kearney 41, 42
Accedo 221
Accenture 41, 42
AccorHotels 92–98
action plans 33
active inertia 127–128
Adidas 102
African SOEs 154
age of anxiety 254–255
agency theory 6
agile mindset 164–165
agility 163–165, 202, 252, 284; *see also* strategic agility and design
Ahlstrand, B. 7
Alibaba 29
alliance strategy 28, 29–32
Alshaya 14
alternatives 88, 91
Amazon 184
ambidexterity 39–40
ambiguity 17, 254
AMO framework 218
annual budget 6
Ansoff matrix 74–76
Apotheker, L. 2
Apple 176, 184; strategic alliance with IBM 29–32
Applebaum, E. 218
Armitage, J. 184
ASEAN 223–224
Ash, C.G. 199
Ashton, J. 37
asset-light business model 26
assumptions 90–91
Atkins, R. 186, 187
automobile industry 63
Autonomy 2

Badik, P. 219
Bailey, T. 218
Bain & Company 41, 42, 43
balance sheet analysis 85
balanced portfolio 73, 74
balanced scorecard (BSC) 231, 232, 236, 237–239
Balticovo 221
Banco Espirito Santo 153
banking 1, 197; top largest banks 146–147
Barbados 152
Barcelona football team 102
Barclays Bank 1
bargaining power: of buyers 56, 57; of suppliers 56, 57
Barney, J.B. 7, 15
Bartlett, C.A. 112–115
Batmanghelidjh, C. 3
Bazin, S. 92
BBC 243–244
BCG growth/share matrix 73–74
behavioural strategy 9, 64
benchmarking 34, 35
Benito-Ostolaza, J.M. 270
Benner, M.J. 271
Bentley, P. 48
Berg, P. 218
best practice/best fit approach 218
betapreneurship 164, 172–175
Beurden, P. van 180
Bharadwaj, A. 33, 201
big data 51–52, 130
Big Society 260
"Big Ten" capabilities 214–215
Bilodeau, B. 34
Bimbo 154
Birkinshaw, J. 40
BlaBlaCar 221
blue ocean metaphor 53
blurring reality 107–108
Bodwell, W. 40

288 *Index*

Bolland, M. 2
Boston Consulting Group 41, 42; BCG growth/share matrix 73–74
bottlenecks 277–278
brain, the 51
brand identity 92–93
brand and marketing ROI 138
Brazil 148; packaging company 168
break-even analysis 85–86
BrewDog 265
Brexit 35
BRICS countries 146, 148–149, 151, 156
British Medical Association 37
Brock, J.F. 188–189
brokers 276
Buckley, N. 201
bureaucratic culture 69
Burn, J.M. 199
business as usual, end of 258, 259
business colonies 281–283
business design *see* design
Business Development Bank of Canada (BDC) 211–212
business ecosystems 13, 256–259
business ethics 17, 130, 178–194; trends in 184–189
business level strategy 28, 32–33
business models 256; multi-sided platforms 270–271, 280–281; redesigning 160, 252, 259–260, 271–272
business production models 105–106
business schools 104, 186–187
business–society relationship 32, 181, 184–189
business strategy: evolution of business strategy theory 5–9; rethinking 259–261
butterfly effect 105
buyers' bargaining power 56, 57

Cable & Wireless Communications (CWC) 47–50
Caldwell, C. 186, 187
Cameron, D. 35
Campbell Soup 161
Canadian SMEs 211–212
capabilities 70–71; "Big Ten" capabilities of growing SMEs 214–215; dynamic 7, 14, 15–16, 70–71, 273; meta-capabilities 160, 252, 272
capital markets 26, 104–105
Carrefour 69
case study analysis 17, 80–98; AccorHotels 92–98; format for 83–91; ten-step procedure 82
cash cows 73–74
Caterham F1 14
cell structure design 168–170
CEMEX 151
chains 166

challenges for strategic management 216
chance 112
Chandler, A. 5–6
charities 3
Chen, X.-P. 272
Chermack, T.J. 40
China 3, 103, 155; economic growth 104, 148; football salaries 109, 110; offshoring and reshoring 105–106; SMEs 222–223; SOEs 153–154
Christensen, C.M. 43
citizens 140
Cleroux, P. 212
climate change 61–62
Clinton, H. 184
Coca-Cola 150–151, 188–189
cognitive dilemma 51
collaboration 260–261, 278–279
collaborative economy 106–107
colonies, business 281–283
Columbus International 47–50
combining dispersed personnel 278–279
Committee Encouraging Corporate Philanthropy 32
common purpose 134–135, 262–263
communication 141, 278–279
communities 140–141
communities of practice 65–66
company-centric view 274
competencies 8, 70–71
complementors 58
complex adaptive system models 271
complexity 17, 254
compliance 189
concierges 170
conduct of the business 122
configurational approach to HRM 218
consulting industry 40–43
consumer services sector 220, 222
contextual ambidexterity 40
contingency approach 32, 218, 229, 231
Continuum Attractions 222
Cook, T. 30
Corbyn, J. 12–13
core competencies 8, 70–71
corporate action 180
Corporate Bribery Act 2010 183
corporate identity 161–163
corporate level strategy 28, 32
corporate planning departments 6
corporate reputation 180
corporate scandals 182–183
corporate social performance (CSP) 179–180
corporate social responsibility (CSR) 46, 127, 187–189, 272–273
cost leadership strategy 76, 240
creative ideas 120

creative problem solving (CPS) 252
Crittenden, V.L. 143
Crittenden, W.F. 143
culture, organisational 68–69
customer analysis 62–63
customer-centric thinking 200–201, 273–275
customer-driven service platform 134–135
customer engagement index 136–137
customer intimacy – differentiation strategy 240
customer relationship management (CRM) 34
customer share 121–122
customer value 119
customer value propositions 240
customers, understanding 137–138
CWC 47–50

data: big data 51–52, 130; mining 52
data overload 127
decision-making, ethics in 189–193
deconsumption 106
deglobalisation 255–256
deliberate strategy 38–39, 215–216
Deloitte Consulting 41, 42
demand conditions 111
Dennison, R. 261
Dentix 222
descriptive schools 7
design: growth with the wrong business design 125; organisational 165–170; strategic agility and design 17, 159–177
design school 10, 16
DESMI 221
determinants of performance 47
development strategy 96
Diamond competitive advantage model 110–112
differentiation stage 167
differentiation strategy 76, 240
diffusion modelling 118–119
digital platforms 54
digital strategy 17, 33, 195–209; *see also* information technology
dilemma management 283, 284
disclosure 180
disruptive forces 41–43
disruptive innovation 162, 172, 173–174
diversification 75–76
Dobbs, M.E. 59, 81
dogs 73–74
Donaldson, T. 120
dot.com crash 8, 11
Dougan, B. 1
Doz, Y.L. 113, 160, 252, 272
dynamic capabilities 7, 14, 15–16, 70–71, 273

Earl, M.J. 199
e-business models 8, 197, 199–200

e-business strategy 196–200; *see also* digital strategy
e-commerce 197
economic growth 220; BRICS countries 148; China 104, 148
economic value 50
economy hotels 94, 95
ecosystems, business 13, 256–259
education 104; business ethics 186–187
El Sawy, O. 201
electric cars 219
Elliott, F. 36–37
emergency healthcare, paying for 36–38
emergent strategy 13, 38–39, 215–216
emerging economies 17, 96, 102–103, 143–156
emerging market multinational corporations (EMNCs) 154–155
emotional engagement 263–264
emotional intelligence 269
employee engagement surveys 34–35
Employee Value Proposition (EVP) 171
empowerment 168–170
enlightening stakeholder theory 133–134
enlightening value maximisation 133
enterprise mobility 29–32
entertainment consumption 203–204
entrepreneurship 72–75, 164; betapreneurship 164, 172–175
entry mode strategies 115
e-organisational dimensions 198
e-procurement 202, 203
Ernst & Young (EY) 41, 42, 43, 184
ethical behaviour 181–184
ethical value 179–180
ethics *see* business ethics
ethics in decision-making (EiDM) 189–193
European Union (EU) 175; SMEs 219–222
Eurotex 221–222
execution 216
exploitation 105, 271
export value chain 255–256
external environment 6; analysis of 52–64

Facebook 108, 184, 195–196, 204, 205, 256
factor conditions 110–111
failures 1–3, 14
fair finances 264–265
fair value accounting 265–266
family firms 152–153
feed-forward orientation 162–163
Ferguson, Sir A. 4–5
Fernandes, T. 14
Fiat auto group 153
FIFA corruption scandal 182
financial crisis of 2008 8, 59, 210
financial markets 26, 104–105
financial measures 230–231

financial situation analysis 85–87, 91, 97–98
firm strategy, structure and rivalry 111–112
Fitschen, J. 1
five forces model 7, 56–60, 199
Five Whys approach 77
flat organisational structure 68
flexibility 196–197, 198, 201–204
Flickr 279
Flow Traders 222
Floyd, L.A. 186, 187
fluidity 160, 252, 272
focus strategy 76
food and drink sector 220, 221
football: FIFA corruption scandal 182; salaries in China 109, 110
Ford, H. 66
forecasts 6
foreigners' payment for healthcare 36–38
formal organisational structure 65–66
Fox, C.R. 8, 64
Fractus 221
"freemium" model 279
FRHI Hotels 97
Friends Reunited 204
functional level strategy 28, 33–34
functional organisational structure 65–66
future, the 17–18, 268–286

G4S 229–230
G5 countries 146, 147
G7 countries 61–62
G8 countries 146
Gale, J. 199
gap analysis 174
Gardner, S. 199
General Electric (GE) 106
generic strategies 14, 76–77, 215
Ghoshal, S. 112–115, 269
Gibson, C.B. 40
global automobile industry 63
global change 26
Global Competitive Index (CGI) 151
global day of service 262–263
Global Family Index 153
global financial crisis 8, 59, 210
global grid 104–105
global organisations 17, 101–117
global strategy 13–14, 103, 113, 114–115
globalisation 69, 102–109; deglobalisation 255–256
Glossopolis 217
Godiva chocolates 161
"good" strategy 216–217
Google 172, 173, 184
Goss, R. 37
Gössling, T. 180
government policy 112

great companies 261–262
Greenberg, D. 169
greenhouse gas emissions 61–62
greening of products 50
Greenley, G.E. 10
greenwashing 178
GreenWay 219
Grosbusch 221
Grossman, R. 200
growth: curses of 125, 127, 128; economic *see* economic growth; focus on customer share for 121–122; just for the sake of it 122–123; path 101–102; SMEs 212, 213, 214–215, 220; traps for emerging economies 151
growth/share matrix 73–74
growth strategies 123–125
Guardian Industries 167
Guerras-Martin, L.Á. 27

Hackbarth, G. 199
Hagiu, A. 270–271
Haier 155
Hamel, G. 7, 8, 12
Handelsbanken 167
Harvard Business School 80–81; oath 187
Havas Meaningful Brands Index 139–140
health: foreigners' payments for emergency care 36–38; impacts of globalisation 104
health tourism 36–38
hierarchies 168
Hilton hotels 153
holographic organisation 271, 283
Holzinger, I. 273
Home Depot 3
horizontal analysis 85
Hoshi Ruyokan 153
hotel sector 26, 115–116; case study analysis 92–98; performance measurement 231–234
HP 1, 2–3
HSBC World Sevens Series 108–109
Huber, G.P. 160
hubs 167
human capital 69
human resource (HR) departments 169–172
human resource management (HRM) 217–218
Hunt, J. 36

ibis hotels family 92, 94, 95
IBM 260–261, 264; global day of service 262–263; strategic alliance with Apple 29–32
idea generation 172
IKEA 139–140
implementation 28, 46, 89, 159–160
in-house law functions 43
income statement analysis 85
incomplete information 90
India 112, 141, 148, 155

individualism view 181, 182–184
Indonesia 149–150
inequalities 105
inertia, active 127–128
"infobesity" 127
information economy 119, 256–257, 258
information technology 33, 41–43; consolidation of the IT function 278; digital strategy 17, 33, 195–209; and entertainment consumption 203–204; IT competencies 70
innovation 94–95, 120; disruptive 162, 172, 173–174; divergent nature of 172; preconditions for 172; from the bottom of the pyramid 279–280; networking and 260–261; new models for 121–125; reverse innovation 253–255
Instagram 195–196, 205
institutional logic 261–262
institutional voids 150–152
intangible assets 69, 107, 230
integration: of core functions 278–279; stage of organizational evolution 167–168
integration/responsiveness framework 112–115
intellectual capital 69
intensity of rivals 56, 58
Intercontinental Hotel Group (IHG) 26
internal analysis 53, 64–72
internal factors 7
international cooperation 62
international strategy 113, 114
Internet 198–199; impact of 195, 196; *see also* digital strategy
Internet of Things (IOT) 206
intrepreneurs 173
iPads 30
iPhones 30

Jackson, A. 1
Jain, A. 1
Japan 106
Jay-Z 9
job creation 220
Jobs, S. 66, 176
Johannessen, J.-A. 271
justice view 181
justification 88–89

Kalleberg, A.L. 218
Kane, G.C. 201
Kanter, R.M. 131
Kaplan, R.S. 239, 240
Ketels, C. 109
Kettinger, W.J. 199
key performance indicators (KPIs) 36
key trends 3, 4
keystone 257–258
Khalifa, A.S. 119

Kickstarter 265
Kids Company 3
Kim, W.C. 53
Kingfisher 13, 179
King's Fund 3, 244
Kiron, D. 201
Klick Health 170
knowledge economy 119, 256–257, 258
knowledge management 8
Kosonen, M. 160, 252, 272
KPMG 43
Krell, T. 199

La Senza 14
Labour Party 12–13
lag indicators 230–231
Lampel, J. 7
lead indicators 230–231
leadership unity 160, 252, 272
legal process outsourcing (LPO) 106
levels of strategy 28–34
Liedtka, J.M. 269
Lifebuoy soap 141
London Stock Exchange 220, 221–222
long-range planning 6
long-term perspective 263
Loux 221
Lovallo, D. 8, 64
low total cost – cost leadership strategy 240
LRN Corp. 169
luxury/upscale hotels 93–94, 95

Ma, J. 29
Maccarone, P. 272–273
macro-environment 53, 54–56
Mahajan, V. 118
Mama Shelter hotels 92, 94, 95
management processes 126–127
Manchester United FC 4–5, 102
manufacturing and engineering sector 220, 221–222
March, J.G. 271
market development 75
market environment 232–233
market penetration 75
market segmentation 54
market share 121–122, 124, 127
marketing 119; changes in 129–138; meaningful 139–142; performance measurement 240–243
marketing dashboards 241–243
marketing profitability analysis 86
Marks & Spencer 1–2
Marriott International hotels 115–116, 153
Mastercard 279
matrix structure 66, 67, 277–278
Mauborgne, R. 53
May, T. 35

McDonald, R. 263
McFadzean, E. 252
McKinsey & Co. 41, 42, 43
meaningfulness: management 175–176; marketing 139–142; strategic thinking 261–263; work environment 253
measurement 171–172; metrics and value creation 135–137; performance 17, 228–248
Mendelow, A. 60
Mercedes Benz 3
Mercure hotels 92, 94, 95
mergers 119, 262
meta-capabilities 160, 252, 272
metrics *see* measurement
Mexico 149–150, 154
MGallery hotels 92, 94, 95
micro, small and medium enterprises (MSMEs) 223–224
micro-environment 53, 56–64
micro-multinationals 107
midscale hotels 94, 95
Miles, R. 6, 14
millennials 106
MINT countries 146, 149–150, 151, 156
Mintzberg, H. 7, 25, 39, 166–167, 215–216
mission statements 35–36
mobile media 129–130, 203
mobility, enterprise 29–32
Mohrman, A.M. 270
Mohrman, S.A. 270
Mondragon 265
moral-rights view 181
Morgan, G. 108
Moutinho, L. 8
Muller, E. 118
multidomestic strategy 113, 114
multinational enterprises (MNEs) 105, 145–146; emerging market multinational corporations (EMNCs) 154–155; national competitiveness and 109–116
multi-sided business tool models 279
multi-sided platforms (MSPs) 270–271, 280–281
MySpace 204

national competitiveness 109–116
National Health Service (NHS) 3, 244; foreigners' paying for emergency healthcare 36–38
nearshoring 105–106
Neilson, G.L. 198
Nelson, J. 187
network organisational structures 67, 167
networking 260–261; and organisational change 275–279; social networks 205, 256, 261, 270
new economy 254–255
new entrants, threat of 56, 57
New Public Management 13

niche players 257–258
niche social networks 205
Nigeria 145, 149–150
Nike 3, 102
no-profit zones 124, 125, 127
Nokia 173
non-employing enterprises 210
non-residents' paying for healthcare 36–38
Norton, D.P. 239, 240
not-for-profits 11; attractiveness of social media for investors 11–12
Novartis 262
Novotel hotels 92, 94, 95
Nutt, P.C. 160

objectives 36
Obstfeld, M. 147
offshoring 105–106
oil prices 144–145
old-fashioned business values 8
Oliver, C. 273
Oliver Wyman 41, 42
optimisation of experiences 138
organisation ecosystems 13, 256–259
organisational alignment 171
organisational capabilities *see* capabilities
organisational competencies 8, 70–71
organisational culture 68–69
organisational design: *see* design
organisational evolution 167–168
organisational flexibility 196–197, 198, 201–204
organisational learning 271
organisational resources 69
organisational structure 65–68, 167, 277–278
organisational success 14–16
orientation 216
outcomes 140
overview, in case study analysis 83
Ozogroup 222

Paddick, B. 48
Palmer, D. 201
Pampers mobile clinics 263
Panama Papers 184
Panasonic 106
Pandora 279
paradigm breaking CPS 252
paradigm preserving CPS 252
paradigm shifts 251–259, 268–269, 272, 273–275
paradigm stretching CPS 252
parallel lines test 14, 15, 134
Parry, B. 231–234
Pasternack, B.A. 198
Pavlou, P.A. 201
payments for healthcare 36–38
Penrose, E. 15
Perera, N. 265

Peres, R. 118
performance blindspots 230–231, 239
performance measurement 17, 228–248
performance measurement systems (PMS) 229, 235; strategic *see* strategic performance measurement systems (SPMS)
perspectives of strategy 38–40
PESTEL analysis 55–56
Petrobras 140
Pfeffer, J. 8
philanthropy 127
Phillips, A.N. 201
Phillips, P.A. 231–234
pioneer stage 167
Pitta, A. 217
planning, strategic 10–11, 34, 35, 270, 275
polarisation 105
Porter, M. 7, 215–216; Diamond 110–112; five forces model 7, 56–60, 199; generic strategies 14, 76–77, 215; value chain analysis 71
Powell, T.C. 8, 64
Powers, C.W. 190
practice approaches 11
Prahalad, C.K. 7, 113
pre-case analysis 83
prescriptive schools 7
Preston, L.E. 120
PricewaterhouseCoopers 41, 42
primary activities 71–72
problem identification 87–88
problem solving 77, 252
process management 271
Procter & Gamble (P&G) 263–264
product development 75
product focus 121
product leadership – differentiation strategy 240
professional services sector 220, 222
profit maximisation 6
profit measures 85, 87
profit sharing 141
profit zones 124, 127, 129
Promoting Sustainable Performance (PSP) research model 214–215, 224
public sector 3; performance measurement 243–244
pull business models 260
Pullman hotels 92, 94, 95
purpose 171, 261–264; common 134–135, 262–263
push business models 259–260
pyramids 166

Qatar 182
question marks 73

radio frequency identification (RFID) 206
Rakuten 102
ratio analysis 85, 86

Real Madrid FC 102
recommended solution 88–89
recruitment for excellence 171
REDF 136
re-inventor companies 128–129
related and supporting industries 111
relational capital 69
relevance 216
report writing 89–90
reputation 180, 282
reshoring 105–106
resource-based view (RBV) 7, 14, 15, 63–64, 69, 217
resource fluidity 160, 252, 272
resources, organisational 69
responsiveness 112–115
Rest, J.R. 190
return on experience (RoX) 137–138
return on humanity metrics (ROH) 135, 136
return on media and channels 138
reverse innovation 253–255
RevPAR 232
Rigby, D. 34
Rihanna 9–10
risk: managing 130; new forms of 103–104
rivalry 56, 58, 111–112
Rometty, G. 30
Ronda-Pupo, G.A. 27
roulette analogy 216
rugby sevens 108–109
Rumelt, R.P. 6, 216
Ruppert-Landscape Inc. 169
Russia 145, 148

sales 122
Samsung 153
Sanchis-Llopis, J.A. 270
Sands, P. 1
Sara Lee 154
Saudi Arabia 145
scale 2
scandals 182–183
scenario analysis/planning 61–62, 269
Schultz, H. 71
scope 2
Segal, L. 170
self-directed work teams 66
self-organisation 264
Semco's Survival Manual 167
sense and respond systems 160, 163–164
service, global day of 262–263
services sectors 220, 222
shareholder value 50, 130, 131–133, 273–274
Sharma, S.A. 199
short-term investors 131–132
Shkreli, M. 182–183
siloed organisations 33

Index

situation analysis 85–87
Six Sigma 231, 232
sizing up the situation 84–85
Sky 203
Skype 279
small and medium-sized enterprises (SMEs) 17, 40, 107, 210–227, 235
smart tourism 51
Smyth, C. 36–37
social dilemma approach 272
social disclosure 180
social media 11–12, 129–130, 203–205, 206
social networks 205, 256, 261, 270
social value 50
society–business relationship 32, 181, 184–189
Sofitel hotels 92, 93, 95
South Africa 148
span of control 65
speed 2
SPS:3–D model 231–234
stakeholder analysis 60–61
stakeholder mapping matrix 60
stakeholder theory 119–120, 159; enlightening 133–134
stakeholder value 132–133
stakeholder value-driven metric 134, 136
Stanford University 186
Starbucks 71–72, 184
stars 73–74
start-up sauna 173
state-owned enterprises (SOEs) 153–154
Storey, D. 216
strategic agility 163–165, 202, 252, 284; and design 17, 159–177
strategic analysis 17, 46–79
strategic behaviour 270
strategic groups 63–64
strategic insight, lack of 59–60
strategic management, defining 27
Strategic Management Journal 9
strategic performance measurement systems (SPMS) 202, 203, 229, 235, 263–243; *SPS:3–D* model 231–234
strategic philosophy 232–233
strategic planning 10–11, 34, 35, 270, 275
strategic sensitivity 160, 252, 272
strategic tensions 212
strategic thinking 17, 259–267, 269–270, 273, 275–284
strategist capability 214, 215
strategy 16, 25–45; content 27, 28; defining 27, 252; levels of 28–34; perspectives of 38–40; in strategy analysis 50–52; tools 34–35; as a wicked problem 160–161
strategy-as-practice (SAP) perspective 11
strategy consulting industry 40–43
strategy maps 239–240

stretch 280
structural ambidexterity 40
structural capital 69
structure, organisational 65–68, 167, 277–278
structure-conduct-performance (SCP) paradigm 14–15, 64
structured case study analysis 83–84
"stuck in the middle" firms 77
substitutes, threat of 56, 57–58
Sun Tzu 5
suppliers' bargaining power 56, 57
supporting activities 71, 72
supply chains 202–203; deglobalisation 255–256
sustainability 105; agenda 53; business ethics 184–185; hotels 96–97
Sutton, R.I. 8
Suzlon 155
Swissair Group 29
SWOT analysis (strengths, weaknesses, opportunities and threats) 54–55
symptoms 91
system lock-in 240
systems 140–141
systems thinking 167–168

talent development 96, 129
tall organisational structure 68
tangible assets 69
tax avoidance 183–184
Taylorism 166, 260
team working 66
technology sector 220, 221
Teece, D.J. 15
ten schools of strategy 7, 38
Tenkasi, R.V. 270
Tesco 36
Thomson Reuters 189
threat of new entrants 56, 57
threat of substitutes 56, 57–58
Toshiba accounting scandal 182
tourism 107, 217; Barbados 152; smart 51
Toyoda, S. 77
trade-off 216
traditional businesses 152–154
training 270
transaction cost theory 6–7
transformational brands 141
transnational strategy 113, 114
Tregoe, B. 252
triad markets 102
triple bottom line 241
triple-filter feedback 233, 234
Trump, D. 184
trust 141
Tumblr 11
Turing Pharmaceutical 182–183
Turkey 149–150

Tushman, M.L. 271
Twitter 11

uncertainty 17, 254
Unilever 13, 185; Sustainable Living Plan 141
United States of America (USA) 219
urbanisation 102–103
user base 12
utilitarian view 181

value-based management (VBM) 126–129
value-based metrics 133
value chain analysis 71–72
value creation 13, 50; in a global context 17, 118–142
value growth 124, 125
value innovation 240
value maximisation, enlightening 133
values 262; old-fashioned business values 8; organisational culture 68–69; *see also* business ethics
van Bever, D. 43
Vasella, D. 262
Venkatraman, N.V. 201
Verizon 52
vertical analysis 85

virtual worlds 256–257
Visco, A.J. 198
vision statement 35–36
Vogel, D. 190
volatility 17, 254
Volkswagen emissions scandal 182
volume growth 124, 125
Voss, G.B. 40
Voss, Z.G. 40
VUCA world 17, 254–255

Wang, D. 43
Warwickshire Police 35–36
Wernerfelt, B. 7
WhatsApp 195–196
Whitman, M. 2
wicked problems 160–161
Wipro 149
Wright, J. 270–271

Xu, F. 186, 187

Yahoo 52

Zeng, M. 272
Zenger, T. 26
Zimmerman, J. 252